Holywood Then and Now

ESSAYS BY AN OLD RESIDENT AT
THE BEGINNING OF A NEW MILLENNIUM

Author & Publisher
CON AULD
2002
HOLYWOOD, COUNTY DOWN

First Published March, 2002.

Published by Con Auld
Martello Corner
14 Victoria Road, Holywood
County Down BT18 9BD.

Printed by
Spectator & Chronicle Newspaper Group
Balloo Link
Balloo Industrial Estate
Bangor BT19 7HJ

ISBN No. 0-9542274-0-9

HOLYWOOD ESSAYS, SKETCHES AND POEMS

CONTENTS

SANCTUS·BOSCUS·

Holywood Then and Now

A few words by way of introduction

Welcome to a collection of essays which attempt to depict the Holywood story over fourteen centuries of recorded history and a few words on how it all came about.

Initially I should say something of credentials. Although my birth certificate records the long-gone angled house at the end of Gray's Buildings on the Marine Parade, in fact I was born at Clanbrassil, the home of my mother's parents.

A plaque on the walls within the Old Priory church commemorates one of my father's forbears – so I can claim to be a hometown product – certainly although I have wandered far and wide, the joy of arrival home in Holywood has always been the best part of any journey.

Although the tides of time have washed away many of the locales, niches and nooks of adolescence, much that is good remains into the twenty-first century. Many of the new buildings are beneficial. Glenlyon and Redburn Country Parks bring back a *"Sanctus Boscus"* we can all enjoy.

It is imperative that Holywood sustains the unique ambience of its auspicious history. Enjoy the manuscript and let me have your criticism or melioration when we meet in the High Street.

CON AULD

HOLYWOOD IS BEAUTIFUL, AND I LIVE THERE

In Holywood - where I live -
Are cornfields and heather
Low hills and high hills
Sitting down together.
Rainbows and dewdrops
And mosses everywhere –
Oh! Holywood is beautiful
And I live there.

In Holywood – where I live –
The sea sweeps by
Far above the ploughlands
The white gulls fly.
Bees in the clover,
Honey in the air –
Oh! Holywood is beautiful
And I live there.

In Holywood – where I live –
The little daisies grow,
They hide their tiny faces
When the sun sinks low.
When the sun is rising
They life their heads and stare
For Holywood is beautiful
And I live there.

A Child's Song - by Rosamund S Praeger

Holywood maypole looking towards Mill Street (now Church Road – c. 1870).

Maypole decorated for May Day towards end of 18th century.

The Holywood Maps - Frontispiece

A curtain raiser for the essays on our town is a selection of the maps from the seventeenth to the nineteenth centuries.
Irish cartography began in the sixteenth century; before then our fringe European islands were mapped by other nations. About 1540 accurate maps of Ireland became necessary to the Tudor administration for security reasons. After the Flight of the Earls (1607) the government required measured plans upon which to base re-distribution of the confiscated territories.

The lands granted to the London companies were mapped by Thomas Raven in 1622, the same cartographer drew the delightful maps of North Down for Viscount Clandeboye in 1625. The Down Survey (1654) – the name means local information was set down on maps – provided Hiberniae Delineatio in 1635. This was the first printed atlas of Ireland's provinces and counties.

An Act of 1774 enabled the Grand Juries to fund area cartography. In 1824 the Duke of Wellington, Prime Minister, authorized the recommendation of the Board of Ordnance in order that its survey should be extended to Ireland. After 1921 an independent Ordnance Survey of Northern Ireland was established in Belfast.
Holywood is fortunate to have benefited from the monumental efforts of both Thomas Raven (Clandeboye maps 1622) and Colonel Thomas Colby (Ordnance Survey 1834) :

(a) A map of Knockfergus Bay in 1599 based on the work of Baptista Boazio for Elizabeth I;
(b) A map of Hollewood in 1625, based on the work of Thomas Raven for Viscount Clandeboye;
(c) A map of Holywood drawn in 1767. It shows the townlands and the major road system of the area.
(d) A map of Cultra in 1775, based on Miss Tate's pen drawing of Belfast Lough;
(e) A map of Hollywood Parish in 1819. This accompanied the Holywood Section of the Parochial Survey of Ireland by William Shaw Mason, Secretary to the Board of Public Records.
(f) A map of the east end of Holywood town in 1834.
(g) A map of the west end of Holywood town in 1834.
(h) A land speculator's map of East Cultra c. 1867
(i) A land speculator's map of West Cultra c. 1867

KEY TO MAPS (h) AND (i)
The artist suggests the following reference key –
[a] Cultra House – large mansion on 5 acres; [b] Mayfield Cottage; [c] North Clanbrassil Villa; [d] South Clanbrassil Villa; [e] [f] and [g] One-storey cottages; [h] and [I] Two-storey cottages; [j] Clanbrassil Terrace – four houses with site for end terrace house; [k] to [l] Three or more villa sites; [m] and [n] Two villa sites; [o] and [p] Terrace site; [q] and [r] Thirteen or more villa sites; [s] and [t] Cottage sites; [v] Site for stable, offices and yard.

Take a look at the pictorial maps. They show the houses and building sites to be let along the coastal path, shortly after the arrival of the railway in 1865.

Among other existing properties the map shows Culdaff, Ailsa, Farmhill, Ardville, the coastguard station and a delightful impression of the re-furbished harbour complete with tall flag staff.

Possibly the agents, George McAuliffe and James Connor, provided clients with an architect's catalogue from which to choose the style of villa residence they would like to build. Many of the specimen houses are remarkably similar to properties under construction in Strandtown at that time.

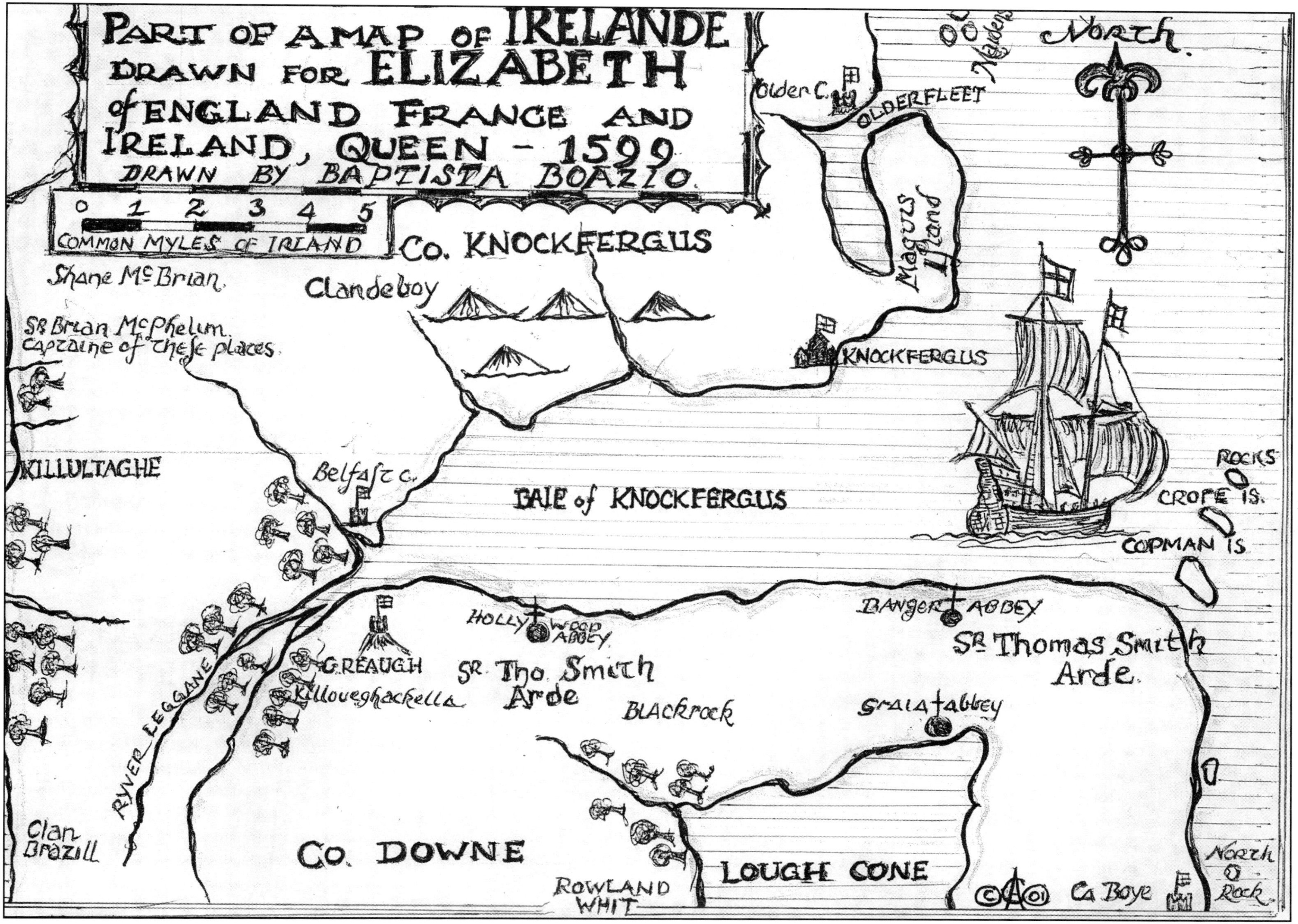
PART OF A MAP OF IRELANDE
DRAWN FOR ELIZABETH
of ENGLAND FRANCE AND
IRELAND, QUEEN - 1599
DRAWN BY BAPTISTA BOAZIO.
0 1 2 3 4 5
COMMON MYLES OF IRLAND
Co. KNOCKFERGUS
Olden C.
OLDERFLEET
Maidens
North.
Magus Iland
Shane McBrian.
Clandeboy
Sr Brian McPhelum
captaine of these places.
KNOCKFERGUS
KILLULTAGHE
Belfast C.
BAIE of KNOCKFERGUS
ROCKS
CROFE IS.
COPMAN IS
Banger ABBEY
HOLLY WOOD ABBEY
Sr Thomas Smith Arde.
GREAUGH
Sr Tho. Smith Arde
Killoueghackella
BLACKrock
Graia abbey
RYVER LEGGANE
Clan Brazill
Co. DOWNE
LOUGH CONE
ROWLAND WHIT
Ca Boye
North Rock

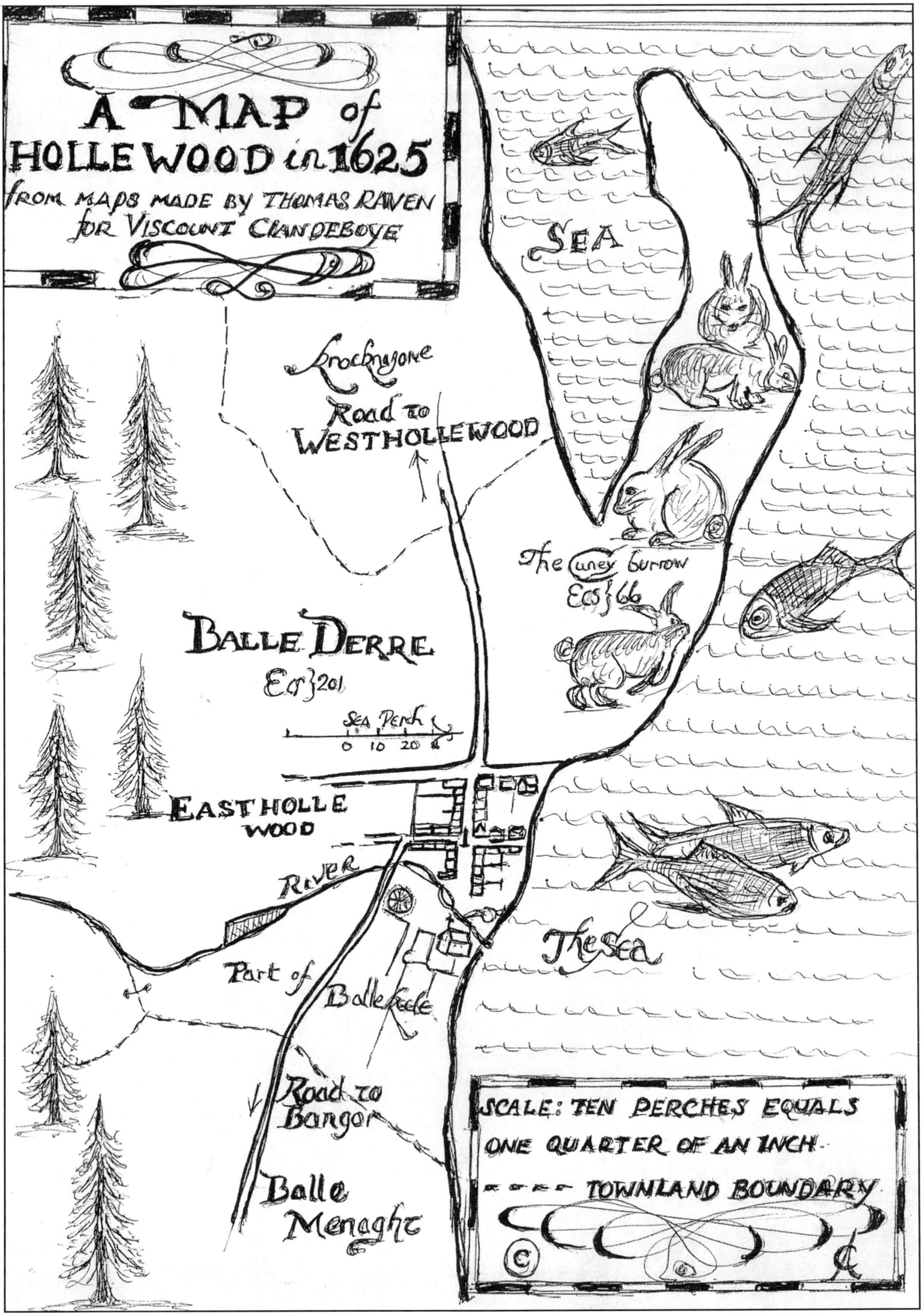
A MAP of
HOLLE WOOD in 1625
FROM MAPS MADE BY THOMAS RAVEN
for VISCOUNT CLANDEBOYE
SEA
The Cuney burrow
Road to
WESTHOLLEWOOD
BALLE DERRE
Sea Perch
0 10 20
EASTHOLLE
WOOD
River
Part of
The Sea
Road to
Bangor
Balle
Menaght
SCALE: TEN PERCHES EQUALS
ONE QUARTER OF AN INCH.
TOWNLAND BOUNDARY

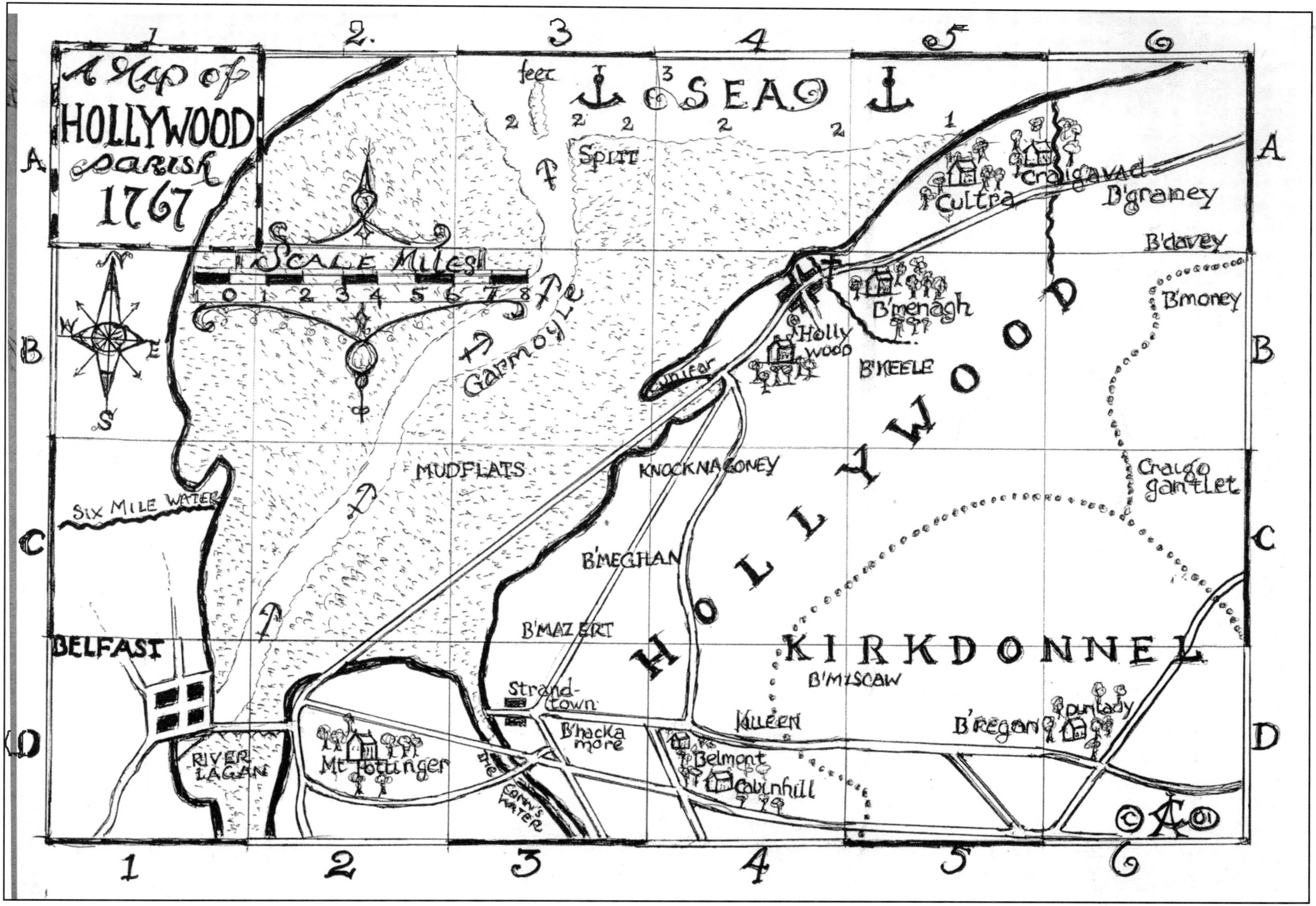

A Map of
HOLLYWOOD
Parish
1767
SEA
feet
Spitt
Scale Miles
0 1 2 3 4 5 6 7 8
Garmoyle
MUDFLATS
SIX MILE WATER
BELFAST
RIVER LAGAN
Mt Pottinger
Strand-town
B'hackamore
Belmont
Cavinhill
Conn's Water
KNOCKNAGONEY
B'MEGHAN
B'MAZERT
Cunifar
Holly wood
B'menagh
B'KEELE
Cultra
Craigavad
B'graney
B'davey
B'money
Craigo gantlet
HOLLYWOOD
KIRKDONNEL
B'M'SCAW
Killeen
B'regan
Dunlady
© AC 01

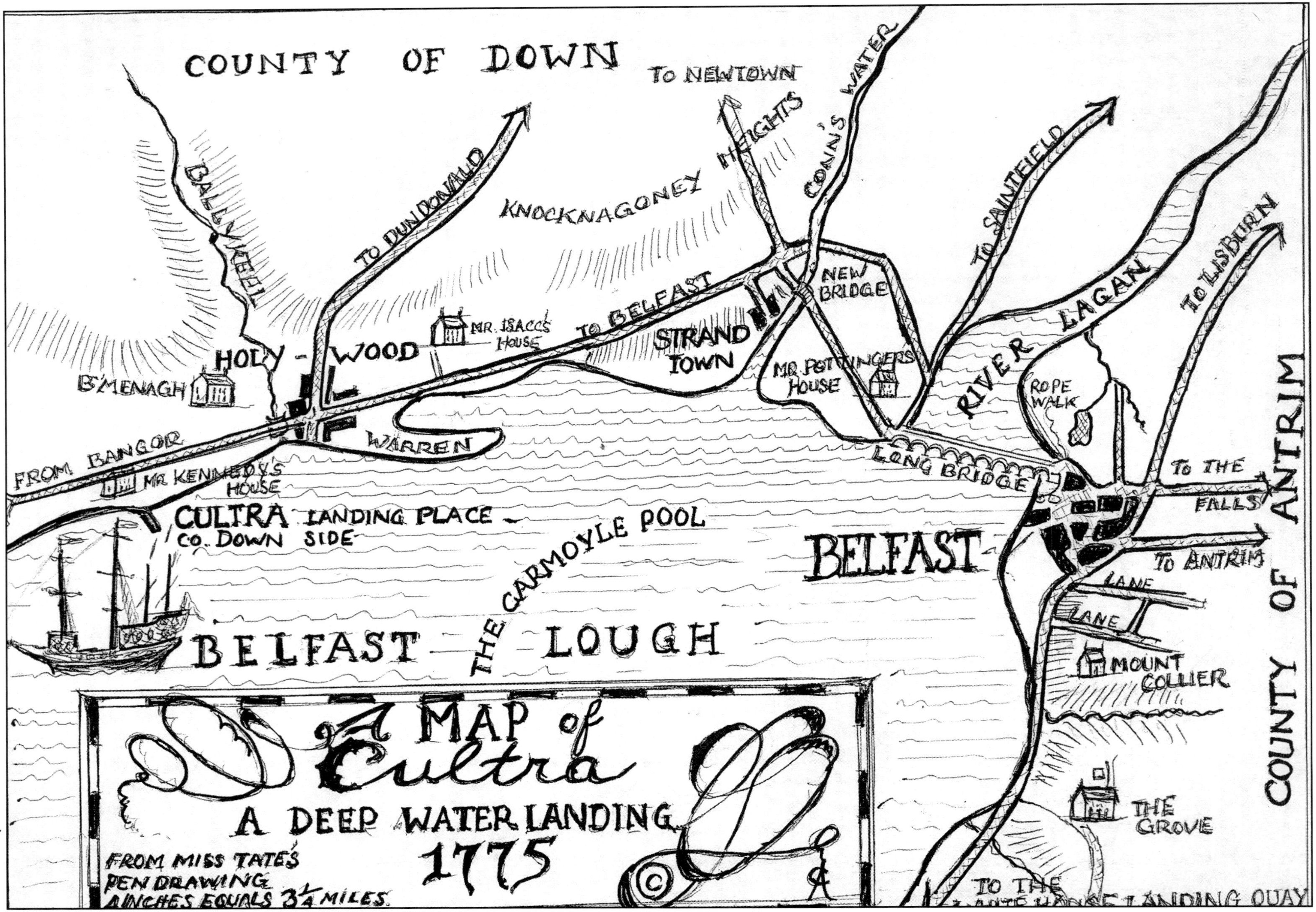
COUNTY OF DOWN
TO NEWTOWN
CONN'S WATER
BALLYKEEL
TO DUNDONALD
KNOCKNAGONEY HEIGHTS
TO SAINTFIELD
TO LISBURN
NEW BRIDGE
MR. ISACCS HOUSE
TO BELFAST
STRAND TOWN
RIVER LAGAN
HOLY - WOOD
B'MENAGH
MR POTTINGERS HOUSE
ROPE WALK
WARREN
FROM BANGOR
LONG BRIDGE
MR KENNEDY'S HOUSE
TO THE FALLS
CULTRA LANDING PLACE - CO. DOWN SIDE
THE CARMOYLE POOL
BELFAST
TO ANTRIM
COUNTY OF ANTRIM
LANE
LANE
BELFAST LOUGH
MOUNT COLLIER
A MAP of Cultra
A DEEP WATER LANDING
1775
THE GROVE
FROM MISS TATE'S PEN DRAWING 4 INCHES EQUALS 3¼ MILES.
TO THE

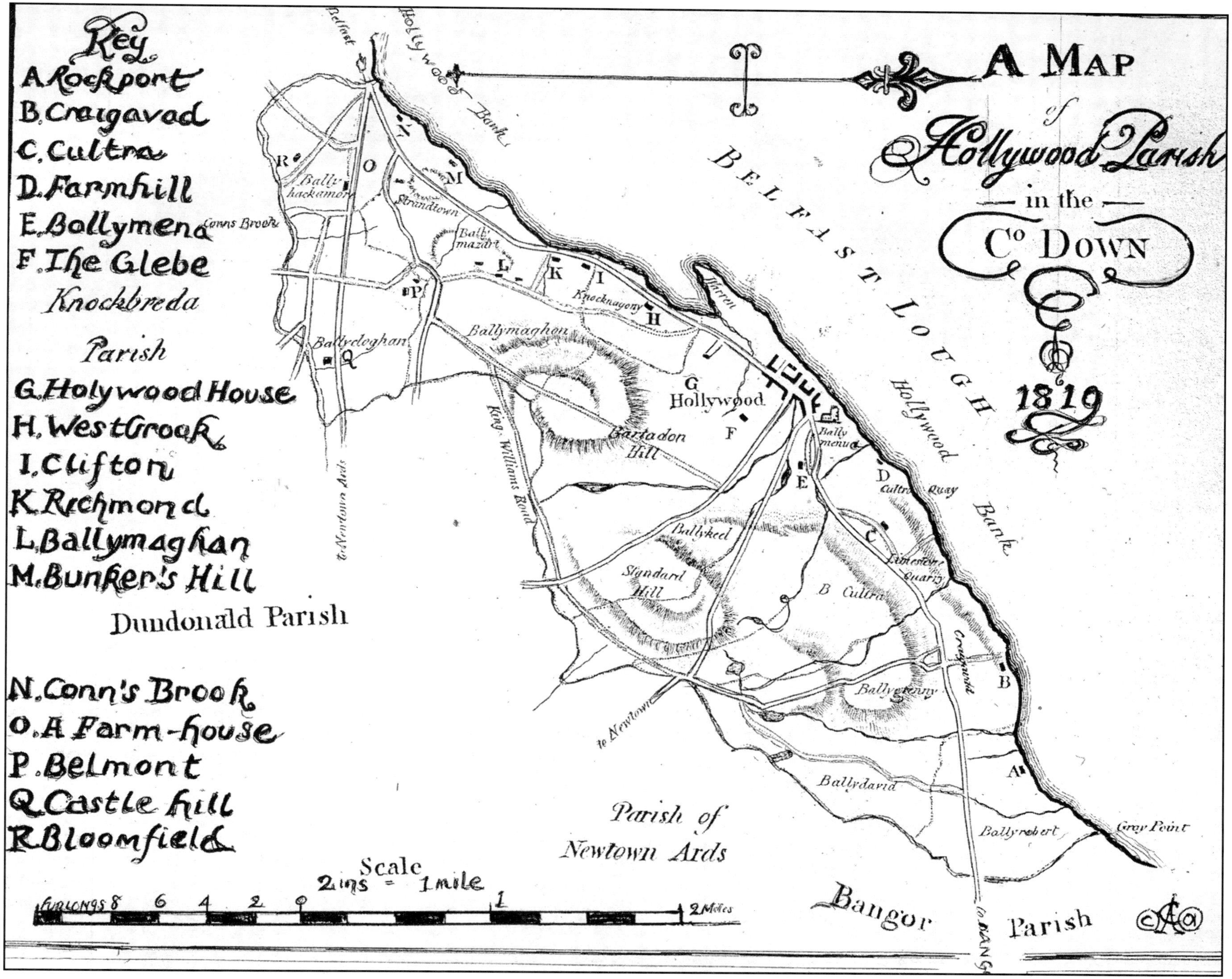
A Map
of
Hollywood Parish
in the
Co Down
1819
Key
A Rockport
B Craigavad
C Cultra
D Farmhill
E Bollymena
F The Glebe
Knockbreda
Parish
G Holywood House
H WestGrook
I Clifton
K Richmond
L Ballymaghan
M Bunker's Hill
Dundonald Parish
N Conn's Brook
O A Farm-house
P Belmont
Q Castle hill
R Bloomfield
Scale
2 ins = 1 mile
Furlongs 8 6 4 2 0 1 2 Miles
Belfast
Hollywood Bank
Belfast Lough
Conns Brook
Strandtown
Ballymaghan
Knocknagony
Ballycloghan
Hollywood
Bartadon Hill
King Williams Road
to Newtown Ards
Cultra Quay
Ballykeel
Standard Hill
Cultra
Limestone Quarry
Craigavad
Ballydavid
Ballyrobert
Gray Point
to Newtown
Parish of Newtown Ards
Bangor
Parish
to Bangor

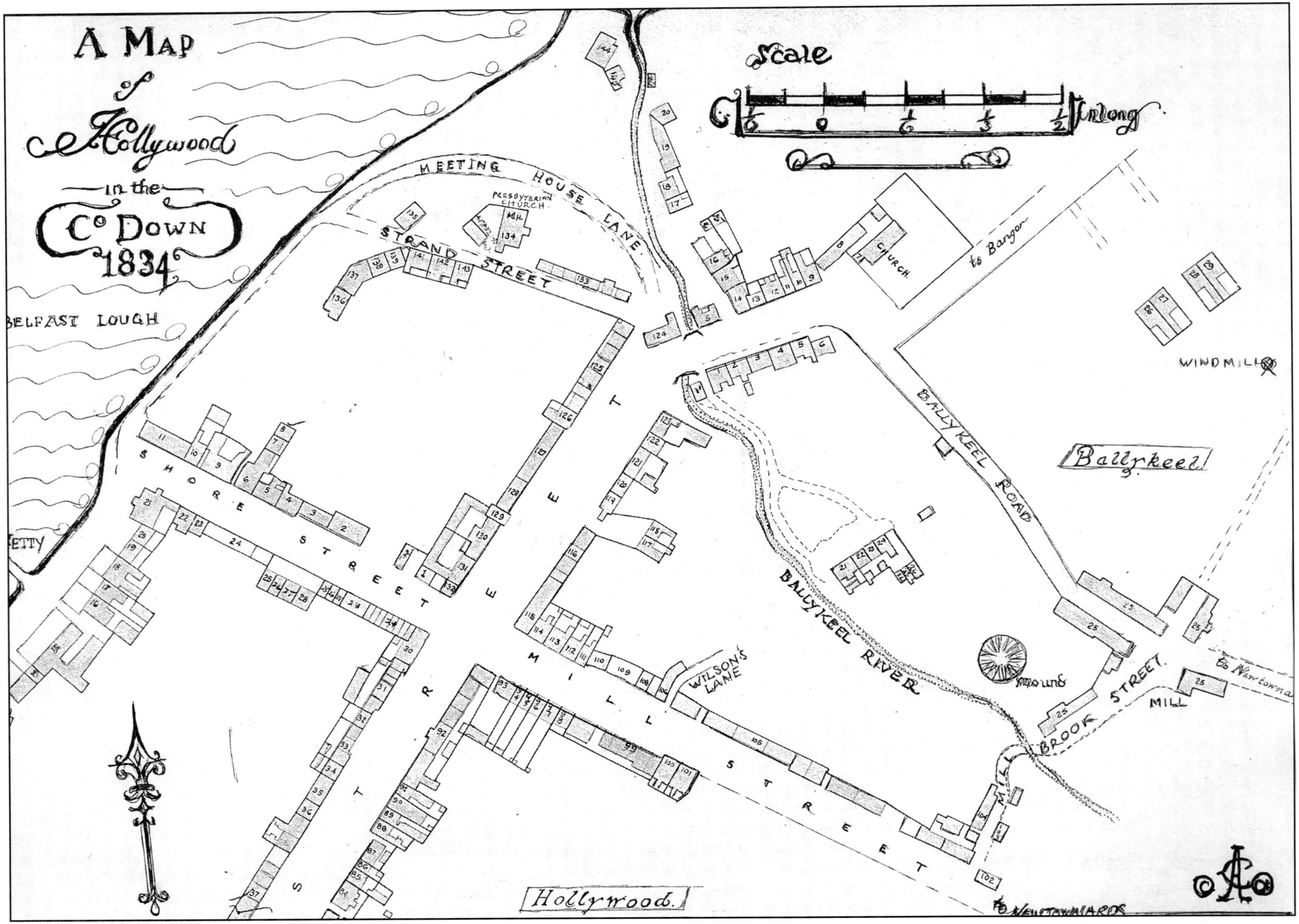
A Map
of
Hollywood
in the
Co Down
1834
Scale
Furlong
BELFAST LOUGH
MEETING HOUSE LANE
PRESBYTERIAN CHURCH
M.H.
STRAND STREET
CHURCH
to Bangor
WINDMILL
BALLYKEEL ROAD
Ballykeel
SHORE STREET
STREET
MILL STREET
WILSON'S LANE
BALLYKEEL RIVER
Mound
BROOK STREET
MILL
Hollywood.
to NEWTOWNARDS

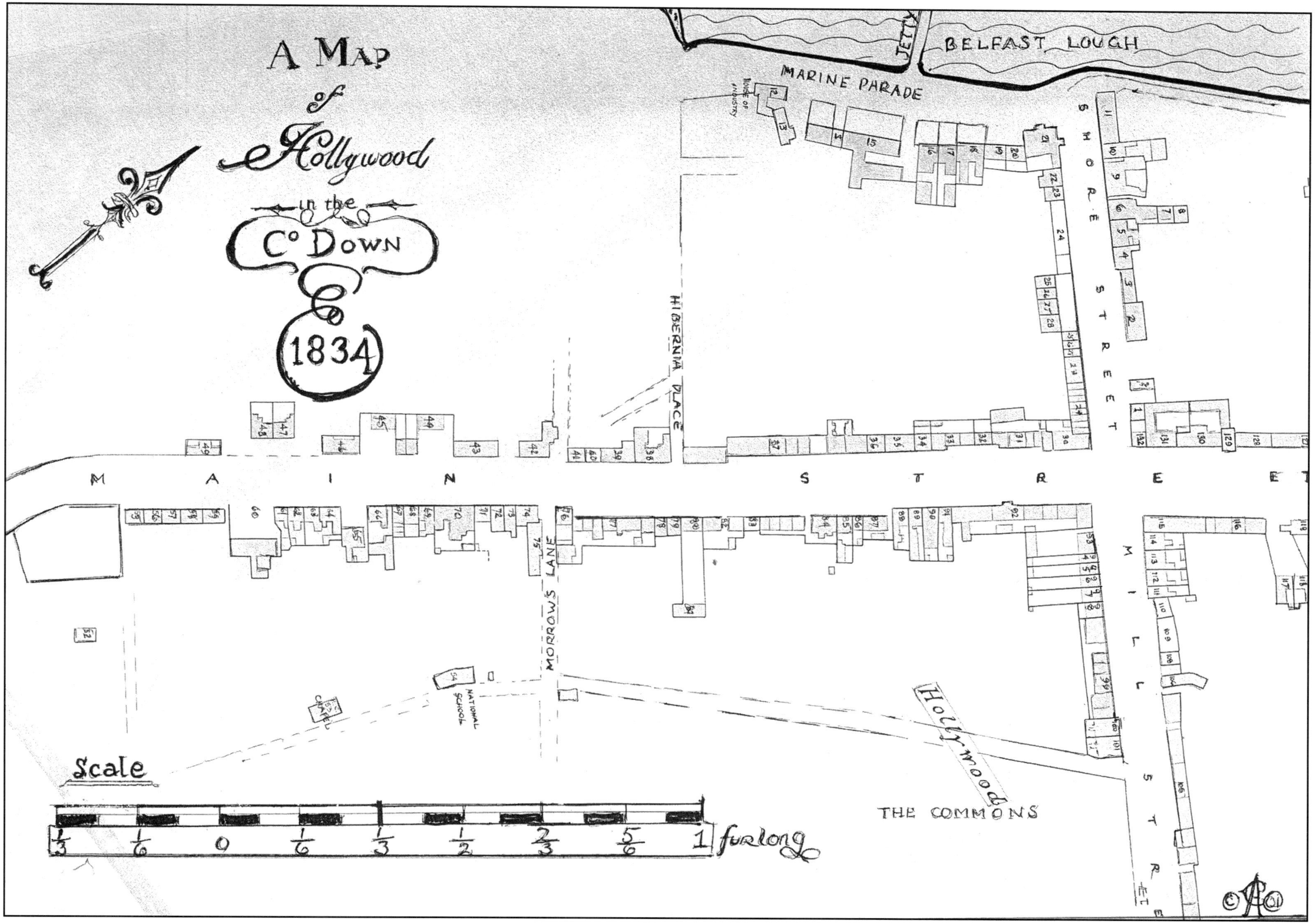
A Map of Hollywood in the Co Down 1834
BELFAST LOUGH
JETTY
MARINE PARADE
HOUSE OF INDUSTRY
SHORE STREET
HIBERNIA PLACE
MAIN STREET
MORROWS LANE
MILL STREET
NATIONAL SCHOOL
CHAPEL
Hollywood
THE COMMONS
Scale
furlong

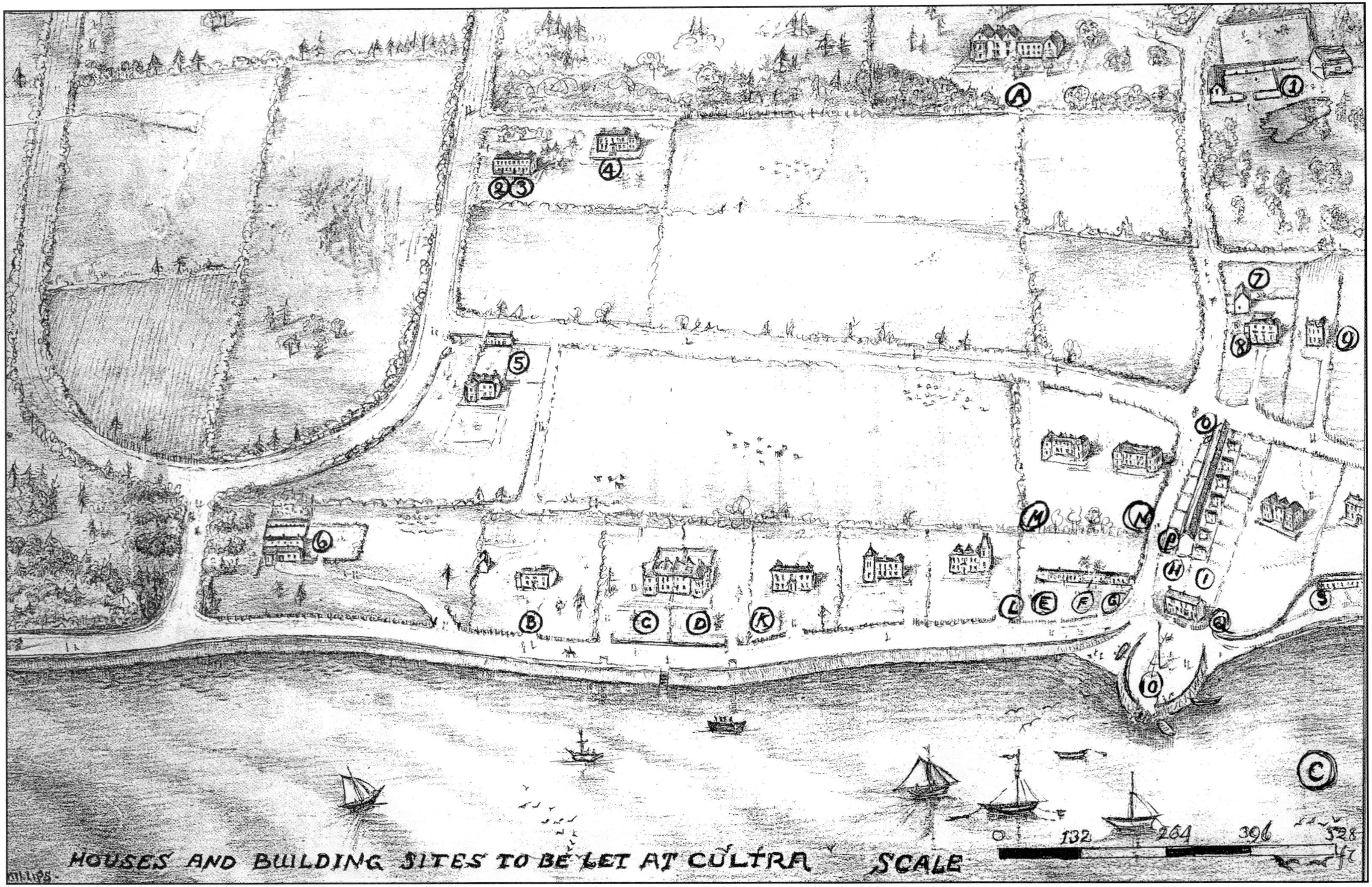
HOUSES AND BUILDING SITES TO BE LET AT CULTRA
SCALE
0 132 264 396 528
A
B
C
D
E
F
G
H
I
K
L
M
N
O
P
Q
S
1
2 3
4
5
6
7
8
9
10
C

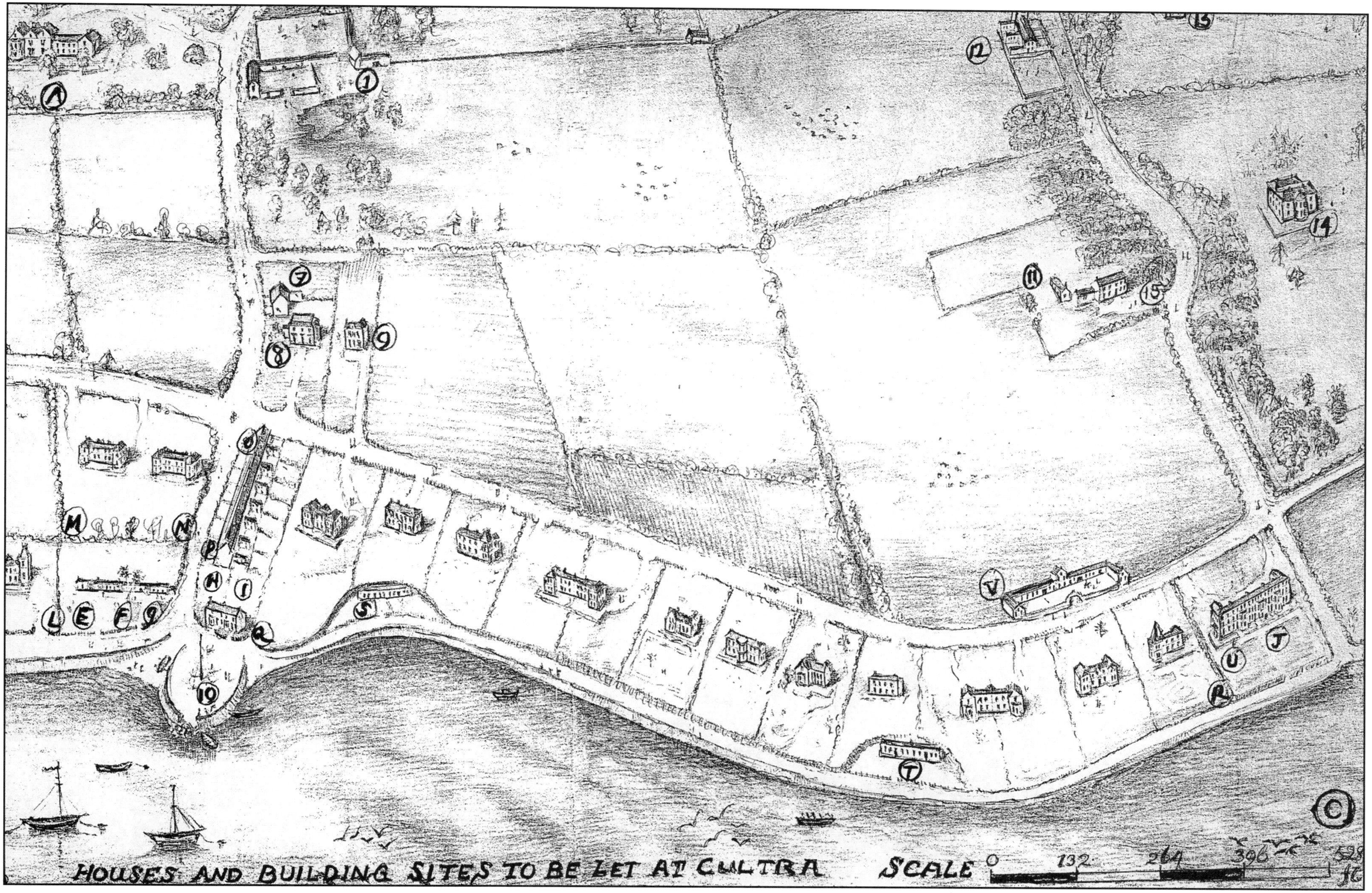
HOUSES AND BUILDING SITES TO BE LET AT CULTRA
SCALE
0
132
264
396
528
ft

ESSAY I - HOLYWOOD - THE MAYPOLE TOWN

To Holywood I'll raise my pen on this momentous day
For now our maypole's back again and everyone is gay.
The little children's cries resound with wonder and delight
To watch the boats go sailing round, Ah! What a pretty sight!

The older folk, too, stand and gaze, then someone starts to cheer,
Another thinks of boyhood days and hides a silent tear.
Now I raise my pen once more before I leave it down
"May God's rich blessing ever pour upon the Maypole Town."

Lines from "Maypole Day" a poem written by Holywood born George Osborough for the presentation of the new maypole on Thursday, 13th October 1949.

HOLYWOOD - THE MAYPOLE TOWN

It does not require a great amount of imagination to decide the subject of the first essay, Holywood is known as the Maypole Town all over the world.
When Rev William Holmes became Vicar of Holywood in 1810, he found his parish rejoiced in the possession of a maypole. Of his new parishioners he recorded -

> *"In their manners a stranger would suppose them to be rough and untractable, but amongst themselves they manifest as much courtesy as is to be met with elsewhere. There is little to distinguish them in respect to customs from the remainder of the Province of Ulster. Their weddings are honoured by hoisting a flag or pennant to the top of a large May-pole which stands in the centre of the village."*

Nowadays, Holywood is the only Irish town to possess a working maypole. However, at the beginning of the nineteenth century, there were maypoles in Downpatrick, Mountmellick, Finglas and Harold's Cross in Dublin. In 1850 Dublin University magazine recorded *"The only authorized pole now standing that we know of is at Holywood, where it used to bear the orange and blue flags and streamers on the Twelfth of July, equally with the flower-decked hoops and green garlands of the First of May."*

May Day festivities go back to the classical Greek goddess of Spring, Chloris, and the Roman Flora, goddess of flowers. From 1644 to 1659, during the Commonwealth Period, maypoles were forbidden by Act of Parliament and May Day festivities strongly denounced by the Puritans. Whether or not the law extended to Holywood we do not know. However, we do know the Holywood maypole preceded and succeeded the lurid life and terrible times of Protector Oliver Cromwell.
In 1625 our proprietor, Sir James Hamilton, commissioned Thomas Raven to survey and draw watercolour maps of his Clandeboye estates. The series is carefully preserved in the Heritage Centre at Bangor Castle. The Holywood map shows the village with a maypole at the crossroads in the centre. The artist has included a flag fluttering in the wind at the masthead. Perhaps a local swain and his colleen were being wed the day Thomas Raven visited Holywood to undertake his cartological survey.

Holywood maypole looking towards Mill Street (now Church Road – c. 1870).

Marcus Ward in 1842 and J B Doyle in 1854 recorded pictorial representation of our maypole. Visit the Holywood Library to see the Ward watercolour and read Doyle's "Tours of Ulster" to discover more of the story. In 1850 Surgeon Thomas T Kelly, our first historian, describes some of the customs which accompanied the jollification of May Day in Holywood and Dublin.

> *"Whenever a lady appeared in the vicinity of the maypole she was liable to be asked to take a turn round the pole; the end of the dance concluded with a kiss. The omission of the latter part of the ceremony was often purchased with*

a bribe! Upon Easter Monday the pole was well soaped from top to bottom in order to render it the more difficult to climb. To its top were attached different prizes in succession, consisting generally of a pair of leather breeches, a hat or an old pinchbeck watch. Whoever climbed the pole and touched the prize, became its possessor.

Other games were running after a pig with a shaved and well-soaped tail, which was let loose in the middle of the throng; grinning through horse collars for tobacco; running in sacks; foot races for men and women; wrestling and dancing reels, jigs and hornpipes. Stewards were appointed to see fair play in the ass races, in which each person rode or drove his neighbour's beast, the last being declared the winner. Blindfolded men attempted to catch a bell-ringer; and there were hopping and leaping races. Twenty or thirty pounds worth of prizes consisting of shawls, hats, frieze coats, handkerchiefs, women's gowns and bonnets were distributed to the winners. In the evening the crowds collected around the maypole, where the boys and girls danced in a ring until a late hour."

Maypole decorated for May Day towards end of 18th century.

Dr Kelly regretted the passing of sports in Holywood *"as the public mind becomes more enlightened"*. Little did he know that the Holywood maypole and its traditions would be in fine fettle in the twenty-first century!

In Holywood on May Day the pole was decorated with floral garlands, a King and May Day Queen were elected. Local children were well coached to dance around the pole, plaiting multi-coloured ribbons down and up the shaft. On summer evenings a table was placed at the base of the maypole, on which a fiddler played for dancing *"where the young people in imitation of their superiors, kept up the revel from eight or nine in the evening until day-break."*

Of the year 1800, Rev Charles J McAlester records

> *"There was a maypole, small in comparison with the one which now graces the centre of our town; yet it possessed an interest which, in progress of our improvements, has disappeared; for regularly on May-Eve a table was placed at the maypole, and on the table a chair was set for the accommodation of the village fiddler, and to his simple music the inhabitants, old and young, dance right merrily."*

The good pastor , like our local doctor, would be surprised to discover that two centuries later, interest in the traditions of the Holywood maypole is as puissant as it ever was! It is impossible to say how often the wooden maypoles have been replaced; the early poles were shorter than the majestic spars of the nineteenth and early twentieth centuries. It seems there were periods when the Holywood crossroads site was without its guardian sentinel.

Such an occasion may have given rise to a local tradition, first recorded by F Sloan in 1930. *" Some Dutchmen were in a small vessel lying off the Holywood shore on May Eve. They came ashore, procured a pole, decked it with garden flowers and danced around it to their hearts' content. The villagers linked hands and participated in the fun."* As time went past, the story lost nothing in the telling. Soon the small vessel had been named "The Dutchman" which had been wrecked on the Holywood shore - the pole became the ship's mast, which has been salvaged from the wreck. By the end of the twentieth century, the fable outshines the story. *"Three hundred years ago ship-wrecked Dutch sailors erected the town's first maypole by way of thanks to local people who saved their lives!"*

Perhaps the maypole depicted by J B Doyle in 1854 was the first of several given to the town by the generous Harrison family who lived in Mertoun Hall, Holywood House and Ardtullagh. Certainly, it was the first pole to be illuminated. Gas street lighting came to Holywood in 1860, for many years our maypole carried four elaborately wrought iron brackets on which gas lamps glittered fifteen feet above the street. It must have been a magnificent sight on dark winter nights, long before brilliant nocturnal illumination became common-place.

Later, four ornamental lamp-posts were erected at the corners of the crossroads to replace the bracketed gas lamps. When gas gave way to electricity, the street furniture was modernised sympathetically.

In passing, one wonders what happened to those four decorated lamp-posts which graced the centre of our town for many years and were replaced by the high lighting stanchions of the present day. Again, it would be good to unearth the donation plaques of the various maypoles, also the Dunville plaque from Monty's spout and many other items of beloved Holywood public minutiae.

During the festivities for Queen Victoria's Diamond Jubilee the maypole was elaborately decorated with flags and emblems. That very year - 1897 - the Belfast Directory describes in detail the maypole which John Henderson had given to the town.

> *"The Maypole, probably the last of its kind in Ireland, stands at the junction of High Street, Shore Street and Church Street, and is the gift of Captain John Harrison, DL. It is an immense Norwegian spar standing about sixty-four feet above the ground and twenty under it. The ceremony of dressing it with bunting and flowers on May Eve is still continued."*

Captain John Harrison used the pole to make a political point against his nephew, Captain Henry Harrison, (1867 - 1954) with whose republican sympathies he was not amused! John Harrison's last will and testament required the upper portion of the pole to be cut away if ever the Home Rule tricolour was flown from it.

In order to appreciate John Harrison's political opinions, we should understand the story of the Tricolour. In 1801 the addition of the Cross of Saint Patrick (red on white) to the Union Flag, symbolised the official unity of the Kingdoms of Ireland, Scotland and England. 'Young Ireland' (1842 - 1848) – were a group of graduates of Trinity College, University of Dublin, who sought to bring about the reconciliation of Nationalist and Unionist colour symbolism in a combination of green and orange separated by neutral white. The emblem was used in the 1848 Rebellion and adopted in 1922 as the national flag of the newly-created Irish Free State.

John Harrison's nephew was an active member of Charles Stewart Parnell's Irish Nationalist Party. In 1890 he was elected Nationalist M P for Tipperary at Westminster. Captain Henry Harrison's regiment was the Royal Irish. He was severely wounded at the Battle of the Somme. Henry supported the 1921 Treaty, which established the Irish Free State and afterwards he pleaded for replacement of the Northern Ireland Government by a Panel of Commissioners.

In his later years Henry Harrison worked with the Anti-Partition League, was Irish correspondence for "The Economist" and edited his own paper "Irish Truth". In 1954 Captain Harrison was interred in the family grave within the walls of the Priory Church. Although born in Holywood, he never came home to reside in Holywood House or any of the other mansions of the Harrison family.

An amusing story accompanies the maypole that Henry Harrison donated on 26th June 1902. The Harrison family, whose choice of first names for their progeny was rather limited, were extremely generous squires of Holywood and particularly hospitable to the many famous visitors they invited to the town. Earl Frederich Sleigh Roberts, V C, of Kandahar, then recently returned from the Boer War, 1899 - 1902, was Henry Harrison's guest at the inauguration of the lofty 1902 Maypole. Eye-witness John R Birch, than an observant Holywood teenager, recorded a story of the event -

> *"Billy McManus was a soldier with Lord Roberts when the Field Marshal won the Victoria Cross at the Khyber Pass. He was at the opening of the Holywood Maypole. When Richard Patterson (Leader of the Town Commissioners and Urban District Council chairman from 1889 - 1904) was making his speech at the ceremony, Lord Roberts recognised Billy McManus in the crowd of spectators. He walked over and shook him by the hand and gave him a golden sovereign."*

Apparently, Billy McManus had been Lord Roberts' army batman. That evening, Billy used his unexpected wealth to entertain himself and his cronies in the local public houses. The following day he was brought before the Holywood Magistrate – quite possibly Henry Harrison himself. The case was dismissed when its circumstances were appreciated with much merriment, by all in the Courtroom.

Another tale connected with the 1902 maypole concerns one Crow Nimmick. The Nimmick family of High Street were the town's leading building contractors. William Nimmick (1819 - 1906) was an eminently competent mason as many local buildings continue to testify. Like every family, the Nimmicks had a "black sheep". Although Crow was a builder by trade, he was addicted to alcohol. When in his cups, his best trick was the ability to shin up the maypole, for which he spent much time in gaol. When discharged the poor lad would go yelling through the town, creating bedlam in the Strand area.

The 1902 pole appears to have lasted for three decades – about the average life of any high-rise free-standing spar, as the meteorological stress is profound. Holywood's maypole is the tallest flag-staff in the United Kingdom unsecured by wire rope support stays. In such poles, the portion submerged under street level tends to rot away and render the upright unsafe.

In 1936 the Holywood Urban District Council replaced the Henderson maypole with a spar which stood some eighty feet about the ground and fourteen feet below street level. Perhaps this was the tallest of all our maypoles – an absolutely straight hundred feet pine tree is not easily obtained in the forests of the world. In that year Mr C B Erskine was Chairman of the Urban District Council and Mr David Bell had already served thirty years as our Town Clerk. He continued in office for another fifteen years. His assiduous loyalty to the town laid the foundations for our present outstanding prosperity. In his speech to the assembled crowd, Mr Erskine paid tribute to the Town clerk's professionalism, and his success in replacing Holywood's famous emblem.

The 1936 Maypole did not survive the Second World War. Local comments on the day of its inauguration were proved correct. *"It is far too tall." "How can fourteen feet underground support eighty feet above?" "It will be the death of all of us!"* Friday, 12th February 1943 was a winter's day in a succession of days of severe storms. At that time, the Northern Ireland Road Transport Board operated its buses from Redburn Square, along Marine Parade to pick up passengers at the top of Shore Road. As the passengers were boarding the twelve o'clock bus, there was a loud crack and the maypole crashed to the ground. Miraculously, no one was injured but many were severely frightened.

It was wartime, and shortly before the disaster a convoy of army tanks had trundled through the town, on their way from Belfast to Holywood Ordnance Depot. In those days, the only way to enter the Kinnegar was through the railway arch at the end of Shore Road. As the convoy crept along the High Street, plate glass shop windows, bottles, sweet jar lids, light fittings and anything else which was movable, shuddered in sympathy with the quaking roadway. One of the tanks may have touched the maypole as it negotiated the corner with considerable difficulty; certainly many people heard a smart smacking sound as the tank passed. The event was the talk of the town for a few days – but those were the war years and we had more important things on our minds!

After the War, the townspeople requested the Council to erect a replacement maypole for the spar which was knocked down in 1943. Councillor William Dunn of Tudor Park, member of a long-established Holywood family, generously donated our first post-war maypole. It was inaugurated on 15th October 1949 before a vast crowd of happy Holywood people. The traditional dancing of children around the pole was revived, the maypole itself being beautifully decorated. The ninety-four feet spar was prepared and finished in Messrs Harland & Wolff's shipyard and towed down Belfast Lough to be unloaded at high tide at the Esplanade by a movable crane.

It is difficult to determine when the maypole was re-sited from the position in the centre of the crossroads, indicated by the Raven map of 1625. James Munce, the town's meticulous Surveyor, took the opportunity to erect the 1949 pole in compliance with the ever-increasing road traffic on the High Street.

The 1949 spar had the shortest life of any of our maypoles. It was removed after only five years. Experts considered it had been attacked by rot. Perhaps, the Council was being over-cautious, as the members remembered the frightening events which surrounded the unexpected fall of the maypole on 12th February 1943!

The Dunn family kindly gave the town a replacement in May 1957. The seventy-five

Maypole looking down Shore Street, c. 1900.

feet spar was inaugurated on a very wet afternoon, the inclemency of which did nothing to dampen the enthusiasm of the spectators. Holywood residents are very proud of their maypole; as William Dunn said to mark the occasion, *"Holywood without our maypole is a town without its heart."* Heart maybe, but twenty years later the pole lost ten of its feet! Again the wet sub-soil of the prehistoric beach line rotted the base of the maypole. It was replaced after the decayed portion had been removed. The remaining fifty-five feet spar appeared very short after all our wooden giants; its shorter height prepared the town for our future maypoles!

During the traffic rush on Monday, 10th October 1995 the maypole literally was the centre of a serious traffic accident – it was chopped off at the base! Fortunately, it fell diagonally along Shore Street. Some weeks before the accident, the Roads Authority had made it illegal for vehicles to turn into Shore Road from the Holywood through-pass. It seems an errant delivery lorry "going the wrong way" collided with the pole. The downfall of the maypole in 1943 was recalled by local folk. All agreed that, once again, the town was fortunate that no one had been injured.

On Friday, 26th April 1996 a long-arm crane used Shore Road as its base to position the new maypole in time for the traditional May Day celebrations. The present maypole was prepared by Harrison Brothers of Darlington from a sixty-feet Douglas Fir tree imported from Denmark. It is our first "hinged" pole, which allows for easy maintenance and prevents underground rot. Proudly it carried the traditional weather-vane, fifty-three feet above the town. Unfortunately the cock flew away when the former pole fell down!

Already in the maypole story we have discussed a couple of our maypole traditions – May Day celebrations and the flying of a flag for weddings in bygone days. Several other customs come to mind.

A tradition peculiar to Holywood is the decoration of the maypole with model yachts. It is difficult to determine when this custom commenced. We know that the pole erected in 1902 carried a cross-tree. It may have been at the ends of this beam that the quaternary sets first revolved in the wind. The present-day boats were hand-crafted by the McCarty family and signify the town's connection with yachting on the Belfast Lough.

Now the Union flag is flown every day from the mast-head. Formerly this was reserved for special occasions. On the request of the bereaved family, the Union flag is flown at half-mast on the death of a resident born in Holywood. It is also flown at half-mast on occasions of national mourning. Flying flags at half-mast was a Chinese custom of the tenth century B C. They were used to signal intentions and identify friends or foes. Nautically, lowering the flag denoted surrender or peace. It became customary for friendly ships, passing at sea, to salute by "dipping" flags in concert. The emblem was lowered slowly from the head of the mast and then quickly hoisted again. In Army parades, regimental flags are lowered before commanding officers in salute and then re-hoisted. When the Union flag is flown at half-mast from the Holywood maypole, it symbolises the town's salute to one of its own. After the honoured daughter or son has been interred, the flag is re-hoisted to the masthead.

After the tragic death of the Princess of Wales on 31st August 1997, the Union flag flew at half-mast for many days, as a mark of the town's respect; the base of the maypole became a colourful garden of floral tributes. The placing of flowers around the pole is a new idea from the people of our town and was used to honour Ulster's motor cycle hero, Joey Dunlop.

Until the 1930's the flag was lowered on to the casket of a deceased Holywood resident when the funeral procession paused at the foot of the maypole on its way to the Priory churchyard. The custom, assiduously carried out by Hugo Shannon, was discontinued when road traffic increased in the town centre.

In former days the lower portion of the pole was used as the town's public notice board – even today notices of meetings and local occasions are posted there. Within living memory Holywood people often enjoyed the sight of an embarrassed young groom, on his stag night, being tied to the maypole and pelted with flour. It seems this laughing stock symbolised the termination of the lad's freedom!

A recent addition to the town's Christmas festivities is the illumination of the Maypole from top to toe with coloured lights. It becomes the cynosure of the County Antrim shoreline, and visitors arriving by air and sea remember their first sight of Holywood with the maypole set in sparkling lights. Perhaps entry into the twenty-first century will see our unique possession illuminated by floodlights to draw attention to the Maypole Town throughout the year.

ESSAY II - HOLYWOOD - SEASIDE FUN TOWN

HER THAT WAVED TILL THE KINNEGAR

On Carrick shore Ah stud an' stud
And luked across at Holywud,
An' luked and luked an' there wuz her
A'wavin' from the Kinneger.

Ah cudn't thole at all, at all
White suds was batin' Carrick wall
But wind and waves ah'd be to dare
To reach my love on Kinneger.

The breakers ris' as high as high
The scrakin' wind got worse forby
But thonder was my guidin' star
A'wavin' from the Kinneger.

Ah tuk me boat an' rowed an' rowed
Across Knockfergus Bay she goed
Nor wind nor wave cud houl me far
From her that waved on Kinneger.

Aye, many years has went an' went
An' now Ah'm oul' and grey and bent,
An' married till a woman, her
That waved me will the Kinneger.

An' whiles Ah stan' and stare an' stare
An' mind thon day in Carrick there'
Ah wish Ah had been drown'd afar
Afore Ah reached the Kinnegar.

(Julius McCullough Lecky Craig)

Our second essay describes the maypole town when it was a leading Irish holiday resort. Come with me on a couple of walks along the coast. We shall stroll towards the Kinnegar and then on some other summer day to Cultra and "the yachting".

Part 1

To raise your expectations for the Kinnegar walk, let me tell you of an annual event which every child anticipated with joy. In Holywood, like every other Victorian holiday town, the summer circus was a long-awaited spectacle.

Every year large posters appeared in the shop windows to advertise the coming event. Excitement crescendoed when mobile cages full of ferocious animals, troops of piebald horses, colourful clowns on stilts and scantily-clad artistes paraded through the town following a brass band. At last the big top had been erected on the Kinnegar and the ring-master presented an amazing programme well worth the visit to our seaside town.

Many years before the circus came to town, Thomas T Kelly, our Holywood surgeon with decided views on a healthy lifestyle proclaimed –

> *"Promenades are the resort of those who come to Holywood*
> *to inhale health from the pure saline breezes!"*

If, like him, you have *"mens sana in corpore sano"*, you will enjoy the Holywood activity events during your day on the Kinnegar "theme park" of the nineteenth century.

Our local surgeon described the Kinnegar in lyrical tones :

> *"On the western side there is a smooth esplanade, formed along the beach, behind this lies several hundred acres of velvet sward called the Holywood Coneygar. Nowhere is there more diversified or beauteous scenery, the views are in no way inferior to the shores of the Mediterranean sea. Here the picturesque beauty of the entire lough can be seen on a clear day. Towards evening when the water is on the beach, the gentle plashing of the waves upon the shingle induces the pensive mood, which poets call 'the voice of the waters'. Towards the close of the day water parties are a major source of amusement, when, for an hour, the glass-smooth sea reflects the rich colours of the western sky. A visitor who knows how to handle the oar leaps into one of the tight little craft which float invitingly at the water's edge. A silent sweep of his oar soon sends him skimming into the sunset."*

Tradition tells us the "water-parties" were rowing-boat picnics, when the occupants of the little craft serenaded each other over the calm waters, the sun sinking behind Cave Hill and the silver moon rising from the Holywood Hills.

In the first part of this essay we shall look at the historic background to the Kinnegar and the recreations it provided for the summer visitor.

Robert Lloyd Praeger studied the Kinnegar as an observant Holywood schoolboy and

The Holywood Ballroom c. 1840 – also used as a Methodist Chapel and the Girl Guides' Hall.

later recorded how the area was home to our first ancestors. Thomas Raven's map, drawn in 1625 for Viscount Clandeboye, shows the Cuney Burrow peninsula quaintly decorated with cheery little bunny rabbits! Conies (from the Latin word coniculus, a rabbit) were bred on sandy warrens by our forbears to provide a rapidly replenishing supply of fresh meat for the table. Possibly the Anglo-Norman John de Saukvill introduced rabbits to the Kinnegar , when King Henry III confirmed his authority in Holywood in 1217. It seems some of the little mammals made their way across the bay to Knocknagoney – "the rabbit hill".

By 1700 ships were beached on the sandbanks and laid on their sides for cleaning and caulking, that is stopping the seams with oakum and melted pitch. Maps of 1743 and 1767 show a four mile roadway running directly from Belfast over the mudflats towards the Kinnegar and into Holywood town, thus avoiding the steep hill to Strandtown.

Mason's map of 1819 marks the warren peninsula and shows the river, which rises in the Holywood Hills and flows into the little landward bay.

In his statistical account, Rev William Holmes, the local vicar mentions *"a new bridge leading to the rabbit warren".* He suggests that Holywood should emulate Holland by reclaiming the many hundred acres of potentially fertile land between the warren and the mainland. His good advice prompted the construction of the Holywood Bank in 1830 and the disappearance of the peninsula.

Reporting on 29th September 1834 Lieutenant G F W Bordes wrote :

> *"A mile from Holywood there is a curious sandbank called the Cunifar. Here large vessels anchor which draw too much water to go up to Belfast.*

It seems the Kinnegar was used to lighten the ships of cargo. Possibly this was why the Customs station was moved from the foot of Shore Street to the Kinnegar in the 1860's.

Perhaps the last time the Holywood shore was used for the off-loading of cargo was as late as 1922. The *"S S Graphic"* sank in Belfast Lough before she could reach Donegall Quay. The ship was carrying the first consignment of Austin Seven motor vehicles brought over to Ireland from the factory in England. *S S Graphic* was raised successfully, beached at Holywood and the little water-logged cars salvaged. After many miles of motoring one returned home to Cultra to be displayed in the galleries of the Ulster Folk and Transport Museum..

A great abundance of edible mussels attracted summer campers to the sand dunes. Their tents, campfires, booths and activities must have provided a colourful sight to summer visitors. During the freezing famine winter of 1739 and again in 1846, some of Belfast's destitute poor lived for many months on the Holywood Kinnegar, devouring shellfish. When Squire Harrison sold the eastern part of the Kinnegar to William Weatherall in 1857, domestic building commenced, the first houses being St Leonard's. An interesting contemporary map called the present-day Esplanade "Park Road" and Kinnegar Road "Milltown Road". Later a frustrated poet changed Milltown to "Milton" and added "Byron Street" to the plan. This map shows the Holywood Music Hall, yet another seaside attraction for summer visitors. Celebrated thespians, comics and singers visiting Belfast theatreland found Kinnegar lodging houses to their liking - many of them found their way to the stage of our little music hall.

In 1865 the embankment, which carried the railway extension to Bangor, bisected Marine Parade and the Kinnegar became a residential suburb of Holywood. Long before Kelly advertised *"the salubrious seaside perambulations and fabulous water-parties of the Kinnegar"*, the young squires of the big houses along the coast had discovered the excitement of wildfowling on the sand dunes. The dining tables of Richmond, Garnerville, Mertoun Hall, Maryfield, Ashfield, Westbrook and Holywood House were accustomed to serve birds from the Kinnegar for the entree at dinner. It was only to be expected that the first official sporting activity would be marksmanship. About 1870 the Ulster Rifle Club started target shooting on the Kinnegar. The club was very successful, and on 30th May 1910 the British Miniature Rifle Shooting Championships were held. The competitors from England won the day. Holywood Scouts and Boys' Brigade acted as stewards - they told stories of *"that day"* for the rest of their lives.

Perhaps it was the Rifle Club which attracted the War Office to purchase Kinnegar land in 1887, and establish a summer drill and target practice camping area. It became a rifle range known as "the Butts", after the Bishop's Palace on the south side of the railway line had been acquired for Army use.

Army personnel were among the keenest participants in the Golf Club and the Cricket Club when the games were played on the Kinnegar. Ireland's first permanent cricket pitch was laid out in Dublin in 1838, and it seems the game was being played in Holywood by the mid-century. A local team was formed in 1871 but only survived a single season. John P Birch records :

> *"The Holywood Club was founded in 1879, the clubhouse being the barn of Eldon House, the home of Robert Erskine, who was practically founder of the Club."*

Documentary evidence sets the foundation date of the Club as Monday, 28th March 1881, following a meeting in the Holywood News Room. The ground beside Eldon House was given by the President of the Club, Captain J R Harrison of Ardtullagh. On 6th June 1883, a pavilion was opened by Mrs Robert Grimshaw Dunville, of Redburn, the Dunvilles being Patrons of the Club.

A highlight of the Holywood society season was the two-day cricket match played on the Redburn lawns by the local club and guests who were visiting the big house. The Dunvilles, proprietors of the Royal Irish Distillery, provided the legendary hospitality for which they became famous in Holywood!

A devastating hurricane in January 1884 broke open the Holywood bank and allowed the tide to ebb and flow over the cricket ground twice daily. A huge tidal wave up-rooted the three-year-old pavilion and carried it half a mile, on to the railway embankment. Only the ingenuity and hard work of the committee reclaimed it and secured the building to its original foundations.

For safety's sake, the Club removed to the five-acre meadow at Spafield in 1885, members again bodily carrying their pavilion across the railway line to the new ground.

In 1899 Holywood won the Ulster Challenge Cup by one wicket over the Ulster Cricket Club. The occasion was marked by a celebration dinner in the Town Hall on Monday, 21st August 1899, the invitation to which reads "Holywood Cricket and Lawn Tennis

Club". The dinner menu shows what Holywood society expected for five shillings at the turn of the last century:

> *"Soup – Puree of Hare (Sherry)*
> *Fish – Fillet Sole Tartare (Hock)*
> *Entrée – Vol-au-vent Toulouse (Claret)*
> *Joint – Roast Sirloin of Beef, Roast Lamb, Boiled Chicken,*
> *Boiled Ham*
> *Sweets – Apple Tart, Orleans Pudding, Macedonia Jelly*
> *Assorted Cheeses. Dessert Fruits (Whiskey)"*

The caterers were Messrs Thompson and Sons of 14 Donegall Street, Belfast. The account for provision of forty guests including wines and spirits was thirteen pounds. The toasts were 'The Queen', 'The Winners of the Ulster Challenge Cup', 'Our Military Friends', 'Our Visitors' and 'The Chairman'.

The J P Birch pavilion was opened on 14th July 1962. The Cricket and Rugby Clubs amalgamated when the new rugby pitch was laid on the fields beside the five-acre meadow. By this time the Holywood through-pass had decimated the cricket pitch. However, the Gaelic players, who used the Church lands beside the main road, co-operated with the cricketers to enable play to continue at Spafield. At the end of the twentieth century, the Gaelic League refurbished their grounds into the finest in the North Down area.

The Tennis Club, which was associated with the cricketers on the Kinnegar, started life on courts beside the Town Hall. The Club does not appear to have survived long into the twentieth century. Many Holywood families owned private courts in their gardens; tennis parties were a definite fixture in the social summer season. The four hard courts of the privately owned Norwood Tennis Club on My Lady's Mile became the cynosure of Holywood teenagers. Its pretty little pavilion was used for the first productions by 'The Holywood Players' and many "hops", the name we used for weekend dances. When the club was added to the campus of Sullivan Upper School, tennis players removed to the municipal courts at Seapark Recreation Grounds. For a short time the title "Norwood Tennis Club" continued at Seapark, now it is only a happy memory of Holywood days long past.

Historically, the most important Kinnegar attraction for visitors to the seaside town was Ireland's first Golf Course. It was founded on 9th November 1881; the original competition being held on St Stephen's Day, 1881.

The Romans called golf a game for rustics – Paganica; Medieval French described it as a 'Jeu de Mail'; the Dutch played it on ice and named it Het Kolven. Scots were forbidden to play 'The Royal Game' in 1457. However, one of them, Sir Hugh Montgomery, brought the game to North Down in 1606 and provided the students of his new school at Newtownards with "A Green for Recreation at Goff".

Marine Parade and old jetty before railway was extended to Bangor.

Mason in his survey of Holywood Parish in 1819 writes

> *"In Holywood a game called by some 'Shinny', by others 'Common' is played with a stick bent at its lower extremity like a reaping hook. The ball, called 'nag' or in Irish 'brig' is struck to and fro. It resembles the game called Golf in Edinburgh. It is played at Christmas and is not confined to any sect as Dissenters and Romanists seem to be equally attached to it."*

I think the sedentary pastor was confusing golf, hockey and hurley.

Golf in its modern form was introduced into Ireland by Rt Hon Thomas Sinclair when he returned from a golfing holiday in Scotland. He was assisted by George L Baillie of Musselburgh who recently had been appointed English Language master at Belfast Royal Academy. 'The Field' magazine of 19th November 1881 records the foundation of the Club. The Holywood Kinnegar was selected as a possible location so George Baillie sought an interview with the landlord, Captain John Harrison. After a good luncheon in Belfast's famous Ulster Club at Castle Junction, the good squire promised *"eighty acres of land for the new links, free of rent or other charge."* Harrison became first President of the Club.

Fortunately, a founder member has recorded his personal reminiscences:

> *" One looks back on those earliest days of golf on the Holywood Kinnegar with mingled feelings of amusement.*

The natives looked on with lofty scorn at the little group that used to come off the train on Saturdays with strange sticks in brown bags. Wet or dry, they tramped the grass and beat the whins. 'Softies' if not 'lunatics' was the verdict of the little town by the sea! Sightseers made little picnic journeys to the Kinnegar to look at the game and went home assuring one another that there was nothing in it. Wagonettes stopped on the Holywood road to survey the golfers through field glasses. On a wet day, if an unlucky stroke at a half covered ball splashed up a fountain of water, the vehicles drove off with bellows and guffaws."

The nine-hole semi-circular course was built around the cricket ground, both clubs working in complete harmony. The inner part of the links ran beside the railway embankment, which area was notoriously swampy. The mid-section was rough grass and fairly dry. The part beside the seashore was covered with gorse and provided a good variety of difficult shots. The main hazard was a small whin-carpeted quarry - a magnet for every ball. Of the quarry, the founder member recalls :

"It was but a brassie shot from the far low brow onto the green, but its whinny depths were fatal to many of us who spent a large portion of our happy Saturdays plying an ineffectual niblick with might and main."

The best holes were those nearest the sea and the greens were surprisingly good.

When the Prince of Wales visited Ireland in 1885 Captain John Harrison took the opportunity to invite his royal patronage for the club; it became The Royal Belfast Golf Club.

Officers from the regiments stationed in Belfast and Holywood began to use the links, especially when the Highland Light Infantry, the Gordon Highlanders and the Black Watch were stationed in Ulster. As with the Army, local clergy were shown special consideration in subscription rates. They were supposed *"to have a controlling influence over the caddies"*, perhaps also over the members! One spectator claimed *"I am not so much here to watch as to listen to the members playing golf!"*.

In 1887 the committee rented one of the semi-detached houses called 'Golf Villas' for a clubhouse, conveniently situated beside the first home green.

By 1890 , membership had risen to two hundred enthusiasts and the links were over-crowded. Increase in the entrance fee to five guineas (£280 in today's money) did not stem the tide of those who wished to take up the sport of the day. As well as over-crowding of the links, the War Office was increasing its use of the Kinnegar. As a result, the Royal Belfast was forced to move to Carnalea in 1892.

The Club returned to the Holywood area in 1925 to enjoy the magnificent course at Craigavad, which has one of the loveliest settings of any in Britain.

Ireland's first lady golfer played the Kinnegar course in 1887. 'The Field' for 1st October 1887 records *"The Club Captain and Mrs Wright played foursome against Colonel Lyon Campbell and Captain Wright. The match attracted quite a turnout of the ladies. At the end of the first round the former were four up, the lady having played particularly well. The second round came down to all even and one to play. The last hole was keenly contested and was won by a long and well-laid put (sic) of Capt Wright."*

Another Irish first for our town was the Holywood Ladies' Golf Club organised in the autumn of 1888 at a meeting held in Hillbrook, Victoria Road, the home of Mrs R Young. Mrs Young became the Treasurer and Miss C E McGee the Club Secretary. The previous year, Miss McGee had been invited by Dr Collier, Headmaster of Belfast Royal Academy "to observe the novel sight of a lady golfer". The "novel" lady golfer was the wife of Capt Wright. Dr Collier introduced Miss McGee to Ireland's first lady golfer and Miss McGee was *'inspired with a wish to play the game of golf'*. Her enthusiasm founded Ireland's first ladies' golf club.

Members of the Royal Belfast encouraged the ladies and gave them free use of the course on specified days. As only five of the fifteen lady founder members were players, it is understandable that one of the first items on the new committee' agenda was "golfing attire". The ladies designed a blazer with full sleeves, tight waist and cut widely in front to display the elegant scarlet and blue club tie!

The first ladies' golf club in Ireland brought even more generous press coverage than its masculine counterpart. The ladies attracted fascinated crowds of spectators to the Kinnegar. The annual St Stephen's Day match with the gentlemen was the highlight of the golfing social season.

Holywood ladies were instrumental in the formation of the Irish Ladies' Golf Union. Miss C Mulligan, a Holywood member, was first Irish Lady Champion. The Holywood ladies moved to Carnalea in 1892 and became the Ladies' Branch of the Royal Belfast Golf Club.

A second golf course was laid out on the south side of the railway line. Few motorists driving over Parkway from Holywood Road at Tillysburn know they are on the second Holywood golf course, a couple of miles from Ireland's first documented course on the Kinnegar. The "Sportsman's Holiday Guide" for 1897 describes Belmont as *"nine holes and rather more than a mile around"*. The course was laid out in the grounds of Garnerville House, the home of the Garner family. The Belfast News-Letter for 5th December 1899 records the Club's annual general meeting. The Golfing Annual records the foundation date as 1892 or 1891, and describes it as *"laid in a pretty park at five minutes' walk from Tillysburn station"*.

The Club is not listed after 1908. Belmont Ladies' Golf Club was founded in 1892 and not listed after 1899. The "pretty" park lay between Garnerville Road, Holywood Road, and Old Holywood Road; the parklands of the Moat House lay to the west. Even now, former children of the area recall with pleasure *"learning to play golf in the sand bunker behind the big house"* during the long sunny summer months. The big house itself made way for special educational purposes - the golf course is long forgotten.

Now we come to the last of the Kinnegar attractions and the only one which continues into the new century. Holywood Sailing Club spread canvas in 1862 under the patronage of Lord Hill-Trevor, Sir Charles Lanyon and the future Lord Dunleath. Craft sailed from the long pier which was built opposite Shore Road in 1855, and rented a triangle of land between Kinnegar Road and the Esplanade on which to store boats.

The Club is one of the oldest in Ireland. Three classes are unique to Holywood - sharpie class, maiden class and junior class. The original burgee was yellow with the Priory motif on a blue circle. In 1923 it was changed to blue and white stripes with the motif in red.

Before 1923 the Club held its shore meetings in the old Town Hall, with social activities in the Kinnegar Hotel. The members erected two large marquees for club guests during regattas.

The sailors co-operated with the Amateur Rowing and Swimming Club, which maintained the timber boathouse on Marine Parade, filled with gigs, ropes and all the equipment necessary to operate an efficient boating organisation. For many years there had been swimming, fishing and sailing from the smaller jetty half-way along the Marine Parade which had been refurbished in 1855. One of the saddest days of the seaside town was in 1873, the day of the tragic Greenisland Regatta. James Withers and Edwin Henderson - a relative of Rev H Henderson, were drowned off the twin islands in Belfast Lough. Early in the morning they set off from Holywood Pier in fair weather for Greenisland on the County Antrim shore. An unexpected storm blew up from the north-west, the gig was swamped and the crew thrown into the waves. The monument at Priory Corner commemorates the disaster. Captain Patty and James Woods were drowned during the regatta. James Shannon, the Holywood stalwart, displayed superb yachtsmanship on that fateful day.

The Sailing Club was using the pier for the Holywood Regatta on 28th August 1883. The successful day was brought to a spectacular end with a splendid fireworks display. Early the following morning the pier was partly destroyed by fire.

During the first decade of the twentieth century the Sailing Club lost its previous enthusiastic supply of Holywood helmsmen. However, by 1923 interest was renewed, and the Club re-organised at the present site on the Kinnegar. A timber shed was erected for time-keepers and storage of equipment. A boatyard was developed and a flag mast hoisted.

By 1929 a distinctive clubhouse was required by the growing membership. A fine wooden pavilion was opened on 11th August, 1931 by Lady Kelly of Ballymenoch House.

The sea front after the railway extension and the Tower was added to St. Colmcille's Church.

By 1932 club membership had greatly expanded, as the seaside town grew in population. The clubhouse was refurbished and enlarged - two years later the name was changed to Holywood Yacht Club. During the second World War the pavilion was requisitioned by the army, indeed the Kinnegar became a military zone. After the war, the Club became famous for social evenings. Memories of the Holywood "squeezes" and coteries were revived, sailors and landlubbers alike enjoyed the fun.

In 1959 Tony Lucy, a club member and a local architect drew plans for a new clubhouse. The old wooden pavilion was jacked up and turned around to face the sea. The new building was constructed around it. Mrs Donnan declared the new building open on 12th May, 1962. Extensions were added in 1989 and refurbishments in 1998 to make Holywood Yacht Clubhouse one of the finest on Belfast Lough.

After 1883 the club used a pontoon which was beached after the season. In 1921 a wooden pier was constructed which proved to be below high water mark and had to be replaced in 1932.

When Sir Samuel Kelly (Commodore 1927 - 1938) discovered that new timber was required, he told the committee to come up to Ballymenoch House and tell the head gardener what was needed to put up a pier!

Over the years, the Club has provided a nautical way of life for many Holywood people. It preserves one of its primary principles - to introduce young people to competent yachtsmanship.

During the twentieth century, military activity increased on the Holywood Kinnegar. Today, most of the area is under Government control. The old butts have disappeared. They were well known to many generations of Holywood teenagers - with diminishing firing points from eight hundred to one hundred yards. Once they were counted among the best in the United Kingdom. Now a modern sewage disposal works has destroyed the site of the former target banks.

The original Laburnum Cottage, the farm of the Greer family, was demolished by the Territorial Army in 1943. Golf Villas, the clubhouse of Ireland's first golf course, was demolished for the buildings of the Royal Army Ordnance Corps. The wartime railway siding has disappeared, as has the Army football pitch. The cricket pitch, the tennis courts and Eldon House are long forgotten.

North Down and Belfast Borough Councils should be congratulated for the preservation of the wetlands between the railway embankment and the Belfast to Holywood dual carriageway. Regretfully, a road bridge has bisected the area, the pipe terminal of a natural gas plant has commandeered part of the area and another commercial park is contemplated on the former mudflats.

However, reed warblers have returned to our wetlands, which once produced the reeds so necessary in the manufacture of linen, a commodity which brought vast prosperity to Holywood in the nineteenth century.

The zone is worthy of bird sanctuary status and the mudflats are returning to a natural habitat. It is essential that the dumping of rubbish beside the sewage disposal plant is prevented, debris removed from the site and the area preserved as a designated nature park perhaps entitled "the Holywood everglades".

I hope you enjoyed the day trip to the Kinnegar when Holywood was a seaside summer holiday town. I hope you do not find the march of time too disagreeable. Tomorrow, if the weather is good, we shall take a walk along the coastal path towards Bangor. By comparison, here time has stood still.

Part 2 - CULTRA

Yesterday, we explored the Kinnegar "the rabbit warren" ; today we stroll along the coastal path to Cultra - "the back of the strand".

Few Ulster towns enjoy as fully documented a seaside saga as Holywood has acquired over the years. An advertisement in the Northern Whig for 13th May 1824 reads:

"Sea bathing - Hugh Stewart of Holywood begs leave to acquaint his friends and the public that he has a few good lodging houses to let and that his hot baths are open to the public."

A year later, on 28th April 1825 his holiday advertisement reads -

> *"H Stewart informs the public that his bath establishment is in excellent repair for the season, consisting of a hot sea water marble bath with shower baths."*

These expensive advertisements may have induced the following extravagant editorial on 1st September 1825 in the Northern Whig -

> *"No watering place can boast so interesting a vicinity as Holywood and remarkably well attended this season. The harbour at Cultra is undergoing improvements and the road from Belfast is to be provided with a convenient side path."*

By 1837 those looking for a Holywood venue could have read in Lewis's directory *"Holywood is delightfully situated. Its fine sandy beach makes it a favourite resort for sea bathing."*

Surgeon Kelly was determined to put Holywood at the head of the holiday resorts lists. In 1850 he wrote -

> *"The hundreds which annually flock to Holywood's shores and the numerous invalids which are daily experiencing renewed health and vigour speak volumes in favour of its high character as a summer retreat. Holywood's climate and advantages are supported by the testimony of many eminent physicians, who affirm the pure water and mild sea air greatly assist in alleviating consumption, rheumatism, psoriasis, herpes, porrido, bronchitis, catarrh, asthma and women's ailments.*
>
> *Watering places helping to perform physical cures should also provide mental stimulation for their patients. In this respect Holywood is peculiarly favoured since the compass of an easy walk introduces the stranger to spots of considerable scenic pretensions and historic interest. Indeed, a few hours spent rambling over the Holywood Hills will exercise healthful influences over disease."*

Sight-seeing added to sea-bathing convinced Kelly that Holywood rivalled the best in the Kingdom as a resort of fashion, pleasure and healing. Arbutus blossoming along the lough-shore, verbena in October and roses still flowering at Christmas, all testified to the mildness of Holywood's temperature and its suitability for sea-bathing.

Dr Knox in "The Irish Watering Places" claims -

> *"the best bathing beaches are at Cultra, where the low tide is close to the shoreline and the sea water is strong, fresh and pure on the open beach."*

Ten years later, in 1860, McComb's 'Guide to Belfast' refers to Holywood as

> *"a rapidly improving village and watering-place much frequented by bathers and invalids. The scenery is pleasing – "quite English indeed". Many handsome houses have been built on the sunny slopes for summer visitants. The rail service is excellent, fourteen trains daily and eleven on Sundays."*

Black's "Watering Places (1871) – "The Guide to the Healthiest and Most Beautiful Watering Places in the British Islands" or "Where shall I go ?" says –

> *"The beach at Holywood is sandy and offers an agreeable place for sea bathing and there are hot baths adjoining. The climate is very good in this pleasant little place to which people are accustomed to resort when they want pure air. The situation is very beautiful and accommodation for visitors is excellent."*

Even as late as 1878, Murray's "Handbook for Travellers" advertises Holywood as -

> *"an agreeable bathing place; its position on the Lough shore offers many advantages."*

So I invite you to come along as a welcome visitor to seaside Holywood, having read the holiday brochures, not long after the railway terminus had opened its doors on to the centre of the Marine Parade in 1848. Remember the railway embankment had not, as yet, bisected the Marine Parade, in order to extend the railway line to Bangor. Turn towards Cultra and imagine the lough waters lapping on golden sands, bathing machines trundling to the waves and health-conscious swimmers splashing in the surf. Hear the summer calls of children building castles on the sands and some of the more adventurous little boys fishing off the jetty. Soon the little pier will be refurbished by good Squire Harrison. You pass the House of Industry, then the pretentious terrace known as Gray's Buildings. For them, Kelly writes *"for comfort and architectural completeness they vie with any"*. Visitors may test this claim as some of the houses may be rented for the summer season. Next door is the holiday cottage of the famous Belfast banking family – the Batts of Purdysburn. Beside the Batts' summer garden is the Marine Hotel, where you may have booked a room with a sea view for your stay at the seaside.

As well as holiday houses and cottages available for renting by the week or longer, there is an excellent selection of commodious hotels and boarding establishments. In a subsequent essay we shall take a stroll around our nineteenth century hostelries.

No holiday visit to Holywood would be complete without a visit to the Assembly Rooms and Baths building, built in 1852. This fine establishment was built on the old site of the Non-Subscribing Presbyterian Meeting House, at the corner of Shore Street. In the large first storey auditorium, visitors and residents alike enjoyed the grand musical concerts, scientific lectures and literary discussions for which the town is famous, and not a few typical Irish political meetings. Possibly the social events known as the Holywood "squeezes" took place in the Assembly Rooms, although some commentators claim "the squeezes" and the Holywood coteries of Rollo House were synonymous. Most likely, kissing and cuddling were common to both! At street level, the Holywood Baths Company later associated with the Railway Company, provided first class concession prices to the public. The well-patronised baths were open seven days a week from 6 a.m. to 10 p.m. The visitor could have a dozen warm salt-water baths for nine shillings, or a dozen cold showers for half-a-crown. An advertisement for 24th May 1854 proclaims *"baths always ready, a female attendant will wait on the ladies"*.
In 1917 the building became the Maypole cinema. On 27th October 1944 it was destroyed by fire.

The 1884 Belfast Directory refers to *"a flourishing amateur boating and swimming club, whose members use the long pier as a base.*

Like the cinema, the long pier was destroyed by fire. The Boating and Swimming Club maintained a wooden hut for equipment at the shore end of the boardwalk.

As you continue your Victorian perambulation along the Strand, you should call into Hugh Stewart's Hot Sea-Water Baths or Ann Rowley's Private Baths. Here, too, are some of the houses Hugh Stewart offers for summer letting. Commenting on such lodgings for visitors, Kelly writes –

> *"No family, however large or small, need despair of meeting with suitable accommodation in private residences, lodgings or respectable family apartments."*

Of Hugh Stewart himself, the chronicler records –

> *"The Stewarts are among the Holywood families who have reared to themselves a considerable amount of valuable house property, by persevering industry. Mr Hugh Stewart, unaided by the blessings a child of fortune enjoys, through unwearied industry and integrity, has acquired an independent annual income of a thousand pounds in household property. Such men are the real benefitters of society."*

The best of the summer "lets" were Ward's cottages at Marino, today the Tudor-style houses in Marino Park. Kelly describes their situation –

> *"The cottages are entirely secluded from public intrusion by their extensive and tastefully laid-out grounds. They partake the character of country residences, being detached and surrounded by luxuriant shrubberies and extensive plantations. For the most part, these are let for summer residences."*

Lieutenant Bordes describes the cottages as built of stone in the Gothic style and generally filled from Belfast for the bathing season.

Indeed, you may have decided to rent one of these holiday brochure delights in order to spend the summer sailing from the nearby yacht club. If so, your daily walk will take you over the area eroded by marine action in the early decades of the nineteenth century to the bathing beach and little harbour, which the Northern Whig claims to be *"so convenient to the lover of aquatic excursions"*.

It seems Cultra had been a yachting centre as early as 1706. The Belfast News-Letter for 19th June 1829 described a Northern Yacht Club Regatta as -

> *"A nine days' wonder of sparkling entertainment which attracted international visitors and great holiday crowds. Long after the yachts had completed the lough races for the day, the booths and stalls, spread over the five acres of sea meadows, attract the crowds well into a night of dancing and carousal."*

The harbour lay within the curtilage of the Kennedy domain. We shall continue the story when we turn to "the Kennedys" of Cultra.

But now, with the westering sun shining on your face and a gentle wind to your back, you take the return journey to Holywood, enjoying the splendid views over the Lough towards the Cave Hill, Black Mountain and Belfast City.
The path will lead you past Cooper's Bay. In the next essay we shall read about many events in our history which could be seen from that lovely little strand. In another essay we shall see how coastal erosion washed away the Point fields that quartered the grand jamboree which accompanied the regatta of the Northern Yacht Club during the final decade of the nineteenth century.

ESSAY III - LOUGH VIEWS FROM COOPER'S BAY

THE SONG OF THE GOOD SHIP CASTLE DOWN

A gallant barque she topped the waves and fearless hearts were we
With guns and pikes and bayonets a stalwart company.
It was sixteen years since Thurot came sweeping up the bay
"The Siege of Carrickfergus" so merrily we did play.

At Greencastle, Whiteabbey and Holywood's Cooper's Bay
Were hundreds waving handkerchiefs with many loud huzza
By that green slope beside Strandtown we cheered and cheer it still,
For we had changed its name that year and called it Bunker Hill.

Cooper's Bay from Seapark (c. 1850) before railway extension.

Just as the twinkling stars shine through God's unfurled flag by night,
By dying fires we sang "Good Night" and "Fare ye well brave tars",
We looked aloft at heaven and sang "Our flag is stripes and stars"
Then into Boston port we sailed beneath those stripes and stars.

Anon – Traditional song

In 1760 Commodore Thurot of the French Navy captured Carrickfergus Castle. In 1778 Admiral Paul Jones of the United States Navy sailed up the Belfast Lough – just a couple of the twenty lough views from Cooper's Bay this essay brings to mind.

As we carry our deck chairs and picnic baskets down to the sandy beach at Seapark, to catch glimpses of our maritime heritage, let us see how the Lough of Belfast (*Beal Feirste*, the Ford of the Sandbank) got its name.

The Irish Annals record *"In the year of the World 3506 Lough Laoigh in Ultonia broke forth."* Adamnan in his life of Columbkille tells how his hero *"requested prayers for some Bangor Abbey monks who were in danger of drowning in the Lough of the Calf"*. Father MacCana in his "itinerary" tells us :

> *the Church at Holywood is built on the Lake of the Calf, the head of which may be forded at Beall-Fearst, when the tide is out.*

At other times in history, Belfast Lough was called Knockfergus Bay or Lough *Beannchor* - Bangor, the pointed peaks..
Before the railway extension to Bangor thrust its embarrassing embankment between

Holywood town and the lough in 1865, a quiet lane led past the Priory church to one of Holywood's best bathing beaches - Cooper's Bay.

A century later, Rosamund Praegar donated the green field beside the beach for children's games and picnics. It became the place for Holywood people to enjoy the view over the Lough to Knockagh and Cave Hill. Viewed from Cooper's Bay, the County Antrim shoreline has provided the backdrop for many of our most important historic events.

The site of a Viking ship buried four miles along the coast at Carnalea and the Viking settlement in Strangford Lough show how close our encounter was with the Scandinavian adventurers of the ninth century. Their first Irish raid was on Rathlin Island in 795. The wealthy Bangor Abbey received attention in 822 and 956; no doubt the longships landed on Cooper's Bay to find what the raiders could pilfer from the Holywood Priory.

On July 29th, 1210 watchers from the beach witnessed our first royal visit. In 1177 King Henry II designated John, his ten-year-old youngest son, 'Lord of Ireland', intending one day to elevate the boy to kingly status. A crown was sought from the Pope, who sent it to England at Christmastide in 1185, when John was eighteen. However, it was never used. A decade after John was enthroned in England he came to Ireland to investigate "the Irish problem". His expedition landed at Waterford and advanced to Carrickfergus Castle, which he captured. A monetary roll preserved in the Tower of London records

> "*Thursday, July 29th 1210 at Holywood - to Geoffrey Luterell to make a prest. to mariners of a ship from Bayonne, 60s. Same day to the same, to make a prest. to mariners and galley-men - £17.*

Such unaccustomed wealth must have brought great merriment to Holywood on the day King John crossed the lough from Carrickfergus. He spent the night in the Government Bailey erected on the Motte. The Motte may have ante-dated Norman times; indeed Monsignor O'Laverty suggests it was a sepulchral mound. Tradition has it that the royal retinue camped on Ardshane - John's Hill. The following day the campaigners trudged King John's Road over the Holywood Hills to Dundonald.

In 1315 beach watchers may have seen the ships of the Bruce invasion at the entrance to Belfast Lough. Edward Bruce was the self-styled King of Ireland. His brother was Robert I, King of Scots. He had some claim to Ulster territory through his mother, which gave him the euphemistic vision of a fourteenth century United Kingdom - Scotland, Ireland and Wales. Edward landed at Larne on 25th May, 1315, and was joined by a few Irish chiefs who proclaimed him King of Ireland. After Edward's capture of Carrickfergus Castle in September 1316, King Robert joined his brother. However, the cruel "scorched earth policy" of the campaigning Scots infuriated the Irish who turned against them. The country was laid waste to such an extent that the Scots were forced to devour their dead to avoid starvation! King Robert returned to Scotland and Edward was defeated and killed at Faughart near Dundalk on 14th October, 1318. Our Scottish

The Holywood lighthouse (1844) built by Alex Mitchell in 1844, demolished in 1891.

cousins returned home, leaving their sordid tales behind them! Apart from a couple of arson attempts by the Scots on Carrickfergus Castle in 1386 and 1402, little more was heard of the United Kingdom of Scotland, Wales and Ireland.

Spectators at Cooper's Bay had a ringside seat for the arrival of our next royal visitor in June 1690. Following the 1688 revolution, Mary, daughter of James II and her husband William were declared joint sovereigns of England, Scotland and Wales. The Irish Parliament continued to support James. In February 1689 General Schomberg's Williamite army landed at Groomsport and captured Carrickfergus Castle on 13th August. In June 1690 King William landed at Carrickfergus and the following month defeated the Jacobites at the River Boyne.

The rival ambitions of Britain and France in America and India led to the Seven Years War -1756 to 1763. On 21st February 1760 astonished Holywood spectators at Cooper's Bay saw three ships of a French national squadron sail up Belfast Lough and drop anchor off Carrickfergus Castle. After a short engagement, Commodore Francois Thurot, the dashing young French naval commander captured the castle. The reason why he had risked this audacious attack was starvation aboard his ships. Provisions were supplied by 27th February and the French weighed anchors at one o'clock the following morning. They sailed from Carrickfergus straight into a British squadron laying in wait off the Isle of Man. Commodore Thurot was killed with five hundred Frenchmen. Three British sailors died and three were wounded.

"The Grampian" off the Holywood Bank; a training ship for destitute boys entering the Merchant Marine.

A few days later watchers from the beach saw *HMS Pallas* anchor off Carrickfergus bringing back many of the French prisoners taken in the sea battle. It may have been that the French attack on Carrickfergus alerted the government to the vulnerability of the North of Ireland.

In 1770 the watchers saw a ship leaving Carrickfergus Harbour bound for America crowded with Ulster emigrants. Among those who left Belfast Lough at that time were the Carrickfergus-born parents of President Andrew Jackson, and the parents of General Stonewall Jackson whose family hailed from Garden Lodge on the Old Holywood Road.

In 1775 the American War of Independence raised the flag of freedom. Holywood people had great sympathy with the New World's religious and democratic principles. Many had relations there and American problems were similar to those of Ulster Presbyterians. It is not surprising that the watchers on the beach cheered with huzzas the redoubtable Scotch-American privateer, Paul Jones, when he paid two visits to Belfast Lough in April 1778 in his sloop *"Ranger"*. Paul Jones became the first Admiral of the United States Navy.
On his second visit, in April 1778, the new-born "Stars and Stripes" thirteen stars and thirteen bars of freedom was flying from U S N Ranger's mast-head. That morning, *HMS Drake* was anchored off Carrickfergus. The audacious Captain Jones attacked and captured the larger British ship. Local folk re-named the escarpment at Strandtown on the road from Holywood to Belfast - *"Bunker Hill"*, in honour of one of the two heights near Boston where the first battle of the American War of Independence was fought on 16 June 1775.

War in the former Colonies and the French Revolution inspired the Irish Insurrection of 1798. When the Society of United Irishmen was established in Belfast on 18th October 1791, it received considerable support from Holywood Presbyterians. Their bravest leader, Henry Joy McCracken, and his family were associated with Holywood town.

Thomas Russell, a McCracken family friend, was out of harm's way at Fort George in the Scottish Highlands during the rebellion. He had been imprisoned in September 1796 following an unsuccessful siege of Belfast. After the rebellion he was released into the safe keeping of James Witherspoon of Knockbracken and Charles Ranken who lived at Knocknagoney, an area which had been searched for illegal arms during the rebellion. On his release from prison, Russell did his best to revive the spirit of insurrection, but without success. While he was in prison, the United Kingdom had been established. Ruthless punishment had been vested upon the rebels and desire for peace in a new century eclipsed the second rising sun of United Irishmen. Russell retreated into hiding, for some time at Craigavad. He escaped by sea from the little Rockport harbour with the help of the local McCutcheon family. Later, in Dublin he pursued his subversive activities and was re-arrested when he was attempting to rescue Robert Emmett from prison. Thomas Russell was transferred to Downpatrick Gaol for trial. There he was found guilty of sedition and executed by hanging - *"the man from God knows where"!*

In that momentous year beachcombers on Cooper's Bay were whispering rumours of a French invasion and gun-running for the United Irishmen. The arrival of a thousand Lancashire Light Dragoons and Yorkshire Fencibles intensified the excitement. The captain of the *"Bull of Irvine"* berthed in Dublin with news of a surreptitious ship he had encountered off the Copeland Islands, flying the American flag and urgently requesting a pilot to navigate the Belfast Lough. Perhaps a pilot was obtained from Groomsport because the next day she sailed past Cooper's Bay and anchored off Holywood. The Holywood Ships' Surveyor, Robert Walpole, boarded her with a company of dragoons. They expected *"The John and Martha" of Virginia*, for that was her name, to yield up a hefty load of smuggled arms; instead they uncovered a cargo of fine Virginian tobacco for the good citizens of Belfast!

The opposite situation occurred a century and a quarter later when little ships brought in mountains of illegal arms which were hidden in the warehouses and mansions of the merchant princes in Belfast and along the North Down coast.

Until 1804, the prison ship *"Postlethwaite"* could be seen lying at anchor between Holywood and Whitehouse. This prison ship was necessary to accommodate the over-spill of United Irishmen rebels from the Belfast prisons. One of the seaboard prisoners was Rev Dr Steele Dickson, Presbyterian minister of Portaferry. He records a spell of shore leave in Holywood on 12th January 1802

"After a pleasant passage, Captain Butterfield landed us near Holywood and escorted us to the house of Sir James Bristow, who received us with great civility and accommodated us with carriages for ourselves and luggage to Belfast."

Sir James' house was at the corner of High Street and Downshire Road; during the 1798 rebellion it was the barracks of the Earl of Westmeath's Yeomanry and was defended by an earth rampart in the back yard. Once it had been Agnes Mawhinney's Inn, later it was owned by Major McDowell, Commissioner of Penang. About 1865 it became the Holywood Royal Irish Constabulary barracks, and in 1934 the site of the New Cinema. In 1994 it was demolished for commercial purposes. Today, Claire House stands on this historic site.

Another reformatory ship, which lay off our shore, was *"The Grampian"*. She was used as a boarding school for destitute boys. From the year 1872 forty or fifty boys, rescued from poverty and crime, were trained to join the Merchant Marine or taught a worthwhile trade. "Grampian" was broken up in 1899, when the boys were transferred to Balmoral Industrial School.

But - to get back to the tale of Cooper's Bay.

Chroniclers disagree which was the first steamboat to pass the Bay. Some record *"Greenock"* out of Dumbarton sailed up the Lough in 1816; others claim *"Rob Roy"* was first to arrive three years later. Europe's earliest passenger steamship *"Comet"* was built on the Clyde in 1812. However, the reliable News-letter assures us that *"The Bangor Castle"* was calling daily at Cultra in 1825 on her way to Bangor. She was the fore-runner of the Holywood and Bangor boats of which we shall read in a later essay.

Little did spectators know that soon Harland and Wolff (1861) and Workman and Clark (1880) would be sending the world's greatest ships down the Belfast Lough.

The most famous of them all, "Titanic" was watched by hundreds of Holywood school children, taken out of class to Cooper's Bay for the big launch on 2nd April 1912. Fascinated, they watched as the huge ship filled the channel - tugs *Hornby* and *Herald* ahead, *Huskisson* and *Herculaneum* astern. Thirteen days later, on 15th April at 2.20 am she sank, taking with her 1,490 passengers and crew.

The fourth royal visit to the Province occurred on Saturday, 11th August 1849. On that wet summer morning, early swimmers at Cooper's Bay saw the Royal Yacht *"Victoria and Albert"* with a squadron of nine vessels, drop anchor off Craigavad. Queen Victoria and Prince Albert sailed up the Lough on the tender *"Fairy"* and disembarked at Belfast about two o'clock in the afternoon. After the visit they returned to spend the night on the yacht. The Royal Squadron sailed at seven o'clock on Sunday morning, but ferocious weather forced a return to lie at anchor off Cooper's Bay, till half-past three in the afternoon when departure for the Clyde became possible. Dense crowds lined the shore, Holywood people peered through the slanting rain hoping for a sight of the royal couple on deck. However, the Queen was not amused by the Irish weather. It took thirty-eight years before Queen Victoria braved our inclement waters again.

When the Prince and Princess of Wales sailed up the Lough in 1885, fifty-three Holywood folk guaranteed the cost of *"illuminating"* the Holywood Hills from Knocknagoney to Craigavad. Presumably this spectacular was accomplished by a series of hill-top bonfires and firework displays.

King George V and Queen Mary sailed up the Lough to open the Northern Ireland Parliament at Stormont in June 1921. They returned amid great rejoicing in 1936 - the last occasion on which the old royal yacht graced our waters.

We got a good view of the new Royal Yacht *"Britannia"* and her royal owner when the young Queen Elizabeth II and her consort visited Holywood on Wednesday, 9th August 1961. Britannia was back to sail the Lough and the coastline to the Giant's Causeway in 1977. Two decades later, on the splendid autumn morning of 27th October 1997, walkers lined the coastal path from Holywood to Cultra to watch that faultless craft make a last visit to the Lough on her farewell voyage around the British Isles.

In conclusion, let me share a couple of personal childhood recollections of Cooper's Bay. Imagine a silver flying-boat rise from mist curtained water and disappear, as swans do, into the early morning blue. These magnificent aircraft were the specialities of Short Brothers, founded in 1936 as Short and Harland's. They inspired us to dream of flights, like migrating birds, to distant domains with magical names. Harry Ferguson had taught the Irish to fly in 1909. By 1933 air ferries were flying from Belfast over Cooper's Bay to Renfrew Airport. In 1971 Short's private aerodrome became Belfast Harbour [later City] Airport and flights over Cooper's Bay became commonplace. My diary for Wednesday, 14th June 1944 reads :

"More battleships anchored here today. The whole lough in front of my bedroom windows is filled with little boats coming and going to attend the great fleet which is assembling off Grey Point."

Each evening a concert of sirens played on the summer fogs. A week later all was magnificent silence; the D-Day fleet had left Belfast Lough for the invasion of the Continent on that historic day, 6th June 1944. This was the beginning of the end of the Second World War.

In the 1970's construction of an inland route for the Holywood through-pass forced re-construction of the railway embankment over part of Cooper's Bay. However, what remains is in-filling naturally with golden sand. On a good summer afternoon, it is covered with children enjoying the beach and the park which Rosamund Praeger gave us.

Perhaps one day when the quality of sea water in the Belfast Lough improves, Cooper's Bay will again provide a premier bathing beach for the people of Holywood.

ESSAY IV - THE KENNEDYS OF CULTRA

The first entrepreneurs of old Holywood

The Cultra Kennedys were decidedly shrewd -
Soon the Clanbrassil debt was bought up and made good
By the first entrepreneurs in old Holywood.

They erected a harbour to expedite trade
And a light house for guidance where taxes were paid
Deep water the asset by which fortunes were made.

They let a new railway line run over their land
Most trains stopped at Cultra by Kennedy command
In the grand railway station built at their demand.

Sir Arthur, the Governor, encircled the sphere,
Australia, Canada, and Hong Kong without fear
To carry principles his family held dear.

Sir Robert the diplomat ruled in the Near East
Lady Bertha beside him whose smile never ceased,
His proud companion at every Embassy feast.

They built a fine mansion house, a second one too,
The first was not suitable for all their to-do,
Now it's a museum for Kennedys are few
At Ballycultra, back of the strand that they knew

C A

I shall always consider myself a fortunate youth to have been born on Kennedy land at Cultra - *"the back of the strand".* Long before Town Planning was invented, the Kennedys were meticulous in the residential development of their estate.

The Cultra Kennedys were a branch of the Cassilis Clan and were a noted Scottish family long before they arrived in the Holywood area from Ayrshire in 1668.

In 1452 Sir Gilbert had been created Lord Kennedy. Later he was appointed a regent to the eight-year-old King James III. In 1502 his grandson David, created First Earl of Cassillis, was killed at the Battle of Flodden (1513). The Second Earl, Gilbert, was killed in an unsuccessful attempt to rescue James V. The Third Earl became Lord Lieutenant of Scotland, as did the Fifth Earl, Gilbert Kennedy.

In 1605 Gilbert was succeeded by his nephew, whose son John succeeded him as Seventh Earl. He died in 1701. It was from this generation that the young John Kennedy hailed,

Cultra old quay showing the lighthouse and cottages for Customs officers.

when he came over to North Down in 1668 to seek his fortune. He was among the second wave of Scottish settlers who came to our shores.

The first John Kennedy arrived in North Down about 1668 among the second wave of Scottish settlers. By then the country had settled down after the Irish Rebellion. Opportunely, Hugh Kennedy's arrival coincided with the Earl of Clanbrassil's disposal of parts of the Hamilton Estates. In 1671 the Kennedys acquired the North Down shoreline from Ballycultra to Ballyrobert. Mason's "Statistical Survey" records the estate comprised 4,000 acres in the townlands of Ballyrobert, Balleydavey, Craig-a-vad, Ballygrainy, Ballycaltre, Carrowreagh and Ballybun.

About that time Cultra House was built on the eminence of the raised beach and commanding the area's best view over Belfast Lough. The canny Scots built their house immediately above a small deep-water harbour. On the Cultra seashore lay exposed the yellow, red and grey sandstone quarries, which had supplied stones for the quoins of Carrickfergus Castle and the walls of the Holywood Priory Church. Perhaps the export of sandstone was Holywood's first business venture. We know the trade continued beyond 1774 as Cultra sandstone was used in construction work on Clifton House in Belfast.

The sale of the quarries and the harbour indicate how insolvent were the pecuniary affairs of the Earl of Clanbrassil. His grandfather, Viscount Clandeboye, would have been horrified; he required *"short leases - the shorter the better".* When the Kennedys arrived the estate was already well settled with small farms.

During the following hundred years few recorded comments concerning the family have emerged. However, there is an interesting note on John Kennedy, the squire during the White Terror which following the heady days of the 1798 United Irishmen's Rebellion. Several local gentlemen did not escape the caustic tongue of Colonel John Joseph Atherton. At the head of a troop of sixty Dragoons and a hundred Monaghans he trawled North Down for rebels and sympathisers. Contemptuously the military man reported to General Nugent, the British Army commander -

> *"Ought we not to punish the gentlemen of the County who have never assisted the well-disposed people, Yeomanry, etc.? For my part, a gentleman of any kind, but more particularly a Magistrate, who deserts his post at such a time ought to be ....I will not say what!*

The Colonel listed Mr Ker of Portavo and Mr Ward of Bangor *"Who is only now to be found."* John Kennedy of Cultra was noted as *"an inactive Magistrate or rather a friend of the United Irishmen."* Squire Kennedy's political leanings were not surprising, as the movement for Civil, Political and Religious Liberty had many supporters in the Holywood area and among the Kennedy tenantry. Earlier, Cultra House had been the venue of a simulated burglary. United Irishmen with blackened faces *"had broken into"* the house and taken away his legally held muskets!

Wily John Kennedy earned himself the epitaph "Sly". In 1797 he was asked to sign the Oath of Allegiance to King George III – *"Faithfully to support and maintain the Laws and Constitutions of the Kingdom, and the Succession to the Throne".* Kennedy replied *"I was a volunteer and know well the use of arms; whenever you are up to me I will join you."*

By the turn into the nineteenth century the countryside had settled down and Ireland became part of the United Kingdom. Like many other leading families, the Kennedys saw the side on which their bread was buttered and took their rightful place in North Down society.

Cultra House, built in 1670, served the family for over a century. About 1817 it was extended and refurbished in the Gothic Revival fashion of the day by Hugh Kennedy (1775 – 1850) who was High Sheriff for County Down in 1802.

Writing in 1850 Thomas Kelly described the manor as *"a building of considerable extent and of some architectural pretensions."*
The three hundred acre demesne was

> *" thickly wooded in the seventeenth century fashion."*
> *Few mansion situations can be more imposing or romantic; it is overshadowed by luxuriant oak trees of gigantic size, the graceful branches sweeping the ground, not unlike the famed banyan groves in the Plains of India. Several rare wild plants decorate the demesne."*

The Park became a tourist attraction for day trippers from Belfast and received many favourable references in the guidebooks of the period. The benevolent proprietors of Cultra and the neighbouring Ballymenoch House encouraged the public to view their beautiful gardens.

Perhaps the visitors caught sight of the eighteen Kennedy children playing under the ancient oak trees in the grounds. It seems after the death of his first wife, Hugh re-married. Grace Dorothea, daughter of Thomas Hughes of Tipperary, gave birth to six sons and five daughters. Sophia, daughter of John Lowe, added two sons and five daughters to the large Kennedy family. This is why the old house required extension and refurbishment in 1817, for certainly the family made the old rafters ring with merriment.

Arthur, fourth son of Dorothea's family, brought considerable prestige to Ireland and the Kennedy name. After days at Belfast Academy and Trinity College he joined the Army and in 1847 became the Poor Law Inspector in County Clare. Those were the famine years and Kennedy's seven-year-old daughter, Elizabeth Henrietta, became famous when her picture appeared in the Illustrated London News on 22nd December 1849 with the caption "Miss Kennedy distributing clothing in Kilrush".
In 1851 Kennedy was appointed British Governor of the Gambia and then Sierra Leone. On the journey home he was shipwrecked off Madeira where his swimming prowess, learned at Cultra Harbour, enabled him to same many lives.

In 1855 he was appointed Governor of Western Australia where Mount Kennedy and the Kennedy range of mountains carry the Cultra family name to this day. His next governorship was Vancouver Island and British Columbia, where he was rewarded with a knighthood.

By 1872 Sir Arthur was Governor of Hong Kong and four years later he was the Queen's representative in Queensland, Australia, where many sites still carry the Kennedy name. Sir Arthur died on the way home to Cultra on 3rd June 1883.

It seems two "tea-houses" supplied sustenance for Kelly's " lounging rusticators" visiting Cultra on day trips from Belfast in the 1850's - one cafeteria was on the hillside opposite the grand entrance gates, the other was beside Cultra harbour.

As we have seen, the little harbour may have been the perquisite which encouraged the Kennedy family to purchase the estate in 1671. As it is significant to the Cultra story, I shall include a few words on its importance.

Generally the North Down seashore shelves very gently to low water mark. Cultra is the nearest point to Belfast where there is in-shore deep water, without the necessity of dredging to obtain a passage for ships. An early Belfast Lough pilotage map, drawn in 1775, shows Cultra and Whitehouse as the customary landing places for passengers from Cross-Channel packets.

The Kennedys re-built the harbour in 1818 and added a small square light house building in the centre of the rather odd arrow-shaped quay.

Writing on 20th September 1834, Lieutenant Bordes reports the spring tides at Cultra Quay rise to twelve feet in calm weather; the rise and fall at neap tides is eight feet. He writes *"Cultra Quay is a small pier for fishing boats".* Nine weeks later Archibald McLachlan, writing from Lisburn, goes into considerable detail about *"the rise and fall of tides at Kennedy's Quay".* He comes to the same conclusion as the good Lieutenant, but in many more words.

Mason's Survey, published in 1819, claims Hugh Kennedy had built the harbour the previous summer season.

> *"Here vessels up to three hundred tons weight can find anchorage.*
> *The quay is highly serviceable to the inhabitants as it affords*
> *cheaper and more expeditious means of obtaining coals and enables*
> *them to export their produce."*

Another interesting import was ice for Ballymenoch House. The mansion's icehouse still exists in pristine condition above the riverbank in the grounds of Leawood, opposite the Eventide Home. Possibly all the big houses in the area obtained ice supplies for food preservation from Scotland via Cultra harbour. So it seems Cultra was a thriving little port in the 1820's. Perhaps the arrival of *"The Bangor Castle"* was a daily high point for the rapidly growing local community. A News Letter advertisement for 23rd June 1825 reads :

FOR CULTRA AND BANGOR

EVERY DAY

THE BANGOR CASTLE

LEAVES DONEGALL QUAY FOR BANGOR EVERY EVENING (EXCEPT SUNDAY) AT FIVE O'CLOCK PRECISELY,

TOUCHING ONLY AT CULTRA

ARRANGEMENTS HAVE BEEN MADE THAT PASSENGERS TO AND FROM CULTRA SHALL BE EMBARKED AND LANDED FREE OF ANY ADDITIONAL CHARGE

THE BANGOR CASTLE SAILS EVERY SUNDAY MORNING AT EIGHT O'CLOCK FOR DONAGHADEE, TOUCHING AS USUAL AT

CULTRA, CARRICKFERGUS AND BANGOR

Even as late as 1843 the Parliamentary Gazette claimed -

> *"vessels from 40 to 100 tons can anchor at high tide at several*
> *places on the shore near Holywood, and vessels of 200 to 300 tons*
> *can float on high water at Cultra, Rockport and Elly's Port."*

In 1850 Dr Kelly tells us *"the small quay, apparently of very early date and now rapidly going to run, is situated at the foot of the demesne."* A quarter of a century later it was completely dilapidated. Possibly the disuse was due to the development of Holywood as a port, and the safe opening of a channel to Belfast passing Mitchell's light-house which was erected in 1844.

In 1855, the fishermen's pier in Holywood, which ran out from the middle of the Marine Parade, was replaced by a 600 feet timber quay. Twelve years later Holywood wharf and pier extending into the Lough for a quarter of a mile from the end of Shore Street, completely eclipsed the pretensions of Cultra Harbour. Eventually the basin was in-filled to provide a yard for the Royal North of Ireland Yacht Club.

A public road ran from the old Cultra harbour to join the main Holywood to Bangor Road at Marino, the western portion of which was called Old Quay Road when the Post Office replaced house names with street numbers. A straight tree-lined carriage drive ran from the house to the harbour.

Cultra harbour has been the venue for pleasure sailing and water sports for several centuries. Kelly records *"the place is of much note for the famous regattas formerly held here."* The Lord Viceroy of Ireland - the Marquis of Anglesey - was Patron. Perhaps he was staying at Cultra House as the guest of the Kennedy family when the Belfast News-Letter described the Cultra Regatta of June 19th, 1829.

> *"The grand affair was the annual social event of the area and*
> *extended over nine days of fun and feasting. The yacht and rowing*
> *races, which were organised from the harbour, attracted competitors*
> *from far and wide. Athletic sports with running races, tug-of-war competitions, jumping*
> *and throwing competitions entertained the great crowds which came down from Belfast."*

The sports and a fun fair with booths, attractions, shies and liquor stalls covered the tree-shaded seaboard meadows which lay between Cultra harbour and the finger of land which is called "Pump Point" today. This stretch of land was eroded in the final years of the nineteenth century - a fact beautifully captured by Rosamund Praegar in the little poem "The Old Pump at Cultra" which I have recorded in another essay.

As we saw, aquatic sports have been enjoyed at Cultra long before the nineteenth century. The Phillips pictorial map, perhaps with artistic licence, shows a yachting mecca. No doubt this was to encourage aspiring residents to build seaside homes in the area, after the arrival of rail transport to the city.

By that time Robert Grimshaw Dunville of whiskey fame had built his great house on the slopes of the Holywood hills. In his poem "North Sea Bubbles" he records a cruise of *" The Black Pearl"*, a 343-ton steam yacht out of the Cultra club to the Norwegian Fjords.

> *"Twenty-five hands on board all hearty,*
> *Were joined from Redburn by our party."*

It seems even then several local families sailed their cruisers and yachts from the inshore deep water at Cultra Point.

In 1889 the Ulster Canoe Club was founded and a few ancillary sheds erected. By 1897 the Northern Yacht Club had completed the first section of its clubhouse on a site which had been occupied by a row of fishermen's cottages. The next two stages of the fine headquarters were completed by 1902. On 2nd September of that year, King Edward VII *"was graciously pleased to command that the Club be henceforth known as "The Royal North of Ireland Yacht Club".*

To give you an indication of the ambience of the Club in those days, let me tell you that on 13th August 1901 several enthusiasts decided *" to get up a new class"* which precluded the necessity of paid hands! The other classes, the *"Stars"* and the *"Birds"* carried paid hands as the sailors were Belfast businessmen *"who did not like to waste their time between the train and the starting gun, and they grumbled at the time needed to hoist and pull out 'the small kite'".* So was born Belfast Lough One Design Class IV, designed by Linton Hope, built by John Hilditch of Carrickfergus and named Fairy Class. The sailing debut was at Royal Ulster on 10th May, 1902. In the early days, Egmont Praeger in *" Sheevra"* was Dux of the Class.

A RELATIVE OF THE SIMMS FAMILY

Conway Ross, member of another well-known local family, described the Club immediately before the Great War

> *"Men dwelling on the shores of Belfast Lough are amongst the most fortunate of their kind. They can make as much money as is good for them in the city, and they can leave it at five o'clock, get down to Cultra, have a comfortable tea, get their boats ready and take the gun at 6.55 pm. It means that in summer we can live two days – a working day and a sailing day. Belfast Lough is probably the best sheet of water in the world for racing. It is a poor place, comparatively speaking, for week-ending; therefore wise men keep racing boats."*

Not long afterwards, *"the racing"* was cancelled for the duration of hostilities.

The two decades after the War were halcyon days for the Club, especially in 1937 when the R N I Y C "Dragon" Class was established.

Two years later in September 1939 Admiralty restrictions suspended all sailing on Belfast Lough. Most owners were on active service or engaged in war work. During the war parachute bombs landed around the clubhouse damaging several local residences. The half-hull model of *" Fiend"* on display in the bar still bears the marks of explosions.

After the war, life returned to the normality of that time. In 1948 Dragon Class *" Ceres II"* brought kudos to the Club by sailing in the Olympics at Torbay. The Diamond Jubilee of Fairy Class exemplified the Club's stride into the sixties with a fancy dress

Cultra Harbour before construction of Lifeboat House.

ball rather than the traditional banquet. The R N I Y C enters the new millennium with the optimism, activity and camaraderie which have epitomized the Club for over a century of excellence in yachtsmanship.

Before we leave the Cultra seashore, I must tell you about one or two harbour events, which are indelibly etched on the memory of your storyteller.

As usual, the few children of the area *"were messing around"* the yacht club on a misty summer holiday in the war years, mostly diving into the extremely cold sea from the end of the old wooden pier. The drone of an aircraft brought music to the morning and soon we saw a Sunderland sea-plane descend through the sun-drenched haze and skim the glass-level lough into a spray of crystal feathers. The boatman took one of the tenders to bring ashore a little group of very important persons in highly braided blue and khaki uniforms. They were hustled into two large military cars and spirited away up Cultra Avenue, to which bellicose encounter we never discovered.

On another misty morning a Sunderland turned over when landing on the lough – the remains were towed into the Yacht Club and broken on the slip-way. Several local children proudly possess wartime souvenirs of that particular example of Short and Harland's most famous product.

When the Belfast, Holywood and Bangor Railway Company was incorporated in 1860, the directors had to negotiate with the Kennedy's representatives – who were assiduous in the proper use of the Cultra estate. The family objected to the construction of a railway line along the Cultra coastline. They thought it would ruin the seascape view from the mansion and destroy *"the yachting"*.

As a result, the railway engineers drew up plans to run a branch line into Bangor from a junction at Conlig on the Donaghadee line – a circular route of some twenty miles! Of course, this ridiculous proposal was abandoned. In 1861 the new Belfast, Holywood and Bangor Railway agreed to build the Holywood to Bangor extension on the present difficult inland route. The Kennedys and their neighbours, the Blackwoods, required elaborately designed stations at Cultra and Helen's Bay. Half the trains had to stop at Cultra – otherwise the Company was liable to a daily fine of £10.

The advent of the railway encouraged the development of the area for seaside villa residences. This was the period before motor transport when every business family living outside the city had to keep a carriage or at least a pony and trap. Railways removed the necessity to build stabling and keep horses and pasture. The business-minded directors of the railway offered concession season and yearly passes to builders of new houses in the area – Cultra became a very popular location for Belfast business and professional families.

Now we return to the Kennedy clan –

The best known of the Cultra family was Sir Robert Kennedy (1851 – 1936). Robert was sent to Harrow School in order to receive an English public school education. At Harrow, he showed prowess in both sport and study. Coming home to Cultra for the holidays was avidly anticipated by the young student, throughout the long terms in England. The voyage home on the Belfast boat became commonplace but Robert never outlived the excitement of jumping down from a first-class carriage on to the family's own railway platform and running up the cinder path to Cultra House, or Mayfield Cottage on the seashore. I wonder did young Archibald Blackwood, Earl of Ava, (1836 – 1900) get the same thrill on arriving home at his Helen's Bay station from Eton College for long summer holidays on the Clandeboye Estate.

For the young Robert Kennedy, the popular Irish boy, Harrow school days blossomed into a good academic and sporting career at Cambridge University. On graduation, he joined the British Diplomatic Service and was appointed Attaché to the British Consul in Spain. During the following years he served in Turkey, Russia, Bulgaria, Rumania, Montenegro and Persia. Cecil Rhodes was a friend who regarded Robert Kennedy as one of the most distinguished diplomats of pre-First World War Britain. His special sphere of expertise was the Balkans and the Near East.

Sir Robert accompanied King Nicholas of Montenegro when His Majesty was received by Queen Victoria in 1897. Five years later, he was in the entourage of the Shah of Persia. Robert retired to Cultra after a brilliant career, and spent his retirement as a Northern Irish Senator and our local philanthropist.

The famous ambassador found time to come home to County Down for the society wedding of the year 1883. Castleward was the spectacular venue. The Hon Bertha, third daughter of Henry Ward, Viscount Bangor, was the blushing bride. It was an outstandingly successful marriage, lasting fifty-three amiable years - ending only in 1936 when the couple died within a few months of each other. Although the traditional family burial place was the Priory, Bertha and Robert were interred together in their proprietary graveyard in the new Cultra Manor parkland.

The Hon Bertha, Lady Kennedy, was the outstanding Ulster adventuress of the Edwardian age and the first European woman to enter Khorassan and Afghanistan.
In November 1882, Robert had come home from a Bulgarian diplomatic mission with marriage in mind. Bertha thought long and hard before she accepted the proposal, which would change her life from the privileged leisure of Castleward to the burning sands of South America and the aridity of Asia.

Robert asked matrimonial advice from his North Down neighbour, Frederick Blackwood, the Marquis of Dufferin and Ava – the leading British diplomat of the day. Frederick said of Bertha –

> *"A sweeter creature I never can wish to see. She carries purity, sincerity and affection in every line of her face. The man who has won that true heart may well be proud of his position!"*

One wonders what Brenda Woodhouse, Frederick's marchioness, thought of this lavish testimonial to his young cousin, Bertha.

The early years at Castleward had taught Bertha remarkable skill in horsemanship. At home, she was an enthusiastic follower of the County Down Staghounds. In Khorassan, Bertha was the first British woman to cover the six hundred miles from Teheran to Meshed on horseback in eleven days.

Bertha became the perfect British Embassy wife – a very demanding and responsible position in the late nineteenth century, when Britain led the world. Her diplomatic career led from Istanbul to Bulgaria, Romania, and Teheran through Central Asia to Samarkand – the toast of every Consulate banquet.

Much in demand on these occasions, Bertha was honoured with the rare royal command from Queen Victoria - *"Dine and sleep"*.

At home in Holywood, Bertha gave her days in community service, especially to the St John Ambulance Brigade and the Soldiers', Sailors' and Airmen's Families Association.

An advertisement in the later years of the nineteenth century offers the letting of Cultra House, along with many others on the estate as well as sites for building villa residences along the coast. Local tradition suggests that the Kennedy headquarters became the family's seaside cottage, Mayfield, so convenient for sea bathing and yachting.

When Robert and Bertha came home from their ambassadorial travels, they chose one of the finest sites on the estate for their retirement home. The new Cultra Manor was built of red sandstone in the grand style. It was the last of the great mansions to be erected along the North Down shore overlooking Belfast Lough.

After another refurbishment and addition of a ballroom with beautiful stained glass windows, Cultra House finally became the home of the popular McCormick family, well known to Holywood folk as the donors of the town's "Johnny the Jig" playground in memory of Hugh McNeile McCormick. This generous family gave the old house for benefit of local people. It became a hospital under the auspices of the Government Department for Health and Social Services. The Department sold it for private housing development, much to the anger of the people of Holywood. Fortunately it was acquired by the Patterson family, who have restored the house to its nineteenth century magnificence.

However, back to the Kennedy story before we lose our train of thought altogether!

After removal to the new Manor House in 1902, the family continued its comfortable and generous life-style, unmindful of the many changes occurring beyond the Manor gates. True to form the Kennedys allowed the superbly engineered main driveway to be used as the first motor-car hill climb course. That tranquil era ended with the deaths of Sir Robert and Lady Bertha. They were survived by four daughters. A few favoured Holywood ladies still treasure the carefully crocheted dolls which the Kennedy sisters made for the Christmas parties held at the "big house" for the children of the Manor staff. The sister I knew best was Miss Maude, a shy and silent lady, who was accustomed to walk the dogs along the shore path to Clanbrassil Terrace where my grandmother lived. On a wet day, or if she was very tired, Miss Maude would come in to drink tea or brown lemonade with ginger biscuits. Not without reason, my brother and I were banished from the sitting room. Miss Maude was easily embarrassed, especially by small inquisitive boys. After fifteen minutes, she would collect her many "things", call to the dogs and continue

> *"beating the bounds of the Kennedy kingdom – Clanbrassil Terrace being at the furthest corner of the estate".*

After the Second World War, Miss Maude and the family found the maintenance of the great house and the hundred acres of pleasure gardens too cumbersome; a smaller easily managed neo-Georgian house was built in the grounds.

Pile lighthouse, built to pilot the Victoria Channel off Cultra.

As a schoolboy I remember cycling up to the Manor for the auction sale of the furniture and paying a precious shilling for a catalogue to gain admission to the house. Among many fascinating sights was the fully extended dining room table piled high with all sorts and sizes of Waterford crystal glasses. In the drawing room there was a small graceful grand piano, the wood panels of which were hand painted and richly inlaid. I still regret that I did not raid my piggy bank to get the ten pounds for which it was 'knocked down' to a fortunate bidder. I often wonder who bought the piano and do they know that it was the prized possession of The Hon Lady Bertha Kennedy who was gifted with an exceptionally fine contralto voice and a passionate love of music.

At the auction, the house seemed strangely small within; I had never before been allowed beyond the front hall. The Kennedys kept clamorous little boys at a distance, preferably at the farthest extremity of the Manor park, where Holywood Boy Scouts were permitted to set up camp on summer weekends.

In another essay I shall tell you more of the Kennedys' generosity to the Scout movement, and the 1st Holywood Troop which rejoiced in the honoured title *"Sir Robert Kennedy's Own"*.

Although the Kennedys have removed from the Cultra scene for many a year, their assiduous butler still keeps a watching brief on the property. Those who came to take care of the estate after the sale frequently met him on the driveway late at night wearing one of Sir Robert's cloaks. He was waiting to catch errant maidservants returning to the big house after staff curfew hour. More recently the butler has appeared in the offices of the Folk Museum to ensure domestic arrangements continue to proceed punctiliously.

Fortunately, the great house and pleasure gardens became the Ulster Folk Museum, an occurrence much appreciated by the local community, as it assures the maintenance of Cultra Manor. Indeed we are fortunate in the number of "big houses" we have in the Holywood area - though that does not excuse the wilful demolition of other examples of our heritage.

Later the Folk Museum was joined with the Ulster Transport Museum on the north side of the Holywood-Bangor road. It was built in the grounds of Sorrento and Dalchoolin, both of which have been demolished.

All these juvenile memories of Cultra, the slipways and the jetty, came rushing back on a morning in the last month of the twentieth century. On Saturday, 18th December the captain of *"Bernice"* deliberately grounded his ship fifty metres from the old Cultra Quay. Two nine-inch holes had become evident in the Dutch cargo ship - she waited at Cultra for passage to Harland & Wolff.

I wonder if any of the visiting sailors from the Netherlands knew that *"Bernice"* was following an eight hundred year tradition, dating back to the years when deep water first put Cultra on the charts of mariners visiting Belfast Lough.

Bernice at Cultra 1999

ESSAY V - WHISKEY GALORE -

THE DUNVILLES OF REDBURN

The Magnificent Clan

The Dunvilles of Redburn were a magnificent clan,
In three generations they reached top with élan,
In ballooning and hunting and yachting and more
There was no one in Ulster could equal their score.
They spent money like water that went with their brew,
The Dunvilles were kind and very generous too,
They gave work to the town and two sons to the War,
They gave banquets and parties and nothing to mar
Dunville's great reputation at home and afar.

They built a great mansion on the Holywood hills
With seventy rooms to entertain the Dunvilles.
Then came Prohibition and Depression as well,
The less opulent Dunvilles were now forced to sell
The "Black Pearl", the "Mascot" and "Banshees" all three
Sixty hunters and the town house, the zoo and the glee.
Then of all their possessions there only was left
The vast echoing house; its last soul laid to rest
In the Priory graveyard with those she loved best.

The house with its furniture, art treasures and all
Now awaited the auctioneer's hammer to fall.
Most of Holywood's townsfolk turned up for the sale
For mementoes of Redburn and "pay on the nail",
A chiffonier here and there a lace-bordered gown.
Now all that remains of that vast wealthy estate
Is a gate lodge, stable yard and a bell by a gate.

C A

In the last essay you read how the Kennedys of Cultra were significant contributors to the history of Holywood for three long centuries. Now we shall follow the fascinating fortunes of the Dunvilles of Redburn who graced Holywood with their presence for three short generations.

In the late nineteenth and early twentieth centuries everyone in Holywood knew the Dunvilles of Redburn. The family's capacity to employ local labour, their patriotic service and their magnanimous generosity made the Dunvilles the toast of the town. The family's quixotic lifestyle gave them fame throughout Ireland and beyond.

The first time I saw Redburn, the big house was scintillating in the snow of a sunny Christmas morning. That day, my father had returned from a long sea voyage. While the festive meal was being prepared, he took my brother and me for a walk in the Holywood woods, and there we saw the good ship Redburn sailing along on a rippling white sea of sparkling frost. My father's uncle, Donald McPherson, was artistic designer of all the brand labels of the world-famous Dunville Irish whiskey. Nowadays these trademark plate- prints are collectors' items.

So it was my sea-faring father who forged the interest of an over-curious little boy in the sad saga of the Holywood Dunvilles and their great house. In the nineteenth century a few Ulster families made vast fortunes from whiskey distilling, linen production, rope making, shipbuilding, tobacco manufacture and banking. All became world leaders; the Dunvilles owned one of the world's largest distilleries.

John Dunville (1785 - 1851) advanced from a young boy apprentice in William Napier's Distillery on Bank Street to owner of the company. As well as whiskey, the firm did a lucrative trade in blending tea. John became a partner in 1808 and re-formed the company under his own name in 1825.

Under John Dunville's management the business prospered and moved from Bank Lane to Callender Street. Further expansion was restricted by current legislation. In those days, whiskey distilling and blending required to be performed in premises at least two miles apart! The law was circumvented by John's brother William setting up a separate company to run the distillery, while Dunville & Company continued to run the blending and retail side of the growing business. By 1884 the firm managed the Royal Irish Distilleries at Distillery Street, bonded warehouses in Adelaide Street, Alfred Street and Clarence Street and duty-paid warehouses in Alfred Street and Franklin Street. In that year the offices were in Callender Street. Twenty-two years later these were extended through to 25 - 29 Arthur Street. The extensive London Office buildings were situated on Shaftesbury Avenue.

The distillery apprentice boy became a town alderman and a manager of the Academical Institution. About 1845 he moved out of town to Richmond Lodge on Holywood Road. That grand mansion was built about 1800 and appears frequently in our local story. Today it is the site of Knocknagoney housing estate.

John married Mary Grimshaw (1789 - 1865) and in May 1838 Robert Grimshaw Dunville was born. Soon the family was moving into the multi-millionaire bracket of society. In 1866 Robert decided to build the finest house on the County Down shore of Belfast Lough for his wife, Jeanie Chaine (1842 - 1914). Their son, John, was the first member of the family to be born in Redburn.

Building the new house a couple of miles along the Old Holywood Road did not sever the friendly link from Richmond Lodge. Local tales tell us when the Redburn stables were fully occupied for the hunting season, visitors' horses were boarded out at Richmond, the neighbouring Mertoun Hall and the other big houses of the parish.

Robert Grimshaw Dunville may have helped to draw the plans for Redburn House as it

Keeper's lodge at Dunville Park - 4 acres of recreation land for the distillery workforce (1891).

seems when he was a youth he spent some time in the hallowed halls of Sir Charles Lanyon's office suite. Certainly he was a gifted amateur artist as his sketches illustrated two of his private publications - *"North Sea Bubbles"* and *"The Norseman Pilot's Song"*. The cantos celebrated the cruise of the family's steam yacht - "The Black Pearl" - *"a spanking little craft of 343 tons with 25 hands on board"*.

R G, a founder member of the Reform Club, was an ardent member of the Liberal Party - until Gladstone advocated Home Rule for Ireland. The Duke of Devonshire, the Liberal M P, was among the many famous guests invited to the extravagant house parties at newly built Redburn.

Redburn was designed by the famous firm of architects - Lanyon, Lynn and Lanyon. The house was the best example and the most opulent of all the North Down mansions. It was built in the Fiddler's Field, part of the Jackson family farmstead, and cost £28,000.

Constructed of finest Scrabo stone, it commanded panoramic views of Belfast Lough and the blue hills of Antrim. Looking from the Lough it was set against the green backcloth of the Holywood hills. When illuminated for evening joviality, it resembled a fairy palace. The well-wooded parkland covered 170 acres, providing pleasure grounds, bridle-ways, a large zoo, kitchen gardens and several waterfalls. There was a small village of stove houses for the cultivation of tropical fruit, and a quaint little dairy for cooling the milk, butter and cream produced from the estate herd of twelve Jersey cows. An elaborate private laundry was headquarters for the army of maids who washed and ironed the steady flow of bed linen, towelling and soft furnishing fabrics the great house utilised every day.

There were seventy rooms, the most beautiful of which were the ballroom and the square entrance hall. At night, the ballroom was illuminated by a magnificent Waterford crystal chandelier, by day the hall shimmered in the blue, reds and green of the stained glass window erected in memory of Second Lieutenant John Spenser Dunville, V C, (1896 - 1917).

Domestic and sanitary arrangements at Redburn were decades ahead of the mid-nineteenth century, as was the comfort of the servants' accommodation. I remember visiting the old house in the 1950's, shortly after it was acquired by Holywood Urban District Council. It was surprising to find some of the bedrooms in the staff wing had never been used - woodwork and plaster walls were just as the builders had left them a century before, neither papered nor painted!

The walled courtyard and stables block with clock tower and grooms' quarters was built in 1879. Perhaps the Scrabo stone quarry at Newtownards was exhausted by then, as the architects decided to build with imported Scottish red sandstone. The buildings provided the best equestrian accommodation money could buy. Today it is a service area for the Redburn Country Park. The yard was dominated by a cupola with bell and clock. The clock still records the passing hours in the Old Priory Tower, the great bronze bell rings out for weddings in the tiny church at Port Braddan on the Causeway Coast.

The stable yard and the Lanyon gate-lodge at the grand entrance to the estate are all that remains of the original Redburn buildings.

The Dunvilles were a family completely dedicated to hunting. Before the Great War their sixteen grooms tended sixty hunters and four carriage horses. An annual Holywood spectacular, before each Irish hunting season, was the sixty hunters trotting through the town from Redburn to the railway station for transportation to Zion in County Meath. For many years the U K railway timetable noted Holywood station as fully equipped for transporting horses - the Dunville horses! Hunting, shooting, fishing, yachting and ballooning all found sporting favourites among the versatile Dunville family.

When the family was in residence at Redburn, usually during the summer months and over the twelve days of Christmas, the Union flag flew from a very tall mast on the roof. Other Dunville residences were No 46 Portland Place in London; Arisay - a shooting lodge in Perthshire, Scotland; Zion - the hunting estate in County Meath; Barry - a sheep-station at Naude in New South Wales, and a farm in South Africa. To this was added a fleet of specialist motorcars; "The Black Pearl" - the fashionable steam yacht moored at Cultra and a collection of hot air balloons.

The ruler of this kingdom was Colonel John Dunville. John loved the mansion - he lived up to the high standards it demanded, and enjoyed the sumptuous lifestyle it provided.

In 1892 Colonel Dunville made an outstandingly successful high society marriage with Violet Anne Blanche Lambert, granddaughter of the Marquis Conyngham of Beau Parc, County Meath.

Family wealth, social position and a diary full of sporting events, set him well above the daily chores of actually running the Royal Irish Distillery. This mundane task was carried out by a Board of Directors and hundreds of contented employees. Whiskey galore provided the immense financial reservoir which ran the Dunville empire. The trusted managers were employed to tend the geese which laid the golden eggs.

John's interest in horses made him the leader of the County Down hunting fraternity. In 1906 Mr and Mrs Dunville became keenly interest in hot air ballooning, a very daring hobby in those days. Together they competed in the Gordon Bennett International Races (1906-1908) and won the Robb and Macclesfield Cups in 1908. "La Mascotte" John's pet name for his wife, was the title he gave to the favourite flyer. As technology increased, "The Banshee" numbers One and Two took to the air.

These were the indecisive years leading up to the Great War. John's aeronautical expertise was demanded when war broke out in 1914. He served as Commander in the Royal Naval Air Service, Balloon Training Wing, specialising in coastal defence. The Service became the Fleet Air Arm. All Holywood rejoiced when the King created John Dunville a Companion of the British Empire for his contribution to Allied Naval Ballooning.

He was one of a very few servicemen to hold officer rank in all three services - Colonel of the Westmeath Militia; Squadron Commander in the Royal Naval Air Service and Wing Commander in the Royal Air Force.

After the war John returned to Redburn to enjoy family life thoughtfully attended by sixteen indoor staff, ten grounds crew and the sixteen grooms.

Life at Redburn was leisured and luxurious. Guest rooms were seldom unoccupied - visitors were met in Redburn Square at Holywood railway station with the elegant Dunville carriage. When motorcars became fashionable the avenues to the big house were lined with Lagondas, Rolls and Belfast Chambers. Visiting chauffeurs and ladies' maids looked forward to the lavish hospitality provided in the Redburn servants' hall by Mrs Black, the housekeeper.

The Redburn day started at 6 a.m. for the indoor staff. House chores in the reception rooms had to be completed by the time the family came down for breakfast - though there was always the morning room for early risers. Family and visitors were wakened by a chambermaid swishing back the curtains and proffering tea or coffee and dry biscuits. Breakfast was an unscheduled buffet meal where heated silver chafing dishes offered a satisfying menu to start the day.

The butler, Eric Thorpe, opened the famous Redburn House bar at one minute past noon every weekday, *"when the sun went over the yard-arm."* Thorpe closed the bar at 3 p.m. and re-opened it from 6 p.m. till midnight. Lunch was a light informal meal often missed by those pursuing their sporting preferences.

Dinner was the formal occasion of the evening for which the cook and her staff prepared all day long. Thorpe sounded the dressing gong at 7 p.m.; drinks were dispensed on the half-hour. Dinner was served on the second gong at 8 p.m. Course followed course, each accompanied by suitable wines. After dinner the company withdrew to the billiard room or to the drawing room for cards or music. Eric Thorpe was kept busy at the bar till midnight, when everyone was supposed to retire for the night.

John Dunville was a generous employer and always mindful of those in retirement who had served the family well. The Dunvilles were ever-conscious of the privileged place their whiskey wealth gave them in society. They repaid business success with generous gifts to the community.

In 1872 John's uncle, William, endowed the Sorella Trust in memory of his sister Sarah, Sorella being the Italian word for sister. The trust sponsored the Dunville studentships at Queen's College and the Sorella Art Exhibition at the Government School of Art. The "Sorella" was awarded through the Municipal College of Technology until the late 1960's, but seems to have been discontinued after the re-organisation of local government in 1972. Today the Dunville Studentship is awarded by Queen's University Faculty of Science and Agriculture to a first class honours scholar for post-graduate research. The £140 award of 1874 is now an annual £2,500 scholarship. So the generosity of the Holywood Dunville family continues into the twenty-first century.

Belfast's first public park - Dunville Park - with its famous fountain, was one of the family's best gifts to the City. The fountain was erected in 1892, similar to the Victoria fountain in Glasgow. It was made in terracotta and decorated in Jacobean and naturalistic ornament - the work of Doulton's of Lambeth, to the design of A E Pearce. Musgrave Foundry made the elaborate railings, a beautiful pseudo-Greek temple lodge, swings for children and shelters for senior citizens completed the idyllic scene. The park was opened in 1892 by the Marquis of Dufferin and Ava, who hoped it would provide *"a place where people of all creeds would meet and help to diminish sectarian strife".*

Aptly named "Distillery" was the Dunville's sponsored football team with its own prestigious grounds beside the distillery itself. The Club continues into the twenty-first century as Lisburn Distillery. Generous as ever, the family presented a magnificent silver trophy, "Dunville Cup", for local competition. Supervised by the Irish Football League Ltd, the Dunville Cup became the League Cup and is competed for under the name of the commercial company which acts as the League sponsor in any given season.

The Dunville fountain (1892) made by Doulton of Lambeth for the Park.

John Dunville died at Redburn on 10th June 1929, aged 62. The town turned out for the funeral, lining the road from the big house to the Priory graveyard, stopping at the maypole for the lowering of the Union flag on to the coffin. Staff and town had always called him "the Colonel" - and indeed he ruled his kingdom with military precision. On his death, the kingdom started to unravel.

Violet Anne Blanche Lambert was born at Beau Parc, County Meath on 14th August 1861. Her father was Major Gustavus William Lambert, J.P; D.L.; Secretary to the Order of St Patrick and State Steward to the Lord Lieutenant of Ireland. Violet's mother was Frances Caroline Maria Conyngham, the Marquis Conyngham's daughter. She had three brothers and eight sisters. Her sister Bertha was a maid of honour to Queen Victoria; Constance was lady-in-waiting to H R H the Duchess of Albany. Amy was a

maid of honour to the Queen. She married the King's Equerry. Of the beautiful Irish Lambart sisters, King Edward was heard to remark, *"No need to be ladies in waiting, my dears!"*
Violet married John Dunville in 1892 when she was 30 and John 26. The wedding ceremony in County Meath was an Irish spectacular; the homecoming to Holywood a Redburn field day. Violet Lambart had always been an expert equestrian – as the newly-wedded Mrs John Dunville she added hunting, shooting, fishing and ballooning to her sporting repertoire.

Redburn and Portland Square in London became centres of lavish entertainment, expertly organised by the fashionable hostess.

The directors of the Royal Irish Distillery enjoyed preference. Like her husband, she was keenly aware of the housing needs of their employees. She even required spacious private baths to be built at Dunville's Distillery headquarters.

Violet was one of the first women in the United Kingdom to obtain a balloon pilot's licence. She was first to fly the Irish Sea and fourth to fly the English Channel. In New Zealand Mrs Dunville was famous for her prowess in shark fishing.

Tommy Thompson (1906–1958) gamekeeper to the estate for 47 years, remembers Mrs Violet ranging the woods, clad in a split skirt, tartan cape and riding boots "toting" two six-shooters to exterminate the feral cat population. On these feline expeditions, she was accompanied by several pet Alsatian wolfhounds. Alsatians were a rare breed at that time, but highly favoured by the animal loving Dunville family.

The Dunvilles were respected parishioners of the Church of St Philip and St James. One Sunday morning driving back to Redburn, Violet took the reins just before the carriage met a regimental band returning to the Palace Barracks from a military church parade. The horses bolted and the carriage was upset. Redburn staff were alerted when the horses trotted into the yard without the carriage. Violet's expert horsemanship averted injury to her passengers.

A generous and colourful character, Violet was extremely popular with her Holywood neighbours. The gracious lady dressed in black continued to welcome guests at the big house entrance doors long after the rest of the family had departed.

In the early months of the Second World War, school children were asked to collect cotton reels of the larger size for the war effort. My brother and I cycled up to Redburn House on this important assignment - obviously Redburn was a repository for such useful items!

Mrs Dunville opened the door herself, asked us to wait in the hall and soon returned with a box of large spools – all complete with coloured thread.

That was the last time I saw Mrs Violet Dunville; the memory remains of a tall straight-backed lady, with very white hair – gentle, jovial and kind to the bitter end. She had withstood all the vicissitudes of the later decades of the Dunville saga and died at Redburn on 7th March 1940. Mrs Dunville was interred under the *"High Victoriana"* memorial she chose for the Dunville family, where for years she had tended the ligustrum bush brought to Holywood from her favourite son's grave in France.

Bobby Dunville's Memorial, Monty's spout at Knocknagoney. It disappeared in the 1970's.

DUNVILLE & CO.
LIMITED,
DISTILLERS,
BELFAST

DISTILLERIES..............Royal Irish Distilleries, Distillery S
BONDED WAREHOUSES...Adelaide Street, Alfred Street, a
Clarence Street
DUTY-PAID WAREHOUSES, Alfred Street and Franklin Street.
OFFICES.......................Calender Street

MRS V A B DUNVILLE, DECEASED
REDBURN, HOLYWOOD, CO DOWN
HIGHLY IMPORTANT SIX DAYS' SALE BY AUCTION
ANTIQUE AND MODERN FURNITURE
2,500 LOTS IN ALL
TO BE HELD ON THE PREMISES ON
20TH, 21ST, 22ND, 23RD, 24TH AND 27TH MAY, 1940

ADMISSION TO VIEW AND SALE BY CATALOGUE ONLY,
PRICE 2/6d EACH

LIGHT LUNCHEONS AND AFTERNOON TEAS WILL BE
PROVIDED ON SALE DAYS
J D NICHOLL & CO LTD
AUCTIONEERS AND VALUERS
43-47 CHICHESTER STREET, BELFAST TELEPHONE 25757

Captain Robert Lambart Dunville (1893-1931); "Bobby", an officer in the Grenadier Guards, first regiment of Royal Household Infantry, was wounded at Gallipolli. During the 1916 Irish Easter Rising he reported for duty in Dublin. The car was ambushed at Castle Bellingham. Irish Republicans put him against a wall, shot him and left him, thinking he was dead. Bobby received a very serious chest wound; fortunately he escaped with his life. He spent many months recuperating at Redburn, but never fully recovered from the effects of his war wounds. On bad days, Jack Farrar, the head groom, would bring Bobby's favourite horse to his bedroom to pay a visit and help him to look forward to better days in the future.

There are many local stories of the young wounded officer who was very popular with the house staff and the Holywood people. The head-keeper, Tommy Thompson, told about the day the captain shot him. They were ferreting rabbits. The keeper was behind a bush. The rabbit got away with a couple of pellets in its fur - Dr Donnan spent three hours removing thirty-three pellets from the keeper's lower body! [The captain had shot him !]

Horses and dogs played a privileged part in the daily life of the Dunvilles. When a horse died in service at Redburn, it was buried with ceremony in full hunting regalia. As Bobby recovered from his war wounds, his love of animals advanced a cherished ambition. In 1920 a circular area behind the house was enclosed with a high wall to protect Bobby's private zoo. Much of the boundary is still in its original position - the railings bearing the Dunville shield.

At that time the housekeeper was Mrs Marshall. As with many members of the staff, she was terrified of the wild animals living at the back doors - sometimes with justification! The collection included zebras, panthers, apes, kangaroos, monkeys, pheasants and badgers. The best-known incumbent was Bruno, a tame bear, who had a special pit in the woods, and of whose cunning many tales are told. Bobby taught Bruno to sit on his gathered tethering chain so that it looked very short. When someone, thinking safety to be no problem, approached to tease the animal, it jumped up and charged to the extent of the chain! Chauffeur Thomas McKeaveney bore the scar of the temperamental beast on his arm till the day he died. There are many amusing stores of how escaped animals surprised local people and soldiers from the nearby Palace Barracks . Eventually, the animals became a core collection for the Belfast Zoological Gardens on the slopes of the Cave Hill, which were opened to the public in 1934. It was the first municipal zoo in the United Kingdom. Before that time, Bobby found that he was no longer able to care properly for the animals under his protection.

In 1930, for health reasons arising from his I R A war wounds, Bobby was advised to voyage on a holiday to the family sheep-station in Australia. The journey was broken in South Africa so that Mrs Robert Dunville could visit her family. Bobby remained in their Johannesburg hotel, where he died on 10th January 1931.

Holywood folk still remember the memorial his mother built at Monty's spout, beyond the Redburn gates on the Old Holywood Road. On many occasions Bobby had watered the horses at the spout. As a memorial, his mother erected a wide horse-trough, a drinking fountain with a chained cup and a basin for thirsty dogs. Recently, without reason, during road works it was removed by a party of travelling people who were camping in the adjacent traffic lay-by.

Captain Dunville's younger brother also died as the result of enemy action. The two brothers grew up in the Redburn paradise for boys, an adventure playground in the Holywood Hills. Both were Etonians. Second Lieutenant John Spenser Dunville (1896-1917) of the Royal Dragoons, was awarded the Victoria Cross posthumously for most conspicuous bravery and disregard for personal danger when in charge of a party of Royal Engineers engaged in the demolition of enemy wire. Dunville placed himself between a non-commissioned officer and the enemy fire. He was mortally wounded but continued in command till the work was completed, setting a magnificent example to all ranks under his command.

A personal letter to John Dunville from Lord Hamilton of Dalziel headed - Fourth Army, B.E.F., France 16.8.17 reads :

> *".....Your son was in command of a raiding party. He crawled up with the engineer to push a Bangalore torpedo under the wire. It required repair and while the engineer was doing this they were spotted by the enemy. Your son lay in front of the expert to ensure success. It was a magnificent thing to do. "*

Thus is recorded the heroic action of Holywood's only Victoria Cross recipient. The posthumous award was made by King George V at Buckingham Palace to his father, Squadron Commander John Dunville, R.N. on 29th August 1917. John is buried in Villers-Faucon Communal Cemetery, France - Row A Grave 21, his Victoria Cross is in the Household Cavalry Museum at Windsor.

The family called this gallant officer "Jonkins". His death was deeply regretted by his home town, which by 1917 was reeling from the number of local heroes who had sacrificed their lives in the Great War. Jonkins' body was not brought home for burial in Holywood. A ligustrum bush from his French grave was transplanted to the new family memorial when it was erected in the Priory graveyard. Previously, members of the family had been interred in the Dunville mausoleum in Clifton Street graveyard.

The Dunville parents were devastated by the death of their second son. The pulpit in the old garrison church, a magnificent stained glass window in Redburn and a memorial in the Parish Church of St Philip and St James were dedicated to Jonkins' memory.

The youngest brother, William Gustavus Dunville (1900-1958) is still remembered as a delightful juvenile who charmed the young people of Holywood with parties at Redburn and chauffeur-driven trips around the town. Tom McKeaveney, who looked after the family's fleet of motors, had some exciting tales to tell of young Master William and his exploits in the years after the First World War. At least one Holywood lady still recalls with pleasure the attention which the handsome young squire from the big house paid to his peers in the giddy days of the 1920's.

William displeased his parents by his marriage to a young lady from East Belfast. The couple were sent off to manage the family sheep farm in Australia, at Barry Station, Nundle, New South Wales. Down under, the young Irish Dunvilles raised a happy family of three little girls. However, the Redburn lifestyle had not prepared William for isolated work in the Australian out-back. The family returned to Redburn and a divorce was obtained. Shortly afterwards, William emigrated to Canada with one of his daughters. It is thought he died there in 1956.

Una, the only Dunville daughter, was born at Redburn in 1903. She was not physically robust and is thought to have suffered from Down's Syndrome. She spent her short life at home when the other members of the family were pursuing their many-sided activities abroad. Of course, this made Una a great favourite with the indoor and outdoor staff at Redburn, where she wandered at will through the great rooms and the pleasure gardens.

The Dunvilles, like other Edwardian families, whose founders had made vast fortunes in Ulster industry, spent money as if it would never run out. Hard work was a long day of hunting, racing, shooting or fishing, followed by a long night of eating, drinking and social activity. All the ordinary chores of cleaning, cooking, maintenance, heavy gardening and simple work were carried out by a loyal army of servants and retainers. The next generation was left to pull what was left of life into some sort of shape and get back the smile into the eyes of the old families, which remained into the second half of the twentieth century.

In the Dunvilles' case, the "next generation" did not survive to pull things together and adapt to the egalitarian society of the sixties. Like Norwood, Edgecumbe, Clonaver and Mertoun Hall, Redburn gave its name to housing developments. Where the pleasure parklands of these fine old mansions once flourished, desirable semi-detached villas blossomed and families moved out from the city and in from the country to populate the new housing estates.

At Redburn, there were no horses left in the stables to be buried in full hunting regalia. The famous circular zoo was reclaimed by shrubbery. The great rooms in the house were shrouded in dustsheets. The greenhouses and the great conservatory were closed down, the gardens ran to weeds, and the staff was dismissed.

The Depression of the 1920's, Prohibition of the sale of intoxicants in the United States, family deaths and delegation of authority resulted in Insolvency and Receivership of the Distillery in 1935, with the loss of hundreds of jobs in Belfast and Holywood.

The big house was rented by the Air Ministry, as billets for Women's Royal Air Force personnel. In 1950 it was purchased with its 170-acre parklands for £14,700 by Holywood Urban District Council. This was half the cost of building the main house in 1866! The town was humming with rumours of a cottage hospital, an early apartment block, or the refurbishment of the zoo, as the main attraction for a pleasure park. What actually happened was less spectacular. A new burial ground was consecrated in 1953. Soon it was followed by a new primary school , a welfare clinic in 1960 and then a Housing Trust estate.

The lovely old house became derelict and vandalised by fire. Although within the "green belt" the site was acquired for the erection of a hotel, which in turn became the British Petroleum staff members' club. In its turn the club building was demolished and the Holywood Private Nursing Home built where Redburn House had dominated the Holywood Hills for over a century.

On re-organisation of local government in 1973, the parklands came under the care of the Department of the Environment for Northern Ireland, who created Redburn Country Park from the remaining woods and parklands. Today, the country park is enjoyed by thousands of walkers and naturalists who are enchanted by the magnificence of the Holywood Hills.

In Belfast today, only one of the prestigious Dunville Distillery buildings continues in pristine condition. It is the magnificent head office of the First Trust Bank in Arthur Street - formerly it was the headquarters of one of the world's largest distilleries. My grand-father, John Morrow of Cromac Square, supplied tarpaulin covers for the fleet of horse drawn and later motor vehicles which carried "Royal Irish" all over the island and to the docks for transportation to a thirsty world. My uncles told colourful stories of the lavish Dunville hospitality provided in the Head Office. They related the sadness and shock of the business fraternity when the unbelievable news of liquidation broke upon Belfast.

It is not our brief in this essay to follow the long story of the departed distillery - that would require an essay to itself. However, it would be unforgivable if I were to omit a paragraph on its downfall and demise.

After 130 years of excellent production, Dunvilles was the last Belfast distillery to close its doors. Many commentators thought the closure was completely unnecessary, even ridiculous.

The immense four-storey distillery building with its dominating 160 foot chimney was the most modern in Ireland. Output around the turn of the century was over two and a half million gallons of "Royal Irish" and other famous labels such as "Three Crowns" and "V R" – in honour of Queen Victoria. The plant had two 160 foot deep wells and a private water pipe to Lough Mourne. The four-storey mill, the maltings, still-house, workshops and offices completed the self-sufficient campus which gave constant employment to almost 500 men and women.

The firm maintained still rooms and storehouses in a building on the west side of Alfred Street opposite St Malachy's Church. These were destroyed in the war-time air raids on the city of Belfast in May 1941. Rumour has it that on that momentous night the whiskey was removed for safety to the basements of a local church!

It seems that some time after 1844 the spire of St Malachy's oak tower was removed *"because the tolling of the great bell therein interfered with the satisfactory maturing of the whiskey in Messrs Dunvilles' adjacent distillery."*

After "the crash" it took twelve years to sell off the whiskey stock and company assets which, in the end, amounted to almost £20 millions at today's valuation. Employers received redundancy payments and shareholders were paid £3.40 for every £1 share. You might say – hardly a justifiable insolvency!

In the mid-1980's the buildings were demolished to provide road space for the M1 motorway, but Distillery Street , Malt Street and Excise Street still remain. The football ground moved to Ballyskeagh and memorabilia of the Royal Irish Whiskey becomes invaluable. However, all is not lost, the Dunvilles may live again in the new century. A Belfast spirit merchant has acquired the title and intends to bottle and distribute Irish whiskies bearing the glorious name.

"Sic Transit Gloria Mundi"

ESSAY VI - THE HARRISONS OF HOLYWOOD HOUSE

The Harrisons of Holywood Fame

The Harrisons of Holywood were kind in their day,
So they bought up the town, then gave it away
A new schoolhouse is necessary – the squire will subscribe
The maypole is missing - the squire will provide.
Fine tennis courts and rugby grounds came straight from his hand
Ireland's first golf course was built free on his land.
Denominational ties were a thing of the past,
When building a church you had only to ask.
The double doors of the great house lay wide to the poor,
For those more discreet there were banquets galore.
They buried their progeny in the old Priory walls
As last of the Parnellites duly recalls.
So three cheers for the Harrisons of Holywood fame
Lift your glass in toast to their generous name.

C A

Imagine a little wide-eyed Holywood boy, his age still a single figure, experiencing his first "big house". At lunchtime I had escaped from Miss Ivy Rowe's kindergarten class at Sullivan Upper School. A few months before that day, the school had removed from the fine old Lanyon building in the High Street to a functional new red brick building on Belfast Road. Our new school was built on half the acreage of the pleasure grounds of Holywood House – the other half was divided from the school playing fields by a weed-infested carriage drive and a fractured rusty barbed wire fence.

To a little boy, the mansion was huge – like an entire street of houses. A flight of yellow lichen-painted sandstone steps framed the full length of the big house. Spikes of thick plate glass littered the wide moss-covered patio. The huge windows were boarded, except for those which bordered the grand front doors. Through these I could see the square entrance hall with an elegant staircase winding around the back wall. The floor was piled high with fallen plaster, but the magnificent cornices and ceiling roses were still visible.

Although the main house was derelict, the Lough family still inhabited one of the mansion's back wings, which stretched out like pointing fingers towards the Holywood Hills. The Loughs used the vast courtyards to byre their famous TB tested herd, which provided grade "A" milk for the thirsty town of Holywood.

Beneath the building stretched a maze of basement kitchens, servants' halls, cellars, sculleries and pantries. These were connected by damp passages, and dimly lit by thickly barred windows. Scary stories told tantalised children about secret passages, which led to the Priory, and of the ghosts which inhabited them. Many foolhardy boys, equipped with candles and torches, patrolled a passage, which led out beyond the basement kitchens to a large vaulted room. This may have been the icehouse of the mansion. J B Birch, a Holywood boy of the 1870's, tells how he followed a tunnel in the direction of the Nuns' Walk to *'a ruined chapel in the hills'* – until fallen earth stopped his foolhardy progress.

Monsignor O'Laverty, parish priest from 1866 to 1906, found various holy relics around Holywood House, which suggests a religious connection with nearby My Lady's Mile and the Nuns' Walk. Denis O'D Hanna, growing up in Holywood a century ago, refers to the White Ladies of Holywood House, one of whom found her vow too indulgent. She retired to a hermit cell at the top of the Nuns' Walk. Perhaps this was the ruined chapel of an earlier generation or an old hearthstone. Apparently the self-chastising woman lived here in abject poverty, food carried up the Nuns' Walk by her indulgent sisters, frequently rejected. On summer nights boy scouts camping in the woods claim to hear her pathetic wailing on the wind.

The Holywood House underground passages still remain, their entrances blocked by Grainger Brothers' construction when the Loughview housing estate was built. Some day archaeologists will unearth them as evidence of an eighteenth century Irish life-style!

Several of the old houses built on the raised beach from Strandtown to Holywood had tunnels leading towards the seashore. The shore ran close to the line of the Belfast Road before the railway embankment was constructed. As well as the Holywood House tunnels, witnesses alive today tell how when they were children they walked *"the smugglers' passages"* to Richmond Lodge and Garnerville House.

When concrete pipes were being laid under Church Road, a vaulted brick tunnel was discovered leading in the direction of the old Vicarage. Recently an elegantly vaulted catacomb was unearthed during road-works at the corner of Victoria Road and Croft Road. Perhaps a less romantic explanation of "smugglers' caves" is the disposal of excess surface water and sewage to the sea. The Belfast Directory of over a century ago claims Holywood was *"exceedingly well served by its sanitary arrangements in every direction"*. A Holywood Planning Report (1960) refers to the antiquated stone sewers and drains which discharge into Belfast Lough.

The story of Holywood House illustrates the land ownership of Holywood town. The Patron of North Down and modern Holywood, Sir James Hamilton, the Lord Clandeboye, died in 1643. The extravagant lifestyle of his grandson, Henry, second Earl Clanbrassil, led to the division of the Hamilton fortunes. On Clanbrassil's death (without issue) on 12th January 1675, his Countess, the lovely but cunning Lady Alice – inherited the estates. The Hamilton family objected to Henry's disposition of the family property; his five cousins instituted expensive lawsuits against Lady Alice, who by that time had married Lord Bergeny. The Hamilton cousins were assiduously determined that the Bergeny progeny would not inherit what was left of the Clandeboye millions! The quintet appointed their cousins James and Hans to manage the Court case. These two gentlemen betrayed their trust and took the estates for themselves. Sir Hans Hamilton acquired Holywood and Ballywalter, with parts of Knockbreda and Dufferin. His daughter married the exuberant Professor Robert Hamilton of St Andrew's University, who was later created a Baronet. Their son Hans succeeded to the Holywood estate. However, Professor Sir Robert's extravagances and the considerable expense of the original lawsuit impoverished the inheritance.

A 1704 Act of Parliament enabled the trustees to sell parts of the Hamilton estates. At the public auction in Newtownards, Simon Isaac, Hans Hamilton's Ballywalter agent, bought Holywood townland, the Priory house, and part of Ballykeel for £1,150. The head-rent was acquired by the Hill family, the Lords Dungannon, who purchased the manorial rights.
Soon afterwards, Simon Isaac chose the beautiful undulating site on the west side of the town on which to build his mansion house. Its backcloth was the woods which clothe the Holywood hills. The view from the front patio was a panorama over Belfast Lough to the Cave Hill, the blue hills of Antrim and Patrick's Slemish Mountain. The house is clearly marked on a survey of County Down in 1740 and beautifully portrayed on the 1775 map depicting the deep water landing places for Belfast.

Simon Isaac bequeathed his beautiful house with the Holywood estate to his son John. His grandson Simon continued the family line and added the townland of Knocknagoney to the estate in 1765. Simon died the following year, leaving the enlarged estate to his nephew Thomas Bunburry of Bloomfield, who took the family name, Isaac. Thomas Bunburry Isaac died in 1802. His son Simon inherited the estates.

Ten years later Holywood House opened its doors to a new owner. On 12th December 1812 Simon Isaac sold the estates to William Kennedy of Bombay in the East Indies for £38,000. William's widow Dorothea inherited the property. She bequeathed the estates to charity and gave a legacy to her daughter, Mrs Higgins. A deeply angry Higgins family filed a Bill in Chancery to recover what they considered to be their rightful property. For the Higgins, charities were a very good idea – provided they did not start at home! The High Court of Chancery ordered that the estate be sold. The newspaper advertisement of the sale paints an interesting picture of our town in the mid-nineteenth century :

Messrs Fairbrother and Clark of London
Donegall Arms, Belfast. Tuesday, 25th October 1854.

Under Order of the High Court of Chancery made in the case of
Higgins v Earl of Shaftesbury and Others

The whole of the rising town of Holywood.
Numerous private residences, shops, hotels, parcels of land and building ground.

The Holywood Demense, most of Knocknagoney, Priory Park,
The Kinnegar and Woodlands.

Gentlemen's residences - Ashfield (the Bishop's Palace), Westbrook, Clifton House, Maryfield, Richmond House, Knocknagoney House, in all about 1,500 acres producing a gross rental of £1,600.

Particularly valuable to capitalists and building speculators from its contiguity to the Port of Belfast and Railway communication thereto.
Holywood is a pleasing and healthy resort, the favourite and most fashionable bathing place on Belfast Lough and the resort of the Residents of Belfast.

Holywood House, with its demesne, was purchased by John Harrison of Mertoun Hall for £37,500. John Harrison was a wealthy Belfast ship-owner and the Irish agent of the National Assurance Company. It was fortunate for the town that he acquired many other lots at the sale - including the Kinnegar.

Harrison's younger son had taken up residence in Holywood House as a tenant in 1851; perhaps this fact encouraged his father to buy the beautiful old mansion at the auction. John Harrison died in 1857 leaving Mertoun Hall to his elder son, Captain John Harrison and Holywood House to his younger son, Henry, who lived there until his death in 1873 at the age of 46.

The family were early philanthropists, sponsoring every good work in the town. Captain Henry Harrison, who was born at Holywood House in 1867, was the last member of Charles Stewart Parnell's Irish Nationalist Party as Member of Parliament for Tipperary. After a colourful life, he was interred in the Harrison family grave within the walls of the Old Priory Church on 23rd February 1954.

Bassett's County Down guidebook records that R D Harrison was in residence in Holywood in 1886. After his death and the Great War, various tenants kept the old place going - the best known were the Loughs with their splendid herd of Jersey and Friesian cows. So the slowly dilapidating old mansion moved into the twentieth century.

My grandmother remembered that momentous week towards the end of the First World War when Holywood was put up to sale to the highest bidder. Like many others, she lived to regret that the Irish politics and European problems of that time precluded a unique opportunity to provide rich pickings for her posterity. But that was not the intention of the Harrisons. During that mild and sunny winter week, Tuesday, 4th - Friday, 7th December 1917, the family hoped *"in as far as possible, to suit the requirements of small capitalists"* especially those who actually lived on the lots which were for sale.

IN THE HIGH COURT OF JUSTICE IN IRELAND - CHANCERY DIVISION
- LAND JUDGES

TOWN AND LANDS OF HOLYWOOD, PRIORY PARK AND KNOCKNAGONEY

BARONY OF CASTLEREAGH LOWER AND COUNTY DOWN
VALUABLE FEE-FARM AND OTHER HEAD RENTS
AND BUILDING SITES

TO BE SOLD BY PUBLIC AUSTION IN 117 LOTS
BY MESSRS R J McCONNELL & CO, AT THEIR PROPERTY SALE ROOMS

ON TUESDAY, THE 4TH DAY OF DECEMBER, 1917
AND FOLLOWING DAYS

COMMENCING EACH DAY AT TWELVE O'CLOCK NOON

BY DIRECTION OF THE RIGHT HONOURABLE MR JUSTICE ROSS

The sale was the talk of North Down for many months and deserves closer attention than opportunity affords in this essay. A meticulously detailed set of coloured maps depicting the lands of the Harrison Estate Act (1883) accompany the sale catalogue. With the script, they paint a fascinating picture of Holywood in 1917, its streets, house names and rights of way, which now are fading memories, vaguely recalled by old residents.

Catalogue lots 1 to 4 covered the 410 acre rentals of Knocknagoney Townland. They included the pleasure grounds of the grand mansion houses at the entrance to our town

Priory Corner c. 1850, demolished in 1971.

- Richmond Lodge, Mertoun Hall, Maryfield and even parts of Redburn and Ardtullagh.

The tenure of Knocknagoney is recorded from the 1674 Clanbrassil Settlement and Reserves to the Earl *"All finds, mines, minerals, hawking, hunting, fishing and fowling"*. It seems the generous Earl and his Lady wife, Alice - Countess of Clanbrassil, allowed some of the tenants to reduce their ground rent by £1. 3s. 4d, if each year they supplied *"one fat beef and one Cunningham bowl of oats"* to the Bailiff.

Because Henry and Alice Clanbrassil concerned themselves with Knocknagoney matrimony, merchandise and money encouraged Randal McDonnell, Earl of Antrim; James Ros of Portavo, Lord Eustace Gascoyne Cecil, Lord Arthur Hill and Lady Ann Jekyll to wander through the Knocknagoney chapter of Holywood history. All these are interesting stories over which we do not have time to ponder in this essay.

The next one hundred and eight lots, numbered 5 to 113, refer to rentals in Holywood town and Ballykeel. These were part of the original Hamilton Estate which Hans Hamilton had to sell *"by Act of Parliament, in the second year of the reign of Her Majesty Queen Anne (1703) for payment of his grandfather's debts"*.

I shall outline eighteen of one hundred and seventeen lot descriptions, to illustrate the careful planning concern the old Squires took for their town.
In 1904 Lot 5 allowed Messrs David Allen and Sons to erect advertising hoardings around the vacant ground at High Street and Sullivan Place corner. However, these had to be removed at a week's notice if the land was required for building purposes

In Lot 14 - Twenty perches were reserved (when required) from the Glenlyon property of Annette Marsh for a reservoir in connection with the Holywood Waterworks. The area is mapped beside Church Road, immediately above Cuillaire, the house beautifully designed by Denis O'D Hanna for his family. Several times in my research for this series of local essays, I have been told *"Holywood's first waterworks was in the Hanna's garden"*. Indeed there is a large quarry pool on that property, now maintained as an exotic water garden. The Glenlyon reservoir site, a few metres along Church Road, is now a shrubbery, covering part of the public park. Possibly it was envisaged as a water control station for the Holywood Waterworks, built in 1882 a kilometre further up the hill. There is a grain of authenticity, though often confused, in all traditional tales. It is interesting to tease out the truth and smile at the confusion.

In Lot 18 on the west side of Alexandra Avenue (now My Lady's Mile) James Munce was allowed to take water from the river which runs through the property, but no sewage should enter the stream. Next door, Robert Beverland was not allowed to expose clothes for drying or bleaching. The Squire seems to have a deep aversion to the display of Monday morning washing lines - this prohibition appears frequently in the local conditions.
In Lot 28 on the Kinnegar, James Pink is not allowed to build on the land, permit the building of houses or sub-let any part of the land.

Lot 29, which included the Orange Hall, still contained a large ornamental garden where Redburn Square is today.

Lot 66 conserved the lands on the west side of Church road. In 1877 John Harrison allowed the Select Vestry of Holywood for sixpence a year to use part of the site for the Parochial National School, provided it was used only for that purpose. Today, the old building has been refurbished as the magnificent Parish Centre.

Next door, James Beggs was allowed to build "Altona", 100 feet back from Church Road, with an ornamental garden in the intervening space. Regretfully, the grand old house was demolished in the year 2001, and the ornamental garden truncated. "Altona" was the only private dwelling in Holywood which boasted a fine pipe organ in the drawing room. Some old residents remember Miss Beggs who went for a daily swim at Clanbrassil on summer days, attired in a voluminous costume. On a cold day she would come into our house for a hot cup of tea before she pedalled her ancient velocipede back to Holywood. The Altona orchards provided great scope for "scrumping" or "raiding", an art local youths cultivated for acquiring apples without being caught. In the late 1940's and 50's Miss Beggs sold a handful of her windfall apples, with the rotten parts carefully removed, to children from the adjoining school for a penny. In the lease the Beggs were not allowed to run a public house in Altona - it is very unlikely that the family would have expended the energy the licenced trade requires!

In Lot 68, the north side of Church Avenue, William Roberts was not allowed to make bricks, except for use on the premises, and he must not convert any part of the plot into a graveyard!

Lot 82 still contained the ruins of the Presbyterian Church on the Strand or Gospel Lane. In the 1834 map this roadway was called "Meeting House Lane".

In Lot 83, number 123 on north side of High Street, Mrs Louisa P Kamcke was allowed to cut turf in Holywood Moss, provided she kept the portion of the bog assigned to her in proper condition.

In Lot 94 Sullivan Schools must use their High Street site solely for a school-house and a teacher's residence. Today the building is the Holywood Library.

In Lot 104 the Trustees must use their Sullivan Place premises solely as a Masonic Hall. If they made openings in any buildings they should not acquire right to air from the adjoining premises, which was Lot 30, Holywood Town Hall.

On the north side of the Masonic Hall a favourite project was sponsored – the Working Men's Club. However, the buildings were not to be used as a hospital for infectious or contagious diseases, a proviso which was included in Lot 66, the Dunlop Memorial Home, now the Abbeyfield Society. The Working Men's Club must not be used by any dangerous, offensive, noisome or objectionable trade which might be prejudicial to the Masonic Hall next door. As usual, the lessees were not allowed to hang out clothes to dry – except in the back yard!

In 1871 by Lot 111, John Harrison leased two acres at an annual rent of £33 for the erection of St Colmcille's Church, on condition that the building should be used only for the purposes of Divine Worship according to the usage of the Roman Catholic Church. In 1895 the Church authorities acquired additional lands along Church View. Here no houses were to be built for letting, the ecclesiastical and educational buildings had to be ornamental and any school or playground had to be built behind a high wall at the southern end of the property.

In 1906 by Lot 113 Henry Harrison granted 41 acres for a term of 21 years to Holywood Golf Club at a rent of £65 per annum. Henry Harrison reserved the right to resume possession if the land was required for building. Perhaps he recalled the generosity John Harrison had shown to the Royal Belfast Golf Club in 1881, on his Kinnegar property, a club which had upped tees and departed to Carnalea in 1892!

The final group of lots, numbers 114 to 117 refer to the Priory Park. These are held under indenture of 1708. In 1812 Thomas Bunbury Isaac, the owner of Holywood House before the Harrison acquired the estate, granted an interest in Priory Park to William Kennedy who came to Holywood from the West Indies. His wife Dorothea, whom we have met before in these essays, granted her stake in Priory Park to Robert Blackwell in

Church Street, formerly Mill Street, east side.

1840. The Harrisons retained an interest in the seven-acre park; in 1917 it came on to the property market with the rest of the Harrison Estate.
It is interesting to note that the diligent Dorothea reserved for her heirs and assigns *"all timber and trees present and future, all mines, minerals, stone quarries, coal, marl clay, brick, gravel and sand, with full liberty to enter with horses and carriages to carry away the same and to make bricks on the premises".* I am unable to find evidence of a brickworks at Priory Park. However, the marl clay appears similar to that used in the brickworks on the Shepherd's Path (later called Alexandra Road and My Lady's Mile). The bricks which line the interior walls of the Church of St Philip and St James were baked in this Holywood brickworks.

Apart from the Harrison family detestation of the sight of washing hanging on a line, frequently the lessees were forbidden to carry on any offensive or dangerous trade or occupation, and they were required to keep their premises in good order and repair. Sometimes they must make or upkeep adjoining roads, build to stated size and valuation, or pay fines for breaches of covenants. All must adhere to rights of way, and rights to light and air.

Holywood was very fortunate to have as its squires a family who dealt with them sympathetically from the highest to the lowest level in town and country planning, as did their friends the Kennedys, in the neighbouring Cultra Estate.

During the Second World War the fields on the west side of the avenue to Holywood House were used as a prisoner of war encampment.

Church Street, west side, showing the Police House, Post Office and Shanks Medical Hall.

The prisoners enjoyed incarceration in the Emerald Isle, far from military activity. Holywood people remember squads of grey-clad detainees tobogganing on the snowy slopes of the golf course during one of those inclement wartime winters. Years later a Holywood holiday-maker met one of our prisoners in Germany. By then he was a coiffeur - the coincidental craic was excellent!

Another prisoner-of-war camp in our area was situated on the coast at Seahill between the Craigdarragh garden wall and Rockport School. Strangely the War Department did not close the coastal path which ran along the camp's perimeter.

On one of those daily sun-drenched misty summer holiday mornings, I remember cycling along that path, when a troop of grey-clad prisoners came down from the camp to swim at the little sandy bay, half-way between the two big houses. Each had a towel under his arm or wound around his neck and all were singing lustily. While they splashed noisily in the sea, a single British soldier sat on a rock listening to pop songs on a portable radio, his rifle lying idly on the sand. Soon the prisoners came out of the water and started kicking a football on the seaside greensward - perhaps the only German team that ever played in Holywood.

The derelict mansion was demolished by the Ministry of Defence in 1941. In 1948 the Northern Ireland Housing Trust built the Loughview housing estate - some four hundred homes were built where the war-time P O W camp had been. Its shopping centre was built over the site of the demolished Holywood House.
A quaint little gate house survived the mansion for many years. Its site is still a green lawn at the Belfast Road entrance to the carriage drive, now Abbey Ring. The back gatelodge, built into the east return wing of the big house, guarded the farmyard gates. Other cottages shared the cobbled yard. The walled garden with its formal box-hedged paths lay beyond the gates and an immense walled orchard stretched up to the Demesne Road. The mansion bell ruled over this pastoral idyll, rung at mid-day to call the workers home for dinner. Many of the orchard and garden walls still bear witness to our Holywood heritage. A partly culverted stream meanders from Holywood Golf Club through Sullivan Upper School playing fields, the grounds of The Firs, and under the new Gaelic football pitch.

In the great days of Holywood House, the little brook was dammed at the foundations of the high wall of the orchard garden to form an ornamental lake surrounded by shrubbery. Some of us around the town still remember jam-potting our first tadpoles for kindergarten classroom display from the lily-clad waters of Holywood House pond. Miss Ivy Rowe, whom we met in the introduction to this essay, introduced her young wards to "nature study" at the water's margins.

As we enter the twenty-first century it is the intention of Sullivan Upper School to re-furbish the area with an aquatic feature in an on-campus nature trail.
The Harrisons of Holywood House would have been enthusiastic supporters of a botanic garden on their cherished turf.

The old mansion house is long gone, but many evidences of our Holywood heritage still remain at Loughview. Let us keep them for future generations.

ESSAY VII - THE SULLIVAN STORY

Sonnet on Ballymenoch House

Fair Ballymenoch, you now inspire my strains
For who can view your scene without delight ?
The circling grove, the lawns and verdant plains,
With rapture steal the astonished sight.
The stately mansion and the fair domains
With verdure drest perennial through the years,
Your towering woods where sylvan beauty reigns -
In every shade fresh glory now appears.
Benignant owners of this halcyon seat,
No sons of penury around you grieve,
With pride you visit Poverty's retreat.
Your hands are always open to relieve.
From them take pattern all you rich and great -
This honoured family strive to emulate.

Robert Sullivan
Juvenile Songs and Poems - 1818

Cunningham Greg of Ballymenoch House sponsored Sullivan's little poetry book and provided a scholarship for his education at the Academical Institution. Today the re-built mansion is the Salvation Army Eventide Home, and the fair domain is Ballymenoch Park - given to the people of Holywood by Lady Kelly.

THE SULLIVAN STORY

Robert Sullivan was born on 3rd January 1800. The family lived in a pleasant little house with a tall chimneystack on Holywood High Street. Today, it is designated by the prestigious plaque of the Ulster History Circle . Now the children's playground, given to the town by the family of Hugh McNeile McCormick and Rosamund Praeger's "Johnny the Jig" occupy the site. The cottage garden ran up to the Ballykeel River, across which the Holywood Motte dominated the skyline. Here Robert played with his brothers and sisters.

The siblings were Daniel - born in 1798; Marcus - 1802; John - 1804; Dennis - 1812; Mary - 1815; and little Elizabeth - 1817. Probably Elizabeth was his favourite sister as she seems to have been disabled. In 1868, Robert's will specially requested brother Marcus to care for her. Daniel, Elizabeth, Dennis and John were interred with their parents in the family grave. The memorial stone is a few metres outside the old Priory Church in which they were christened and within which Robert was buried in July 1868.
Daniel Sullivan, the children's father, was born in County Kerry in 1764. He died in

Sullivan National School, 1862, the upper school was added to the east gable in 1877.

Holywood on 4th January 1853, aged 89 years. Rev C J McAlester, Mrs Mary Sullivan's minister, claims *"Daniel was stationed in Holywood in the Revenue Service".* Writing in 1886, the parish priest, Monsignor James O'Laverty said he thought *"Sullivan was an ex-marine with "some small situation called Harbour Master of Holywood, which would require an antiquarian investigation to discover the utility of".* Research indicates a Customs or Coastguard Station was situated on Marine Parade, later in the century similar posts were sited on the Kinnegar and at Marino. The appointments provided adequate remuneration for the Government officers who manned them.

The Kerry naval man fell in love with a Holywood lass - Miss Mary McClement. A testimonial which comes from those who knew her says, *"Mary was a woman of amicable disposition, gentle manners, rare good sense and unaffected piety".* Mary and Daniel married in Holywood and set up house in the little cottage with tall chimneys and long back garden. The house became a happy home for the family of eight, ringing with laughter and stories of the sea. Here Robert learned the first lessons of family life. In May 1833 Mother Mary was the first of the large family to die. She had seen her precocious son become a Dublin University Master of Arts and a Government Inspector of Schools.

Robert's introduction to education was a nursery school taught by elderly Mrs Bannister and her daughter Molly close to the Sullivan's cottage. His second school seems to have operated in the Session House of the Presbyterian Church, which had removed to Strand Street in 1726. Presumably, he transferred to the Established Church School as the family were members of the Church of Ireland. When Robert was four or five years of age his father went off to fight the French. In 1798 Holywood supporters had encouraged the United Irishmen with jubilant shouts of "Liberty, Equality and Fraternity". They sang a different song when Napoleon Bonaparte threatened invasion of the United Kingdom in 1803.

The Napoleonic Wars required a constant supply of recruits for the major British force - the Royal Navy. Frequently, an armed force would come ashore at a selected town, seize all the likely young men they could find and carry them off to serve King George, under a harsh discipline and for a small remuneration.

Such a press gang descended upon Holywood and recruited twenty men, including Daniel Sullivan. At that time Daniel would have been at least forty years of age. He was a happily married man with six children and employed in a good Government job - not the usual type of press gang recruit. However, local evidence of the event is compelling, perhaps he volunteered for the job!

Daniel Sullivan seems to have served in the Navy from 1805 until 1811 when he resumed his Customs post. During these formative years, Robert Sullivan was bonded completely with his mother, a deep love and respect which remained all the years of his life.

News of the wars and the Battle of Trafalgar (21st October 1805) was avidly sought by Holywood people, especially the Sullivan family and young Robert. In those days, the only means of communication were the Belfast News-Letter, the Commercial Chronicle and the Belfast Daily Mercury. Such newspapers cost about fivepence, far too expensive for the local folk. In any case, many of them were unable to read. A society met in the home of Mr James Hogue in Shore Street, sharing the price of the news-sheets or receiving out-of-date "papers" from the big houses. Robert Sullivan was only too eager to be appointed reader to the group of interested men and women. No doubt, the remuneration supplemented the family funds when his father was off at the Wars.

When Robert was seventeen, he attended Mr Hugh Kennedy Greenfield's *"English and Classical School"*. For some time he had been employed as general factotum at the new Vicarage or Glebe House which had moved from Priory Park to Church Road in 1813. It was the vicar, Rev William Anthony Holmes (1810 - 1825) who had discerned young Sullivan's potential and arranged for the boy's attendance at Greenfield's Holywood Academy. Here, Robert's superior intellect and industry made him the star student.

Again, Mr Holmes came to the assistance of his prodigy. One evening the vicar was dining with Mr Cunningham Greg and his wife Ellen at Ballymenoch House on Bangor Road. After dinner he showed his host a scrap-book which Robert had been writing in his spare time. It was a neatly scripted volume containing juvenile poetical compositions. Cunningham Greg was deeply impressed by the intellectual ability of the young man. As a result the vicar and his parishioner decided to assist him in two ways - the publication of the poems and the gift of a scholarship to the Belfast Academical Institution.

The book was called "Juvenile Poems, with a few Songs". It was printed by Mr Francis D Finlay of Cornmarket, Belfast in 1818. Robert Sullivan prefaced his first publication - *"I wrote the pieces during my vacant hours, solicitations from my friends prevailed upon me to offer them to the public."* Ninety-two subscriptions of one shilling covered the cost of printing the little volume. Some of the verses are adolescent love poems, some show his deep social concern; others are inspired by sea stories and the Napoleonic Wars. The Holywood theme runs through eight of the poems. The sonnet which prefaces this essay is a sonnet dedicated to his benefactor, Cunningham Greg.

His position in later life convinced Sullivan that the published poems of puberty were an embarrassment to a leading educationalist! About 1830 Robert Sullivan acquired and destroyed as many books as possible. Today, the only known copy is preserved in the Belfast Linenhall Library.

Fortunately for Robert Sullivan, Cunningham Greg was a member of the Belfast Academical Institution, which was founded in 1810 and opened to students in 1814. Cunningham Greg's subscription of one hundred guineas permitted him to nominate a scholarship student for education at "Inst". In February 1819 Robert Sullivan entered the classical school, a few weeks after his nineteenth birthday.

Much has been made of the nineteen year old student's daily walk along the new Belfast Road to attend classes at 'Inst'. The Academical Institution had a boarding department - students from as far afield as Dublin, Glasgow and Jamaica were enrolled. For Robert Sullivan and another clever Holywood boy, John Wightman, daily lectures at the embryonic University of Belfast commenced at 7 a.m. in summer-time and 7.45 a.m. in the winter months. In 1819, two coach services connected Holywood with Belfast. Neither would have taken up passengers for such an early start but would have provided a return journey. In seems unlikely to me that the Faculty of the Institution or his rich Holywood sponsors would have allowed a scholarship student to walk five miles every morning to attend lectures. Other boys from Holywood attended the Academical Institution or the Belfast Academy, which had been founded in 1785 in Academy Street. Most likely, students were driven up to the city in the family trap, a light two-wheeled one-horse carriage on springs. No doubt, "lifts" to school were as common as they are today! Possibly Sullivan boarded at "Inst", we know that later he lodged in the city.

Soon Robert Sullivan made his mark on his masters and the two hundred and fifty students. His fellow classmen awarded him, by popular acclamation, the coveted silver medal for Logic. He was selected by the Classical School to read his Latin translations in verse at "Common Hall" - a Saturday morning communal tutorial. Sullivan's name appears six times in the list of prizewinners at the Institution's public examinations advertised in the News-Letter for 30th June 1820. Here was a young man who having attended "Inst" for eighteen months, is able to win class prizes in Mathematics, Greek Elocution, Ancient Geography, Latin Extempore and Speaking, also Latin Juvenal and a prize in French Language. This is a worthy achievement in any school. At "Inst" which Sullivan afterwards called *"Ireland's first really great National School"*, it was amazing, and says much for the high standard of his early education in Holywood.

Sullivan's competent apprehension of Euclid's elements attracted the attention of the Master, James Thompson, father of Lord Kelvin (1824 - 1907), the Institution's world-famous physicist. When Sullivan left "Inst", James Thompson obtained the position of Tutor at Tyrell's Pass, County Westmeath for his favourite student. There Robert Sullivan, now twenty-one years of age, far away from the restraints of home and family, fell in love with the gentle lady who was to be his devoted partner for over forty years.

A second tutorage took him from Westmeath to Thurles, County Tipperary. As well as tutoring and paying court, Sullivan found time to study for Dublin University examinations. He matriculated into Trinity College in 1824, when he and Mrs Sullivan removed from Thurles to Dublin. Dublin University conferred Baccalaureate in 1829, Magistratus in 1832 and Legum Doctor in 1858.

Robert Sullivan's mother became ill and died in Holywood on 19th May 1833, aged 56 years. Her son returned home immediately. A light went out in his life as he stood in the Priory graveyard with the sorrowing family she had held together, through thick and thin, for thirty-five years. Mary Sullivan had made it possible for a talented boy from a lowly home to attend a distinguished school and university. She accomplished this at a time when most children were required to earn their keep at the earliest date possible. Robert Sullivan spent the rest of his life attempting to repay the debt he owed to his mother.

When Robert and his wife came to Dublin in 1824 it seems his intention was to study for the Irish Bar. Rev C J McAlester, who knew Sullivan and his family very well, claimed Robert was called to the Bar in 1838 *"but without any intention of applying himself to the legal profession"*. Possibly the reason for this was a commission from Mr Cummins, a Dublin publisher, to revise school textbooks. At that time Sullivan was editing a book on the meaning of words, which became the basis for the popular "Spelling Book Superceded". Sullivan soon realised his career lay in the world of modern Irish education rather than in dusty Hibernian Law Courts.

In 1832 the Chief Secretary had introduced the National System of Education for Ireland, under an interdenominational Board of Commissioners. The Board provided state support for the parish schools and the previous "hedge schools". The parish schools were operated by the local Church authorities; the hedge or pay schools came from the early 1700's when Roman Catholic Church schools had been prohibited. In the "Black North" Presbyterian schools often fell into the same category.

The name "Hedge School" persisted even after the schools moved into makeshift buildings or pupils' homes. 1824 Estimates suggest 9,000 hedge schools were attended by ten thousand children. Teachers were itinerant, depending on fees in coin or kind. Subjects were reading, writing and arithmetic; textbooks were whatever came to hand.

Obviously it was necessary for Government to introduce a viable education service. It was not surprising that Robert Sullivan elected to assist in establishing the foundation

Sullivan Street (1863). It replaced Wilson's Lane and was demolished for car parking in 1969.

for a modern system of education for Ireland and to provide authorship for the textbooks which secured the project's success.

The Board particularly welcomed denominationally mixed schools where pupils could receive a "literary education" together, and scripture reading separately. Co-operating schools received building costs, teachers' salaries, textbooks and an efficient inspectorate. Each of the three ecclesiastical bodies criticised the arrangements for their own peculiar reasons. Had he still been alive in 1870, Sullivan would have been very disappointed that the Board accepted the denominational nature of most schools.

The 1832 Board introduced a *"payment by results"* scheme for teachers; this inoperable provision was discontinued by the Belmore Commission in 1898. In 1833 the total number of pupils in national schools was estimated at 107,000 - by the end of the century over half a million children were in attendance.

To understand fully the Sullivan story of education in Holywood and elsewhere in Ireland the reader should remember that the United Kingdom government was responsible for the whole island until 1921.

The Kildare Place Society played a valuable part in the story. This society was founded in 1811 by a group of philanthropic lawyers and businessmen, for the promotion of education among the Irish poor. As it was non-sectarian, it attracted state funding, and soon was advocating teacher-training, textbook publication and a rigorous inspectorate. Model schools were established on a monitorial system with residential accommodation for the candidate teachers.

A fundamental requirement of the Society was *"Bible reading by all the children together 'without note or comment'."* Increasing criticism came from the Roman Catholic clergy and state support was withdrawn. The Board accepted this method of Bible reading without comment for its national schools, teacher training and model schools. However, the Board's training institution in Marlborough Street, Dublin was declared unsuitable for the training of Roman Catholic teachers.

In 1883 the Government granted state aid to denominational Irish teacher training colleges. When the Irish Free State was established, the Marlborough Street College was closed. In the early 1920's Stranmillis Training College was established to train teachers for the state sector in Northern Ireland. St Mary's College and later St Joseph's College were founded to train teachers for denominational Roman Catholic schools. These few brief comments should help to clarify some of the difficulties Robert Sullivan had to face as Board Inspector and later Professor in Marlborough Street Training College.

In 1832 Robert Sullivan applied for one of the four inspectorships the Board intended to cover the island. When his application was refused, his good friend and member of the Board, the Archbishop of Dublin - Dr Richard Whately - suggested he should consider preparation for Holy Orders. McAlester records the resulting conversation *"Sullivan replied he could not do so as he was married. "No objection to that", said the Archbishop. "But my wife is a Roman Catholic" replied Sullivan.* In May 1832 Robert Sullivan was elected to the post of Inspector, with responsibility for the northern counties, as he hailed from Ulster. The Board required its four inspectors to be strict, efficient and totally dedicated to the profession. The annual salary was £250, which included charges and travelling expenses - soon this was increased to £300. In comparison, a national school master received about £30 per annum; the difference in salary shows the importance the Board placed upon its Inspectorate.

Although Sullivan had been appointed as second choice in May 1832, on the recommendation of the Established Church, his academic qualification, his church membership and his Ulster background made him the obvious choice out of 38 applicants. His area of responsibility was Ulster with an occasional straying into Leinster.

The new inspector's greatest difficulty must have been how to travel rapidly to visit his schools, many of which were in the most remote places. The first railway in Ulster opened on 12th August 1839, between Belfast and Lisburn. By that time, Sullivan had been promoted to professor in the Dublin Training College - so the inspector missed the first train by one year! Walking, riding on horseback or pony and trap were the only means of transport from the stage coach points.

By 1834 there were 28 lines operating forty coaches out of the capital. Dublin to Belfast took twelve hours, tickets cost 27s 6d for a seat inside and 15s outside. Journeys were accurately time-tabled and efficiently conducted, subject to penalty clauses imposed by the Post Office. Sullivan may well have patronised Daniel Miskelly who started a coach service to Holywood in 1810, and whom we shall meet again in another essay. Miskelly hired post-chaises, gigs, jaunting cars and horses. His *"Waterloo"* coach served Randalstown, the *"Union"* went to Cookstown, the *"Lark"* to Ballymena. Miskelly also ran the *"Antrim"* and a speedy, cheap conveyance from Coleraine to Belfast; all good means of vehicular transport for His Majesty's Inspector of Schools. Sullivan seems to have coped successfully with a peripatetic life in the northern counties.

However, the inspector's life was not an easy one! Usually they were on circuit for nine months of each year; the other three months were used for training and technology revision in the Dublin Model School. The details of every school visited on circuit had to be recorded meticulously in "the Road Book". If the inspector made mistakes or left his work uncompleted he was required to discharge the expense himself. Every statement he made was scrutinised for ulterior meanings. In fact, inspectors were called before an officious Board for rigorous inquiry. The inspectors were themselves inspected! An inspector's visit to a country school was a dreaded event and pupils and teachers alike expected the worst. Inspectors felt very much the same way when they appeared before the Board!

Newspaper reports of opposition to the National School system and foolish misunderstandings by Presbyterian and Roman Catholic clergy make interesting and amusing reading. They illustrate the extreme prejudice with which Robert Sullivan had to contend in a few places in his native Ulster. Belfast Daily Mercury for 7th October 1859 claimed *"Sullivan's prudent and conciliatory conduct did a vast deal in rendering the national system popular throughout Ulster."* The Londonderry Standard for 20th December 1861 recorded *"Sullivan established the national system in Ulster in the face of difficulties which few other men would have attempted to meet."*

Obviously, the workload of the inspector was impossible to achieve in so large a sector, later the system was rationalised. Sullivan made the best of an impossible task. It says much for his schooldays in Holywood and at "Inst" that Robert Sullivan did not possess a sectarian or prejudiced bone in his body.

His tact and patient perseverance were quite unbelievable during the six years he spent in the Inspectorate. The time fully equipped him for the most important part of his career - teaching teachers how to teach!

In 1838 Robert Sullivan was appointed Professor of the Marlborough Street Training College in Dublin. Here he could freely propagate the national education system for Ireland, in which he devoutly believed. McAlester wrote *"The influence of his instruction extended to every part of Ireland and his name became known in the most remote corners of the land for the promotion of unsectarian education."*

Here I should give you a précis of the twelve practical rules which Sullivan instilled into his trainee teachers. These were the basis of education and the way in which they should conduct themselves as instructors of the Nation's children.

"Avoid politics; keep a time and a place for everything
and always keep it in its proper time and place.
Promote cleanliness, neatness and decency.
In yourself and in your words require truth and honesty
with kindness and firmness.
Always observe a love for animals."

These golden rules were taught to the students long after Sullivan's days in the College. A schoolteacher aunt of mine who trained in Marlborough Street in the first decade of the twentieth century learned the rules by heart and lived out the remainder of her life by their dictates.

The Board opened the Model Schools and Teacher Training College in Marlborough Street in 1835. The original concept was to establish five professorships; by 1838 only two had been appointed - Father W M McGanley and Robert Sullivan. They had one full-time assistant - John Rintoul and two part-time specialists, teaching Art and Music. The two professors shared control of the Model Schools and the Training Department. Sullivan was responsible for lectures and course work in Teaching Practice, Schools' Organisation, English Literature and Composition, History, Geography and Political Economy. To this impossible workload was added Head of Inspections, compilation of detailed reports and compulsory attendance at meetings of the Board.

At first the length of teacher training in the College was a mere three months, later it was increased to a six-month course. Between 1838 and 1854 some 4,000 students were trained. A typical day in the life of a student teacher was :

"Rise and shine at 6 a m for a meagre breakfast (tea was forbidden). Lectures were arranged between 10 a m and 4 p m. After dinner, (tea allowed twice a week) a study period from 5.30 p m to 8.45 p m was timetabled. At 9.30 p m the students retired to bed.

It seems training was not only academic; it also prepared teachers for the social life to which they might look forward on a salary of £20 per annum!

Nineteenth century students were much the same as students of any age. Some were industrious - others indulgent. We read of Professor Sullivan's disappointment in Mr Aston, who was brought before the Dublin magistrates *'on charges of intoxication and being found in company with women of improper character'*. Another Marlborough Street trainee-teacher was fined ten shillings for drunkenness. A serious problem for the good professor was students who inclined themselves towards party politics. Those were the days of the Ribbonmen, so called in 1811 as *"a new name for the United Irishmen"*. Ribbonism was a sectarian movement seeking to achieve an independent Ireland by armed insurrection. In fact, Ribbonmen expended their energy in feuding and elaborate secret rituals - the very stuff of student activity. Things got so dangerous that the student

Conjectural interior of Priory Church c. 1835. Rafters were used for Parochial School building.

teachers were forbidden to leave Marlborough Street College on St Patrick's Day 1848 - the doors were firmly locked!

Much of Professor Sullivan's time was taken up in attempting to better students' prospects and rewards from the Board. The Belfast News-Letter for 13th July 1868 recorded *"Sullivan not only succeeded in making good teachers but in securing them as personal friends."* Faculty work load and employment description defy reason; how Professor Sullivan efficiently performed his duties and continued annually to produce carefully prepared textbooks shows the stature and tenacity of a true educationalist.

On 7th October 1859 Belfast Daily Mercury claimed

"Dr Sullivan became an author to supplant immoral
publications, introduce improved methods of teaching
and provide the necessary literature. As an author,
Sullivan's unparalleled success in Great Britain and
the Colonies comes from the working out of an original
idea and the elaboration of a new method!"

Although verbose, this newspaper cutting summarized a brilliant career in education. Sullivan realised that the national system of education would perish if an adequate supply of recognised textbooks in every subject was not available to the pupils. He saw a window of opportunity, filled it by amazing industry and unintentionally made himself a millionaire in the process.

The Board encouraged aspiring authors, under strict rules. All books had to be in sympathy with the national system. The text had to be completely free from opinions or allusions which might offend members of any religious communion. The books were required to be available at the lowest possible cost. Each pupil in Ulster could expect 3.1 pennies (1.5 pence) to be spent on his school books each year. It says much for Sullivan that he offered his textbooks to the Board without commission in order to save public money. Fortunately for him, his generous offer was refused. When Sullivan published his books at his own expense, he supplied them to schools at 20% less than the booksellers' cost. He even went the third mile and supplied the unbound printed pages for local school binding to save pennies for the Board.

In the Ulster Observer of 26th January 1867, Dr Sullivan commented – *"I repeatedly urged the publication of a complete set of books for school use."* In this, Dr Sullivan was successful. As early as 1835, the Board had published fourteen titles – many from the pen of Robert Sullivan. The efficiency of the textbooks was tested in the Model School and found to provide the required results. They were used from First Year to Teacher Training and beyond.

To show the academic versatility of the man, take a look at a list of his works –
Juvenile poems, Manual of Etymology, Spelling Book Superceded, Dictionary of Derivations, Papers on Popular Education, Dictionary of the English Language, Geography Generalised, Literary Class Book, Knowledge of Common Things, Manual of Etymology, and *Words spelled in Two or More Ways.*

In 1847, Robert produced an educational game called *"Game of England in a Box"*. J Robinson suggests that this may have been a letter game played with cards or wooden blocks. Examples of a mid-nineteenth geographical card games are extant. I wonder did our Holywood hero hold copyright to the game!

In the foreword to the 23rd edition of *"The Spelling Book Superceded"* Sullivan notes that copyright laws were being broken by printers in Canada. Over six million copies of Sullivan's works were sold. By 1846 the Irish publications were greatly in demand in Canada, Guiana, Newfoundland, Gibraltar, Malta, with a possible Modern Greek translation for Corfu.

Publication did not cease on Sullivan's death. He bequeathed £4,000 to his nephews, John and Marcus Sullivan, whose publishing undertaking received the copyright of his books and all the stock in hand. The books continued to be published well into the twentieth century as *"Dr Sullivan's Series of Improved School Books".*

It is not surprising that the massive workload and responsibility of office were claiming a heavy toll on the sixty-seven year old professor. Modern retirement pensions would be many years in the future!

On 24th December 1867 Professor Sullivan was working in his study in Marlborough Street. It was typical of the man that he should be working on Christmas Eve! Suddenly he suffered a seizure, which resulted in temporary paralysis and loss of memory. Sullivan realised he was unable to control his pen. The power in the fingers of his right hand has disappeared. The first Mrs Sullivan had died some time before this tragic event. Fortunately, Dr Sullivan had re-married. Now Lucinda Sullivan, nee Brady, cosseted the professor back to health at Kingstown, outside Dublin. One can imagine how frustrating it was for the author of *"Words spelled in two or more ways"* published that very year, should be unable to remember the words he wished to employ! In the new year, the Sullivans thought a visit to the whirlpool baths at Spa in Eastern Belgium might help the invalid.

While in London on the way to the Continent, they took the opportunity to consult an eminent physician, who advised the professor to return home as soon as possible. Back home in Kingstown, it seems his strength was restored. The following spring he was able to return to work in Marlborough Street, even though that was against the wishes of his wife and the advice of his doctor. In July he suffered a second severe seizure. Dr Robert Sullivan died on 11th July 1868.

Rev C J McAlester, an intimate friend of Dr Sullivan was one of his executors. Both were Instonians, although McAlester was the junior by ten years. Sullivan's mother had been a member of the Presbyterian congregation in Holywood to which McAlester was called in 1834.

On 24th November 1868 a public meeting in Holywood resolved *"to erect a granite obelisk in a conspicuous situation in the town as a memorial to our greatest benefactor".* The Sullivan Memorial Committee estimated the obelisk would cost £250 and requested subscriptions in March 1869.

I am unable to discover from Holywood folk evidence that the obelisk materialised, although we have a very pleasant sketch of what the Committee intended. I surmise the donations were used to erect the memorial within the walls of the Old Priory Church, in which Robert Sullivan was christened and where he attended Divine Worship as a youth. The Memorial Committee reminded the Holywood people that Dr Sullivan had given £2,000 to build the National Schools, a bequest of £4,000 to enlarge and endow his schools, also a £2,000 bequest for the relief of the poor of the parish - £8,000 in all.

By his will, Sullivan bequeathed £4,000 to endow three scholarships in Queen's College, Belfast. McAlester claimed the residue of his property, possibly this was as much as £8,000, became available for the promotion of unsectarian education in Holywood, depending upon the judgment of his executors.

The gift of £4,000 to his nephews assured the success of "Dr Sullivan's series of Improved School Books". The Sullivan family in Holywood and his wife Lucinda were remembered generously; several small bequests made an estate of £45,000, over two million pounds in monetary value today.

Fortunately, J Watkins of Dublin sculpted a head and shoulders of Dr Sullivan in 1867, the year before he died. The bust has an honoured place in the foyer of Sullivan Upper School. Rosamund Praeger, a former student, carved a fine profile and title plaque for erection above the main doors of the new school building when it removed from High Street to the Belfast Road site.

No essay on Robert Sullivan would be worth its salt without a description of the schools he founded in Holywood.

The Sullivan National Schools were opened on 28th April 1862, six years before Dr Robert Sullivan's death. In 1859 he had entrusted to Thomas Greg two thousand pounds *"for the erection and endowment of a National School in Holywood".* Thomas was the son of Cunningham Greg – Robert Sullivan's benefactor.

The famous firm of Lanyon, Lynn and Lanyon was engaged as architects and John Ross of Belfast as construction engineers for the new school. It is built in the Venetian Gothic style, using yellow polychrome bricks relieved by black banding. Carved sandstone was extensively used for door and window lintels. The graceful staircase tower and entrance gives the building an ecclesiastical appearance.

A nursery school was situated in the south wing, however it soon became evident that the infant accommodation was inadequate. The 1868 Inspector's report advised enlargement. A building site behind the school was purchased for the erection of an additional class-room, a lavatory and a water closet, costing £310.

The boys' school met on the ground floor of the main building. The girls' school was upstairs. In an 1853 report, Sullivan had declared *"I consider girls' education of equal and indeed greater importance than boys."*

The Belfast News-Letter, 29th April 1862, covering the official opening recorded

> *"Male and female schools are fitted out in first class manner – eight desks in each school, each seating seven pupils, fifty-six in all. In the boys' school there are forms, in the girls' school there are individual seats to protect the girls' modesty."*

Robert Sullivan's concern for the girls extended to the boys in a different way.

At that period in some schools, and for a long time afterwards, corporal punishment was the norm. Dr Sullivan utterly disapproved of beating or caning. Lecturing to his students, he taught

> *"Some teachers think boys can no more learn without thrashing than tops spin without whipping – such teachers who govern by fear are unfit for office."*

The Sullivan School managers attempted to enforce this principle. In April 1887 they ruled that assistant teachers could be dismissed from office if they used corporal punishment on a pupil. It seems a Mr Small avoided dismissal by agreeing to keep an accurate punishment book! Parents had complained to the Headmaster, Mr Adam Speers, concerning the case of some country boys *"who had to fast for ten hours".* It seems they were arriving home with swollen faces, discoloured fingers and throbbing hands and wrists, resulting from Mr Small's beatings. Mr Small, by name and nature *"was a famous caner and had habits unbecoming to a gentleman of education and culture".* One day an exasperated student, driven beyond endurance, threw his slate at the irascible little man. The slate missed the master's cranium. There is no record of what he wrote in his punishment book on that memorable day!

The managers frequently ran into financial difficulties. Some commentators suggest that the actual building costs consumed most of Sullivan's donation, leaving little for endowment. Had they vested the school property in the National Board, two thousand pounds might have been available. Wisely, the members preferred to keep their independence and rely on the Sullivan gift.

Dr Sullivan intended that there should be good accommodation on campus for the teaching staff. A letter from Greg to McAlester in November 1859 comments on the unavailability of finance for this important project. In 1883 money was not available to pay water rates. Holywood Town Commissioners requested twelve pounds per annum to supply water to the school by cart *"for drinking and scientific experiments".* The principal teacher, Adam Speers, decided the school would collect and use rain water. The Town Commissioners reduced the charge to £6! In 1867 the Managers found it difficult to pay the school cleaners. The teaching staff were requested *" to look to the cleanliness of their own classrooms!"* That request soon brought proposals to increase school fees to pay the cleaning ladies.

Of course, fees were very reasonable: labourers' children paid one penny a week, artisans' children twopence. Professional and business people were charged five shillings a quarter for the education of their children. Dr Sullivan himself offered to meet the fees for any child whose parents needed help.

Teaching staff salaries were five, three or two pounds per quarter, accordingly to status. After 1869, Dr Sullivan's additional bequests may have allowed increases in staff remuneration. However, teachers could win a salary supplement based on the performance of scholars at the public examinations: an early form of payment by results.

The teaching syllabus included reading, writing, arithmetic, geography, spelling, grammar and needlework. An additional fee was charged for agriculture, book-keeping, music, art, algebra and geometry. The Bible was read daily without comment – local clergy had the opportunity to instruct their own parishioners one day each week.

The Management Committee endeavoured to adhere to Dr Sullivan's requirements to the letter. All supported the ideals of non-sectarian education, and the principles of the national system of education. Along with the Sullivan trustees, local members of the clergy and a representative of each church in the town were eligible for membership of the Management Committee.

A new operational scheme was introduced after 30th October 1889, which eventually became the Board of Governors of Sullivan Upper School. The Sullivan National School provided primary education in the town centre until 1954, when it was united with the Parochial National School and became Holywood Primary School.

In his will, Robert Sullivan bequeathed the residue of his estate *"for promoting national unsectarian education in Holywood"* at the discretion of his executors. After his generosity to the town, his family and education in general, it is unlikely that Dr Sullivan realised the magnitude of the residue. When the will was drafted, it appears over £8,000 was available to the executors for this purpose.

By March 1869 John Anderson, Secretary of the Sullivan Memorial committee, confidently wrote *"Dr Sullivan bequeathed a sum of £4,000 for the enlargement and endowment"* of the Sullivan schools. Another opinion was that the annual income from £4,000 was intended for the augmentation of Holywood teachers' salaries, the building of additional classrooms and provision of staff accommodation.

Monsignor O'Laverty, the parish priest who elected not to take his seat on the School Management Committee, thought some of the Sullivan bequest should be used for the Parochial School which his congregation had opened in the Strand in 1869.

In 1873 the executors announced they wished to erect an Intermediate or Upper School linked to the existing National School and adjacent to it. At that time, many of the local business, professional and farming families sent their children by train to the Belfast Academy (1785), the Academical Institution (1810), St Malachy's College (1833) and Victoria College (1867). They wanted a school of similar category in Holywood, unconnected with the National School and built on a different site. However, the executors persisted with their intention to build the Upper School in association with Sullivan's National School.

Lanyon, Lynn and Lanyon were commissioned to draw plans for a completely sympathetic addition to the original building of 1862, which had proved to be architecturally acceptable to the High Street scenario.

So successful were the architects in the task set by the Executors that only to the rear east gable can one detect the junction of the two buildings. The Upper School had its own entrance hall, a fine clock tower containing two rooms, a semi-hexagonal stair well, three teaching rooms and a commodious first storey assembly hall. Separate toilets and a wall dividing the playgrounds were erected.

Later, a red brick wing was added to the south of the Upper School, to accommodate a science laboratory and a domestic economy department. At first, the school was not successful. Two years after the official opening, which took place with great pomp and ceremony on 1st October 1877, there were only twenty-seven scholars on the roll. By 1884 the School was severely in debt!

In 1886 the Management Committee took the bold step of appointing the efficient principal teacher of the National School, Adam Speers, as Headmaster of the Upper School. He remained in the post until 1911 – a quarter of a century of devoted service. Mr Speers was a firm but fair disciplinarian, a science graduate of London University and an outstanding educationalist.

Within the year, numbers increased to 109 scholars. The Upper School remained on the High Street site, with ever increasing success, until 1939 when a new building was erected on the extensive playing fields in the grounds of Holywood House, which the Board of Governors had assiduously acquired some years before the removal.

Before the Belfast Road grounds became available for school games, the Sullivan boys played a form of rugby football on the vacant ground opposite the old school, on which the Kearney Brothers building was erected in 1936. School hockey was played at Seapark, on an excellent pitch over which a new road has been constructed. The grounds beyond Spafield were available for cricket and the important Annual sports Day; tennis was played at the Norwood Club. For budding helmsmen there were two yacht clubs and two golf courses for those who wanted to learn the Royal and Ancient game. A highly competitive inter-Church League provided entertainment for badminton enthusiasts. For those with Thespian ambitions, the School organised concerts and Shakespearean productions in the High Street Church Hall, later the Holywood Players looked to the School for its star performers.

Sullivan Upper School on Holywood High Street provided an excellent academic curriculum and sports programme for its students.

The Second World War broke out in September 1939 – at the beginning of the Autumn School Term. The necessity for military accommodation forced compulsory occupation of Redburn, Ardtullagh, Oakley and even St Helen's in the High Street. A little bird, probably the School's emblem robin red-breast, informed the Governors that the unfinished new school building was to be commandeered as a military hospital.

After Assembly the following morning, the school marched crocodile-style from the old building to the new twelve-acre campus on Belfast Road. Each of us conveyed items of vital equipment. I recall carrying a flower-pot holder with a perky pixie attached to its side. My brother's task was to bring the school hand-bell, the clapper of which he sounded from time to time to accompany our pilgrimage!

The formal opening of the new Sullivan Upper School did not take place until Wednesday, 29th May 1940, when the new building was completed. The Vice-Chancellor of Queen's University, Dr D Lindsay Keir, performed the ceremony. In sixty years the school has grown from one hundred to over one thousand students; the staff from twelve to more than 65 members. It is a story of continual academic and campus progress. Immediately after the war, a much-needed dining hall was added and extended two years later. Norwood Tennis Club pavilion and courts were acquired in 1948 and a new staff common room added the following year. The Grant Wing was built in 1950. In 1952 the campus almost doubled in size with the purchase of the upper playing fields.

In 1953 Dromkeen House was acquired for the Preparatory School. In 1959 three laboratories, an art room and the library block were added to the main school. The War Memorial Pavilion was erected to commemorate the twenty-two "Sullivanians" who had given their lives in two World Wars.

The extensions of 1964 more than doubled the facilities. A common assembly hall was built, four additional laboratories, the swimming pool, a music lecture room, the administrative block, study rooms, classrooms and sports centre changing rooms. Provisions necessary for the twenty-first century continue. The sixth form centre, outdoor pursuits centre, all-weather pitch and sports areas, the cricket table, an estate maintenance block and ancillary garages make for a well-ordered school community. Well edited specialist school publications illustrate modern progress, especially *"Dr Robert Sullivan and Sullivan Upper"* edited by M Keown and published in September 2000. Robert Sullivan would be proud to see how his Upper School has developed.

At the beginning of the twenty-first century the School's academic reputation is supreme – the Irish motto *"Lamh Foisdineach an Uachtar – the gentle hand foremost"*, recalls the founder's teaching dictum – *"Some teachers think boys can no more learn without thrashing than tops can spin without whipping – such teachers who govern by fear are unfit for office."* This pronouncement, with its insistence that *"The education of girls is of equal and indeed greater importance than boys"* is the best note on which to conclude the Sullivan Story and in our next essay to consider the other schools in Holywood.

ESSAY VIII - A PROFUSION OF HOLYWOOD SCHOOLS AND SCHOLARS

A Critic Storm

"The critic storm that proudly rends
The oaks of learning's hill
Shall pass my shrub, that lowly bends'
Nor deign its growth to kill.

Some words of Miss Brooks which Robert Sullivan selected to preface his first book "Juvenile Poems with a Few Songs" published in 1818.

Contains –

THE EARLY SCHOOLS

The happy description of early Ireland as *"a land of saints and scholars"* may come as much from early missionary endeavour as guidance for students. Men entered religious communities to praise God and seek wisdom, then to propagate that learning. So it would seem the earliest school in Holywood was connected with the Priory and the great Abbey of Bangor. It was a Celtic school associated with Laiseran's foundation operating about the year 640.

This was replaced with a school established by the order of the Hermits of St Augustine some time after Thomas Whyte had built our Priory in 1190. Probably Niall O'Neill replaced the Augustinians with Franciscans in 1490 – they were his favourite religionists. The third order arrived in Ireland about 1425. Tertiaries were men and women living in a community associated with a religious order; they assisted the secular clergy and may have been involved in education. Throughout the period, Holywood Priory remained subordinate to the Augustinian Bangor Abbey.

The Dissolution of the Priory on New Year's Day 1541 by King Henry VIII brought an end to ecclesiastical poor relief, medical care and education. Dissolution brought much less money than expected into government coffers. However, pensions for displaced superiors averaged £28, and the ordinary monks received about £2 in compensation. They were allowed to ply a trade and some may possibly have set themselves up as schoolmasters! The Old Priory continued to be used for public worship until October 1572, when Sir Brian MacPhelim O'Neill burnt the roof to prevent government forces using the church building for shelter against an inclement Holywood winter. I suppose local education was put into abeyance during those difficult days.

In the early years of the seventeenth century Sir James Hamilton, North Down proprietor, re-established the Holywood School. One of the conditions of the Patent Royal was the provision of schools in Bangor, Killyleagh, Dundonald, Ballyhalbert, the Ford at Belfast and in our town.

The Hamilton schools followed the Scots system. One school was situated in each area supported by parental contributions where possible. Sir James allowed five pounds per annum from the Parsonage tithes to support the school. The remaining tithes were given to

> *"goodly and religious uses, church maintenance, breeding scholars and preachers and for poor and charitable works, special consideration to be given to the poorer sort."*

Accordingly in the second decade of the seventeenth century a Parish School was established adjacent to the Priory Church which Sir James had re-roofed and refurbished for worship.

For the support of university education in Ireland, Sir James required his little town of Holywood to pay *"Eight pounds per annum to the University in Dublin"*. Hamilton, a classicist himself and a Fellow of Trinity College, would have been pleased to know that his provision for the University helped many Holywood students, especially Robert Sullivan and Lloyd Praeger, to benefit from their years in Dublin. Today the Friends of the Holywood Library pay the traditional annual subscription to Trinity College - University of Dublin.

EXPANSION IN THE NINETEENTH AND TWENTIETH CENTURIES

When Rev William Anthony Holmes was appointed Vicar in 1810, he found five well-attended schools in Holywood, two of which were for girls. He reported that parents were anxious for the education of their children. Books in use were *"The Speaker"*, *"Murray's Reader"* and a translation of *"Telemachus for Advanced Students"*. Telemnachus was the son of Odysseus, who waited, along with his mother Penelope, for his father to return from the Trojan Wars. It says much for the level of education in Holywood, three centuries ago, that the Classics were being studied - if only in translation. Students also read the Bible and the Presbyterian Shorter Catechism.

School fees in 1810 were from four shillings to six shillings per quarter, according to the classes which the students attended. The Vicar records, rather testily, that *"although all the school masters were Protestants, none of them attended the Established Church!"* This was rectified by 1836, when the Clerk to the Vestry was Master of the Parochial School, which was organised in a barn situated between the Priory Church and the seashore. It seems he was paid two pounds per annum for his pedagogic services to the Parish.

The statistical report written by Lieutenant G F W Bordes on 29th September 1834 gives a detailed account of the five schools in the town and six in the surrounding area. **Holywood Public School** was built on Bank Lane (upper Church View) in 1821. The building cost Two hundred pounds, which was covered by a government grant of Fifty pounds and generous local subscriptions. Mr J Patten donated the building site for the school. By 1834, Schoolmaster Wylie was teaching 130 boys and girls of all denominations.

Although parents made a contribution towards the education of their children, the major cost of maintenance came from public subscriptions. Lieutenant Bordes records without comment *"The poor are attended to one hour in the morning and one hour in the evening."* The Holywood Schoolhouse with two teachers' residences is marked clearly on the first Ordnance Survey map (1834). Today it is the 1st Holywood Scout Group headquarters.

In the upstairs rooms at the east end of the building, in 1834, Susan Hanna taught a school exclusively for girls, some 26 in number, who paid one penny per week for the privilege! The girls' school was opened in the same year as the public school, which met downstairs. It was sponsored by the London Hibernian Society. The Society contributed ten pounds per annum for school maintenance; generously they provided books for the girls. The Society was a Protestant missionary association which sponsored free elementary education at a time when the ability to read and write was increasingly in demand.

Information from the 1841 Census indicates only 47 per cent of persons over five years of age were able to read; by 1911 the number had risen to 88 per cent. The London Hibernian Society was founded in 1806 – by 1823 it had 61,387 pupils in its schools. The **Holywood Girls' School** came completely under the care of the Society in 1834 – presumably at that point the girls were no longer required to give Ms Hanna, the weekly

penny on a Monday morning!
It seems the Presbyterian Church in "Gospel Lane" operated a school for 39 fee-paying girls and boys of all denominations. It was established before 1832; the master was Mr Riddle. The schoolroom was in the Kirk Session House beside the church building. Mr G Scott adds to the Lieutenant's information –

"The schoolroom is over a room in which the Synod meets.
The master receives three shillings and threepence to four shillings and fourpence per quarter from the forty children and two pounds a year from the Synod.

On the north side of the Main Street, Miss Knowles taught 20 fee-paying pupils in a school established in 1832. Mill Street (now the lower part of Church Road) was the venue for Miss Blair's Nursery School. Here she taught 35 boys and girls from all denominations in a school established in 1818.

The largest of the schools in the extended parish was at **Knocknagoney**. According to Lieutenant Bordes, it was built by public subscription in 1818 under the patronage of the Turnley family of Richmond Lodge, whose garden parklands are the site of the present Knocknagoney housing estate. However, the records of First Holywood Presbyterian Church claim the school was established in 1812 by public subscription and enlarged in 1818. This may explain why the building is marked on the first edition of the Ordnance Survey map as 150 yards to the north of the site shown on subsequent maps.

The Knocknagoney school catered for 88 boys and girls of all denominations who paid a penny, threepence or sixpence a week. The Master, Hugh Macready, received a monthly salary of thirteen shillings and four pence. The school was granted £7.00 per annum from the London Hibernian Society, who also provided textbooks for the children. In 1923 the Knocknagoney Sunday School had an attendance of seventy scholars, in 1950 the Sunday school transferred to Garnerville Church, a daughter church of First Holywood. It was demolished shortly after the Church of the Annunciation was built to the north of the site. By that time, Knocknagoney Primary School had removed to a fine new building on the opposite side of the "Doctor's Road".

First Holywood Presbyterian Church sponsored two other schools -**Creighton's Green** and **Ballymiscaw**. Creighton's Green was established in 1827 and placed under the National Board in 1831; the Board provided an annual grant of Ten pounds. A quarterly fee of one shilling and sixpence provided education for 86 boys and girls of all denomination. An interesting letter landed on the desk of Rev. Henry Henderson on 1st November, 1866, it shows the tenuous tenure of the teaching profession a century and a half ago!.

"218 Creighton's Green National School

Reverend Sir,

We are to inform you that the Commissioners of National Education have ordered that salary be withdrawn from Andrew Frazer, teacher of this school from 30th November 1866. In consideration of his services, however, they will allow him a gratuity of twenty-seven months salary on condition that he shall then finally retire from the office of Public Instructor, giving up possession of the School-House and leaving the free stock and the school records in a satisfactory state.

We remain, Reverend Sir
Your obedient servants".

Teachers came and went. In 1923 the Sunday School boasted some fifty scholars. In 1935 the property was transferred back to the Church. Electricity was installed in 1953. Numbers on the school roll had decreased after the Second World War, even the Sunday School closed in 1971 due to lack of numbers. The old school house on Upper Whinney Hill road was sold and re-furbished as a private dwelling house.

A small school for boys and girls was erected by public subscription in 1810 at **Ballymeekan**. It was situated on the west side of Belmont Road opposite the junction with the Old Holywood Road. In 1834 there were only 13 pupils in the little school. This

St. Laiseran's Academy, 1873, converted to Parochial House in 1877.

may well have been because *"the school was supported by the scholars and the master lives day about with the farmers!"*
Another small school which has disappeared was **Ballygrainey** *"on the road from Holywood to Bangor at Crossroads".* The first edition of the Ordnance Survey map shows an important crossroads where Craigavad Post Office continued in business until the end of the twentieth century. Lieutenant Bordes was unable to discover when this school was established, but noted that the master, Mr J Johnston had been teaching at Ballygrainey since 1831. It was a fee-paying school for thirty boys and girls in the vicinity of Craigavad Station Road.

A mile further along the Bangor Road, **Ballyrobert**, later called **Glencraig**, School was built in 1820 at the gates of Rockport House, the residence of Mr John Turnly. Mrs Turnly donated ten pounds a year to the school and its 39 scholars paid one penny per week in fees. Classes were taught by a mistress trained under the Kildare Street system of education. The building was enlarged and re-modelled over the years . In 1965 it removed to the Seahill residential development. Today it is one of the best primary schools in North Down. The old school house and residence still stands on its original site, refurbished as a private dwelling.

Lieutenant Bordes' final reference is to **Ballymiscaw** school *"in the south part of Ballykeel, established in 1827 and placed under the National Board in 1834".* The Board made an annual grant of Ten pounds and the 86 boys and girls of all denominations paid quarterly fees of one shilling and sixpence. The building included a Master's residence. The narrow Ballykeel townland extends down to Holywood directly across the road from the schoolhouse. It seems the Holywood and Dundonald Presbyterian parishes shared responsibility for the property, and both benefited when it was sold in 1985. Today it is the private residence of a former student.

An amusing story is told around the Dundonald area about recruitment Day 1914 in Ballymiscaw School. Kitchener's posters called citizens to answer the needs of King and Country, but only one man turned up at the schoolhouse table - Thomas Gray.

The recently knighted Robert Kennedy of Cultra Manor, an uncompromising local magistrate, was invited to make the inducement speech. Sir Robert's pony was sent back to Cultra Manor without its owner, and the trap was abandoned in the middle of a ploughed field. The schoolroom was filled with pepper and the door tied. It seems the Squire was not as popular in Dundonald as he was with his Boy Scouts and the people of Holywood.

Some sixteen years after Lieutenant Bordes survey, Surgeon Thomas Kelly was collecting information for his "History of Holywood". He writes :

> *"In Holywood the invaluable boon of education, on terms*
> *almost gratuitous, is offered to all that will avail themselves*
> *of it. Two schools on the National system of Education - one*
> *for boys and one for girls, and a similar one under the Church Education Society, have been established and are in effective operation.*
> *To assist in the management of these, several benevolent ladies and gentlemen devote no small portion*
> *of their time."*

By 1886 George Henry Bassett's "Guide" reports

> *"The compensations for residence at Holywood are numerous.*
> *It has first-rate public and private schools, one founded by the*
> *late Dr Robert Sullivan. Another is under the National Board*
> *of Education in the Parish Church grounds, of which Mr Richard Doak is the Principal.*

The Belfast Directory for 1897 praises both these schools and *"the first-class ladies' and boys' boarding and day schools in the town".* However, a full list of the private schools, their locations and dates is very difficult to determine accurately.

We know that Greenfield's English and Classical School was in existence in 1817 as Robert Sullivan attended classes there before his days at the Academical Institution in Belfast. It must have been a very good school, as Sullivan became a highly proficient scholar under the tutorage of Hugh Greenfield.
The Rev John Poole established his English Mercantile and Classical Academy in 1854.

Victoria Road - the old Ballykeel Road in High Holywood - was a favourite location for private schools. At Hillbrook, Mrs Bankhead ran a school for young ladies before 1854; by 1864 the property became John Turpin's school-house and in 1877 Dr R Farrell removed there from the High Street. Miss Stitt operated a ladies' school in Glenside Place which was replaced in 1858 by Shepherd's Mercantile and Classical Academy.

Ardmore Terrace at the top of Victoria Road sported Mrs Marshall's Ladies Seminary in 1858. In the same year in Millbank, at the corner with Millbrook Street, Mrs Thorn ran a ladies' school. It seems that this school was taken over by the Misses Bleck in 1877, and by Miss Lodge ten years later. In 1976 Brookside Nursery Playgroup was opened in Millbank House and continues to serve the community into the new century. On the other side of Victoria Road the Misses Robinson ran a school for boys and girls at Martello Terrace until 1935.

Beyond the country end of Victoria Road at Woodcroft Park a play group was opened in 1970 to overcome transport difficulties and provide an opportunity for local children to come together in a structured and regular way. Eventually the playgroup removed to Glenview Farm at the top of Church Road.

The town centre itself provided the venue for another group of private schools. Miss Kennedy opened a School for Young Ladies at 28 Shore Street in 1852, nearby was Miss Mulligan's Preparatory School. As early as 1805 Mrs Bannister and her daughter were running a school in High Street. Here Robert Sullivan was introduced to education. The High Street also provided school houses for Mr Foster's Seminary, Miss Love's Ladies School at number 122, and Mrs Summers' School at 116. These three High Street schools were operating during the 1870's.

As we shall see, Rev C J McAlester opened a remarkably efficient school on Marine Parade in 1834, and removed to High Street in 1849 where it gained the affectionate title "the Underground Academy".
Hibernia Place was chosen by Miss Reid for her Ladies' School in 1877. It was selected in 1897 for a Girls' Boarding School run by Miss Russell and Mme Dommell of Paris.

On Church Road Miss White ran a school for girls and well into the last century the Misses Bosworthicks operated a boys' and girls' school in Church Hill Terrace. At number 1 Bangor Road, Mrs Biddle opened "The Warren School" in 1936.

The Warren was the most recent of our private preparatory schools. It is remembered by many boys and girls who commenced their education under the tutelage of Mrs Biddle and her staff. Churchfield House was built about 1845 on part of the ancient Priory yard. Five years later it was described by Surgeon Kelly as two extensive and commodious family mansions, one the residence of the Misses Dawson, the other of Mrs Cairns, situated at the corner of the Ballykeel Road. The good doctor's text proceeds to take us, on a fine summer day, for a romantic stroll up Ballykeel Road to our picturesque hills. Every Holywood resident of the twenty-first century would do well to read the poetic picture in his History of Holywood.

The Warren School prospered and extended into the third house of Victoria Place, that fine terrace built in 1855, which seems to have changed the name of the historic Ballykeel Road to present day Victoria Road.

The Warren closed its doors for the last time in July 1971. In its heyday it provided a disciplined education for about one hundred boys and girls instructed by eight members of staff and other specialist instructors.

Other Holywood scholars dimly recall little single teacher private schools in The Crescent, My Lady's Mile and at Seaview Terrace.

The shortest lived of any of our educational establishments was the **COUNTY DOWN AGRICULTURAL COLLEGE**. Monday, 22nd January 1844 was the date set for the annual general meeting of the Holywood Teetotal Society. Dr McKittrick, Holywood's Medical Officer, appraised the members of their duty *"to see that those who were to live by agriculture be instructed in its principles."* The town supported the project. Later Thomas Kelly recorded :

> *"a splendid model agricultural school, under the National Board,*
> *has been erected, and is now in effective operation. The school is superintended by a teacher of superior acquirements - it promises*
> *well to fulfil the ends for which it was established."*

The 1837 Irish National Commissioners' Report had required agricultural schools to produce *"an intelligent class of farm labourers and servants".* Knowledge of the science of agriculture was to be promoted in special schools as it formed *"the only source of employment*

National School on Church View, 1822. Later it became the Masonic Hall and then a Scout Hall.

for many labouring poor." For this purpose the Commissioners divided the island into twenty-five districts, each received a Government grant to establish an agricultural college with a model farm.

Dr McKittrick wanted the County Down grant to come to Holywood, and the town supported his application to build a school suitable for one hundred students. The County Down Agricultural School was opened at the corner of Victoria Road and Croft Road in 1849.

Mr William McMeekin, who had five years' experience as a national teacher, was appointed Master with responsibility for organising the model farm. The farm's seven Cunningham acres were situated on the north side of the Ballykeel Road below the school. At that time Croft Road was a country lane.

Here Mr McMeekin looked forward to instructing his students in the practical science of agriculture - digging and fertilising the soil; propagation and rotation of seven varieties of edible crops and animal husbandry. He acquired the model farm stock from the local area - two cows, a calf, a donkey, nine piglets, twenty-three hens and a rooster. What the master did not attract was a satisfactory number of willing students !

Although he said *"The school is making a great contribution to local farming methods"*, the Commissioners were not impressed by his optimism. Dr James Patton, Her Majesty's

Head Inspector, visited the school on Friday, 31st October 1851. He inspected the two-year-old model agricultural project in detail. He commended the fine new building with its excellent rooms capable of accommodating one hundred students. He admired the animals and the farm. However, he recorded that on the day of his inspection, only seven pupils were in attendance; two boys under seven, two under eleven and three under fifteen years of age.

In his report to the Commissioners, Dr Patton judged the school *"valueless, possibly injurious and certainly a waste of public money".* He attributed its total failure to the managers, the distance of the building from the village and the many good schools in the area. The Commissioners closed the school in June 1852.

The cows and chickens, the donkey and pigs found good homes in the Holywood area. Domestic wings were added to the re-furbished school building which was divided into the semi-detached residences, "Crofton" and "Burnleigh".

The model farm became the property of the McKibben and later the Ballagh families. In 1866 "Croft House" was built on part of the seven Cunningham acres where the seven crop rotation experiments had taken place. Croft House, later a residence for senior citizens, was demolished in 1989 to make way for present day housing. The Holywood Agricultural College had been a miserable failure!

To complete the survey we should take a quick look at the background stories of the other Holywood schools, many of which continue into the twenty-first century.

PAROCHIAL NATIONAL SCHOOL

The Church of Ireland Parochial School removed to Church Road, opposite the new Parish church, in 1845. The roof timbers of the Old Priory were re-designed for use in the new school. By 1875 it was over-crowded. Mr John Brown, owner of the surrounding land, refused to allow expansion. Squire Harrison donated land on the west side of Church Road for the erection of the required larger school building. The fine old Parochial School had residences for teachers at either end. Mr James Joyce was the master for many years. He operated the school under the Church Education Society. The carefully preserved building became the church hall and later the headquarters of 2nd Holywood Scout Group. The Parish Office was located in one of the residences, formerly occupied by Miss Maud Thompson, caretaker of the church and school buildings.

In 1878 the new Parochial National School was opened by Rev Dr G R Wynne, Vicar of Holywood. The Boys' School was in the larger hall; the Girls and the Infants' School had equally suitable accommodation. Modern blackboards and desks which could be converted into dining tables were provided. The building, in Scrabo stone, designed by William Batt, was built by William Nimick, the local contractor.

The fine pine ceilings were revealed in 1999 when the building was completely refurbished as "The Parish Centre".

HOLYWOOD PRIMARY SCHOOL

In 1954 the Church School combined with the Sullivan National School to establish Holywood Primary School. Holywood Urban District Council found it very difficult to acquire a suitable central location for a school to accommodate 520 pupils. Eventually, the school was built to the west side of the Parish Church.

Holywood Primary traces its history to the school established in the early years of the seventeenth century when King James I gave our local government into the care of the Lord Clandeboye. Accordingly its crest carried the Priory motif, the De Saukvill star, Laiseran's cross and the red hand of the O'Neill family.

The 1997 official inspection report found *"a caring and well-ordered school where there is a strong sense of community. High standards of behaviour are expected and received. The children demonstrate a keen interest in their work and apply themselves purposefully to the tasks assigned. Their best efforts are recognised within class and at morning assemblies."*

The school aims to provide an inspiring, secure and happy environment in which the girls and boys can learn effectively and realise their potential. Parents are partners in school life and in the children's spiritual and moral well-being. Pupils are encouraged to express themselves with confidence, cultivate tolerance and fair play towards others, record accurately the knowledge they acquire in language, numeracy and science; also to participate happily in physical activity.

At present the enrolment is 523, teaching staff numbers 24 and annual attendance rate is 96.2%. There is a varied range of enjoyable and educational extra curricular activities. The pastoral dimension required a caring commitment by all teachers to guide and advise pupils on personal and educational matters.

The Robert Sullivan tradition continues into the twenty-first century in Holywood Primary School.

ST LAISERAN'S ACADEMY

St Laiseran's Academy was opened on Ean Hill in 1874 by Rev James O'Laverty, parish priest of Holywood. In 1904 he recorded :

> *"During 1873 and 1874 I erected, under the superintendence of Mr McMullen, Clerk of Works for the Church, St Laiseran's Academy for the education of boys and girls whose parents did not wish them to commingle at the National School with children of a humbler class. The introduction of tramcars into Belfast induced many of the Belfast merchants, who hitherto resided in Holywood, to select other suburbs of the city for their places of residence. The average attendance became*

consequently much reduced, and after considerable monetary loss I had to close the Academy. The building remained, for a short time vacant, but in 1877 I changed it into a parochial residence. The total cost of that building was borne by myself."

When Father O'Laverty took up residence in the Academy building he used the tower for the pursuit of his favourite hobby - Astronomy. The building was vacated when new clergy residences were built in the church grounds beside My Lady's Mile and completely renovated in 2002.

THE CONVENT SCHOOLS

The Convent School was established in a beautiful old family residence called "The Firs" which was built in 1889 on Belfast Road, Holywood. It remains one of Holywood's best examples of the Arts and Crafts Movement, which stressed the value of artisanship. The house became the home of the Maguire family who bequeathed the property to the Sisters of the Cross and Passion. In 1944 the Sisters opened a private school, "Mount St Mary's" which closed two years later. In June 1948 a residential hostel was opened and in January 1953 Sister St Francis re-opened the private school. However, by July 1971 circumstances again forced the closure of the little academy. In September 1971 the Order of Sisters of the Sacred Heart of Mary opened a grammar school for girls. By 1975 the enrolment was 325 students and there were twenty-five members of teaching staff. The Priory Singers, the Convent School Choir, were very popular in the town and achieved many successes in Irish musical festivals. This very successful girls' grammar school amalgamated with St Patrick's College at Knock on Upper Newtownards Road. The beautifully preserved building became the headquarters of the Council for Catholic Maintained Schools.

HOLYWOOD TECHNICAL AND COMMERCIAL COLLEGE

The 1947 Education Act provided universal free secondary education. The Sullivan building became the Centre for Adult Education and an embryonic Holywood Technical and Commercial College. However, the Urban District Council considered the old school building to be *"totally unsuitable to the needs of modern education"*. The Councillors decided to build a new Technical College in the playground behind the Sullivan building. Classes were to be removed to the new building simultaneously with the gradual demolition of the old School! Fortunately, re-organisation of local government prevented the demolition of one of the town's best loved buildings, our Sullivan Schools.

PRIORY COLLEGE

In 1954 the Secondary Intermediate School was built to accommodate 320 pupils, on a site in Church View where agricultural allotments had produced vegetables during the War. The purpose-designed buildings provided an assembly hall/gymnasium, special subject rooms, classroom blocks, staff rooms and a library. The Education Authority found it necessary to include a school meals kitchen on the site to serve the other schools in the town and surrounding district. Two decades later, and after major refurbishment, the School changed its name to Holywood High School. In September 1998 it took the

St. Patrick's Church, 1830. It became a National School and then a Church Hall, demolished in 1977.

title "Priory College". Today the College continues to be a co-educational integrated school with a teaching staff of 30 specialists instructing 400 students. It has a well-stocked library, two computer suites, a new technology facility and a state-of-the-art fitness suite. The mission statement of Priory College is

"to develop the full potential of each student in partnership with home and community".

HOLYWOOD NURSERY SCHOOL has an interesting history. After the Second World War the Urban District Council acquired two large properties for community use while a new Civic Centre was under construction in Sullivan Place. These were the Patterson family home in High Street, where the Health Centre is situated today, and Riverston House at the corner of Brook Street and Church Road. In August 1946 a meeting was held in the Warren School during which it was agreed that a proposed Holywood Nursery School would operate in Riverston House. A fund-raising project was initiated to equip the new school; the first teacher was appointed in May 1947. The Nursery School opened in Riverston House on Monday, 16th June 1947 with five children on the attendance roll.

The school prospered, numbers increased, and on 11th February 1954 the Committee applied for a grant from the Down County Education Committee. This was refused even though the old house was showing signs of wear and tear. The following year the Committee was forced to look for new and safe premises, and in October 1956 an approach was made to the County Committee to assume responsibility for the viable and growing nursery school. On 14th January 1957 the County Education Committee agreed to take control, however six months later it changed its mind!

After much deliberation, on 6th December 1988 the Down County Education Committee did take control - almost five years after the first application. A few weeks later an official inspection recorded - *"The premises of the Holywood Nursery School are in extremely bad condition."* Even so, it was not until July 1989 that the Ministry of Education *"directed the closure of the school on account of the dangerous state of Riverston House"*.

In September 1960 a site for a new Holywood Nursery School was at last acquired - it was the lower garden of Riverston House where the nursery school children had played for twelve happy years. Riverston House was demolished in 1960. The house area was used for Holywood's fourth telephone exchange building. In the lower garden a purpose-built nursery school was opened on 5th September 1963.

Today the Principal has two assistants for an enrolment of 52 happy children who attend in two sessions, morning and afternoon - 26 at each session. In Holywood Nursery School children learn naturally through play, which enables their skills, knowledge and fundamental concepts to develop. The staff work as a team, sensitive to the individual needs of the child, to plan an exciting, stimulating and structured environment. The purpose of nursery education is the learning and development of skills, attitudes and understanding so that children will live full and satisfying lives and become confident and useful members of society. Consideration is given to the effective transition from nursery to primary school. An environment is created in which the children feel happy and secure in an atmosphere of warmth., love and understanding. Good relationships among other children, staff and parents are essential. Holywood is happy to be among the towns which pioneered the nursery school movement. We are proud to possess one of the finest nursery schools in the Province in the year 2002.

THE HOLYWOOD RUDOLF STEINER SCHOOL

In 1975 the Holywood Rudolf Steiner School was founded in "Highlands" on Croft Road. Highlands had been the home of the Heyn family - owners of the Ulster Steamship Company. The old mansion has been re-named "Saralies House" in honour of a beloved member of staff. Academic curriculum is based on the principles of the Austrian philosopher and educationalist Rudolf Steiner (1861-1925). The school's intake is comprehensive and co-educational, for children between four and seventeen years of age, from all social, religious and economic backgrounds. Students are encouraged to focus upon a wide understanding of the world, with awareness and sensitivity. In a Rudolf Steiner school intellectual progress is no more important than physical, emotional, spiritual and artistic development. Close co-operation between parents and teachers is emphasized in order to achieve the school's mission statement. There are three departments - kindergarten, lower and upper schools, in each the aim is to stimulate scholars to give their best in a wide range of skills and personal gifts.

REDBURN PRIMARY SCHOOL

Redburn Primary School occupies a most picturesque location. The elevated site surveys the Lough and the Antrim Hills, its backdrop is the tree-clad Holywood Hills. Until 1940 the area lay to the south of the main driveway to the Dunville mansion house. Where the boys and girls play today, the sixty hunters and team of carriage horses browsed grass beside the grand entrance avenue. In 1950 Redburn was acquired by the Urban District council for £14,500. The council used part of the parklands for playing fields, a cemetery and the campus of Redburn Primary School. The spacious building was opened in the early 1960's to accommodate 350 children from the Palace Military Barracks and the rapidly growing residential housing estates on the western side of Holywood. The parents of about 150 of the children are military personnel. The principal is assisted by ten teachers, supported by thirteen general staff members.

The ethos of the school promotes education for mutual understanding and development of links with the local community. Redburn pupils and their teachers combine to develop self-independence, self-esteem, courtesy, independence and inter-dependence. The school is an integral part of the community supporting local charities, choral work, inter-schools sports and quizzes. Special education support is available for children who need help with their studies. Where possible, coaches are employed to encourage the boys and girls in keen sports participation. The school maintains a close working relationship with the parents and guardians of the pupils. Violet Dunville of Redburn House would have been very proud to see her lawns used for the education of children - a subject which was always very close to her heart.

HOLYWOOD ADULT EDUCATION CENTRE

In 1998 the Holywood Adult Education Centre opened at the gates of Redburn Primary School. The Redburn Pavilion is a purpose-built unit to provide daytime and evening courses for people who wish to improve career prospects, pursue a hobby and enjoy the company of others who share similar interests. Under the aegis of North Down and Ards Institute of Further and Higher Education, the aim is to create effective and efficient learning opportunities for those who wish to realise personal goals in learning, recreation and employment.

The curriculum offers thirty electives in the Redburn Pavilion and eight courses in the computer suite

ST PATRICK'S PRIMARY SCHOOL

St Patrick's Primary is the school of St Colmcille's parish. Its roots go back to the pre-reformation school of the Augustinian Priory (1190) the Third Order of St Francis (1490) and possibly the hedge schools of the early eighteenth century.

Repeal of the Penal Laws in 1829 encouraged the Roman Catholic residents of the area to lay the foundation of St Patrick's Church on Church View. Shortly after the Church was dedicated, a school was opened in the Strand area of the town.

Later the Strand school removed to the house of the sexton of St Patrick's, which was adjacent to the Church itself on upper Church View. When St Colmcille's Church was dedicated in 1874, St Patrick's became the new home of the church school, after suitable alterations - where classes continued for over sixty years.

In 1937 a purpose-built five room schoolhouse was erected on the present site at the top of Church View. Sixty years later, the spacious building provides ten classrooms, an assembly hall, a canteen, library and a music room. There are 516 students in the school, and the annual admission is 45 boys and girls. Present teaching staff includes the Principal and eight assistant teachers with music tutors, classroom assistants and thirteen supporting staff members. St Patrick's mission statement affirms -

> *"Governors and staff of St Patrick's Primary School believe the school to be a vital part of our parish and of the wider Catholic community. As such, we are firmly committed to the aims and ideals of Catholic Education and the provision of quality education for all our pupils. St Patrick's affirms its commitment to a positive and caring pastoral system and to foster an atmosphere of praise, encouragement and mutual respect."*

St Patrick's provides a wide-ranging sports programme for the boys and girls. Music is an essential part of school life and has won respect and reputation through the choir and orchestra far beyond Holywood.

ROCKPORT SCHOOL

Rockport House was associated with local education almost a century before Geoffrey Bing founded an independent preparatory school there in 1906. John Turnly built the mansion in 1817; his wife sponsored the day school which was established at the grand entrance gates in 1820.

John was related to Francis Turnly of Richmond Lodge, four miles nearer to Belfast and to the famous Batt family of Purdysburn. John Turnly (1764 - 1841) is memorialized in Holywood Parish Church as *"unostentatious and retiring, who lived a useful and happy life"*.

The Ordnance Survey memoirs of 1834 state *"the whole shore of Belfast Lough in Holywood Parish is studded with gentlemen's seats, all of which are ornamented with gardens and plantations."* Both Richmond and Rockport are included on the list. Today *"the ornamented plantation"* provides an exquisite seaside campus.

In 1906 the first enrolment was four boys; Headmaster Bing was assisted by one master and a matron. Today, Rockport is a boarding and day school for boys and girls, from pre-prep to tenth-year - General Certificate of Secondary Education level. There are 209 students on campus with 30 members of staff and several visiting specialists. Often Rockport is described as *"an extended family"* which prepares boys and girls for life as well as tertiary education.

The school seeks to provide the highest academic standard for the individual student, emphasizing the moral, spiritual, cultural and sporting aspects of life. It is a community in which students, staff and parents play as a united team.

Rockport House and its extensive grounds have grown from a Georgian mansion to a fully equipped school campus.

In 1910 an extension to the east side of the house became necessary. By the middle years of the First World War there were twenty-seven boys in attendance; one master and four former students paid the supreme sacrifice, a further nineteen Rockportians served in the Forces. In 1918 a memorial room was erected. During the Second World War sixteen old boys were killed, many times that number served.

In 1918 the land lying between the house and the railway line was acquired, the Rockport magazine reported *"the supply of potatoes, garden produce, milk and in the future it is hoped, of butter, is assured"*. By then there were forty-eight hungry students eager to devour the produce from the Home farm, further expansion was demanded and the playing fields were refurbished.

Athletic activity always has been an integral part of a Rockport education, frequently culminating in University colours and national status. Activities range through rugby, cricket, hockey, trampolining, swimming, golf, netball and table tennis.

In 1967 a Board of Governors was appointed and the Charitable Trust established - three years later the Parent-Teacher Association came into being.

In 1970 the Board embarked on an ambitious building programme which included a classroom block, additional changing rooms and shower areas. The year 1974 brought the Pre-Preparatory Department which later was accommodated in its own purpose built classrooms.

As Rockport continued to prosper, once more additional classrooms became necessary; a gymnasium, assembly hall, craft centre, dining hall, sports hall and all-weather pitch were added on campus.

In recent years a home economics department, staff houses, state-of-the-art computer suite, expansion of the modern languages, music and drama departments all make Rockport a leading independent school. It is a member of the Incorporated Association of Preparatory Schools and the Headmasters' Conference.

Q Horatius Flaccus would have been pleased that Rockport chose from the Odes, the school motto - *"Virtus Rupulsae Nescia Sordidae"* - True manliness knows no disgraceful defeat! (Liber Tertius Carmen II). The Latin poet's little farm, near Tivoli in the Sabine Hills - *"the apple of his eye"* - was rather like the rolling Rockport campus.

GLENCRAIG CAMPHILL COMMUNITY

In his short history of Glencraig Manor and the community, "The Spreading Flame", D M Wright tells how Miss Mary Simms built Childhaven on the Glencraig site in the later years of the seventeenth century. There she provided sanctuary for needy children from all over Ireland. Childhaven was destroyed by fire in 1688, Miss Simms removed to a cottage at Seahill and in 1700 sold the property to the Craig family, who had arrived from England in 1648. The Craigs completed the building of Glencraig Manor by 1743; the family remained in residence for 127 years, then returned to England, having sold the property to the Lindsay family. The Lindsays refurbished the façade of the old house about 1827 and in 1901 Sir Daniel Dixon bought the property, the Lindsay family by then being extinct.

We know that in 1889 Sir Daniel Dixon bought Ballymenoch House, its demesne and the coastline from Holywood Pier to Clanbrassil Terrace. He was elected first Lord Mayor of Belfast and died in 1907. The generous Craigavons took up residence at Glencraig in 1923. By 1944 the Swains, followed by the Nobles, were training racehorses on the broad green Glencraig acres.
In 1954 the Friends of Glencraig purchased the estate; ten years later a porch inspired by the organic movement was added to replace the original façade. By 1993 the building returned to a more traditional style, making provision for a wheelchair lift and a series of therapy rooms. By then the house had been re-named Comgall. Comgall (517 - 601) was the son of Setna, a nobleman of the Kingdom of Dal Riada, South Antrim and North Down. He founded the great monastery of Bangor in 558, and ruled over it for half a century.

Other sources record that Glencraig House was built in 1833 by Miss Mary Symes who resided there until her death in 1863. In 1858 she donated a site for Glencraig Parish Church at the gates of her thirty-one acres of seaboard parklands. Although the mansion is situated between Craigavad House (c. 1783) and Rockport (c. 1800) it is not included in the long list of "Gentlemen's Seats with which the whole shore of Belfast Lough is studded" - Ordnance Survey 29th September 1834 by Lieutenant G F W Bordes. However, G Scott added a memoir - *"Glencarrick in the townland of Ballyrobert is the residence of Miss Sims."*

After the death of Mr Noble in 1950 (William Noble and Company Ltd, Belfast - bag and sack manufacturers) Glencraig was acquired by the N I Hospitals Authority, and two years later it was transferred to the Royal Victoria Hospital.

On 18th September 1954 the Dowager Marchioness of Londonderry opened Glencraig Curative School. Shortly afterwards, the neighbouring Craigowen House on the shore cliff was added to the magnificent Glencraig Camphill Community campus. Now the campus covers over one hundred acres of seaside woods, fields and parklands. There are nineteen houses, schools, workshops, a village centre and a working farm at the heart of the two hundred strong community.
The school provides education for young people aged six to nineteen, the training scheme continues to twenty-five years of age. Some adults who require a sheltered environment find both a home and daily work on the campus at Glencraig.

Creation of a healthy therapeutic environment is enhanced by the use of biodynamic agriculture and total attention to the natural world. The campus provides the community with whole foods and household products. Farm and garden produce are grown without the use of pesticides or artificial fertilisers.

In the schools the Waldorf curriculum and curative education inspired by Rudolf Steiner bring science, art and religion into harmony, allowing the students to develop their full potential. Specific therapies, under medical supervision, art, massage, horse-riding, curative eurthmy along with speech, music and play therapy help residents to master individual difficulties.

Volunteers can attend the one-year foundation course in anthroposophy, curative education and Camphill community life. Those who come with previous experience in these fields may proceed to the three-year training course in curative education and social therapy.

The Camphill Movement, founded in 1940, works to create communities in which vulnerable children and adults, many with learning disabilities, can live, learn and work with others, in healthy social relationships, based on mutual care and respect. Camphill is inspired by Christian ideals and recognises the spiritual uniqueness of each member of the community, regardless of disability, religious or racial background.

There are nine Camphill communities in the Republic of Ireland and four in Northern Ireland. Two of these hold a valued position in the wider Holywood Community - Glencraig and the Organic Shop, Cafe and Bakery at 8 Shore Road.

SOME OTHER PLAYGROUPS

Glencraig Playgroup is one of the oldest nurseries in the area. It originated as a private enterprise in mid-twentieth century in the old Glencraig Schoolhouse. Today, the children meet in the nearby Scout Hall. It is a registered as a non-profit-making school organised by a Parents' Committee and run by professional staff. It seeks to prepare children for primary school in a safe and satisfying atmosphere, where confidence and imagination are developed by free play and free expression in art and music. Glencraig Play Group's mission statement is to provide a stimulating environment in a homely atmosphere; to develop self-esteem, respect, tolerance and self-control; to promote a holistic approach to education and life.

Teddy Bears Playgroup dates back over twenty years. It is a community project organised by a committee of parents. The Group meets in the Orange Hall in Redburn Square. Recently, another play nursery has been opened in the former private nursing home at Plas Merdyn on upper Church Road.

Mother And Toddler Groups in growing numbers are available in the town. One uses the halls of High Street Presbyterian Church. The Ark for Mothers, Minders and Toddlers meets in Rev John Poole's tall house in the High Street and a third group for Toddlers is organised in the Community Centre at Redburn.

You will find accounts of the Sullivan Schools and the Palace Barracks School in other essays. I hope I have covered all our educational establishments - I find the number quite surprising. Large or small, every school and its teachers meant everything to each of us as scholars in our infant and teenage days. The collection makes me realise how much we owe to those who shaped (or in an very few cases marred) our childhood days in Holywood.

Our town claims an excellent educational history and continues to provide the best possible opportunities for future generations.

The Sullivan Schools, Holywood.

SCIENCE CLASSES.

SCIENCE AND ART DEPARTMENT.

SESSION 1879-80.

DURING the ensuing Session, Classes in the following subjects will be conducted at the Sullivan Schools, by

MR. A. SPEERS, B.Sc. (Lond.)

INORGANIC CHEMISTRY—Theoretical and Practical.
ORGANIC CHEMISTRY—Theoretical and Practical.
ELEMENTARY MATHEMATICS.
PRINCIPLES OF AGRICULTURE.
MAGNETISM AND ELECTRICITY.

The hours of meeting of the Classes will be as follow :—

Elementary Mathematics—Monday Evening, from 6.10 to 7.10.
Principles of Agriculture—Tuesday Evening, from 7 to 8.
Magnetism and Electricity—Tuesday Evening, from 8 to 9.
Inorganic Chemistry—Friday Evening, from 6.30 to 7.30.
Laboratory Practice—7.30 to 9.
Organic Chemistry—Saturday Evening, from 6.10 to 7.10.
Laboratory Practice—7.10 to 9.

Intending Students are requested to meet in the Science Room of the Sullivan Upper School, on Tuesday Evening, the 14th inst., at Eight o'clock, when their names shall be registered.

Queen's and other Prizes will be competed for at the Examinations of the Department, to be held in May, 1880, at which all Students are expected to present themselves.

Further information may be obtained from Mr. SPEERS, or from the Secretary of the Local Committee, the Rev. HENRY HALLIDAY. M.A.

ESSAY IX - HOLYWOOD HIGHWAYS, BYWAYS AND RAILWAYS

Will you come to Holywood, dearest Jenny O ?
Then along the shores we'll stroll
While the bright waves near us roll
Making music for our soul, dearest Jenny O.

Then to the hills we'll turn, dearest Jenny O
And as o'er their heights we roam
You will see my cottage home
Where I hope you'll mistress come, dearest Jenny O.

In conclusion I've to tell of sweet Jenny O
That her lover next day went
To the clergy for consent
His union to cement with sweet Jenny O.

Lines from "The Holywood Guiding Star"
sung to the air - "Kelvin Grove"

The Annals, a chronically arranged record of Irish events from the eighth century, claim, *"In Ireland, well built roads existed from the early Christian period joining religious houses, town, harbours, fords and palaces"*. The most important roads were paved "slighe" radiating from Tara to Gartan, Armagh, Dunseverick, Derry and Downpatrick. From Downpatrick there was direct communication with Bangor and Holywood.

Even in those far away days, when the highways crossed over bog land the local people were required to provide road maintenance. From the twelfth century, English law required enlarged, safe and unobstructed highways. By 1613 the Irish Parliament made road building and upkeep an urgent responsibility for parishes. In theory Irish roads had verges and were metalled to a width of several metres. By 1729 Turnpike Trusts levied tolls for road maintenance. A traveller from Belfast to Holywood would have passed the tollgate at the Strandtown end of Holywood road. Tolls were very unpopular - as late as October 1814, Holywood farmers successfully engaged in Court proceedings to abolish the toll charged on country traffic entering the city over the Long Bridge. By 1765 Grand Juries were able to levy rates for up-grading the road system, which soon extended to eight thousand miles throughout the island.

As the centuries rolled on, mail coach and motor transport required an ever-increasing standard of road construction. As we move into the new century, Motorway Three (the M3) is scheduled to by-pass Holywood to the south, joining the Dargan Bridge and Sydenham By-pass with the present Bangor Dual Carriageway at Ballyrobert.

The earliest roads in Holywood were tracks worn by the feet of monks and friars travelling from the surrounding religious houses to the Holywood Priory. Greatly frequented was the path to the parent Abbey in Bangor, founded in AD 558 some seventy years before St Laiseran settled in Ard-Mac-Nasca. An embryonic Ballykeel Road wound its way over the Holywood Hills to Movilla Abbey and onward to the religious houses at Greyabbey and Black Abbey. By the thirteenth century, the steep road leading over Standard Hill to Dundonald had developed, and is clearly shown on the 1775 map as a high road.

Communications between Holywood, Downpatrick and Belfast existed from earliest times. The 1775 map shows the Belfast Road climbing to Strandtown, crossing Connswater River by a new bridge and the River Lagan by the Long Bridge. However, *"a new and correct map of 1743"* indicates a more direct approach to Belfast straight over the mud flats from the Kinnegar.

The 1767 map shows the present day Old Holywood Road merging into Jackson's Road to gain easy movement between Belmont and Holywood. Demesne Road, running over Holywood House demesne from the Old Holywood road junction, did not materialise until the 1870's. In 1830 a lane ran from Church Road through Lemonfield to the Shepherd's Path. The Shepherd's Path became Alexandra Park and then My Lady's Mile about 1890 – the lane became the town end of the present-day Demesne Road.

Apart from Thomas Raven's drawings of 1625, perhaps the most interesting maps illustrating the development of our area are Williamson's Survey (1810) and the Hollywood Parish Map which accompanies Mason's Statistical Account in 1819. They show "King William's Road", along which the Duke of Schomberg's Army marched from Groomsport, to meet King William III in 1690. Moss Road climbing over the Holywood Hills is clearly marked, branching off from Church Road half a mile from Holywood town centre.

Some commentators claim the first stagecoach service in Ireland started between Belfast and Newry on October 4th, 1704 for a fare of one guinea. Although there was a coach service between Belfast and Dublin as early as 1742, the first permanent and reliable service was established in 1788. The following year the Post Office awarded prestigious mail contracts to the most efficient coaching firms. Until the 1820's important coaches were accompanied by military detachments and armed guards to forestall highwaymen. Journey times were advertised and contractors' penalty clauses operated.

The Belfast News-Letter for 30th June 1820 carried an invitation for proposals to *"convey His Majesty's Mail in coaches, drawn by four horses, carrying four inside and three outside passengers at the rate of five or six miles an hour from Newry to Belfast for a term of seven years."*

The same year, 1820, Daniel Miskelly's advertisements proclaimed –

> *"Cheap travelling:*
> *Coleraine to Belfast – Mondays, Wednesdays and Fridays*
> *at Four O'clock. Arrives Belfast One O'clock.*
> *Leaves Belfast Two O'clock the following day!"*

As we saw in the essay on Robert Sullivan, Miskelly ran *"The Lark"* to Ballymena; the *"Union"* to Magherafelt; the *"Waterloo"* to Randalstown; and the Antrim coach. In 1810 he started a coach service to Holywood from Pottinger's Entry in Belfast. At the same time, John Rowley was operating a daily service in his 'long coach' drawn by four horses from his home in Holywood to Campbell's Tavern in Ann Street. The fare in 1810 was one shilling and sixpence for an inside seat, and one shilling outside on the box. By 1819 Robert Duffin was

> *"respectfully requesting passengers for his car which started from Holywood to arrive at Mrs McCully's in Lower Church Lane at ten o'clock each morning, returning from Belfast at one o'clock."*

An advertisement in the Northern Whig on 13th May 1824 proclaimed :

> *"Hugh Stewart intends to carry the mail between Holywood and Belfast every day at 8.45 a m returning 10 a.m. starting 2.45 p.m. returning to Holywood 4 p m. Seats may be taken at Mr Dunlop's in Ann Street or at the Post Office in Holywood."*

On 29th September 1834 Lieutenant G F W Bordes described the Holywood conveyances:

> *"There is one coach and one regular car. The coach is the property of farmers and innkeepers, the shares are Ten pounds. It starts at Donaghadee at seven o'clock a m, collects passengers at Holywood at half-past nine and arrives in Belfast at half-past ten It leaves Belfast at five o'clock every evening except Sundays. The time of starting is one hour earlier in summer than in winter.*
> *The regular car takes the mails from Belfast at half-past seven a m passing through Holywood at half-past eight a m arriving in Bangor at ten o'clock a m returning through Holywood at half past four p m and arriving in Belfast about twenty past five o'clock p.m.*
>
> *There are a great number of cars running in the road between Belfast and Holywood at different hours, twenty-five in the summer and fifteen in the winter, besides others which occasionally run between Bangor and Belfast."*

It seems Holywood had an excellent commuter service – a daily choice of twenty-five daily runs, the journey time one hour and the cost one shilling.

And so began road timetables and competition which eventually came to a head with the Holywood omnibuses in the 1920's, but that road rage was a century in the future - I shall tell you about it later in this essay !
The Northern Whig for 1st September 1836 reports –

> *"We are glad to find that the road from Belfast to Holywood is about to be improved with a convenience which has long been a deterrent – a side path – which is in rapid progress and promises to be the most substantial benefit."*

The result of this appears to have been an Ordnance Survey memo, which recorded:

"The drive from Belfast to Holywood is agreeable. On Sundays vast numbers drive from one town to the other several times in the same day for the pleasure of the drive!"

The Holywood road became a paradise for summer promenading and a goldmine for David Miskelly whose hired post-chaises, gigs, jaunting cars and horses made him a very wealthy citizen. Soon he removed from the Holywood coach terminus at 30 Pottinger's Entry to Bunker Hill at Strandtown, where *"his vehicles ran past his lofty entrance gates."* He died in his great house on 22nd September 1845. A few months after his death, the County Down Railway Act was passed at Westminster.

Belfast's first railway ran to Lisburn. It was opened on 12th August 1830. However, as early as 1834, G Scott in the first Ordnance Survey had observed -

"It appears much land might be reclaimed along the Holywood shore – or a railroad made from Belfast without causing any other level than that which at present exists to be made."

The possibility of a completely level four-mile line encouraged Belfast's famous entrepreneurial Montgomery Brothers to apply the amazing theory of atmospheric transport for the construction of a railway from Belfast to our seaside town.

The idea was mooted by John Vallance in 1826 and used on the line between Teignmouth and Dawlish in Devon. The carriages were propelled by a piston working in a vacuum pipe laid between the rails. Suction was created by stationary engines at intervals along the line. The suction system had been considered for use in Ireland's first railway – the Dublin to Kingstown line of 1834. Soon it became evident that rats always devoured the tallow lubricated suction points as quickly as replacements could be installed! The clever Montgomery solicitors immediately got rid of their franchise to the directors of the Belfast and County Down Railway. The Belfast to Holywood steam railway line opened on 2nd August 1848. The News-Letter reported –

"Holywood Railway – this branch of the Belfast and County Down Railway was first opened to public traffic on Wednesday. The line runs parallel with the Belfast Bay, on the County Down side, and being a perfect level, the movement is very easy. The carriages are fitted up very elegantly, and with every regard for comfort. The arrangements for the transfer of traffic are carried out with the utmost satisfaction and punctuality."

The Holywood terminus was situated on Marine Parade – the sea and sandy beaches of our town ready at the doors to greet the holiday travellers. Charles Lanyon was the Railways Company's official architect. Holywood Station was the first of many buildings his office designed for our town. Like so many Englishmen, Lanyon found employment in Ireland as a youth, fell in love with the country and married an Irish lass. Charles Lanyon was born in Sussex in 1813. In Dublin he was apprenticed to Jacob Owen of the

Holywood motor train 1912, gas works in background.

Board of Public Works. In 1835 he was appointed Surveyor for County Antrim where his most outstanding project was construction of the world-famous Coast Road. Sir Charles Lanyon became Ulster's leading architect.

Other Holywood buildings which are associated with the family firm – Lanyon, Lynn and Lanyon – are the Non-Subscribing Presbyterian Church, the Sullivan Schools, the Parish Church, Redburn House, Craigdarragh, possibly Martello Terrace and other private residences.

The Belfast and County Down Railway Company directors appointed the expert engineer, John Godwin, to overcome subsidence problems on the line at Ballymacarrett and Tillysburn. Godwin had come over to Ireland from Swansea as Engineer to the Ulster Railway Company. In 1849 he became Professor of Civil Engineering when the Queen's College was opened in Belfast.

The famous surveyor who worked on the Belfast to Holywood Railway was William Dargan. Dargan (1799 – 1867) was the son of a Carlow farmer who sent his boy to England for education and an apprenticeship in surveying. Love for his native land called him home and in 1831 he won the contract for Ireland's first railway line – Dublin to Kingston – he rapidly became the leading railway engineer. Many Holywood leisure seekers enjoyed themselves on Dargan's famous island in Belfast Lough. In 1839 Belfast

Harbour Authority commissioned William Dargan to cut the first stretch of Victoria Channel – the excavated material from which was deposited to form Dargan's Island. It was tantalisingly visible from Holywood Kinnegar and many Holywood people resorted there for entertainment. After Queen Victoria's visit in 1849 it became the Queen's Island. The Island's seventeen acres of gardens, amusements and bathing facilities became a fashionable summer pleasure resort. The central attraction was a gigantic glass-house, the Belfast Crystal Palace. Other features were a menagerie and amusement arcade. The People's Pleasure Park was taken over for ship-building in 1870. Dargan's enterprises soon spread to seaside town developments – Portrush is one of his jewels.

Today it is appropriate that the railway line which once again joins our seaside town with Larne should cross the Dargan Bridge, opened by Queen Elizabeth on 9th March, 1995.

Robert Lloyd Praeger, a Holywood man writing in 1898, tells us that:

> *"In 1848 Holywood railway traffic was worked by two little tank engines about eight feet long weighing eight or nine tons. High speeds were not encouraged. On one occasion, the only available engine being out of repair, all ten hands of the permanent way staff were called out to push the three o'clock train to Holywood!"*

Two years after the arrival of the railway, Surgeon Kelly describes it as an additional attraction to the seaside town. *"The distance to and from Belfast is performed by this locomotary mode of travelling, in from eight to ten minutes. In summer months a train leaves each terminus hourly from seven o'clock a.m. till half-past nine p.m."* Obviously the good doctor chooses to travel by road.

> *"Those who prefer the gentle and healthful exercise of driving can have their feelings amply gratified, on very moderate charges, as the village is well supplied with vehicles for this purpose, which are in readiness at any moment of the day. It is but just to state, that the Holywood car-drivers have always been found extremely civil and accommodating."*

Within the year, ten trains a day were bringing fun-seeking day trippers to Holywood for swimming, sunning, sailing, spas and seaside holidays. The Railway Company made arrangements with the Holywood Baths Company to issue first-class return tickets from Belfast which included a warm bath and a day at the seaside, all for one shilling and sixpence. In 1856 the Railway Company took over direct control of the Baths Company.

Fast and frequent transport offered to busy Belfast businessmen the opportunity of all the year round living in their favourite holiday town. Formerly this superior lifestyle was reserved for week-ends and the summer months, now their second houses became permanent homes.

Fine terraces and grand mansions sprang up on the rising ground behind the village – soon called "High Holywood".

Around these, the mild climate and fertile soil afforded the cultivation of beautiful gardens and parklands. Washed sea sand, sandstone and bricks from the local works provided building materials; gravel containing iron salts from the spas made miles of weed-free private avenues.

Many a jarvey who had lost the Belfast road trade as a result of the arrival of the railway made a better living driving the new residents to and from Holywood station. There was a car stand at the foot of Hibernia Street and another in the High Street. In 1866 twelve hackney carriages and nine drivers were licensed to convey the good folk of Holywood over the rather muddy streets.

All was progress and prosperity for the fashionable residential town until 1860 when the Belfast, Holywood and Bangor Railway Company was incorporated to construct an extension of the line to Bangor town. The good old B C D R had cash-flow problems at the time, resulting from an attempt to win the Royal Mail run from its Donaghadee Station to Portpatrick.

Fortunately the environmentally-conscious Kennedy family of Cultra refused planning permission for a coastal railway to Bangor. Unfortunately, the inland route bisected Marine Parade and isolated the town from the Kinnegar and our sandy seashore.

The new company took over the Holywood branch of the County Down Railway for £50,000 and a rent of £5,000 in perpetuity. The two companies had adjoining but completely distinct termini at Queen's Quay in Belfast. For a short time, Holywood also had twin termini. Passengers for Bangor from Belfast changed trains at Holywood and ascended a broad flight of steps to the upper platform. Soon the gradient was altered to make a rail track connection and a grand new Holywood Station was added to the Lanyon-designed building.

Passengers entered the station through the booking hall which accommodated a ticket window, stationmaster's office, newsagent's kiosk and a battery of penny slot machines. A wide covered corridor led past gentlemen's toilets and ladies' comfort rooms to the timber canopied Belfast platform with its coffered ceiling adorned at each end with B H B R monograms. Here first class and general waiting rooms were available for the convenience of passengers.

A subterranean passage led under the railway line to the Bangor platform, again there was a canopy and a waiting room. Fires blazed in all the rooms, porters kept the area scrupulously clean, looked after the passengers and tended the flower baskets. A palm tree shaded the station-master's house; a signal box and an extensive goods-yard completed the Holywood Station complex. The prestigious "United Kingdom Handbook of Railway Stations – 1912" recorded "Holywood – goods, passengers and parcels, livestock, horse-boxes, prize cattle vans, carriages by passenger train".

Some of the buildings were destroyed by fire in 1965; others were demolished to provide space for the through-pass in 1970. When Northern Ireland Railways assumed responsibility, Holywood was "normalised" to reflect the standard of present-day lifestyle and transport service. The Holywood line had been transferred to the Ulster Transport Authority in 1948 - exactly a century after it opened for business. In 1951 diesel rail cars were introduced. Northern Ireland Railways replaced the U T A in 1967. At the end of the twentieth century re-opening the Belfast Central Railway re-connects Holywood with every railway station in Ireland.

The Belfast & County Down Railway provided seven stations in our area. In 1864 Glenmachan is shown as a rather elaborate station on J H Connop's lithograph "View of Sydenham, Belmont and Glenmachan". Today its site is approximately where the line passes under the Sydenham By-pass bridge. It was approached by a wide avenue joining Holywood Road at Garnerville Road junction. It may have been built for limited use by season ticket holders and their dependants who lived in the surrounding mansion houses.

Sydenham station platform was not built until 1851, perhaps at that time Glenmachan was moved four hundred yards down the line nearer Holywood and re-named Tillysburn. At Tillysburn Station footpaths to the Holywood Road were provided for passengers, some of whom were members of the Belmont Golf Club which was advertised as *"five minutes walk from Tillysburn station"*.

Kinnegar Halt (1905) was built for the railmotor service, which challenged the opposition which came from Belfast's electric tramway system. It was patronised by military personnel resident at Palace Barracks. The "down" platform at Marino was built in the 1860's, the "up" platform in 1900. It had a useful suite of buildings and a small station house. Its flowers, shrubs and shady arbours were the joy of the Bangor line. Cultra, also of 1860 and 1900 vintage, was *"of ornamental character"*. It was destroyed by fire in 1896 and replaced by more prestigious buildings. Originally half the number of timetabled trains had to stop at Cultra - under a penalty of ten pounds a day! The station provided transport for members of the Royal North of Ireland Yacht Club - now it serves the Ulster Folk and Transport Museum.

Today the Craigavad station building is used as a private residence. Once it was an important station on the line with cross-over points for railmotors and a post office. After 1925 it provided transport for members of the Royal Belfast Golf Club, whose gates were beside the railway. Formerly, Girl Guide companies using Lorne Training Centre found Craigavad station a very convenient transport connection.

Two nineteenth-century transport proposals, both concerning Holywood, failed to come to fruition. The first was the Strandtown and High Holywood Railway Company. Erection of many large mansions along the hill sides, overlooking the Lough, encouraged speculators to consider building the High Holywood line in 1880.

Seven years later a more viable project almost succeeded. On 8th March 1897 Holywood Town Commissioners approved a proposal of the Belfast Street Tramways Company to

Bus in Redburn Square - stationmaster's house in background.

extend a system of electric trams from Campbell College to Holywood maypole along Old Holywood Road and Demesne Road. Of course, the Belfast and County Down Railway objected. The Grand Jury approved a Draft Order in Council, subject to undertakings which were to be given by the Company. In 1896 Lord Pirrie and the Lord Mayor inspected the Dublin "electric cars", the following year the Laganside site was selected for a generating station to supply electricity for tramways. The privately owned horse-drawn tramway was acquired and electric cars operated officially from 5th December 1905.

Holywood had missed the electric tram but not the "motor" train. In 1905 the railway company introduced a frequent steam railcar service to Holywood with rapid return to Belfast. The railcar units combined a little tank engine with a long comfortable centre-aisle coach - the beloved Holywood motor train.
Soon stronger competition challenged steam transport. While the railway won the battle over electric trams, it sought to win the Holywood omnibus war by joining the battle. The directors of the B C D R endorsed the axiom *"If you can't beat them, then join them."*

Ulster's first omnibuses came on the roads about 1905 and were operated by the Northern Counties Railway, although their adaptability and economy soon threatened the innovator. All the railway companies were forced to follow suit. Holywood's first bus arrived at the maypole in the early 1920's. It was operated by Tom McClements in red Dennis vehicles. Dorothy Tait was a passenger on the first bus from Holywood to Belfast

"It was a cold bleak day when a man arrived with what looked like a tramcar body on rubber-tyred wheels and propelled by a motor engine. The contraption was without a door, passengers merely walked up a few wooden steps at the rear of the vehicle, which was lined with wooden seats on either side.
Interior temperature was of two varieties. If you preferred fresh air and cold (and it was cold!) you sat at the back; if you preferred heat (and it was hot !) you went up to the front where a large electric heater gave a fierce glow. Of course, the heat went straight out at the open other end. The "craic" to and from the City was excellent – comments mostly in favour of 'bus as opposed to rail travel. The return fare was five pence."

Soon J Russell and then George Gregory were operating rival services. A fourth entrepreneur was Samuel Gillespie who ran the famous 'Maypole Queens'.

The Belfast terminus for all Holywood buses was Oxford Street – the kerbside! Here the rival operators drastically cut their fares to attract trade. Another eye-witness, J B Birch, described the exciting journey home after work in the City.

"Competition between the services gave the Holywood Road the appearance of Derby Racecourse, the various buses attempting to pass and re-pass each other. The rickety vehicles raced along - their drivers encouraged by the exclamations of the passengers.

Cut-throat competition forced rival operators off the road. The Bangor Queen, Enterprise, Tonic and Pioneer buses joined in the competition and having reached Holywood, continued the race down the Bangor Road.

By 1927 the Belfast and County Down Railway was operating a punctual and safe service in clean and comfortable Leyland Lion vehicles. The *Northern Ireland Road Transport Board* took over the service on 23rd August 1935. The *Ulster Transport Authority* assumed responsibility on 1st October 1948 and *Ulsterbus* on 17th April 1967. Holywood passengers from Belfast had to wait for the bus on the wet and windy Oxford Street kerb until 15th July 1960 when a terminal building was erected on the site of the former Central Railway Station. The spacious Laganside Bus Centre was opened in 1996.

The B C D R became an integral part of Ulster Transport Authority on 1st October 1948. Hundreds of acres of railway land, 76 miles of track, more than 30 stations, with residences, impressive termini at Queen's Quay, Bangor and Newcastle, several catering establishments, rolling stock, locomotives and all the rest was acquired by the government for £485,989. The only part of the system which remained in operation was the Holywood and Bangor line – literally a going concern, which in 1958 was making an annual profit of £68,000. The other Belfast commuter lines, Newtownards (14 miles – 30 minutes), Comber (8 miles – 18 minutes) and Donaghadee (22 miles – 50 minutes) were closed down on 24th April 1950. In its heyday the company carried four million passengers on 600,000 train-miles annually.

One nineteenth century Holywood transport story immediately claims local interest. It is the *Grand Holywood Pier*, and deserves detailed attention. Every Victorian seaside holiday resort required a pier on which visitors could promenade during sunny summer days.

For many years a small jetty had served the sea-fishing community; Holywood's major landing place was at Cultra Harbour. The Irish Parliamentary Gazette of 1846, while congratulating Holywood on *"its beautiful situation, cleanliness and cheerful appearance"* required *"the town's small pier to be repaired and extended".* Accordingly in 1855, the prosperous little town demanded a more prestigious anchorage.

Holywood resident, John Getty McGee, the Belfast master tailor who made the "Ulster" top coat a world-wide dictionary derivation, organised a subscription list for the new jetty. The £260 subscribed paid for the erection of fifty yards of wooden planks which the builders pointed towards the Cave Hill from the middle of stylish Marine Parade. The rather steep berthing fee was a half-crown. Local fishermen got "freebies" if they gave a couple of days a year to keep navigable the channel which led out to the middle of Belfast Lough.

After the Holywood Gaslight Company was incorporated in 1856, the managers realised that a substantial wharf on which to off-load coal-boats was necessary. A public meeting on 30th October 1863 was amazed to learn two significant facts: In 1862 thirteen thousand tons of coal had to be beached on the Kinnegar for delivery to the Gasworks and private homes because there was no adequate coal quay in Holywood. As well as this piece of information, they discovered that a third of a million passengers had travelled by rail to Holywood over the same twelve months.

It appeared that a landing stage for passenger boats and a coal quay would provide a goldmine for local shareholders. The Holywood Pier Company came into being, and local investors rushed to become subscribers. Shares costing two pounds each raised a proposed working capital of seven thousand pounds. The plan was to run an L-shaped pier into the sea for a quarter mile from the foot of Shore Street, incorporating a coal quay of some 300 feet in length.

Months before the official opening, an eye-witness, writing on 8th May 1867, described the excitement of the crowds, as they ran down the uncompleted boardwalk to greet the inaugural visit of the good ship "Erin". The first passenger to disembark was the famous John Getty McGee himself, who called for three hearty cheers as the "Erin" continued on her voyage to Bangor. The construction was completed in 1869.

Captain R H Davis reported :

"The pier extends from the railway embankment for 1,360 yards

over the seabank, even at low tide a vessel of moderate draft can call. It is of very great strength and rests on round metal pillars, so placed and transversely bolted together most effectively to resist the action of the water.

A fine promenade has been erected on one side, which is protected from the main roadway of the quay so that no danger can arise from the horses and carts. It is the intention of Mr Brown, the spirited owner of the Erin steamboat, to place a first class saloon vessel of high speed on the service to run every hour.

The first regular Holywood boat was the "Devenish", re-named "Lady of the Lake". She was a 132 feet 60 horsepower iron paddle steamboat, maximum speed 13 knots, draft 3 feet, 75 ton registered, carrying 500 passengers. Devenish had been built by Henderson & Coleman of Renfrew for the Lough Erne trade.

The August 1869 advertisement, which encouraged passengers to voyage to Holywood by sea, read –

"The Lady of the Lake will ply (weather permitting and casualties excepted) between Belfast and Holywood from the foot of High Street (Belfast) – seven trips each day and on Sunday three trips.

Fares : Single cabin – Fourpence
Steerage - Twopence"

Unfortunately, it proved impossible to keep the channel cut unsilted. It led out to the main Belfast Lough channel, and ran at right angles to the tidal flow. No sooner was it dredged, than it silted up again. The little tugboat "Wonder" and a dredger from Dundrum Bay fought a losing battle with nautical nature. Eventually, on 15th December 1873, the "Lady of the Lake" left Holywood for the Blackpool trade. Meanwhile the "Gareloch" became the Holywood boat. She was jinxed by a series of accidents which included a collision with the Queen's Bridge!

A public meeting was held in the Assembly Rooms on Marine Parade to discuss the inefficient marine service, which had been inaugurated in such auspicious circumstances just a few years previously. One speaker shouted angrily *"The Gareloch is an insult to the intelligence of the Holywood people."* However, still confident of the viability of sea transport, a limited liability company was formed *"to raise funds to procure a steamboat to ply between Holywood and Belfast".*

The owners of the pier agreed to lease a berth to the new company for £200 per annum. The directors added a rather parsimonious clause to the agreement *"The rent will be £300 if the steamboat profits exceed ten per centum."* A maximum of one thousand shares at five pounds each went on offer to the public. By April 1871 the company was operating "Lily". She was a lively 150 feet craft of 56 tons, draft 30 inches, capable of sailing to Holywood in twenty minutes on twelve pounds of steam with 300 passengers on board. Silting interrupted the service in 1872. Other vessels used on the Holywood run were "Vesta", "Shamrock", "Renown" and even the little tugboat "Wonder" was called into service on occasions!

Holywood Pier, 1867, almost a quarter of a mile in length.

The 1875 tourist guide was sorry to report that the Holywood boat service had been discontinued. *"And so the vultures started to gather."* In 1876 Messrs Priestly and Company of Liverpool, on poor legal advice, purchased the pier with the intention of sailing a small swift steamer between Belfast and Holywood. Messrs Rae & Young of London acquired it in 1877. Three years later, they had to hand it over to the Imperial Credit Corporation for £775. You should remember that the entire operation – pier, breakwater, channel cuts and quays cost £9,400 in 1864. That was a mere sixteen years previously.

About that time, a rogue card was played by the Belfast Central Railway. It is a company redeemed from complete oblivion by the present-day pedestrian passages in Oxford Street through which the Central Railway Company's permanent way once ran. Although the Central Railway was formed in 1864, by 1875 it controlled only two miles of suburban track; linking the three Belfast termini. Unfortunately, its exciting project to build a grand central terminus on a site reserved beside the Town Hall in Victoria Street was discarded. The travelling public had to be satisfied with a modest little platform off Oxford Street called Queen's Bridge Station!

The Central Railway Company's principal interest was the movement of cargo traffic. The Directors leased the Holywood Pier with the intention of diverting trade from Belfast Harbour to Holywood Pier and thence via the railway line from Holywood and Ballymacarrett Junction to the entire Irish railway network - bold stratagem indeed!. *"The Belfast Harbour Authority was not amused."* However, the ambitious plan did not get on track as in January 1883 the tailpiece of the Holywood Pier was carried off in a fierce north-easterly gale. A few months later a large sailing vessel dragged its anchor and breached the structure. Rapid repairs were effected before for the cruellest cut of all.

Holywood Sailing Regatta on 25th August 1883, was operated from the Pier. In the evening a splendid fireworks display was enjoyed by crowds of spectators on both sides of Belfast Lough. The coffee kiosk did a roaring trade that day - sadly some hot ashes ignited the floorboards during the rush to serve the crowds with refreshments. The proprietor thought he had extinguished the fire before he and his staff went off duty. At two o'clock the following morning the fire flared up on a brisk breeze. Belfast's horse-drawn fire engines were on the scene as quickly as possible - one sucked water from an ebbing tide, the other connected pipes to a street hydrant and sprayed water from Holywood's new Waterworks, then under construction. The fire blazed for five hours. On that holiday August morning of 1883, crowds arrived from all around the Lough. Wags said it was the world's best fireworks exhibition ever witnessed! The fire completely destroyed two hundred feet of the Pier and rendered it inoperable. In 1889 the owners sold the fire-scarred ruin to Sir Daniel Dixon, who resided in Ballymenoch House and owned the shoreline as far as Clanbrassil Terrace at Cultra.

Soon nautical nature had submerged Holywood's magnificent pier, the coal wharf and the passenger boat quay under the sands. However, when the railway embankment was moved farther north in the 1970's to facilitate the Holywood through-pass, the flow of sea currents was altered and the stanchions of the old pier rose above the mussel-beds of the Lough.

Today, the foundations are visible at low tide from the Esplanade end of Shore Road. Old Holywood folk say on stormy winter nights, at the full of the tide and moon, you may hear sailors sighing for their lost ships and Presbyterians singing their sad Hebrew psalms, for their meeting house which, like the Pier, lies under the waves at the foot of Shore Road.

In the next essay we shall investigate the commercial enterprise which engendered the wealth to sustain Holywood's viable transport system.

ESSAY X - HOLYWOOD - TOWN OF TRADE AND COMMERCE

The Boys of the 9.15

A song of 1920 for "The boys of the 9.15" to be sung daily in the "Harmony Compartment" of the Belfast and County Down Railway -

"A new song I shall sing to you about the nine-fifteen,
Concerning boys who journey on the train from Bangor town,
Subscribers who are noted on the good old County Down -
They are men of very great distinction on the nine-fifteen.

CHORUS

On the nine-fifteen, on the nine-fifteen
They are men of very great distinction on the nine-fifteen."

(My grandfather and uncles were among the group of twenty-one businessmen who travelled daily to town from "down the line".)

HOLYWOOD - TOWN OF TRADE AND COMMERCE

The story of any town would be incomplete without an attempt to examine the money supply and background economy of its hinterland. As with so many topics, we are fortunate that the trade and commerce of the Holywood area are well documented.

There may have been a market in the village which grew up beside the Holywood Priory, especially after King John's visit in 1210 and when King Henry III allowed John de Saukvill to make Holywood a centre of local government in 1217. We know that John de Courcy, the sponsor of our Priory, was issuing coinage at Carrickfergus and Downpatrick by the end of the twelfth century. Some day a Holywood gardener may unearth a hoard of de Courcy pennies!

The earliest recorded evidence of Holywood's commercial ventures, apart from the fishing industry, seems to be the weekly markets and annual fairs of the early sixteenth century.

Patents of King James I from 5th November 1606 granted permission to Sir James Hamilton to hold weekly markets in Bangor on Mondays, at Castlereagh on Thursdays *"and also one other market at Holywood on every Wednesday, weekly, for ever; and one Fair at Holywood aforesaid annually, on the twenty-fourth day of March, and for two days following, for ever with Courts of Pye Powder.*

The title *"Court of Pye Powder"* comes from the French words pied *"a foot"* and poudrieux *"dusty"*. The Court was held at fairs to administer instant justice to buyers and sellers. Suitors were country folk with dusty feet; justice had to be administered with as much speed as the dust could be shaken off the feet of the miscreant. Ancient law tracts called a pedlar *"pede pulverosis"* or dusty-footed and required that if he were a vagabond *"he should have justice administered to him within three ebbings and three flowings of the tide".*

I wonder how many felons waited the sentence from our local court while the tides flowed over the Holywood sands!

Conditions of the seventeenth century Royal Land Grant required Hamilton to advance the prospects of the Scottish settlers. The three strategically placed markets in North Down encouraged a steady trading pattern and supply industry for the surrounding farming families of each town.

The long established Irish fairs had an ancient and colourful history to which the locals came to enjoy a holiday or Holy Day. Accordingly, fairs were held on the feast day of the local saint. As Hamilton was the son of a Scottish Presbyterian Manse, our proprietor did not know that St Laiseran's red letter day is celebrated on 25th October! For Hamilton, 24th March was as good as any other date! Fairs were attended by crowds of merrymakers and professional hawkers who travelled from fair to fair pedalling their wares and skills. Frequently, fracas broke out and pilfering was common. As in Holywood, some fairs were allowed to hold Courts of Pye Powder to redress the disorders committed during the fair-days.

For many years in Holywood, traders set up their stalls and booths in the widest part of the High Street between the maypole and the Ballykeel River. Today the breadth of that part of the street indicated the market square.

A pipe-dream industry which never materialised concerned tales of the Holywood coal mines. When Sir Robert Walpole, Prime Minister 1721 – 1742, appointed Arthur Dobbs, Surveyor General for Ireland, a government exploration hoped to find lead and coal on the shores of Belfast Lough. In a letter dated 28th November 1725. Arthur Dobbs recorded

> *"I went along the shoar to Hollywood to view the freestone there which just crops our at the sea mark and dips to the sea. It lys too steep [for coal] and if any be there I take it to be more into the country."*

Most likely the memories of borings in the winter of 1725 engendered the fable of the Holywood coal mines!

An older and viable trade came from Belfast Lough and indeed several nineteenth century commentators describe Holywood as a fishing village. Surgeon Kelly, who lived on High Street and had a penchant for sea bathing, tells us that the watering places along the coast share a common origin. He claims a few straggling huts of fishermen become the summer haunts for health-seekers and before you know it, the hamlet becomes a seaside resort.

Water mill on Ballykeel Road (Victoria Road) – demolished to build Millbank on the site.

Rev William Holmes says *"Fish, especially the mussel, is used in the season"*. Lieutenant G F W Bordes records *"In 1834 there were six fishermen and two fisherwomen"* living in the village. However, the earliest reference to the fishing industry in Holywood is in the 1333 Inquisition which records *"a fishery worth three shillings and fourpence at Holywood".* Considering the Inquisition valued the famous fishery on the River Roe at twenty shillings, the Holywood fishery must have been of considerable importance in 1333 !

Rev C. J. McAlester paints a picture of our market town towards the end of the eighteenth century and emphasizes the value of seafood for the local residents –

> *" There were no regularly constructed side paths; householders occupied much of the space now neatly formed into footways, patches of grass here and there at the side of the streets afforded a resting place, if not a grazing ground, for the geese, of which literally, and perhaps, figuratively, there were a great many. Conspicuous in the front of many houses were large bluish heaps, which a stranger passing through the village might have puzzled to understand, were the shells of what was the staple commodity of the place – mussels – which the adjacent banks yielded much more abundantly than they now do."*

The weekly markets and annual fairs fitted comfortably into this rustic idyll. The Holywood market experienced fluctuations of depression and success. When Rev William Holmes took up duty in 1810 he found *"a new fair, which is as yet badly attended, is held quarterly in the village of Holywood".* The vicar gives an interesting sidelight on the purchasing power of the Holywood villagers at the time. *"At present labourers average 8 shillings and 6 pence per week; a man with horse and cart receives 3 shillings and 9 pence per day. Fifty years ago he was paid 8 pence for the same period. In 1705 for a fat hen 4 pence was allowed – at present that article would be valued at two shillings sterling.*

We get a good idea of the actual cost of living about that time from items listed in the weekly account book of Woburn House, home of the Dunbar family at Millisle, twelve miles from Holywood as the crow flies. The housekeeper's book records life at the big house from 1829 to 1840. Money matters in Richmond, Holywood House, Cultra and Ballymenoch would have been much the same.

The "woman in the laundry" received a guinea per week and "the charwoman" 9 shillings for 3 days a week.

Buttons for the Primate, Lord George Beresford, Archbishop of Armagh	*3/-*
Five pounds of cheese	*4/10d*
Ice for wine	*6/6d*
A shovel for the laundry	*3/6d*
Seven pounds of sugar	*4/1d*
To the groom for turnpikes	*£1.8s.3d*
Paid for a letter	*2/8d*
One pound of tea for the schoolroom	*7/-*
A barrel of oysters	*6/6d*
Twenty-eight lbs of soap	*£1.8.0d*
One pound special green tea for the parlour	*12/3d*
One pound of mustard	*2/-*
Wax candles	*£6.14.9d*
A chicken	*2/9d*
One pound of rice	*6d*
Muffins for Lord George	*5d*
Half-pound of brown candy	*8d*
Pound of sugar candy and liquorice	*2/10d*
Flowers for the Drawing room	*6/-*
Coffee	*£4.10.0.*
One pound of tea for the room	*7/-*

Purchase of dry tea for the school-room, the parlour and the room (servants' hall) is frequent and very expensive, as is lamp oil, supply of candles and chimney sweeping. It seems each week the housekeeper defrayed the books of other head servants and tradesmen: fishmonger, coachman, iceman, grocer, poulterer, milkman, baker, brewer, miller, butcher, greengrocer, and the pastrycook. All the accounts were audited weekly by the butler or house manager and give us an interesting portrayal of life "downstairs" in a great house in the first half of the nineteenth century.

The "upstairs" account book of the same family, for the years between 1833 and 1841 is even more fascinating. Here are a few examples taken at random from the record :

A new carriage in 1834	*£135*
Annual subscription to Christian Knowledge	*One guinea*
Black satin gown for Susan	*£5.1s.6d.*

Over the decade Susan was showered with flowers, gowns, shoes, gloves, ribbons and bonnets! She was the daughter of the Archbishop and wife of George Dunbar.

Annual subscriptions for almanacks (presumably this refers to newspapers)	*£5*
For a present	*£50*
Eber's opera box	*£100*
The last of the lady's maid (what event that payment settled defies speculation)	*£9.18s.6d*
To a distressed Highlander	*£5*
To Sampson for J's picture	*£2.18s.*
Two saws and one pair of scissors	*15/6d*
Doctor Southey's visits	*Eleven guineas*
Concert subscriptions	*One guinea*
Courier des dames	*£3.0.0.*

A note for the year 1833 records the capital investments, the annual interest on which provided finance for household and family expenses. It seems £2,565 was required annually to run Woburn House – its equivalent today – £100,000

The economic importance of the twelve big houses in the Holywood area should not be under-estimated. They supported the local traders, provided centres of industry for the villagers and maintained a stable society.

As we have seen, the vicar recorded in 1810 there was a badly attended quarterly fair in the village. By 1834 Lieutenant G F N Bordes recorded *"There is a fair on the first Monday in February, May, August and November of each year for cattle, pigs and horses of an inferior description. It is more a fair of pleasure than of business."*

Fourteen years later, the Parliamentary Gazetteer of Ireland, 1846, complained *"A badly attended fair is held every three months in Holywood."* However, the publication redeemed its criticism by describing the village as *"having a remarkably clean, neat and cheerful appearance and occupying a beautiful site".* Even the poorly attended fair seems to have run its course by the middle of the century. By then, Holywood was an "up-market" seaside resort with a railway terminus. Perhaps in 1850 the fair in the High Street *"for the sale of horses of an inferior description"* did not concur with the aims of the tourist trade and the aspirations of the proprietors of the new fashionable hotels.

Two other Holywood markets deserve mention. In 1867 Squire Harrison encouraged the growth of an open market to benefit the local economy. For many years the area between Shore Road and the Strand was known as "the markets". Today the through-pass crosses the expanse.

Pedestrianisation of Hibernia Street promised the town a twenty-first century weekly market. Perhaps it will succeed where others have failed and return to the town the Royal Charter of weekly market and annual fair. Of course, a better location would be the old market square between the maypole and The Crescent on High Street. Traffic-wise, the area has three by-pass routes – to the south Brook Street and on the north side the through-pass and Strand Avenue.

In their heyday, fair days and market days were family fun days for young and old. However, holidays were unusual for hard-working farmers; they combined labour with pleasure bringing their corn for grinding at one of the Holywood mills while their wives and children bargained and made merry at the fair.

There were four mills in Holywood town – three operated by the water-power of the Ballykeel river – one driven by the winds that whistled around Ardshane. The earliest mill may have been worked by the religious community of the Priory, founded by Laiseran about 640. As early as 630 monastic settlements had water-powered grain mills; wheels were set horizontally catching the water flow to turn the millstones.

Holywood Windmill, may have been used as a Martello or watch-towner.

Rev William Holmes in 1810 records -

> *"It is said that the first flax-mill erected in Ireland was in this parish. The writer has conversed with a person who remembers to have seen it, and informs him that the wheel was horizontal, but he cannot vouch for the correctness of his description. There are four windmills and five watermills in the parish.*
> *One of the watermills is now used for the manufacture of flour, and another is a flax mill; the remainder are what are called common grist-mills."*

You should remember that during Mr Holmes' ministry the parish extended from Grey Point to Connswater.

Writing in 1834, Lieutenant Bordes expands our knowledge –

> *"There is a large flour mill at the south-western point of the parish called Beer's Mill, with a mill pond. There is a windmill in the townland of Ballymenagh and one in that of Ballykeel near the village of Holywood, and two small water mills in that village: one overshot wheel 16 feet diameter, one breast wheel 15 feet diameter."*

Of the mills featured in the Lieutenant's survey, only the walls of the Ballykeel windmill are extant. A painting by A Nichol, 1834, in the care of the Ulster Museum, presents an accurate impression of the working windmill. The artist painted his view looking across the Holywood mill-dam towards the Belfast Lough. The present-day back drive to Martello Terrace was the road up to the mill. The Raven map, 1625, seems to suggest the lane continuing over the hill to meet the road to Bangor.

A land map drawn for John Hunter in September 1831 shows both sides of the Windmill Lane, Ballykeel Road and Millbrook Street, lined with buildings, possibly the mill-workers' cottages. The present Mill Moat House adjacent to the cottages may have been the mill-owner's house. The windmill seems to have produced flour for the bread of Holywood folk from the seventeenth century until the 1840's. Today it is known as "the Martello Tower" from which the nearby terrace takes its name. You may ask how the Italian word for a hammer came home to Holywood.

Martello watch-towers were small circular forts built for defence against invasion during the Napoleonic Wars. The name came from Cape Martella in Corsica, where such a tower was captured, with great difficulty, by the British Fleet in 1794. A sandstone parapet added to the Holywood windmill stump indicates that it may have been refurbished as a watch-tower – however, it was not required to protect the Maypole Town from an invasion by the French Emperor!

Lieutenant Bordes' *"water-mill with a sixteen feet overshot wheel"* was situated at the corner of Ballykeel Road and Millbrook Street. Mill Bank House, Victoria Road, was built on the steeply sloping site before 1850. Water-power was diverted from the Ballykeel River by a sluice constructed behind the old Manse on Victoria Road. It flowed in a conduit beside Victoria Road into a two-acre mill dam situated behind "Martello Corner". The skilful fabrication of the channel was revealed in 1998 when gas pipes and telephone cables were laid along the road. Numbers 16 to 18 Victoria Road occupy the site of the old mill dam. The architectural subterranean mill race still runs under the grounds of Martello Terrace. The race emerged at Millbrook Street corner providing a waterfall of over twenty-five feet to rotate the sixteen feet vertically set wheel. The mill tail race returned the well-used water to the Ballykeel River.

In 1924 Miss McAlester, a daughter of Rev C J McAlester, then an elderly lady, recalled the days of a happy Holywood childhood, especially the mills.

> *"I remember Church View was known as the backs of the gardens and a double ditch ran parallel with it. The Martello Tower was a windmill. Another mill stood where the houses known as Millbank are now. To the east of this was a mill dam which on one occasion overflowed its banks, the water rushing down what is now Victoria Road towards the sea. In its course a cow was drowned in Stewart's Place and the house of Mr Hodgson, the Belfast bookseller, was flooded. Mill Lane was not much more than a path, the stream which now runs under it had to be crossed on stepping stones. There were a few cottages on both sides of the path. A favourite and somewhat adventurous walk for children was to begin on the shore and make their way up the river to what for many years we have called Marsh's Glen. The most exciting part of this expedition was creeping beneath the archway under the main street before reaching the grounds of The Crescent. Across the foot of Gospel Lane, that is Strand Street, there were two houses and here were warm baths kept by a Miss Rowley. On the sea side of the houses there was a little jetty with a ladder for the use of bathers. Of course, there was as yet no railway bank."*

"Mill Street" became "Church Street" after the Parish Church was built on its present site in 1844. The street took its original name from the water mill which Lieutenant Bordes tells us was operated by a brest wheel of fifteen feet diameter. Like its two counterparts, the Ballykeel River provided the water power. The mill and adjacent cottages were demolished about 1858, when Riverston House was erected. It is interesting to note that site demolition removed the Connor family coach house, which was used for the Celebration of Mass in 1815.

Riverston House was acquired by the Urban District Council for social purposes after the Second World War. The house was removed, before 1960, to accommodate the new Telephone Exchange and the Nursery School. Perhaps the best-known resident of Riverston House was Bernard Hughes Esq, founder of the Belfast Bakery. The house was typical of the rapidly disappearing merchants' mansions, which were built in Holywood in the nineteenth century, and contributed greatly to the prosperity of the town. During the past century, more than twenty of the merchants' mansions have been demolished. However, many examples still remain, especially the graceful terraces and huge semi-detached villas. It is imperative that these beautiful examples of Holywood's heritage are not desecrated with the permission of the Planning Authority!

Before the Ballykeel River turned the wheels of the two water-mills in the village, it operated the grindstones at Glenview Farm. Three-quarters of a mile up the steep road which led towards Standard Hill, now Upper Church Road, Samuel Houston's mill served the local community. Private housing development in the 1990's removed the old mill building. Evidence of the mill race and small dam, depicted on a land map of 1830, can still be seen in the picturesque bower which lies at the head of Glen Lyon Gorge. I am unable to find the site of *"the windmill in the townland of Ballymenagh"* to which the Lieutenant referred.

The five local mills depended upon the farming community to bring commerce into Holywood. The tourist trade depended upon satisfied visitors returning to enjoy the golden beaches year after year. Throughout the nineteenth century, our major summer industry provided employment for Holywood folk in the hotel trade and in leasing holiday homes. Rev William Holmes records –

> *"The wealth of the villagers consists principally in the accommodation which they lay out for lodgers in the summer season. They have either small houses fitted up for the purpose, which are let at a good profit, or apartments prepared in their own dwellings."*

Lieutenant G F W Bordes agrees –

> *"The inhabitants derive their chief support from the profit of their houses which are let in the summer season to the sea bathers."*

However, we have followed in other essays the commercial advantage the lucrative tourist trade brought to the town.
As the hospitality business declined, the gainful occupations which it had engendered continued to prosper. The specialised building trade developed into a local ability to erect fine mansions for the merchant princes of Belfast.

Tradesmen and shopkeepers welcomed the opportunity to meet the needs of the wealthy new residents. Good domestic service was at a premium. The farming community continued to prosper by meeting the needs of the affluent recent arrivals to the town in the same way in which they had supplied the hotel owners with fresh food for their summer guests. Of course, agriculture has been the staple employment of the Holywood area from the earliest times.

The early life style of the Holywood monks required the personal maintenance of both soul and body. Travellers to the Priory would have introduced new methods of horticulture from all over Europe to our area from the seventh to the tenth centuries.

Holywood's vicar paints an interesting picture of agriculture in the Holywood Hills three centuries ago.

> *"The natives live principally by tillage. There are a few weavers and hosiers amongst them, but their employments seem to take up their time only when they cannot employ themselves in agricultural pursuits. Almost every weaver, except those who live in the village, has a piece of ground sufficient to furnish his family with potatoes, oatmeal and milk."*

Rev W Holmes compared his Holywood parishioners with those of Belfast city.

> *"Nothing can be more distressing than to see the pale meagre appearance of the city artisan whose constitution is undermined*

Water mill on Mill Street, demolished to provide site for Riverston House, now site of telephone exchange.

> *by a sedentary life. When he is transplanted to the country and employs himself in cultivating a piece of ground, the exercise gives him new vigour to his frame and elasticity to his mind."*

High praise indeed for our neighbours in the Holywood Hills! The vicar continued :

> *"Holywood farmers are in general a wealthy class of people, the bad seasons which have prevailed of late and their vicinity to the Belfast Market, have contributed to enrich them. However, some who hold their farms at high rates are beginning to feel the effects of reduced prices. The extent of farms is from 80 to 10 acres; the greater number are from 40 to 20 acres. As they are principally laid out in tillage, the stock of cattle is not considerable. Farmers seldom keep more than from two to six cows and from two to five horses."*

> *"The farmers manure with seaweed which gives them crops of potatoes and wheat in succession. By adding stable manure the soil is strong enough to afford four-fold rotation – potatoes, wheat, ryegrass and oats. Beyond the hills, where the soil is poorer, they use lime and alternate flax and oats with the potatoes. Most of the gentlemen who have villas on the shore cultivate*

field turnips, field peas and beans. However, their uncertainty renders them an improper kind of crop to be dealt in by the common class of farmer.
By the exertions of the gentry, the
black cattle of the Irish breed may be improved."

Obviously, the vicar was very conscious of the class divisions of his parishioners and completely unconscious of political correctness! He goes on to describe the implements used by Holywood farmers, farm rents and wages paid to labourers.

"Implements of agriculture are of the very best description, the
Scotch plough is every where to be met with. Even farmers
who have not more than twenty acres have one or more carts -
so that the Irish plough and car are fallen into disuse. The roller,
an implement of great service in agriculture, is in general use.
In Holywood village there are three cart and plough makers, each
of which finds sufficient employment for an establishment of tradesmen
whose work is scarcely inferior to that imported from Glasgow."

Commenting on Holywood rentals on 29 September 1834 Lieutenant Bordes adds the information that *"Rents range from £4 per acre for the best agricultural land to £1 for the worst. Building ground along the coast can command £8 per acre.*
He describes

"Holywood at work - farm holdings vary from two to seventy
acres, the land is well manured to produce a rotation of potatoes, wheat,
oats, barley with clover and ryegrass. The cattle generally used are
the Devonshire and Ayrshire breeds. The fences generally are banks
with a ditch on one or both sides. The farm buildings appear good
and commodious. The low ground and along the shore the soil is good,
deep with a sandy or clay bottom, in the hills it is light with a rocky bottom.
With the usual village tradespeople there are eight fishermen and six
fisherwomen who catch cod and plaice off the coast in winter and
codling in the summertime. There is not much hand-spinning in the
parish but there may be fifty weavers. Spinners receive a penny or tuppence a day,
weavers earn up to one shilling and tuppence."

To illustrate rents for the period, Holmes used the account books for the Kennedy family who owned the four thousand acre estate around Cultra House. In the year 1705 the Ballycultra lands were let to the tenants upon leases of three lives and 31 years, for a total sum of £300. By 1802 this had risen to £1,850 per annum. In 1814 the rent role brought in £5,300 per annum. The vicar estimated by 1820 the Kennedy family would have an annual income of £9,000 from the Cultra estate - a quarter of a million pounds at today's valuation. Holmes uses the 46 acres of Woodside Farm in Ballycultra to illustrate his case. In 1741 it was let at half-a-crown per acre, by 1809 the farmer was paying £2.10.0 for the same area of land.

Holmes records

"In the year 1741, eightpence per day was the rate of wages for
a man and horse, by 1810 the wage had risen to eight shillings
and sixpence. In 1705 a fat hen cost fourpence - in 1741 sixpence
and by 1810 that article would be two shillings."

It seems inflation is not a modern problem. Strangely enough, two of the indicators frequently quoted are the cost of *"a fat hen"* and *"how much a man with a horse* (presumably his own animal) *receives for a day's work"*. Mr George F Platt of the Ulster Bank has ascertained figures which show comparative values at fifty-year intervals from 1700 to November 1999. The figures are derived from the Retail Price Index, based at January 1987 equalling par. The index covers the combined cost of a number of specified items but does not take into account other factors relevant to a comparison of values - such as the cost of real property or the level of wages. The estimation is interesting as a comparison with the various monetary values quoted in our period of study. As we enter the twenty-first century the pound sterling of 1700 was worth £72.48; 1750 - £79.38; 1800 - £29.25; 1850 - £47.63; 1900 - £53.77 and 1950 - £19.85.

In this essay we have taken a quick look at the way in which our forebears earned their livelihood. We have seen the prosperity produced by the Holywood markets, the milling and agriculture industries, the building and retail trades - with comparative modern valuations. We have met with the fortunate few who lived in luxury on the ground rents which their estates produced, and the considerable employment their life-style provided. Then we welcomed the special affluence which the merchant princes brought to our town.

Today Holywood is proud of its excellent community relations, erudite schools, specialist shops and excellent road, rail and air communications. The choice of sports clubs, golf courses and yacht clubs is unparalleled in the Province. The town has two purpose-built doctors' surgeries, three state-of-the-art dental surgeries and several nursing homes. We have the choice of more than twenty alternative medicine and therapies centres and three health clubs. The Queen's Hall complex and the Mertoun Hall site will add two additional purpose-built activity gymnasia.

We were the first town in the United Kingdom to be presented on the internet as a "virtual town centre". The aim of this project is to give residents private ownership of the town centre on the Internet. The website introduces Holywood businesses to the Internet and brings them closer to residents for shopping and services. So Holywood adds another "first" as we enter the twenty-first century, and our 434 business outlets present themselves at home and abroad.

Several essays have stressed the importance and salubrity of a vibrant tourist trade when visiting Holywood was a leading seaside holiday experience.

Now we return to the story of Holywood hospitality as we take a stroll around the town to visit our taverns, ancient and modern. - So let us take a walk on the wild side!

ESSAY XI - HOLYWOOD HOSPITALITY - A HIKE AROUND OUR HOSTELRIES

In the last essay we looked behind the scenes of our town's enterprise. Now we shall enjoy a walk around our hotels, taverns and restaurants – a particular Holywood forte.

A Bacchanalian Song

"Come now, let us drown melancholy
And care – we shall banish it too;
Draw near to us, boys, and be jolly
We'll show you what liquor can do.

What though you have met with affliction
I've drank of the draught long before
Come now, my boys, off with restriction
And let us have one bottle more.

Come, landlord, come send in a barrel;
Come, come now, my words don't control,
For liquor it will end a quarrel
And cherish both body and soul.

Robert Sullivan – Juvenile Poems

Perhaps when Dr Sullivan was appointed Professor of the Dublin Teacher Training College he regretted the words written by an eighteen-year-old student!

When Rev William Holmes came to Holywood in 1810 he found ten public houses open for business. Four were in the village of Holywood, only one of which had good accommodation as an inn. Perhaps this was the house which Miss McAlester, daughter of the Presbyterian minister, said *"stood at the corner of Church Road and High Street"*. Miss McAlester claimed a hotel guest had scratched on one of its windows *"Ye winds and waves pray cease your anger that Thomas, James and John may get to Bangor"*.

Another early tavern may have occupied the corner at Morrow's Lane and the High Street. During site renovation a swinging inn sign board was discovered. It bore the name "Agnes Mawhinney". Perhaps Agnes was the original lady inn-keeper who paved the way for the traditional Holywood land-ladies of later days.

Of course, Holywood hospitality goes much further back in history – right to the seventh century religious foundation. One of the duties of the Priory was to provide a safe resting place for wayfarers, especially those travelling between the monastic settlements. Even then, Ard Mac Nasca was a convenient place to spend the night.

Hibernia Street (formerly Place) showing the Railway Hotel. The gardens became Redburn Square.

When the town became a summer retreat, the tourist trade was a major source of income and a demand for holiday accommodation flourished. In a previous essay, a walk to Cultra took us past the Marine Hotel. Surgeon Kelly depicts it in glowing terms :

"The Marine Hotel provides ample accommodation for those whose brief sojourn, or other circumstances, disincline them to encumber themselves by the cares of house-keeping or with a separate establishment. At this hotel there has been established an American bowling alley; and we are informed that the village now contains many players of no mean proficiency."

In 1865 the golden sands which spread before the Marine's welcoming doors were cut off by the railway embankment. The Marine Hotel was converted into semi-detached houses when Holywood ceased to be a holiday resort. In 1970 the houses were demolished to make way for the through-pass.

Surgeon Kelly described the accommodation provided in the Belfast Hotel as *"ample and in the first style. It is a spacious building in the Main Street giving unfailing attention and civility and attracts a large concourse of the highest respectability of strangers and visitors.* The building is one of the oldest in Holywood. Valuation documents show that the third storey was added about 1840, perhaps it was already the town's leading hotel at that time and its expansion indicated its success. John Power (1797 – 1874) was the proprietor of the Belfast Hotel. The Power family lived in Eldon House on the Kinnegar. As well as being proprietor of the Belfast Hotel, John Power had many business interests in the town. He married into the Ballagh family. A grandson became Sir John Cecil Power,

Member of Parliament for Wimbledon from 1924 to 1945. Sir John was born in Eldon House on 21st December 1870. He crossed to London and made a vast fortune. His donations helped to found the Institute of Historical Research and the Royal Humane Society. The impressive local story reads like a Holywood Whittington saga! Sir John died on 5th June 1950.

The Belfast Directory of 1897 records "*The Belfast Hotel in High Street is Holywood's principal hotel. It is an extensive building with large stabling and carriage accommodation. The proprietor, Mr Robert McKelvey, conducts it in the best style at a reasonable tariff.*" The name was changed to Central Hotel in the early years of the twentieth century, however an interesting letter of 28th February 1895 calls it the Imperial Hotel. A lease of 2nd September 1918 indicates that the building was rented to Mrs Elizabeth J Murray for £60 a year, then to a Mr Griffen. The Lynch family became proprietors in the early 1920's. The Hotel with its public bar, restaurant and its roadside petrol filling pumps remained in operation until the mid-twentieth century. Then the old building became an office block with provision for shops and a restaurant on the ground floor.

The Bangor Hotel was a few doors along the High Street, in the direction of the Priory Church. The proprietors were Mr and Mrs Anderson, who continued in business until the 1850's. The building became premises for William Miller's construction business. In the 1970's the former Bangor Hotel building and its neighbours were demolished to make way for the then Housing Trust's apartment buildings.

A few steps along the High Street towards the Priory Church brings the visitor to the Belfast Bar - in the 1920's it became the popular "Old Priory Inn".

In our walk along the seashore to Cultra we met Ann Rowley supervising her Spa and energizing Bath-House. Ann's father was one of the main property owners in the town during the middle years of the nineteenth century. Among John Rowley's holdings was a row of thatched cottages beside the road bridge which crossed the Ballykeel River. About 1840 John Killops opened the Belfast Bar in one of these cottages in order to catch the growing tourist trade. After John Killops died in 1853 his wife Jane ran the business until the 1880's, offering the finest hotel accommodation on the first floor to her happy clientele.

John Rowley used the ground on the other side of the river to erect the two tall round-cornered town houses which have resisted the ravishments of demolition and remain a Victorian feature in the town. The Belfast Bar prospered and soon was extended over the Ballykeel River to provide a room of some thirty square metres, between the bar and the neighbouring tall town house. At first the room was approached from the public house. Soon a door was opened into the street, but not before it received its traditional name *"the room behind the bar"*. Over the years it became a Methodist Chapel, the famous Holywood Ballroom, the Guide Hall and a motor cycle repair shop. In 1982 it was incorporated into the refurbished Old Priory Inn when the Brady family sold the property. The Inn was renovated once again in 1998 and today it is one of Holywood's prestigious restaurants.

The Maypole Bar is situated at the High Street corner of Shore Road. The building dates back to the early years of the nineteenth century and retains its traditional ambience. In 1834 the proprietor was Thomas Read, by 1854 the ground was leased by a Belfast solicitor, Adam Macrory. At that time, the house was called The Duke of York. There are many stories of the part the Maypole Bar played in the Holywood story. During the construction of Saint Columcille's Church the stonemasons retired to the Maypole Bar where they received a bottle of Guinness and an ounce of tobacco when they finished each week's hard work - something by the way of an incentive bonus! Recent refurbishment of the Maypole Bar meticulously maintained the genuine interior of an Irish public house; its amity has travelled over the world.

A few doors down Shore Road from the Maypole Bar was the Cyclist Arms Hotel, which was run by Fred McDonald between the years 1898 and 1907. The house was a hostel for bicycle enthusiasts who had adopted the new fangled safety machine, which arrived in 1890 complete with gears, chains and pneumatic tyres.

The first proper bicycle was invented in 1861 when pedals were added to the dandy horse. John Boyd Dunlop, who had Holywood connections, was a veterinary surgeon in May Street, Belfast. In 1889 he invented the pneumatic tyre so that his delicate son could ride a bicycle in comfort. Dunlop's brilliant idea was to stick a sleeve of Irish linen to the wheel, fit an air-filled tube inside the sleeve and protect the running edge with thick strips of rubber.

The Dunlop Pneumatic Tyre Company manufactured its product in Belfast, but soon removed to the centre of the bicycle industry in the English Midlands. Many of the bicycles which graced the Holywood hostel were made by the Gordon Brothers of Hillsborough, who by the end of the century were turning our seven hundred "racers" each year.

Today, Wine & Company is opposite the Maypole Bar on High Street, at the top of Shore Road. Although frequently refurbished, it still retains much of its character. In the early years of the nineteenth century the building was a row of cottages. By 1849 William Kincaid was operating a public house there with hotel accommodation on the first floor. At first it went under the name Kincaid's Hotel. In 1852 when the town prospered with the summer holiday trade and day trippers arriving on the train, the house took the title The Railway Hotel. Patrick Burns became the proprietor in 1860 and served the public for eighteen years. After his death, his widow Ellen Burns kept the business going until 1897, adding to it a tobacconist's shop in the house next door.
Before the turn of the nineteenth century, the Railway Hotel was re-named the Victoria Bar and more recently The Seahorse Inn. It was modernised in 1975 and again in 1998. Today, Wine & Company is an exclusive restaurant and wine merchant's business. The cigar store and tobacconists was taken over in the early years of the last century by Mrs Sheridan who added a lending library to the business. Recently this building was brought back into the licensed premises.

Nineteenth century visitors progressing along the north side of High Street would have arrived at Mrs Nimick's *"little public house at the top of Killop's Court"*. Then continuing the tour of the town taverns, they could have called into James Gourley's Ale House at the top of Hibernia Street. Holywood people who remember Fahy's newsagents' business and Miss Winnie Barr's grocery store in that area of the town, will recall stepping down into the shops. One wonders how James Gourley's customers negotiated the stairs to the street after an intemperate evening!

Both the Gourley and Nimick establishments have disappeared with the passing years. However, the mid-century house opened by James Withers in Hibernia Street is still open for business. In 1848 Hibernia Street was the town's main approach to the new railway terminus, as Sullivan Place or "the new road" did not materialise until 1870. The foot of Hibernia Street provided a hackney carriage rank for passengers arriving in Holywood by train – so it was natural for James Withers to call his adjacent public house "The Railway Tavern". Trade was brisk, and soon the tavern was added to the growing list of holiday resort hotels. When James Withers died in 1870 aged 90, his wife continued to run the business. Mrs Mary Withers made up a quintet of Holywood landladies – with Mrs Jane Killops, Mrs Ellen Burns, Mrs Nimick and Agnes Mawhinney. One wonders if the five landladies were unique among Ulster's seaside resorts.

In the twentieth century, the name was changed to "The Railway Bar". The buildings in Hibernia Street were demolished in 1970. The present "Railway Inn" which was re-built on the original site, brings to mind the nearby Belfast and County Down Railway. Today, the Carmichael family provide cordon bleu cuisine for every individual taste from traditional to daring on the site of the old Tavern. Yet another refurbishment brings the old inn into the twenty-first century under the destination : Platform Holywood.

Our walking tour of Holywood taverns takes us up Hibernia Street once again and across High Street to the "Old Palace Bar" at Patton's Lane. Here we are in very good company for one of the nearby shops was a Medical Hall owned by our good friend Surgeon Thomas Kelly, whose words of wisdom have been quoted frequently in our text. Nearby Mr Claude Henfrey, who captured on film the early years of the twentieth century, ran one of the first ice-cream parlours in County Down. Henfrey's Holywood home-made ice cream won many prizes. He introduced the first chocolate coated ice-creams to Ireland. The parlour became Tog's Ices, run by the Togneri family. Angelo introduced his Holywood customers to the delights of "knickerbocker glories" and other glamorous sounding confections. It was a regular meeting-place for teen-agers in the 1960's with a coffee bar and jukebox! Nowadays the premises are used for commercial purposes.
As early as 1860 Mr J McMurray was operating as a spirit-dealer in his house beside the entrance to Patton's Lane. The Jefferson family acquired the business and changed the name to "The Old Palace Bar", after the Bishop had removed his Palace from Ashfield to Culloden in 1890. In later years it was known as the Palace Bar and was the favourite house for military personnel stationed in the Palace Barracks. At one time it was the meeting place of the Antedeluvian Order of Buffaloes – the "Buffs". For many years its forecourt boasted a maypole or flagstaff crowned with a weathercock. A few old residents

High Street (north side) showing Bangor Hotel, Belfast Hotel and the Duke of York (Maypole).

insist this was the pole which Crow Nimmick shinned successfully when inebriated.

Patronage by British Army soldiers drew the attention of terrorists – the building was destroyed by bombs in 1974. Reconstruction brought a new name to the town – The Martello Inn. In recent years it has become a specialist wine and spirit store called Winemark.

Returning to our "crawl" towards the maypole, along the south side of the High Street, the visitor came to The White Star Inn. The Trainor family owned the property. It was situated beside the entry to Alexandra Place in a high Victorian semi-detached house. In 1870 the building had replaced the first two houses of a neat little terrace, the remainder of which was demolished in 1999 to make way for an apartment block known as Lesley Mews building. The popular White Star Inn became The Holywood Bowl, The Bear and then The Gallery Bar. Today it is a café bar which specialises in good food and select wines, and has spread its curtilage into the second half of the original building which has been carefully restored.
In the 1850's the visitor would have discovered yet another public house beside Alexandra Place, now long forgotten, as is its name. By the turn of the last century, the building had become premises for the extensive business of the Ballagh family who opened their High Street coal importing firm in 1855.

When the railway line severed the town from the sea in 1865 it reduced pretty little Bath Terrace to a narrow street on the town side of the embankment, leading to the Strand

and Stewart's Place. Until 1850 the unculverted Ballykeel river flowed through Stewart's Place to enter the Belfast Lough at Conaty's Arch. Local entrepreneur Hugh Stewart developed the area about the year 1830. In 1870 Henry Godbey opened his hostelry in one of Hugh Stewart's houses which faced the new railway arch at the estuary of the Ballykeel River. The tavern was acquired by the Conaty family who gave their name to the arch and the public house. In summer time, Conaty's public house served the fishermen and thirsty swimmers who used the nearby jetty. Their best customers in the freezing winters of the 1890's were the hungry stevedores who unloaded coal on the sands at low water beyond Conaty's Arch. Readers will remember that the coal wharf operated by the Holywood Pier Company was silted up by this time. However, unloading on the Strand did not last very long. By the turn of the century, coal was brought by railway and unloaded in the Holywood goods yard. This arrangement added greatly to the price of a bag of coal at the door! Conaty's public house successfully survived the protrusion of the railway embankment towards the sea in 1971 so that the throughpass could be built over the original Bangor railway line. Today, the Seaside Tavern is a traditional Irish public house, providing true Irish hospitality. The building is meticulously maintained in its original condition.

Unlike the Seaside Tavern, the Star and Garter did not survive the construction of the Holywood throughpass. For many years it stood at the Marine Parade end of Bath Terrace. Originally called The Pier Hotel, the proprietor, Patrick Burns, provided superior accommodation for those who continued to patronise Holywood for summer holidays even as late as the year 1870.

Timothy Hevey designed the hotel, his preoccupation with designing for church buildings was evident in its ecclesiastical mode. It was built by William Nimick's local firm in red brick with the yellow polychrome door and window surrounds, which were popular in Holywood public buildings at that time. Patrick Burns died in 1878; he had called his house The Pier Hotel, commemorating the pier which had been commissioned with great ceremony a few months before Burns opened the hotel.

When a tragic fire ignited the unguarded ashes of the pier's coffee kiosk and started its gradual decomposition, the hotel assumed the fashionable name Britannia. As today, in 1893 many Holywood people were sailing enthusiasts. Possibly the hotel took its new name from the Royal Yacht Britannia, which was launched in 1893. By that time, Thomas Archibald was proprietor.

At the turn of the century the hotel altered its name once again. It became The Star and Garter, and was a favourite rendezvous for local sporting gentlemen. In 1970 the attractive old building was demolished by the Roads Authority to make way for the Through-pass.

Today, a walk along the Esplanade brings the visitor to The Dirty Duck. Originally called the Kinnegar Hotel, it dates back to the years when the Esplanade was under construction on the sea side of the new railway embankment. A new road and railway arch was necessary to rejoin the bisected Marine Parade with the town. The Kinnegar Hotel was opened by Daniel Shipp in December 1865, and shortly afterward it was acquired by Charles McCadden, a new resident who had removed to Holywood from Rathmullan in Donegal.

An interesting advertisement of 1874 calls public attention to the sale of Daniel Shipp's Kinnegar property between Park Road, Milton Street and the Belfast and Holywood Railway line.

IN THE LANDED ESTATES COURT, IRELAND

SALE

ON FRIDAY, THE 20th DAY OF NOVEMBER, 1874

IN THE MATTER OF THE ESTATE OF DANIEL SHIPP (OWNER)

RENTAL AND PARTICULARS OF

PARCELS OF GROUND, WITH DWELLING HOUSES, AND PREMISES THEREON

PARK ROAD AND MILTON STREET, HOLLYWOOD, COUNTY OF DOWN

(HELD UNDER LEASE 4th DECEMBER 1865 FOR A TERM OF 900 YEARS)

TO BE SOLD BY PUBLIC AUCTION IN ONE LOT BEFORE

MR. HUGH HAMILTON, AUCTIONEER, AT HIS SALEROOMS,

ANN STREET, BELFAST

AT THE HOUR OF ONE O'CLOCK IN THE AFTERNOON

When Joseph Boyce acquired the property in 1894 he re-named it "The Kinnegar Bar". During the First World War Alexander Steen, the fourth proprietor reverted to the original name, but Holywood people always knew the public house colloquially as "Steen's".

In its early days the hotel served the needs of sportsmen, the crowds and military personnnel who used the nineteenth century Kinnegar Theme Park with its golf course, shooting range, tennis courts and cricket grounds. Holywood's Victorian Music Hall lay directly across Milltown Road. Happy theatre-goers patronised the house after, and perhaps during the evening stage shows!

When Alexander Steen, a sailor himself, acquired the licence, the hotel was favoured by Holywood yachtsmen, the Club having moved to the Kinnegar in 1923. The building was refurbished and became "The Clipper" in 1984. It gained an international reputation for its excellent cuisine and brought back to the Kinnegar some of the nineteenth-century marine vivacity. More recently the Clipper was re-named "The Dirty Duck Ale-House".

Before 1971, visitors entering Holywood by road from Belfast would have seen "Sandes Soldiers' Home" on the cliff-face of the ancient raised beach. Built in 1905, the building was a good example of the popular Arts and Crafts Movement - a style of architecture prevalent in the town at that time. The Arts and Crafts Movement stressed the value of artisanship. Designers felt that the growth of industry and the increasing tendency towards machine production was threatening the quality and especially the individuality of the applied arts in general. The movement attempted to unite the arts in a common excellence of design and sound traditional workmanship. Holywood is fortunate to possess several good examples of the style. Tragically, our best example - Abingdon - was needlessly demolished in 1995.

Sandes Soldiers' Home was a purpose-built community centre for military personnel from the Palace Barracks. After the First World War the building was acquired by the Williamson family, who opened "Loughview Café" on the ground floor. The business prospered and by mid-century it became the "Loughview Hotel". A car hire and garage service was added. After the Second World War the Toner family bought the property and transformed it into a first class hotel called "The Strathearn". The building was destroyed by fire in 1971. Its attractive garden became the site for Strathearn Court - a select private housing development.

Less than a mile along the Belfast Road from Strathearn Court the Windsor Hotel provided excellent cuisine and comfort during the middle years of the twentieth century. Formerly Clifton House occupied the elevated site overlooking Belfast Lough and the Antrim Hills. Clifton was built in the eighteenth century by the Haliday family. The best known member of the family was Alexander Henry Haliday, born in the house in 1806. He became Ireland's foremost field naturalist, and in 1833 published an interesting thesis on "Insect Life" using his observations around Holywood as the basis for the study.

Another famous student of natural history and botany, John Templeton, also used the Tillysburn area for research. In 1795 he found a previously undiscovered species of rose growing on the coast-lands at the foot of the Doctor's Road - now Knocknagoney Road. An eye-witness, Rev William Holmes recorded in 1819 *"the rose formed a beautiful bed to near an acre in extent"*. Templeton cultivated cuttings which, in 1797, won a coveted prize from The Dublin Society, which called it *"Rosa Hibernica - the Holywood rose"*. The plant grows to twelve feet, produced blushing cream flowers, pear shaped cherry red hips and grey-green leaves. By 1900 railway and road construction had decimated the acre plantation to a single hedgerow; Roads Authority completed the annihilation in the 1960's. Fortunately, the last Holywood rose bush was cosseted by Queen's University Department of Botany in the Derryvolgie Experimental Garden. When the garden was demolished in 1993 the uprooted bush was transferred to the Botanic Gardens *"where it still grows among the flaunting foreigners - a greatly treasured modest little plant, Rosa Hibernica - the Holywood rose."* It is believed that Hibernia Street in the town was named to honour the rose. As this book goes to press our local rose has come home and is growing happily at Martello Corner on Victoria Road.

High Street (north side) showing Gourley's, Nimick's and the Victoria (Wine & Company).

Clifton House was demolished about the year 1880 and the elevated site used to erect Knocknagoney House. That huge red-brick Victorian mansion became the home of the McCance family, wealthy linen manufacturers, who contributed much to the life of Holywood town. In 1956 the grand house became the Windsor Hotel under the expert management of Mr and Mrs Harry Toner of Holywood it soon became a leading North Down hotel. Unfortunately it fell victim to the troubled times of the 1970's.
In 1978 it was acquired by the Police Authority to be used for educational purposes. Twenty years later, part of the extensive grounds were given over to the construction of a vast supermarket.
For a short time after the demolition of Redburn House on the Old Holywood Road, the Redburn Hotel occupied the site. Before the new building was demolished, it was used by the British Petroleum Group as a social club for its employees. Now the purpose-built Holywood Nursing Home occupies the location.

The spacious grounds of the Province's premier hotel lie a mile from Holywood town centre at Cultra. Culloden was built in the early 1880's by W A Robinson (1816 to 1898). The wealthy Scottish stock-broker came to Holywood about 1870; as with many other visitors he remained for the rest of his life. Robinson's great house was built in the baronial style of his homeland, with a central tower and spectacular reception rooms entered from a central hallway. From the tower, Robinson had a fantastic view of the entire Belfast Lough and beyond. An interesting feature of the estate was a private entrance on to the covered footbridge of Cultra Railway Station.

The Robinsons bequeathed the mansion to the representative body of the Church of Ireland, to be used as a palace for the Bishops of Down and Connor and Dromore. The old Palace on the Belfast Road was sold to the Government for use as a military barracks in 1887. That year Bishop Welland removed to Ardtullagh and in 1899 to Culloden, which then became the Palace. Bishop Welland died there in 1907. His successors, Bishop Crozier and D'Arcy enjoyed the comfort of the modern and convenient new Palace. During these years the beautiful little private chapel was added and a fine stained-glass window inserted above the grand staircase. In 1923, the Palace was sold to Sir John Campbell, an eminent gynaecologist. The Campbells lived in Culloden until 1955 when the mansion was acquired by the White family who operated a lucrative catering business in Belfast.

Belfast Telegraph for 13th April 1956 records

> *"that Gothic mansion, Culloden, Cultra, once the Palace of the Bishop was sold by auction today with 12 acres of ground for £18,500. The property includes a pleasant little woodland and a big walled garden with greenhouses and a vinery. The question of de-consecration of the private chapel to allow development of hotel amenities is not likely to arise as it is considered that this action was taken years ago."*

Later it was brought into the Hastings Group and The Cultra Inn was built in the grounds. The hotel building was extended to include accommodation suites and the Elysium Leisure Complex. Today the Culloden's five-star grandeur has won for it a world-wide reputation as one of Europe's finest hotels.

We started the story of Holywood hospitality with the seven century Hospitallers in their Priory hostel, offering accommodation to weary travellers. In this essay we have told the tales of the twenty-eight hostelries which have traded in the town over the centuries.
We enjoyed the halcyon days of resort hotels in the Victorian fun town. We envied the abundant liberality of the merchant princes; we acclaim Holywood's endless choice of accommodation, coffee houses, restaurants, taverns and bistros.

So perhaps you would relish a ramble to our modern rotisseries after your peripatetic cruise of Holywood's venerable hostelries. Indeed you may have visited some of them already on the original walk.

Grouped around the maypole you will find an interesting choice of restaurants. At the top of Shore Road the Camphill Coffee Shop has replaced Bell's Home Bakery, formerly the town's first "tea shoppe", here organic foods are the quintessence. The Water Margin (Cantonese) and Ganges (Indian) have replace Chiccarino's American Tavern. Next door, in the old Central Hotel building, is the Lapamanza Steakhouse. Across the market square Jiggery has replaced the Schooner and the nearby Butler's Fish and Chip Restaurant provides excellent cuisine. Turning the corner into Church Road, Dynasty (Chinese) is situated next door to the former Pepper Mill and on the other side you will find Bistro Iona and Panini., and on Demense Road try Rayanne House for breakfast.

A walk up High Street from the maypole will bring you to the Fontana Restaurant, directly opposite the former Holywood Milk Bar - now only a happy memory of local teenagers and bobby-soxers of forty years ago! Keeping on the south side of the road you can sample the dishes available in Wilson's Hot Bread and Coffee Shop, the Sultan (Indian) beside the Gallery Café Bar and Grill, Holywood Pizzas, close to the former site of Henfrey's and Tog's Ice Cream Parlour, Pizzini Burgers, the Bay Tree in Audley's Court and the Silver City Restaurant (Chinese).

On the north side of High Street you may try the succulent delights of Country Fried Chicken, Rita's Kebabs, On Kee (Chinese) and Sullivan's Restaurant in Sullivan Place. In Hibernia Street you will find Ventnor's Gourmet Sandwich Bar, Bobby Mac's Hot Food and the Platform. Passing the former venue of the town's first milk bar in the Kearney building you will come upon the China Inn (Cantonese) and Bokhara (Indian).

Beyond the town centre, near the former Clanbrassil Hotel on Seafront Road is the Cultra Inn which offers casual dining in the spacious grounds of the five-star Culloden Hotel. Across the road at the Ulster Folk Museum you can banquet in the splendour of the Manor House. Here, if your happy group numbers more than fifteen members, you can book for a stay in the residential centre.

Further along the road to Bangor, Crawfordsburn Country Park sponsors the Conservatory Restaurant, the Rambling Rose Café is open for business at Dickson's Garden Centre, and the Old Inn (1614) welcomes you to the village.

To bring our gastronomic tour to an end I should mention two Holywood tea-shops of the War years. In 1940 the population of the garrison town was increased by hundreds of military personnel in billets and barracks. The Redburn Café was opened for the security forces in the single-storey building behind the tall house at the corner of the Square and Hibernia Street. At Laburnum cottage on the Kinnegar, beside the Army Ordnance Depot, a railway carriage became a tea shop with a plentiful supply of home-baking for resident regiments. Traditionally, American "diners" are converted from carriages, even today they are built in the railway style. I am sure the war-time tea shop on the Kinnegar made our American G I soldier visitors feel at home on Holywood's Kinnegar.

So perhaps you will relish many of the restaurants and taverns which carry accolades and special culinary awards. Which ever you choose in Holywood, Egon Ronay's seal of approval is never far away - come and enjoy !

ESSAY XII - TOWN TABLEAUX

Holywood

By fancy led, I oft did rove
To yonder hill above the grove
That crowns the wood and verdant plain,
The fertile fields and azure main
Come, fancy lead me to its brow
That I may gaze on all below.

Thrice hail, you great and generous few
Philanthropists benign and true
That with a firm unwearied care
Unawed by fear did persevere
To check contagion's poisonous blast
And distribute a rich repast.

(Lines written by young Robert Sullivan from the hill behind Holywood House praising those who ordered the happy working of the town in the early nineteenth century)

I raise the curtain on this essay with a picture of Holywood as it might have been had not local government been re-organised in 1973. Like many other small towns in Ulster, Holywood was absorbed into one of the twenty-six District or Borough Councils.

After the Second World War, the Stormont government enacted the Planning Act (N I) Preliminary (1945). Although this Act was intended to address urgent projects and repairs resulting from the difficulties of the war years, the ever-vigilant Holywood Urban District Council immediately commissioned a preliminary planning report, the proposals of which were intentionally planned to fall within the structure and compass of a Regional Plan.

The North Down Area Plan duly arrived in 1972 - Holywood was considered to be a part of the Belfast Urban Area. When the North Down and Ards Area Plan for the years 1984 to 1995 was printed, it included detailed proposals for Holywood. Perhaps the most contentious of these was the inland route to "by-pass" the town.

The twenty-first century greets yet another Regional Plan - this time for the Councils' areas which lie within "Greater Belfast". Formerly "small" was beautiful - now "big" is "better" for those who plan our future!

In the middle years of the war, I remember being taken by my father, home from the sea, to look at the neglected Sydenham by-pass. Work had commenced on the by-pass before the war started and by 1939 had progressed as far as Sydenham railway station. There it ended, in heaps of ashes, a profusion of weeds and crazes of rusty ironwork. I viewed with amazement a road with a field running down its centre; it was the first dual carriageway I had ever seen!

The Holywood Urban District Plan had envisioned continuation of the Sydenham by-pass and the Belfast-Bangor trunk road - motorways had yet to be denominated - on the sea side of the railway. It ran across the Kinnegar, passing Holywood some three-quarters of a mile into the sea beyond the Esplanade, where the main multi-level slip roads into the town were to be constructed. The proposed by-pass 'came ashore' at Seapark, crossing Old Quay Road, Farmhill, Cultra Avenue, the railway cutting and joining Bangor Road at Culloden.

I remember when we lived at Clanbrassil, my parents were denied planning permission for a family bungalow in the corner of the upper garden - *"the proposed new road may stray nearer to the sea"* was the reason given by the Planners for the refusal.

The proposed reclaimed land between the new road and the Holywood shoreline was to be used for a yachting centre and basin, a conference centre, a concert hall and a five-star hotel. The marine park was to be extended to Seapark, where the recreation grounds were under construction at that time. An open-air swimming pool was proposed - excavations for which are still visible in the car park beyond the Seapark tennis courts.

In fact, things turned out diametrically opposite to the Council's plan for our town. In the early seventies an inland through-pass replaced the proposed seaside Holywood by-pass. Redburn Square, Marine Parade, Bath Terrace and several fine houses on Bangor Road disappeared. The railway embankment protruded sea-ward and the Bangor Road re-joined at Croft Road. In 1865 a railway embankment had isolated the seaside town from its golden beaches - a century later the Roads Authority compounded the atrocity, in the teeth of local opposition.

The present-day proposal for the arterial Belfast/Bangor highway is "Motorway Three - M3", the continuation of the road crossing the Dargan Bridge and the Sydenham by-pass. The route of Motorway 3 lies from the Tillysburn intersection over Knocknagoney to the south of Holywood Golf Course. Its route will devour the excellent farmlands of the Holywood Hills to meet the existing Bangor dual carriageway at Ballyrobert.

A land use map which accompanies the Holywood Urban District Council's day-dreams shows Spafield and Seapark reserved as extensive recreational adjuncts and the Kinnegar designed for industry and sewage disposal.

Loughview, Ballymenoch and Olinda were on the map for housing development.

The later North Down survey comments favourably on what had been achieved before re-organisation – that was in the days of Urban District administration – houses for senior citizens, the new Fire Station, Civic Hall, Creighton's Green reservoir, the Secondary Intermediate School [now Priory College], the Primary and Nursery Schools and a Technical College (now the Library). The Holywood Council had built more than eight hundred houses. It had purchased the one hundred and seventy-four acre Redburn Estate for a Country Park and Cottage Hospital. This complemented Lady Kelly's generous gift of the Ballymenoch Municipal Park to the town.

Had the Holywood Council been able to demand the current high domestic rates which resulted from re-organisation, modern Holywood might have sported its own Marina, Hospital, Concert Hall, five-star Hotel, swimming pool, and a Grand Corniche Scenic Highway. I leave you to muse upon the idyll!

Now let us take a brief look at the figures and the way in which local administration has developed in Holywood. Ireland's first official numeration of citizens was calculated in the early nineteenth century. The "census" of 1659 was a political statement calculating the number of native Irish and settlers' families in each of the townlands. Although a 1764 document sets the town's population at 1,671, we should remember that in those days the Parish ran from Grey Point to Connswater, and early head-counts were usually based on the Hearth Tax returns. The reliable count made by Vicar William Holmes in 1810 claims there were 1,255 people living in the town and 734 in the adjacent townlands –1989 residents in all.

An official census was proposed for 1813, however the Grand Juries would not co-operate. Local numerators conducted the census of 1821 and 1831 over a period of several weeks They are valuable but inaccurate.

In Holywood Parish the 1831 Census was taken by Mr H Patten in January of that year. For each of the fifteen townlands it records the number of houses, families, employment, sex and age of individuals. The figure for Holywood and adjacent townlands was 2,760.

The 1841 Census was a single-day project, carried out by the officers of the Royal Irish Constabulary. Holywood returned 1,532 inhabitants.

From 1851 a Census was recorded each decade -

1861 - 2,422; 1871 - 3,462; 1881 - 3,293; 1891 - 3,389

The Urban District Council made returns on various years –
1901 - 3,840; 1911 - 4,035; 1926 - -4,823; 1937 – 5,050;
1947 - 6,345; 1951 - 6,316; 1961 - 8,060; 1971 - 8,011
1981 11,696 -

The 1981 census was the first taken after the Holywood area was increased by the re-organisation of local government, which brought Holywood into the Borough of North Down.

The 1991 Census records that the 8,158 hectares of North Down Borough had a population of 71,832 persons (34,284 males and 37,548 females) living in 26,619 households, or a little more than three households per hectare of the Borough.

In this census, the five wards of Holywood stretch from the Belfast boundary at Tillysburn in the west to Sheridan Drive and the Ballysallagh Road to the east, and have a population of 14,104.

CRAIGAVAD is our largest ward, having 1,928 hectares in which there are 2,698 people (1,342 males and 1,356 females) living in 929 households, or about 2 hectares for each household.

CULTRA ward has 649 hectares, in which 2,689 people (1,334 males and 1,355 females) live in 892 households, or one house-hold per hectare.

PRIORY ward is next in size, with 451 hectares, 2,663 residents (1,270 males and 1,393 females) living in 974 households, two per hectare.

LOUGHVIEW ward has 339 hectares, 3,076 citizens (1,481 males and 1,595 females) in 1,186 households, which means there are three households per hectare.

DEMESNE is our smallest ward having only 180 hectares; 2,978 people live there (1,400 males and 1,578 females) in 1,127 households. This has the densest population – 6 households per hectare.

It will be necessary to await the 2001 Census to obtain a breakdown in ward figures. However, the annual abstract of statistics for 1999 records the population of the Province as 1,688,600 and an estimate for the Borough of North Down as 75,000. Males born in 1998 can expect to live for 74.2 years and females until they are almost 80 years old. Over the decade to 2006 there is an estimated 16 per cent decrease in the number of births, an increase of 6 per cent of those aged between 60 and 74 years and a 15 per cent increase in those aged over 75. A 3 per cent increase in the population overall is predicted. So it seems we shall be able to enjoy our lives in Holywood a little longer as the years pass !

The town lies outside the Belfast Urban Area Stopline, which forms the limit to development of the urban area. The continued application of Stopline policies remains a basic tenet of regional strategy, therefore the future growth of Holywood will be constrained by the policy of containment of the Belfast Urban Area. The Policy will limit future population growth and should prevent the outward sprawl of Belfast. *"The green wedge separating Holywood Town from the reminder of the Belfast Urban Area will continue to be kept free from development, to allow the town to retain its separate identity and character."* Such were the aims of the original North Down and Ards Area Plan. Future generations must continue to enforce the aims, and in fact they are included in the twenty-first century "Greater Belfast Plan".

If you take a walk to the end of High Street you will see the interesting boundary post with a compass device fashioned on its cap. It guards the entrance to the new Gaelic football grounds and proclaims *"Holywood Commissioners 1859".* On the other side of the gate a milepost records *"Belfast 4 - Holywood - Bangor 6".* This is a definite boundary of 1834. The bounds were extended on 14th January 1865 by order of the Lord Lieutenant. Other extensions took place in 1920 and 1946. As we have seen, in 1973 the town was brought into the North Down Borough Council - Holywood's electoral area stretching from Tillysburn to Ballyrobert.

In order to understand the growth pattern of our town and its social administration, we must go back to the earliest years. We have a fascinating pedigree, well worth the hours of interesting study it deserves in specialised books. Here I merely touch the fringes of the subject and offer a few stepping stones for your guidance.

Most commentators seem to agree that from earliest times, Holywood was a natural seat of local government. Probably it was a centre of Irish Druidism, whose Magi held the knowledge of law and advised the local Ri (King). Holywood lay in the Sub-Kingdom of Dal Fiatach and Over-Kingdom of Ulaid - the capital of which was Emain Macha, Navan Fort. Assemblies of the people elected or deposed their leaders - in turn the leaders organised the good government of the people! From the mid-seventh century, Holywood looked to the Priory and later to the O'Neill's of Clandeboye for leadership.

The Anglo-Norman Conquest of Ulster in 1177 replaced this early form of Irish "democracy" with the continental system of land tenure, local government and ecclesiastical oversight. In Holywood, the norm was exemplified by John de Courcy's agent building our Augustinian Priory in the year 1190. In the same way, the visit to Holywood on 29th July 1210 by King John himself and the appointment of John de Saukvill as our Overlord by King Henry III in 1217, showed the colours of the modern way of local government.

The Anglo-Normans introduced the Grand Jury administration system of territorial divisions, which we call *"Counties".* The High Sheriff (Shire Reeve) nominated a Jury of up to twenty-three property owners; one of their main functions was *"to rule on the validity of indictments".*

Royal Charters of James I in the early 17th century required the new proprietor of Holywood, Sir James Hamilton, to guarantee good government and to establish schools and churches in the area.

It is interesting to note that the Grand Juries continued in operation after the settlement in North Down - which in other places was called a Plantation. In 1634 the Jury could levy a local tax for road and bridge maintenance, by 1708 it was responsible for the upkeep of jails and courthouses. In 1765 the erection of county infirmaries was added to its responsibilities. Grand Juries lost their administrative functions under the Local Government Act (1898) but kept a role in criminal proceedings. They survived as Assizes until 1969.

Holywood Cinema, 1934. In 1789 site of Yeomanry Barracks, by 1864 Police Barracks, now Claire House.

Until 1869 in small towns such as Holywood, where an Established Church existed, the General Parish Vestry attended to local affairs. The Parish Vestry could arrange the collection and expenditure of Parochial Rates. The tax was used for poverty relief, control of vagrants, provision of Constables and the Watch, maintenance of streets, sanitation and oversight of public houses. The Select Vestry consisted of members of the Established Church and only attended to Church matters. On the other hand, the General Parish Vestry could include representatives who were not communicants of the State Church - in Holywood such members usually turned out to be the Clergy of other congregations. After 1869 only members of the Church of Ireland could be elected on to the Parish Council; by that time Holywood was governed by Town Commissioners.

Under the Lighting of Towns (Ireland) Act 1828 Holywood acquired Commissioners to undertake proper illumination of the streets at night-time.

The Irish Poor Law (1838) provided a system of relief based on a property tax administered by the Poor Law Commission and Guardians. Eventually the island was divided into 163 Unions, each with its own Workhouse, Holywood being set within the Belfast Union. Although Belfast Workhouse opened in 1841, Holywood's *"House of Industry"* had operated on the Marine Parade from 1810. In the year 1851 the Poor Rate provided funding for dispensaries and other public health matters. Holywood Dispensary *"was founded for the purpose of alleviating the ills of suffering humanity by affording gratuitously advice, medicaments and attendance to such as require its aid, within the town and the adjacent country".* The Poor Law and Poor Law Valuation continued until 1946.

The Local Government Act of 1898 introduced democratically elected County and District Councils. The following year in Holywood the Town Commissioners became the Holywood Urban District Council. For the first time, women were able to stand for election as District Councillors. After 1911, women could be elected as County Councillors.

Today a Rate Collection Agency receives a regional rate and a district rate based on property values. This is utilised by local and central government for domestic and social services.

In Holywood voluntary "social services" pre-dated the modern system by several centuries. Over many years, the generosity of local people is well documented in charity donations. *The Holywood Bequest Fund* was established long before Hugh Wright of Philadelphia remembered his home town with affection and bequeathed the interest on £230 for the poor of the parish. In 1794 Simon Isaac of Holywood House left the same capital sum to the fund. Miss Isabella Eggar of Philadelphia bequeathed £312 to the fund, reserving two-thirds for education of poor children. By 1837 the Kennedy family had donated another £240. The donations amounted to £1,000 capital for the fund, a considerable sum of money in those days.

Income derived from the Bequest Fund was distributed through the *Holywood Society for the Suppression of Mendicity*. Its purpose was *"to encourage honesty, industry and frugality; to relieve distress; to promote a reverent observance of the Sabbath and to better and improve the condition and morals of the poor".* Members met for the last time in Downshire Road's Loan Fund Office on 27th December 1841. The Poor Law Act (1838) had rendered the Society redundant. The Committee resolved to use the fund to establish *"The Holywood Destitute Sick Society"* – its purpose was to aid those *"who could not receive the relief offered in the (Belfast) Union workhouse".* The members divided the parish (Grey Point to Connswater) into six districts and appointed official visitors.

The re-formed Society started life with a healthy capital of £1,048. It appears that subscribers who preferred the defunct "*Suppression of Mendicity Society"* confined their charitable actions to the distribution of blankets and clothing among the poor at Christmas-time. We always have had our independent thinkers in Holywood! Perhaps they were proved to be in the right. By the famine year of 1846 funds of the Destitute Sick Society were running out. On 28th February the Treasurer reported *"Receipts - £72.13.41/2d ; Expenditure £74.5.7 1/2d - Overdraft 12s.3d.* - a veritable Holywood Micawber scene!"

As a result, the members resolved

> *"The funds arising from charitable bequests should be applied for the aid of a larger class than the Destitute Sick Society embraces and that the various Ministers of Religion should have their attention called to cases of distress. It is thereby resolved - that the Holywood Destitute Sick Society be now dissolved."*
>
> *Signed – Rev. Joseph McCormick – Treasurer –*
> *(Vicar of Holywood - 1839 to 1856)*

Surgeon Thomas T Kelly, proprietor of a medical hall near the High Street end of Patton's Lane, who knew all about poverty, wrote in 1850 –

> *"In worthy imitation of many large towns, a Relief Society is established which in times of scarcity, affords wholesome and nutritious food to many needy families. During the severity of winter, coals are distributed among the poor."*

Kelly goes on to eulogize the Holywood Loan Fund –

> *"The Loan Fund has been established for many years to foster habits of industry and frugality; its condition speaks highly for the industrial portion of the population."*

The Loan Fund was a highly successful private bank for Holywood people before the advent of the Northern and the Ulster Banks, founded in Belfast in 1824 and 1836 respectively.

The town sported several Teetotal Societies and an Agricultural Society. It is claimed that Ireland's first ploughing match was organised at Holywood.

A few words on the Holywood Nursing Society concludes this brief account of nineteenth century voluntary social services in Holywood. In the 1870's the possibility of opening a cottage hospital appealed to Holywood residents. On 4th December 1880 a children's bazaar raised over £100 towards the project. The idea never came to fruition, although it was still a local aspiration when the local Council purchased Redburn House in 1950. For short periods, there had been private nursing homes in Hibernia Street and at Salernum on Croft Road.

In 1884 the Holywood Nursing Society was formed to care for the sick at home. A hostel for nurses in association with the Society was built on Church Road in 1903 – today it is the Abbeyfield residence, formerly known as the Dunlop Memorial Nurses' Home. It was erected by the people of Holywood in memory of Dr Archibald Dunlop (1834-1902) Town Commissioner and Medical Officer. This popular medical practitioner, who originally hailed from Derriaghy, built St Helen's on the High Street in 1876.

The Belfast News-Letter of 17th May 1957 records the final meeting of the Nursing Society. When the National Health Service came into existence in 1946 – the sick poor became the responsibility of the Welfare State. The Dunlop Memorial Home was sold and the considerable assets of the Society were vested in the Holywood Nursing Society Trust, to provide annual donations to the social work of the Holywood churches. The benevolent funds of the various congregations also benefit from the bequests of Robert Sullivan. He left £2,000 in trust to the Lord Bishop of Down, the interest from which was to be given to " *the deserving poor, without religious distinction."* The relief was distributed annually at

Christmas time to Holywood folk, whose parents had been born in the parish. The generous intentions of yesterday's independent benefactors are in the best of health at the beginning of the twenty-first century. As with most Ulster towns, each weekend brings teams of voluntary collectors into the High Street appealing for donations for every deserving charity under the sun. Holywood continues to be one of the most generous places in the Province per capita of our population.

As the most important scene in the tableau of any town is the standard of the services which local government and the private sector provide for the citizens, we shall take a few minutes to look at our water supply, gas and electricity, sewage disposal, telephones and public buildings.

Holywood has been extremely fortunate in the provision of utilities from the days of the old Parish Vestry, through the years of the Town Commissioners and the Urban Council to the services supplied by North Down Borough Council today.

WATER

"Water is life the whole world over". As the third millennium progresses, water becomes an increasingly scarce commodity. Fortunately, Holywood has both water and life in happy abundance.

Twelve millennia ago, the water of the Ballykeel River gouged out the valley we call Glenlyon as the ice cover melted from the Holywood Hills. In later days the stream provided drinking water for the Priory and the village.

The spacious terraces and large houses of eighteenth-century Holywood obtained water supplies from private spring wells and large rain-water storage tanks positioned in attics and courtyards. Smaller dwellings had communal manual pumps. In the Cultra and Craigavad areas, families continued to obtain water by petrol and electric pumps until utility mains were laid in the 1950's.

In 1854 Viscount Dungannon, whose family had bought the manorial rights of the area in 1765, provided a public fountain at the corner of Church Road and Church View. The site is now occupied by the gates of the Methodist Church. It was an elaborate structure with wrought iron railings upon which the local children were wont to swing, in a game peculiar to Holywood. The fountain was demolished in 1925. The granite finials, emblazoned with the Hill-Trevor escutcheons, are preserved in the garden at Martello Corner.

On May Day 1865 the newly-elected Town Commissioners undertook the drilling of wells in Church View and Church Avenue. The spring which fed the Dungannon fountain still spills its waters over Church View at the junction with Birch Drive.

The first public reservoir was constructed before 1880 in the catchment area of the Ballykeel River on Upper Church Road. It served a population of 1,000 citizens with

House of Industry (1813) on Marine Parade. Extension of railway to Bangor (1865) created the swamp area.

twenty gallons of pure water per head every day. In 1899 the interior of the reservoir was deepened and the catchment dam raised, increasing the storage capacity to twelve million gallons.

The land around the reservoir was Holywood's first public park. Many Holywood lads with their dads remember Sunday afternoon walks around the old artificial lake and the upper water meadows which supplied it. I seem to remember, when it was completely full, children could race model yachts on the reservoir waters. The boats were launched at the bank from which the wind was blowing, then the competitors ran to the opposite side to await the winner!

In 1921 a second reservoir was constructed above the first, with a storage capacity of thirty-two million gallons. Even this failed to assuage the thirst of the rapidly expanding town! In dry summers the old spring wells had to be resuscitated, pumps re-appeared in the streets and water-rationing came into effect.

In 1946 a catchment area of four hundred acres was acquired to construct the Creighton's Green reservoir. The new reservoir has a yield of a third of a million gallons each day; and it provides excellent sport for the Holywood fishing fraternity.

Re-organisation of Local Government (1973) required ownership of the three Holywood reservoirs and the parklands to be devolved to the Department of the Environment's

Water Service. Eventually, the Department sold the Church Road waterworks, Holywood's first public park, into the private sector.

In recent years, the western part of the town had been serviced with water from the Silent Valley in the Mountains of Mourne.

GAS

Gas and water, in reliable supplies, were early requisites for the comfort-seeking residents of Holywood town. From 1765 the General Parish Vestry had been able to raise money for lighting the streets at night-time to prevent crime. The Lighting of Towns (Ireland) Act (1828) brought the town's first representatives into being, principally responsible for street illumination. The Town Improvement Act (1854) extended their responsibilities.

From 1820 gas lights had replaced oil lamps in the major County Down towns. Newtownards received a gas supply in 1846, Bangor in 1855. In 1856 The Holywood Gaslight Company was incorporated with a capital of £2,000 in four hundred shares which were rapidly taken up by local residents. The contract for gasworks and the laying of mains was given to Messrs Laidlaws of Glasgow. Installation work took three years, the gasometers, retorts and works buildings were situated on the Kinnegar. It is interesting to note how often Holywood exploited the private sector to improve the life-style of the townsfolk.

On the evening of 1st December 1860 the townspeople followed the lamp-lighters round the town as Holywood was illuminated with "the new-fangled gas". The crowd cheered as each lamp sprang to life.

The Parish Church was among the first large buildings to install gas lighting; the Railway Company received considerable criticism because the terminus continued to be illuminated by oil-fashioned oil lamps. The most spectacular gas lights in the town were supported by four huge wrought-iron brackets attached to the Maypole.

The gas mains were extended throughout the town and by 1867 had been taken as far as Craigavad. Colliers supplying coal to the Gasworks were run on to the shore at low water and the heavy cargoes loaded into carts. At high tide, the lightened ships were floated off the sand. In 1855 Captain Harrison, Chairman of the Company, in order to avoid the difficult unloading operation, refurbished the Marine Parade jetty. However, the water depth was inadequate for coal boats. In 1867 the Belfast and Holywood Steamboat and Harbour Company opened a purpose-built coal quay, which solved the problem for a short time.

Gas supply was an efficient method of home heating, lighting and cooking. Many houses had switches beside the doors of living rooms and bedrooms "to switch on the light". Refrigerators, fires, cooking stoves, and water heaters all brought high profits to the fortunate share-holders of The Holywood Gaslight Company.

The undertaking was acquired by Belfast Corporation on 30th April 1937. The Department of Economic Development decided to terminate the production of Belfastgas on 14th November 1985 – the operation plant at Sydenham was officially closed down on 14th November 1988. Phoenix Gas laid its pipes through the old mains in 1999 – having brought a pipeline under Belfast Lough from Newtownabbey to Kinnegar.

ELECTRICITY

Electricity was being supplied to Holywood from the Belfast grid as early as 1924, although the Northern Ireland Electricity Board was not established until 1931. Soon an office and showroom were opened in Sullivan Place, which was extended on to the old Town Hall site in the 1950's and removed to High Street in 2000. The electricity supply was carried through the town on elegant iron poles, regularly painted *"Holywood green"*. The poles sported coped street lights on swan-neck brackets; the naked bulbs magnified by a myriad tiny mirrors. Many of the original poles remain in service – now painted battleship-grey! When the Department of the Environment assumed responsibility for the service in 1973, a policy of replacement with inexpensive wooden poles was adopted.

ROADS AND FOOTPATHS

Roads and footpaths were the responsibility of the Commissioners and Council. Provision of adequate street lighting was merely one of the many safety services the demanding Holywood electorate required in return for town rates. As we have seen, the first action of the Town Commissioners was the provision of additional public water pumps on May Day 1865. At the June meeting of that year, the Commissioners applied to the Grand Jury for a grant to replace the town footpaths. At that time, Holywood roads were constructed from water-worn rounded stones carted from the shore. Cobble-stones attracted layers of dirt and dung. Early pedestrian crossings consisted of flat granite stepping stones, laid across the roadways.

It is interesting to note in 1934 Holywood High Street, at the Sullivan Schools, was an experimental venue for the first officially recognised pedestrian crossing. These were the invention of Leslie Hore-Belisha MP, Minister of Transport from 1931-1937, as a method of safely crossing busy roads. Experiments were conducted all over the United Kingdom. At that time, Holywood High Street was the main artery road which carried all the traffic between Belfast to Bangor. Holywood was a successful site – the yellow globes and road stripes of the old Belisha crossing remain in situ to the present day.

In the eighteenth century, the condition of Irish roads was notoriously bad, in spite of the efforts of Grand Juries and expensive road toll gate charges. Improvements were achieved by John Loudan MacAdam, who gave his name to the successful system of road maintenance first used in London in 1817. The system was superceded by bitumen and later asphalt laid on concrete when motorised transport became popular. One of the first experimental concrete roads in the Province was laid on the Holywood road between Strandtown and Tillysburn. Like the Holywood Belisha crossing, it continues to provide good service to the public into the twenty-first century.

On 18th September 1865 the Commissioners struck a rate of eightpence in the pound on a town valuation of £8,333.11.3d. - it brought in £277.15.9d. and paid for satisfactory public services. In 2001/02 the rates demand is £2.4406 pence in the pound on greatly increased property valuations. Our Victorian ancestors would have been incredulous!

SEWAGE

As we have seen, sewage disposal in Holywood received high praise in the Belfast Directory for 1897. As early as 3rd September 1866 the Government Loan Commissioners had granted £1,000 for the construction of a local sewage system. The firm of William Nimmick, the local building contractors, were commissioned to lay 5,383 feet of main sewers with connections to 350 houses. Although before 1866, night-soil was collected by cart for disposal in Belfast Lough, the Commissioners had to threaten legal action against those who were dilatory in taking advantage of the new arrangements! Today the top-ranking Kinnegar treatment plant serves the town adequately. However, on occasions evil-smelling emissions fall far short of clean-air standards set for the twenty-first century.

CEMETERIES

Today, cemeteries in Holywood rate among the best in the Province. However, in former years the Commissioners were not outstandingly successful in providing public burial grounds for town use.

Perhaps the town's earliest burial place was at Glenview Farm on the Upper Church Road. A collared urn from Glenview was in the Ulster Museum collection in 1965 when excavations of the gravel pit exposed a ring-ditch in which a sherd of pottery (possibly from a Bronze Age urn) was found. There may be a cemetery of Bronze Age burial mounds at Glenview, where our ancestors rest in peace. Three miles away on the Cairn Hill we buried our Princes, some four thousand years ago.

The Priory Graveyard dates back to Laiseran's seventh century foundation. Tradition tells us it extended to Churchfield and even as far as The Crescent area, where a memorial stone dated 1706, was unearthed in 1969.

The familiar stone wall which surrounds Priory Corner was built about 1826. Several grass-carpeted foundations indicate the westward extension of the graveyard during the second half of the nineteenth century. In 1879 the Board of Guardians assumed responsibility for the grounds. After a few years the Town Commissioners replaced the Board and opened 'The New Cemetery' in 1890. It was extended in 1938 by the Urban District Council.

The grounds at Redburn were consecrated in 1950 and extended when all our cemeteries came under the care of the North Down Borough Council.

TOWN HALL

The Town Hall was the most grandiose project of the Commissioners. Before 1872 they met for their deliberations in the Assembly Rooms on Marine Parade. The Commissioners

The fountain (1854), corner of Church Road and Church View, demolished in 1925.

looked to the private sector for financial support to build a new headquarters for the rapidly developing town. A prospectus of 15th June 1871 outlines local need for an auditorium in which to stage concerts, lectures and public meetings, all of which should provide a fair rental income. With the Holywood Loan Fund's promise of £400 and the donation of a free building site, £1,200 was thought to be a sufficient capital sum. Accordingly the Holywood Town-Hall Company offered six hundred shares at £2 each. Public duty was the main inducement; however a healthy dividend was anticipated. Should the project fail, the sale of the building would reimburse the shareholders. The 1872 list of interested local societies which accompanied the publicity literature, included the Pier Company, the Rowing Club, Musical, Literary and Temperance Societies and the Loan Fund Company. The Commissioners considered the support promised by the local societies and the public in general would guarantee a good return on investments. It is interesting to note that the Secretary of the proposed Town Hall Company was Mr W C Praeger.

The new Town Hall was designed by William Batt, and opened for public use in 1876. It was built by William Nimmick of Holywood in the Lombardic style which complemented the adjacent Sullivan Schools building. The Town Library, News Room and Town Commissioners' Chamber occupied the ground floor. Double stairways led to the Concert

Hall. The elegant auditorium provided seating capacity for an audience of four hundred, with a further hundred in the gallery.

The concert hall and stage were completely refurbished in 1917. Murals of Holywood, the pier and the Priory decorated the proscenium arch. Again the complete building was magnificently refurbished in 1938 – two years later it was a burnt-out shell!

In the first year of the Second World War the hall was leased to the Holywood Garrison Theatre.

The Belfast Telegraph for Christmas Eve 1940 records -

> *"Holywood Town Hall was gutted early this morning by the most notable fire in the history of the town. A member of the Telegraph staff who was on his way to the train station, raised the alarm. The caretaker, Mrs Thompson, and her family were extradited with great difficulty. The blazing building made an awesome spectacle in the darkness of the early morning. Its beacon-like glow could be seen far out at sea. Belfast Fire Brigade, the local auxiliary Fire Service, Army personnel from the Palace Barracks and local people made heroic efforts to save the famous old building without success!"*

During the war the Urban District Council operated from offices in the High Street where the Tesco Supermarket is at present. Post-war regulations prevented re-building the Town Hall on the original site.

In the early days of the Second World War the Council had built a Civil Defence gas cleansing station opposite the Town Hall ruins. Cessation of hostilities rendered the ugly brick building redundant. Plans were executed to use the cleansing station as a town library with a council chamber and administrative offices on a second storey. The purpose-built council chamber was oak-panelled, the desks and furnishings carefully handcrafted in oak. The furnishings were removed to the Bangor Hamilton Hall in 1973 when local government was re-organised and Holywood councillors commenced deliberations in Bangor Castle council chamber.

As the central part of Holywood's Festival of Britain celebrations, the assembly hall with seating capacity for 500 people was built adjoining the civic building and library. With its suite of ancillary rooms, the Queen's Hall complex provided an imposing headquarters for Holywood Urban District Council. The official opening ceremony took place on 14th October 1953 by Lord Wakehurst, Governor of Northern Ireland. Queen Elizabeth II and the Duke of Edinburgh visited the Queen's Hall on 9th August 1961. As a special part of the Borough Millennium celebrations, the Queen's Leisure Complex was added to the existing civic provisions for Holywood people.

LIBRARIES

Libraries and reading rooms in Holywood have a long and meritorious history.

In the early years of the nineteenth century, a young Robert Sullivan was reading the daily newspapers to the group which met in the Short Street home of Mr James Hogue.

In 1837 the First Presbyterian Church opened a library in "Gospel Lane" – the amusing title given to the Strand when the congregation moved there from the Sea-Meadows.

Five years later a News-Room was operating in the Temperance Hotel on High Street. When the new Assembly Rooms were built at the corner of Shore Street and Marine Parade, a Library and News-Room were made available to Holywood readers.

In 1862 Dr Robert Sullivan required his representatives to conduct a library for artisans in his National Schools. No doubt, Ireland's leading educationalist remembered the early days when he read the newspapers to the townsfolk in Shore Street.

When the Town Commissioners built the Town Hall on Sullivan Place in 1876, the library, which had operated in the Assembly Rooms, was removed to that prestigious location.

Two years later, the Holywood Parochial Library was opened in the Church School on Church Road; this removed to the Working Men's Reading Room at the corner of Church View and Church Road in 1883.
St Patrick's Library and Reading Room opened on Church View in 1895.

As we have seen, the old Town Hall, with its well-used library, was destroyed by fire on Christmas Eve 1940. After the war, the Urban District Council replaced the public library with a location in the former Civil Defence gas cleansing station as a part of the new civic buildings. This opened on 17th May 1948. The library provided an excellent service to the Holywood people for 44 years in that old building. At re-organisation of local government, the library service was taken into the central administration.

The Holywood library removed to the former Sullivan schools in 1992. It was *"just coming home"* as such a change would have delighted Dr Robert Sullivan, especially *"its use by the whole community, its educational purpose and its free access to learning for all"*. Today, the library in the Sullivan Building is the flagship of the South-Eastern Education and Library Board

TELEPHONES

The Telephone Exchange in Belfast was opened four years after Alexander Graham Bell exhibited the world's original telephone in Philadelphia in 1876. Holywood's first telephones were installed in 1885, the local exchange was situated in the Town Hall. About 1888 the switchboard was removed to the second house in the terrace beside the Priory Church. Photographs of the final years of the nineteenth century show the High Street festooned with wires strung between excessively high poles, all leading to Priory Corner.

My grand-parents were among the first to install a telephone when the lines reached Cultra. The quaint old instrument remained in use for many years. It was fitted into a small box above a writing desk attached to the wall in the hall. There was a cranking handle which the subscriber turned furiously to contact Miss Annie Houston, the exchange operator, who knew and communicated all the latest Holywood news.

The first submarine cable was laid from Donaghadee to Portpatrick in 1893. Ten years later, the Post Office assumed responsibility for the service.

The first automatic exchange in Northern Ireland was installed at Groomsport in 1929.

The Holywood exchange removed to a fine purpose-designed building on Victoria Road. When a fourth removal took the exchange to its present site on Brook Street, the Victoria Road building was converted into a "ranch-style bungalow". Belfast Area transferred to the subscriber trunk dialling system (STD) in 1961. In 1980 the service was taken into the private sector under the title 'British Telecommunications'.

Eighteen years later, Holywood was supplied with the Cellnet system which is available to every house and business premises in the area.

In the town tableaux essay I have tried to illustrate the development of our town. I hope it suggests the debt we owe to those who ordered affairs for community benefit down the centuries and encourages us to maintain the Holywood tradition of public service in the years to come.

SEAL OF THE TOWN COMMISSIONERS OF HOLYWOOD.

HOLYWOOD TOWN COMMISSIONERS
1853 - 1899

The seal of the Holywood Town Commissioners was designed by R.M. Young, M.R.I.A., a nephew of John Anderson, J.P., who was chairman of the Town Commissioners from 1869 to 1883.

At each of the angles of the Gothic trefoil shape is a sphere representing the world of John de Sancto Bosco, one of the founders of Oxford University. John de Sancto Bosco was a philosopher and mathematician of great reputation who flourished early in the 13th century and is supposed to have been born in Holywood.

The Rosa Hibernica is also on the design. This was a new species of rose discovered in the Parish of Holywood in 1795

ESSAY XIII - EARLY DAYS IN THE HOLY WOOD

The Old Crown Memel Pine

It stands in solitary state, upon the jutting coast:
Like some brave faithful sentinel who will not leave his post.
In vain his foes, the elements, opposing him combine;
They cannot force him to bow down, or make submissive sign:
In vain the angry hurricanes to humble him essay:
In vain the wily water creeps to sap his strength away.
He calmly watches whilst around huge boulders shattered fall,
And stands more proud to think that he is stronger than them all.
Alas! Old friend, your day will come, howe'er you fondly dream,
Tomorrow, and you prone will lie, a helpless wave-washed beam.

S R P.

The town of Holywood is situated on the County Down shore of Belfast Lough and is backed by an extensive range of hills which rise gradually from the water's edge to a height of some 700 feet. The Ice Age had a notable effect on the physical features of the area. As we celebrate our entry into the second modern Millennium, it is easy to forget that for hundreds of millennia ice masses were pushing over the Holywood Hills, advancing and retreating until the final melting took place some 12,000 years ago. As the hills became clear, fast-flowing sediment bearing streams gouged deep channels into the hillsides and spread fertile alluvium over the lowlands. Today, the streams are known as the Ballykeel River (Twistle Burn), the Croft Burn and the Redburn. In the west of the old parish are the Yarrow River, Tillysburn and Rory's Burn. In the east, Ballymenoch Burn, the Glen River, Glencraig Burn and Craigdarragh River flow on to sea.

With the final retreat of the ice, Belfast Lough remained blocked for a time and glacial lakes were formed. Probably, a small lake emerged in the Holywood Glen and a large lake at the head of the Lough, where its flood waters emptied through the Ballymaghan Gap, a line followed today by Parkway - the outer ring of the dual carriageway. Raised beaches were formed, indeed much of the town of Holywood is built on the shore area of a raised beach, while the Kinnegar is a raised submarine bank – its sands, gravels and shells resting on thick deposits of estuarine clay. It is interesting to note that west of the town, deposition was the order of the day, while to the east – towards Cultra Point – there has been extensive erosion.

Nine millennia ago our first ancestors arrived on the scene. They were hunters and gatherers who sought their food supply on the forested hills and along the seashore. They hunted wild pig and deer, fished for salmon and eels and collected shellfish, birds' eggs, nuts and berries. Here and there they have left clues to their activities – flint implements and wild boar bones in the Kinnegar sandbank; the possible remains of a six thousand year old dwelling on the former shoreline at Knocknagoney and a family hearth on the landing approach of aircraft into the City Airport. Other Mesolithic sites have been found at Glendhu near the end of the Ballymaghan Gap. Though the climate was pleasant enough, the Mesolithic population was small and the economy could not support large numbers of people.

Radical change came some 5000 – 6000 years ago with the arrival of Neolithic farmers who introduced cereal cultivation and domestic animals to Holywood. On the highest part of the Holywood Hills - Cairn Hill - they buried their important tribal leaders in an impressive stone cairn, possibly other cairns are still to be excavated on that high hill. A small Bronze Age burial site was excavated in 1965 near Church Road, opposite the lower reservoir.

Some hundreds of years before the advent of Christianity the first Celtic-speaking peoples reached our shores either directly from the Continent or via Great Britain. They heralded the Iron Age. This was a time of raths, defended farmsteads, and their stone counterpart, cashels. It was an age of myths and legends, like Cuchulainn and Medb of Connacht, who came to take the Bull of Cooley, and of warring kingdoms.

To show how close we are to our history, let me tell you about Douglas Davis, a member of staff at the Royal Belfast Academical Institution. One summer day, Douglas was digging in the back garden of his Upper Croft Road home when his spade struck stone, nine inches under the vegetable patch. It was an unfinished quern – a small hand mill for grinding corn. Soon Douglas was unearthing areas of cobbling which showed the place where his early Holywood neighbours had lived. Partly overlying the occupation layer, a course of massive stones came to light. This Croft Road rath has been dated to the 6th Century AD and seems to have been occupied for a considerable time by our Holywood ancestors. Later excavation produced some 150 pieces of souterrain ware, perhaps best find of all was Douglas's discovery of a small bronze pin. Imagine his delight! Prehistory and history are indeed just under our feet if we take the trouble to look around us.

Ten years ago Neil and Connor Patterson were playing in the Croft Burn when suddenly in the loose soil around the roots of an old beech tree, the tooth of a straight-tusked elephant appeared! The find is unique in Ireland and comes from the inter-glacial period, one hundred millennia ago. The history of the Holywood tooth is being researched by the Ulster Museum. Who knows what other surprises the Holywood terrain holds for the hunters and gatherers of the twenty-first century ?

You must not think that landscape changes ended with the disappearance of the Ice Age and prehistoric farmers. A stroll from Holywood along the coastal path, past Clanbrassil Terrace to Cultra, only three generations ago, would have given a very different view from the present one. In 1893, Mary K Andrews described marine erosion of the Point Fields at Cultra Bay. She tells us,

> *"Much land has been washed away of which no trace would have remained had it not been for one insignificant landmark, a shaft of Crown Memel pine, 23 feet high, standing on the beach opposite the Point. It forms part of a windmill pump erected in 1825 to remove water from a sandstone quarry situated in the Point Fields. Now it is 50 feet from the high water mark and at high tide is surrounded by three feet of seawater. In 1829 the sea was 50 feet from the quarry and a broad carriage drive passed through the Point Fields to Cultra Quay".*

The eroded fields covered several acres and were used for the tents, marquees and side shows of the nine day Northern Yacht Club Annual Regattas, as we have seen in another essay. The major portion of the pump disappeared in the great storms of December 1894. I remember seeing the base of the stump in the mid-1940's.

Holywood folk – Robert Lloyd Praeger and his sister Rosamund - commented on the interesting shoreline at Cultra. Robert wrote

> *"One of the few exposures of Permian Age Dolomite in Ireland occurs at Cultra. Formerly it was exported to Glasgow for the manufacture of sulphate of magnesia. The red and yellow sandstone was a favourite building stone as it is found in local houses, the Old Priory and in St Nicholas' Church at Carrickfergus."*

Rosamund saw the coastal erosion from the artist's point of view and penned the little poem lamenting the loss of her friend, the old Crown Memel pine shaft, which introduces this essay.

Holywood has rejoiced in a series of names. In pre-Christian days it was called *Bally Derry* – the townland of oak grove. In 819 the Felire of Aengus the Culdee, on a list of the Festivals of Irish Saints, called Holywood *Ard Mac Nasca* – the height of the Son of Nasca, situated on the shore of Lough Laoigh in Ultonia. When King John visited us on 29th July 1210, our town was recorded on a Treasury Roll in the Tower of London as *Sanctus Boscus* – the holy wood - using the fashionable Latin of that time.

By 1300, the taxation of Pope Nicholas translates the Latin into Early English – *Haliwode.*

In the 14th century the O'Neill family restored the Irish name, *Ard Mac Criosq* ; by 1490 this had been abridged to Ardince. Edmund MacCana in "Irish Itinerary" returns to Latin *Collis Sancti Mac Nissi* – correctly this time, as Classical Latin does not admit to the word 'Boscus'.

After the Reformation, an inquisition at Ardquin in the Ards [15th November 1605] changed the name to *Holliwood.* Six years later, the Plantation Commissioners recorded the building of a new house for Sir James Hamilton at *Hollywoode*, while in 1625 his cartographer called the place *East Hollewood*. The mapmaker's name was Thomas Raven and he painted a little village called *West Hollewood* a few miles nearer Belfast Ford.

A pilot chart of Carrickfergus Lough showed Holywood as it was seen from the sea in 1693. In this map, the town was situated 4 miles from Belfast and could be approached over dry sand at low tide. The Tillysburn River ran into a wide marsh protected by the Kinnegar peninsula, and the hill behind the present-day flyover bridge was clearly indicated as a navigation mark.

The 1767 map of County Down used the name *Hollywood*, however Williamson's map of 1810 records *Holywood*, as do the Ordnance Survey maps of 1834 and 1859, although a map devised for the auction of Kinnegar sites on 20th November 1874 still reads *Hollywood*!

By the mid-19th century the spelling has become established as *Holywood*. However, most of us continue to call our town "*Hollywood*". My grandmother always said "Holy wood" as did many of her contemporaries. On the re-organisation of Local Government, in the 1970's, the Borough Council encouraged the 'holy' pronunciation, without success.

Now let us take a look at the three churches and the townlands of the old parish, which bounded the Loughshore from Grey Point to Conn's Brook.

Our townlands are -
Ballyrobert – Robert's townland; Ballygrainey – town of the sunny places; Ballydavey – David's townland; Craigavad – the rock of the boat or the dog rock; Ballycultra – the town at the back of the strand; Ballyderry – the town of the oak grove;Ballymenoch – the monks' townland; Ballykeel – the narrow townland; Holywood – the town of the sacred wood; Ballyknocknagoney - the town of the rabbit hill; Ballymaghan – the town of the O'Mahony family; Ballymisert – Ballymajor – the homestead of the plain; Ballymachoris – Strandtown; Ballyhackamore – the town of the big field or the wide ford; Killeen – the little glen; Ballycloughan – the town of the stone house. The townlands on the plains of Belfast ran into Dundonald parish.

Our three churches were situated in Craigavad, Ballymaghan and Ballyderry. In 1626 they were united into the Parish of Holywood.

Cragger Church at Craigavad occupied a site between the Royal Belfast Golf Clubhouse and the Lough shore. It measured 48 feet by 18 feet and was valued at ten marks in the taxation of Pope Nicholas (AD 1306). *It was esteemed to be a Rectory* and possessed a town glebe, a holy well and a graveyard. Cragger paid five shillings in proxies, five shillings in refections and two shillings in synodals. Proxies were the provision of necessary entertainment for a Bishop or other official visitors to the Parish. Refections paid for food, drink and spiritual comfort during the visit. Synodals were payments made by the inferior clergy to a Bishop at an Episcopal visitation. It seems the Bishop did rather well in those far-off days!

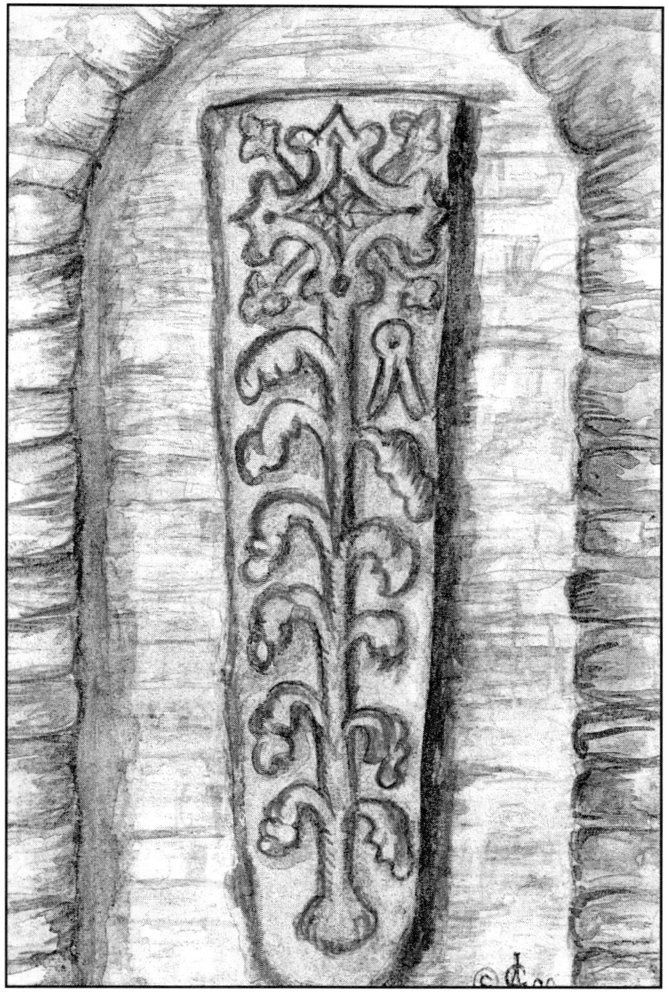

Twelfth century coffin lid found in Priory graveyard in 1879.

In 1622 Robert Echlin, Bishop of Down from 1613 to 1635, wrote –
"Craigavad Church is in ruin, Sir James Hamilton possesses all the tithes."

Cragger was entitled to the tithes from the townlands of Craigavad; Ballyrobert; Ballydavey; Ballygrainey and – according to the 1627 Inquisition – Ballymoney.

In 1844 the tombstone of James McGee, who died in 1714, was standing in the old Craigavad graveyard. Later it was removed to Clifton Street cemetery. When I was an inquisitive teenager, parts of the ivy-clad walls of Cragger Church could still be explored among the trees and shrubs which border the south side of the fairway to the twelfth green of the Royal Belfast Golf Course. I wonder how many club members realize they are playing over the ground where worshippers once walked to Cragger church on the Sabbath day!

Ballymachan Church was at the west end of the Parish – it was the poor relation to the other two. The taxation of Pope Nicholas valued it at a mere four marks. The curate was required to pay 20 pence in proxies, 20 pence in refections and two shillings in synodals. Like the others, it came under the supervision of the great abbey at Bangor. Ballymachan was entitled to the tithes accruing from the townlands of Ballymachan, Ballymachoris and Ballymisert and the plains of Belfast.

The little Church was built beside the old Holywood Road; an Anglo-Norman Motte is some metres to the East. The ruins were pillaged shamelessly as a convenient quarry for local garden rockery stones when residential building commenced in the area. Evidence of the graveyard emerged in the gardens of Moat House. Two stone coffin lids were discovered, ornamented with eight point floriated crosses. One is marked with shears to denote a lady, the other with a sword to indicate a gentleman.

Tradition has it that Con O'Neill, who died in Holywood in 1618, was interred in the Ballymachan graveyard. It is thought that his memorial stone was built into a field wall when the graveyard closed. On 5th November 1625 the castellated mansion on the nearby Motte was the venue for Sir Foulke Conway's Jury Inquisition into the lands which had passed to the Crown on the Dissolution of the Monasteries. When the present Moat House was built, the old mansion became a fernery. As a small child I remember being entranced by its tropical splendour. Perhaps this was the remains of Balimichgen Castle, which an Irish Pipe Roll reported to be in the possession of King Henry III in 1221. Today, traffic on Parkway speeds past what present-day civilisation has made of Church, Castle and our heritage!

Holywood Priory is the best documented of our three churches. The taxation of Pope Nicholas valued it at six marks. Proxies were twenty pence, refections twenty pence and synodals two shillings. To appreciate the fascinating story of Holywood Priory, we should understand the colossal impact in 432 of Patrick's advent into this Druid-controlled land of warring kingdoms.

In 431 Pope Celestine sent Palladius to Ireland to minister to Christians in a pagan country. Patrick returned to Ireland about 432 to convert those pagans to the Christian faith. A decade earlier the Christian British teenager had been captured from his father's farm by an Irish raiding party. After six years as a slave in Ireland he escaped and returned to bring the faith to the pagan Irish living "*In Ultimis Terrae, Usque Ubi Nemo Ultra Est*". Two Latin texts written by Patrick are possibly the oldest documents in Irish history. No other pagan nation received Christianity so vigorously: within three generations the newly formed Irish church was commissioning missionaries to overseas lands. At first these enthusiastic Irishmen went to Scotland and England, then they voyaged to continental Europe where they contributed to the re-construction of Western Christendom after the breakdown of the Roman system under barbarian invasions.

Columcille left Ireland for Iona; Columbanus and Gall left Bangor for France, Switzerland and Austria. Today the Borough of North Down is twinned with Bregenz in Austria where Columbanus founded the church in 610. Euphemistically the great stone from which Columbanus boarded a boat in Bangor Harbour to commence his continental mission now stands beside his Church in Bregenz.

Because Ireland is on the fringe of Europe we embraced Christianity relatively late, and comparatively peacefully! The same fringe geographical position guaranteed that while the rest of Europe descended into what was called *The Dark Ages,* we developed an outstanding standard of Art, Music, Poetry and independence, between the sixth century and the Anglo-Norman Conquest.

Such then is the backcloth to the year 640 when Laiseran established the Holywood Priory, under the aegis of the Great Monastery of Bangor, which had been founded in 558 and was the greatest university in Christian Ireland.

Laiseran appears to have been the son of a local sixth century chief, Nasca, whose royal residence was Galway's Fort at Ballymiscaw. Although this magnificent rath was desecrated by the construction of a silo in 1984, letters patent of 1620 identify it as *Ballisnesca – the homestead of Nesca.* Most likely, Laiseran commenced studies at Bangor monastery with his siblings Gobhan and Graphan. They were three of the twelve monks who served their apprenticeships in Spike Island Monastery, founded in 620. Some time before 642 Laiseran returned home to Holywood and established our Priory.

In the ecclesiastical history of the English Nation (735), The Venerable Bede lists Laiseran among the Irish Clergy who received instructions from Rome in 642 regarding the correct method of calculating the annual date of Easter. Laiseran's festival day is 25th October, which by association becomes Holywood's red-letter day. The Belfast directory for 1897 claims Laiseran's foundation was served by four hundred monks. However, the Belfast Directory was not noted for its exactitude! If indeed the Priory was so extended, it cannot have failed to attract the attention of invading Vikings from the year 795, especially as it was built near the seashore. However, the raiders did not have it all their own way as they left some of their companions in graves four miles along the coast at Carnalea.

One positive result of the Viking raids was the preservation of the Antiphonary of Bangor, a late seventh-century collection of Irish hymns and poems written in Latin by Bangor scholars. Before one of the sudden Viking attacks, a sagacious monk escaped with the treasure to Bobbio in Italy, a monastery which Columbanus had established in AD. 612. The manuscript remains in the Library at Milan, in spite of all attempts to have it returned to its proper home in North Down. One might say it is our equivalent to the Elgin Marbles.

The Holywood community followed the Bangor life-style. A circle of wattle and daub thatched huts provided accommodation for groups of six monks – three old and three young men. Continuously and in rotation, one of these "families" was offering worship in song and prayer. Vegetable gardens surrounded the dwellings. There was a large assembly house for communal worship, a school, a hospital, a guest house and a graveyard. The campus was enclosed within a strong wooden fence. Today the Holywood Priory palisade is indicated by the famous "S" bend on the Bangor Road at the foot of Victoria Road. Our little town grew up at the Priory gates on the banks of the Ballykeel River, where the monks' water mill would have been situated. So in Holywood life proceeded with Irish art, learning and missionary endeavour, punctuated with raiders from overseas and natural disasters. Little did our ancestors know the unnatural disaster which was about to occur.

The Normans conquered England in 1066; partly subdued Scotland in 1174 and almost vanquished Wales in 1280. They saw the British islands as a geographical unit but strangely they failed to create the desired United Kingdom.

In 1156 Pope Adrian IV gave Henry II the Overlordship of Ireland. The Pope hoped that the Celtic Church would be brought into line with modern continental practice.

In August 1170 Richard de Clare - "Strongbow" -the king's henchman - landed at Waterford in response to an appeal from a disgruntled Irish Chief, Dermot Mac Morrough, who was begging for foreign assistance to defeat his personal local enemies. The English Henry found the window of opportunity for conquest too good to ignore! Strongbow brought over an army of 1,200 to augment an advance force of 500, under the leadership of Robert Fitzstephen, who had landed at Wexford in 1169. Strongbow's easy success in curbing the native Irish alarmed the king. Henry himself landed near Waterford in October 1171 with an army of 4,000 men to advertise his kingly supremacy.

Six years later John de Courcy, one of the king's young and eager knights, with 300 soldiers and Irish auxiliaries, captured "*impregnable Ulster*". De Courcy thrice thrashed the last King of Ulster, Ruaidri Mac Donlevy, at Downpatrick in February 1177. Then started the exciting De Courcy tale of victory, building prowess and formation of local government in which Holywood played its part. As with Strongbow, De Courcy's astonishing success captured the attention of the successor to the throne, King John (1199). It also caught the envy of Hugh de Lacy, younger son of the Lord of Meath.

The two Norman knights fought the piece out for fully five years; no doubt much to the amusement of the local Irish peasantry! Then on May 2nd, 1205 their royal master granted John de Courcy's hard-won lands to Hugh de Lacey.

De Courcy, never a man to give in without a fight to the end, retreated to his wife's country - the Isle of Man - to recruit assistance. Soon he renewed the war with an unsuccessful attack on Dundrum Castle. Paradoxically, John de Courcy was defeated by the ingenious defences he had invented himself for Dundrum.

Eventually John regained the favour royal; but only as a humble knight, bent on the defeat of his enemy and successor - Hugh de Lacey.

Holywood Motte and Bailey which King John visited on 19th July 1210.

As Irish history repeats itself *ad nauseum*, the de Lacy family soon lost its privileged position and King John came to examine the Irish problem personally. He landed at Waterford on June 20th, 1210 with a grand army and explored the island northward to Carrickfergus. The castle was taken, along with thirty disloyal Norman knights, three of whom were of interest to Holywood. These three were the disgraced Hugh de Lacey and his friends William de Braose, Lord of Limerick and Robert de Weldebuef. From Carrick prison, Robert could see his Edereskel estates stretching from Holywood to Ballyoran on the south side of the Lough. No doubt he wished he had remained safely in North Down !

De Lacey and De Braose escaped to France but Matilda de Braose and her baby son were captured at sea and thrown into prison where both starved to death. It was John de Courcy, the sponsor of our Holywood Priory, now a humble and pardoned knight, who had brought the wretched mother and child to the King.

At this point we lose sight of John de Courcy. However, if you drive the fourteen miles over the Holywood Hills to Greyabbey, you can visit the religious house his wife built in 1193. Affreca de Courcy, the daughter of Godred, King of Man, is buried in Greyabbey - perhaps her famous husband lies beside her.

As we have seen, the King landed at Waterford in 1210 and explored the island northward to Carrickfergus Castle, the erection of which de Courcy had started in the 1180's. King John spent the night of 29th July 1210 at Holywood and the following night at Dundonald where he passed the time gaming with the Earl of Winchester, to whom he lost two pence!

In 1217, Henry III confirmed John de Saukvill, a favourite Anglo-Norman adventurer, *"in possession of Holywood"*. The de Saukvill eight-pointed star appears on the Holywood coat-of-arms beside St Laiseran's cross and the red hand of the O'Neill's of Ulster.

The de Saukvill family enforced the fortification of the motte, and organized the Anglo-Norman system of government and jurisdiction under itinerant justices - a novel scheme for the Irish natives! The new regime attempted to fulfill King Henry's promise to the Pope for the reform of the Celtic Church. Papal legates visited Ireland to launch a vast ecclesiastical building campaign. Benedictine foundations replaced decaying Celtic establishments, Cistercian monasteries were established – one at Greyabbey, another near Ballywalter at Temple Finn, White Abbey was erected. Earlier, John de Courcy had founded the Priory of St Andrew of the Ardes at Black Abbey. Leper houses were built. For the first time, Ireland experienced the good works of Knights Hospitallers and Templars. Fifteen miles from Holywood at Castleboy, Hugh de Lacy established the Ards Preceptory of the Knights of the Order of St John of Jerusalem.

Augustinian Friars took over the houses at Bangor, Movilla and Holywood. Holywood people must have been deeply impressed by the fine stone building which replaced the old wattle and dab structures of the Celtic monastery. About 1190 Thomas Whyte, John de Courcy's Holywood agent, built our Priory for the newly-arrived Augustinian Brothers. Measuring some 78 by 24 feet the beautiful new church was carefully built of Cultra stone ashlar with some red sandstone.

Originally the door was at the village end of the south wall; in the 15th century the west end was re-built and a more elaborate entrance provided. At that time the fine lancet window with ogee arch and square drip-stone was inserted into the rebuilt west gable, and the elegant traceried east window added. The fifteenth-century refurbishment may have been executed when Niall O'Neill introduced the Third Order of St Francis to the Priory. The 12th century windows had been extremely narrow – those nearer the east end are original. However, in the 17th century, several large windows were let into the south wall. Possibly the second refurbishment was under the instruction of Sir James Hamilton when the church was re-roofed for his Scottish Presbyterian tenants. A number of thirteenth- century carved masks or corbels were built into the new eaves-cornice, three were placed outside and two inside.

In 1800 the tower on its square base with bell and clock octagonal upper stage was constructed on the wrought stone platband, which truncates the west gable, a fine example of eighteenth century architectural skill.

In 1879 a thirteenth-century sandstone coffin lid was unearthed in the graveyard. It was inserted into the external south wall for public display. A cross with foliated head and leafed shaft is carved on the stone. The eleven leaves symbolize the six sons and five daughters of the deceased; a pair of shears indicates their lady mother. The North Down Borough Council removed some of the corbels and the coffin lid for display in the Bangor Heritage Centre.

The Priory site has accommodated the Celtic community of Laiseran. Thomas Whyte chose it on which to build a fashionable Augustinian religious house. James Hamilton refurbished it as a meeting house for his Presbyterian settlers. They were succeeded by the Anglican Church in 1661.

Let us look behind the scenes of parish life before the dissolution of the Priory on 1st January 1541. Our parish priest lived in the Parochial House, within the Priory Park. He received fees for baptisms, weddings and funerals, and possibly a good meal after the event! This would have been welcome remuneration, as the local clergy were very poorly paid. The Diocesan priests usually came from families intimately connected with the church, possibly the family of the local clan head-man. Some were graduates of the Studia Particularia – substitute for a university in later medieval Ireland. Other priests were graduates of overseas universities. Although canonically unlawful, priestly marriage was widely accepted.

The Church was a well-ordered community. The local bishop was required to visit every parish at least once each year to oversee the work of the ministering priest, the bishop in turn was responsible to the Archbishop of Armagh for his work. The local congregation's duty was to provide hospitality to pilgrims, travellers and the needy. Some had special guesthouses, some even provided hospitals.

The Priory church court heard suits on marriage problems, libel, debt, disputes over wills, adultery, fornication and perjury. A discontented litigant could appeal to the Archbishop or even to the final court in Rome. Suitable penances were imposed on those found guilty, sometimes the penance had to be performed in public. Churchgoers on a Holywood Sabbath may have seen a local penitent standing at the church door, dressed in white linen, candle in hand, while the mass progressed inside the Priory church!

As we have seen in other essays, fourteenth century confusion in England brought the decline of Norman power in Ireland. The Hundred Years War with France began in 1337. The corrupt legal system, rising taxes and the break-up of feudalism encouraged popular rioting. Most of all, the Black Death by bubonic plague (1348 – 1350) claimed the lives of a third of the population and respected neither lord nor labourer. The whole structure of life changed radically. The Irish and the few overlords who remained were left to their own devices – "*Hiberniores Hibernicis Ipsis*". Without a constant inflow of settlers and a firmly established government, the Anglo-Irish lifestyle fell apart.

Then came the unsuccessful Scottish invasions. Edward Bruce, with grandiose ideas of a Celtic united kingdom of Scotland, Ireland and Wales, landed at Larne in 1315 with 6,000 veteran Scottish soldiers. The Scots took Carrickfergus Castle in 1316 but were completely defeated in 1318. The Scottish invasion showed the native Irish the impotence of their English rulers and encouraged revolt against a feeble government.

Into North Down the O'Neill clan extended from Tyrone, eventually establishing headquarters at Castlereagh. Their overlordship was symbolized in Niall O'Neill's endowment and refurbishment of the Holywood Priory church. In 1490 he established his favourite Third Order of Franciscans in our town. You must not assume this was the first time the O'Neill family had expanded into North Down. During the first half of the seventh century Congal Caech, the short-sighted one, of mid-Antrim Dal N'Aridi was King of the Cruthin, the old Irish name for Picts. Northwards, towards the Causeway coast, was Dal Riada and to the south Dal Fiatach, in which territory lay Holywood and North Down. Although the populations were mixed, scholars generally claim North Antrim and North Down residents were Gaelic and the mid-Antrim people were Cruthinic.

The Dal Riada dynasty had established a colony in south-west Scotland in the fifth century and eventually ruled their Irish estates from Scotland. It seems that in the year 627 the myopic Congal became Overking of Ulaid, that is Antrim and Down, but after the Battle of Moira, in which he was killed, the O'Neill family claimed dominance over the whole of the north of Ireland by force of arms.

The sixteenth century brought revival of English interference in Irish affairs. In 1536 the Irish Parliament made Henry VIII *"Supreme Head of the Church in Ireland"* and in 1541 it conferred upon him *"most willingly and joyously, the title "King of Ireland"*. Between these years, the Irish monasteries were dissolved because *"they remained loyal to the Pope, performed superstitious ceremonies and disregarded the praise of God and the welfare of man"*. The townlands of Holywood Parish reverted to the Crown and the Franciscan Friars were turned out on the country-side. On 1st January 1541 Connogher O'Hamill was forced to resign his charge. He was the last Prior of Holywood. The Government Commission set up in April 1539 decreed that *" the lands of the Holywood Priory, Ballykeel, Ballymenoch, Cultra, Knocknagoney and Ballyderry became Government property for the time being"*, although the Exchequer obtained little additional revenue as a result of the dissolution of the Irish monasteries, superior monks and friars were granted pensions calculated on the annual income of their monasteries.

King Henry's policy was to reject the Pope, but not to destroy the Catholic faith or religion, so parish worship continued in Holywood, although it seems to have ceased in Craigavad and Ballymaghan. That was until Sir Brian McPhilm O'Neill destroyed the Old Priory by setting fire to the roof – a veritable red-letter day in 1572, the story of which we shall read in another essay.

Pump which extracted water from Cultra Quarry. Surrounding land was eroded c. 1875.

ESSAY XIV - ENGLISH TUDORS AND SCOTTISH STUARTS IN IRISH HOLYWOOD

A little town called Holywood

"There's a town called Holywood in the County Down,
A place of charm and great antiquity;
It lies sequestered by the shore of lovely Belfast Lough
Where the hills of Antrim you can plainly see.

And high above the town the Holy Wood looks down
On scenes of quiet beauty and repose;
When the red sun sinks in the west behind the Antrim Hills
With a glory 'ere the evening shadows close."

Written by G A Osborough for his article on Historic Holywood

G A Osborough's father, Constable Andrew Osborough, (1860 - 1942) Royal Irish Constabulary - was the only Holywood policeman to be mentioned in Hansard (Third series, Vol 313 - 4th April 1887.

> "The Chief Secretary, Mr A J Balfour [Manchester, E.] said the County Inspector had given an order that Constable Osborough be transferred and the Holywood magistrates asked that he should be sent back on the ground of his good conduct, local knowledge and good service."

In 1541 Henry VIII ennobled Conn O'Neill, 1484 - 1559, first Earl of Tyrone. The Virgin Queen invited Conn's legitimate son, Shane, 1530 - 1567, to her London Court in 1562.

Shane was as clever and unscrupulous as his English hostess - she was a twenty-nine year old virgin, and he a very handsome thirty-two year old Irishman. Shane arrived in London with an escort of gallow-glasses armed with battle-axes, bare-headed with golden curls flowing down their broad backs. They wore yellow shirts dyed with saffron, large flowing sleeves, short tunics and rough frieze cloaks. Shane and his entourage made an immense sensation in London. At Court, the English followed them around with as much wonderment as if they had come from China or America! Shane submitted to Elizabeth, without any intention of keeping his royal pledges. This flamboyant Irishman was murdered on 2 June 1567; leaving twelve landless McShane O'Neill's to terrorise the countryside.

In Ireland the early decades of Elizabeth's reign were remarkably tolerant of religious affiliations. However, after 1570 when the queen was ex-communicated by the Pope, Jesuits became active throughout Ireland, encouraging opposition to the Protestant persuasion. No serious attempt had been made to enforce the doctrinal changes of Edward VI (1547 - 1553). Queen Mary had restored the Catholic church and clergy but there had been no persecution of Protestants. Now Elizabeth had to act against a counter-Reformation.

The new Queen continued her father's policy of rewarding the outwardly friendly Irish chiefs. In 1567 Brian McFelim O'Neill was granted an English knighthood as "*a good and loyal subject*", even though his vast and scenically magnificent North Down territories were derelict and *"sparsely populated with a wicked, barbarous and uncivil people, some Scottish and some wild Irish"*.

In 1571 Elizabeth's principal secretary, Sir Thomas Smith, a dedicated disciple of Sir Thomas Moore's utopian ideas, was fired with a fancy notion to establish a "*model community in North Down*". The Queen granted Smith "*what he could take in seven years*" provided there was no charge on the Royal Exchequer!" The necessary finance was raised through a joint-stock company and promotional literature for an early '*Enterprise Ulster*'! Sir Brian O'Neill, still profusely professing loyalty, was affronted, even though most of his estates lay vacant and untenanted. In October 1572 O'Neill defended himself by torching the churches where Smith could billet his troops - Bangor, Newtownards, Movilla, Dundonald and our Holywood Priory.

Seven weeks before the conflagration - 10 August 1572 - Secretary Moore's son Thomas had landed at Strangford, bright-eyed and bushy-tailed, to take possession of *"the model community"*. A year later Thomas was murdered. A letter written at Carrickfergus Castle on 20th October 1573 by the Earl of Essex, reports the shooting of young Thomas at Comber. His body was brought to Holywood for safety. Later we shall read the actual letter in the essay entitled "A Garrison Town". Smith's expedition was a dismal fiasco - his model community never saw the light of day.

Elizabeth, who could not brook failure, granted Ulster to Walter Davereux, first Earl of Essex [1541 - 1576]. As with Secretary Smith, the conquest had to be at his own expense. Essex mortgaged his English estates to get the money. He posted garrisons at the Belfast ford and at Holywood, with a Lieutenant Moore in charge. Walter's unsuccessful attempt to colonise the area was the most viscous of all the English onslaughts. His customary tactic was a surprise attack followed by a total brutal massacre. The worst example of his malevolence was on Rathlin Island where he slaughtered all the women and children of the MacDonnell clan, who had been sent to the island for safety. Sea currents prevented Sorley Boy MacDonnell coming to their defence. All MacDonnell could do was weep on the heights of Fair Head.

Elizabeth created Essex to be her Earl Marshal of Ireland and gave him a Barony in Monaghan as a reward for his efforts. The bestiality of Essex laid the foundations for the hatred of the English nation, which still persists in certain areas of Ireland to this day. The second Earl of Essex was Robert (1567 - 1601) who came over to Ireland in 1599 as Lord Lieutenant. At the age of 20 he became Elizabeth's favourite toy-boy - the ageing Queen was 54 at that time, but that is another story of little concern to Holywood.

Again, the O'Neill contested the probity of yet another Sassenach to challenge his manorial rights. They fought it out at the ford over the river Lagan, and Essex defeated O'Neill. The two men reached a settlement in 1574 and the ever-hospitable Sir Brian O'Neill threw a celebration Irish banquet inviting Essex as the chief guest. During the feast the perfidious Albian had his host arrested. Later O'Neill was executed in Dublin on a charge of conspiracy with his wife and his half-brother. After the Battle of Belfast Ford the supercilious Essex had commented scathingly on the local women's ear-splitting dirge for their dead husbands and sons. This was a mere whisper in comparison to the Irish coronach which followed the atrocious murder of Sir Brian O'Neill and his lady wife.

Lex Telionis saw that the Essex incursions came to naught. North Down remained O'Neill territory under the leadership of Sir Conn O'Neill of Clandeboye.

In 1589, by right of Tanistry, the area passed to Sir Brian O'Neill's cousin, Con McBrian O'Neill. All over the country the upkeep of the established churches was neglected - no effort was made to re-roof the Holywood Priory. Even after *" the flight of the Earls"* which was the final scene in the Elizabethan conquest of Ireland, the building remained open to the sky. As late as 1st December 1598 the parsimonious Queen was weeping over precious money wasted in Ireland.

> *"We receive naught else but news of fresh losses and calamities.*
> *We shall not suffer our subjects any longer to be oppressed by*
> *those vile rebels".*

Although the O'Neill Hugh, Earl of Tyrone, had submitted to the Crown in 1603 and was allowed to retain his lands, much to the chagrin of the English army, he decided to go into voluntary exile on the continent. With his ally Rory O'Donnell, the Earls of Tyrone and Tyrconnell set sail from Rathmullen in Co Donegal on 4th September 1607 in a ship flying French colours. Of course, their lands became forfeit to the Crown. Robert Kee records *"It is here that the history of official modern Northern Ireland really begins."*

The London Companies formed *"The Honourable the Irish Society"* to colonize or plant the lands forfeit to the Crown. To this day, The Society continues to fulfill its commission with amazing efficiency. Derry became the London with Derry to its tail. The Maiden City and surrounding country prospered through the wealth of the London Companies - Drapers, Salters, Fishmongers, Haberdashers and all the rest!

Holywood was not part of the 1610 Plantation of Ulster. North Down and the Ards were privately organised settlements of Scots Presbyterians. Hypothetically Con O'Neill remained in possession of Clandeboye for the time being, but Con O'Neill was a yesterday's man, and could not comprehend the brave new world of the seventeenth century, which was dawning over North Down. He squandered a vast inheritance and is thought to have died at Holywood in 1618. He was interred in the old graveyard at

First Presbyterian Church, Bangor Road, built 1842.

Ballymaghan, where his gravestone was found built into a field wall.
Richard Hayward wrote of O'Neill –

> *"There's little known of him round the hills of Castlereagh,*
> *And the grass has hid his grey old home this many's a day:*
> *But they tell me out at Holywood they sometimes see the man*
> *Late afoot and sorrowing for his yellow-haired Clan."*

As we shall see, two years before his death Con transferred the Castlereagh property to Sir James Hamilton and Sir Moyses Hill, ancestor of the Downshire family. O'Neill's widow Ellice married Henry Savage of Ardkeen in 1628. Ellice and Con's son Daniel were unsuccessful in their efforts to recover the family silver. Daniel joined the Court of James I, fought in the Civil Wars under Charles I and Charles II, and married the Countess of Chesterfield. He became Postmaster General of England, Scotland and Ireland and also Master of the Powder and Groom of His Majesty's Chamber. Daniel O'Neill died in 1663, aged 60 years, and was interred at Brompton, England. It seems he never wanted to return to the grey old home at Castlereagh or worship in the family pew at Holywood.

Now let us re-trace our steps to discover how Daniel O'Neill's father lost Holywood and his North Down estates.

Parish Church, Church Road, built 1844.

James Hamilton was the son of the Presbyterian Minister of Dunlop, Argyle, in Scotland – Rev. Hans Hamilton. With another Glasgow University graduate, James Fullerton, he came to Dublin in 1587, ostensibly to open *"a Latin school"*. In reality, they came *"to negotiate among the gentry and nobility of Ireland for promoting the knowledge and right of King James' interest and title to the Crown of England after the death of Queen Elizabeth"*. In other words, Hamilton and Fullerton were spies for James IV, King of Scotland.

Their Dublin school was successful and even attracted the patronage of James Usher, later Archbishop of Dublin. The two schoolmasters were well rewarded – both were knighted; Fullerton became Ambassador to France. Later Hamilton became Viscount Clandeboye, owner of the broad acres of Holywood, Bangor, Ballywalter, Ballyhalbert, Craigavad and Dundonald with interests in Cavan and Killyleagh.

Rev Andrew Stewart of Donaghadee, whose father came to Ulster with Hamilton's first settlers, recorded the dramatic story of how Hamilton had gained possession of the O'Neill lands.

It seems a few months before the death of Queen Elizabeth some of Con O'Neill's servants killed a soldier in Belfast town when they were bringing back wine for a banquet at Castle Reagh. Con was accused of levying war against the Queen and imprisoned in Carrickfergus Castle. Through the tact of his wife, O'Neill managed to escape. While visiting her husband in prison the good lady brought him

> *"two big cheeses, the meat being neatly taken out and filled with cords. These she left him to hank himself down from a window when, by moonshine, he might see a boat ready to carry him over to Bangor".*

At Bangor Con lay concealed in an old steeple. Most likely the steeple cache was the tower of Bangor Abbey. From Bangor harbour Hugh Montgomery, Laird of Braidstone, effected Con O'Neill's escape to Scotland. Montgomery sought the aid of James Hamilton to secure a royal pardon for the refugee. In return, Con agreed that each of his benefactors would receive parts of his lands in North Down. King James granted a Royal Pardon to O'Neill on 16th April 1605. *"O'Neill has his life and a third part, Montgomery has a third part and Hamilton has a third part of Con O'Neill's estate in Down. In this way Holywood came into the hands of Sir James Hamilton."*

Here we should pause for a minute to meet our new King and friend of our proprietor. James I was the son of Mary, Queen of Scots and the unfortunate Henry, Lord Darnley. At the age of ten the erudite James could read a chapter of the Latin Bible extempore in French and then translate from French into English and back to Latin. His speeches were subtle and vigorous – one, a counter-blast on tobacco, was extremely clever! James desired toleration and cessation of religious controversy. His motto was *"Beati Pacifici"*. Perhaps tactless and conceited, he is considered the most learned man ever to occupy the English throne. Louis of France considered him *"the wisest fool in Christendom"*.

Sir James Hamilton received North Down by Royal Patents in the early years of the seventeenth century *"from the creeks of Groomsport to the sea roads of Holywood; from the Lough shore to the Holywood Hills."* The area represents approximately the present extent of the Borough of North Down. Conditions of the Royal Patents required our proprietor to provide churches, schools, markets and suitable settlers to populate the estates.

About 1609 Sir James began the exciting experiment of reviving Holywood – a place which already had a history of some thousand years. The O'Gilmores, the local native Irish tribe, must have watched the canny settlers with some amusement, as the Scots accustomed themselves to their new situations. Craftsmen, tradesmen, farmers, labourers and speculators paid the eight pence fare to the boatman for passage from Portpatrick to Donaghadee.

Rev Andrew Stewart, who told us how Hamilton won his land grant, described the "blow-ins" as they disembarked at Bangor Quay–

> *"the scum of both nations who for debt or breaking and fleeing from justice or seeking shelter, came hither".*

To the Scottish settlers it seemed as if they were American colonists being observed by Red Indian Aborigines; except that the sea voyage from the old country lasted hours rather than weeks.

They took up their allotments, set up shops and built cabins. Perhaps the foundations of Farmhill Cottage at Marino date back to those early days, and possibly parts of other Holywood farmsteads, considering it was only twelve generations ago.

In 1625 Hamilton commissioned Thomas Raven to paint a set of water-coloured maps of the estates. This beautiful collection is carefully preserved in Bangor Castle Heritage Centre. Raven portrayed East Holywood as a village of some forty cottages, meeting at a crossroads, where a high maypole stood. The eastern stretch of the wide main street provided a market place. Mill Street, Shore Street, Hibernia Street and the Strand show their early emergence into history. The Ballykeel river divides East Hollewood from the church, already re-roofed and surmounted with cross finials, perhaps the decorations were by artistic licence!

The name of the surrounding area is shown as Ballederre. On the west a road leads towards Knocknagone, eastwards another path goes to Ballymenaght. Apparently Brook Street and the back avenue to Martello Terrace are the old Ballymenaght Road leading towards Bangor. The Cuney Borrow (Kinnegar) is drawn as a peninsula and beautifully decorated with little rabbits. On another page, Raven shows West Holywood a couple of miles along the road to Belfast. It is a small village - a high mast with cross-tree stands at its center. The road system suggests the situation of West Holywood was the high ground, later called Bunker Hill. An earlier map drawn in 1580 shows Holywood Abbey marked on this situation and Haliwood Abbye indicated further eastwards along the coast. The 1767 map gives the name Strandtown to West Holywood. In 1850 Kelly describes our homologous village - West Holywood as

> *"an obscure hamlet possessing no objects of interest further than being surrounded by a beautiful district of most fertile soil which extends to the Hills of Castle Reagh".*

Sir James Hamilton sponsored other town settlements - Bangor, Dundonald and Ballywalter; they developed as quickly as Holywood. News of sweet success got back to Scotland and encouraged additional settlers to follow their friends - to such an extent that over forty immigrant families overflowed to Hamilton's land interests in County Cavan.

Sir James appointed schoolmasters and clergy in each of his North Down towns. At that time, called the "Prescopalian period", Presbyterian clergy possessed the churches and tithes, though they did not use the liturgy or conform to the usage of the Established Protestant Episcopal Church. North Down settlers were Presbyterians and their ministers came with them from their home parishes in Scotland. The Presbyterian Church was established by Act of Parliament (114 Act James VI Parl 12 Anno 1592). These early Presbyterian ministers were comprehended within the State Church of Ireland, established by Henry VIII in 1536. They conferred with the Bishop concerning the common interests of religion; some were members of the Convocation.

St. Colmcille's Church, High Street, built 1847. Destroyed by fire 1989.

Robert Echlin, ordained in 1601 by Dunfermline Presbytery in Scotland and consecrated Bishop of Down and Connor in 1613, ordained Robert Cunningham on 9th November 1615 into the Parish of Holywood. On 9th November 1619 he ordained John Lowthian in Dundonald. On 3rd March 1626, James Hamilton - Sir James' nephew - was ordained in Ballywalter. The same Bishop ordained Robert Blair on 10 July 1623 in Bangor to replace the deceased Dean Gibson. Blair had been Professor of Greek at Glasgow University; he came to a large Irish congregation of twelve hundred communicants.

All went well in Holywood Priory Church until William Laud, Archbishop of Canterbury and the Lord Deputy, Sir Thomas Wentworth, procured the Act of Conformity. In 1636 Rev Robert Cunningham of Holywood was deposed for refusing to sign the 'Canons'.

Kelly records an important event which occurred in Holywood on 8th or 9th April 1644, eight years after Cunningham's removal from the parish.

> *"An eminent minister of the Church of Scotland, Rev Patrick Adair, was sent over to administer the Solemn League and Covenant in Ulster. The object of the Covenant was to declare allegiance to the Throne of England and for the protection of the Protestant religion, etc."*

After a sermon preached by Patrick Adair the Covenant was subscribed by the parishioners. The Holywood document is in safe keeping in the Ulster Museum. Descendants of some of the subscribing families are still resident in the area.

An article in the Centenary Volume of the Belfast Natural History and Philosophical Society records seventeen of the sixty-four names subscribed on the Holywood pages of the Covenant. It claims there were many more signatures on the pages which have been lost.

The seventeenth century document was presented to the Society by Mr Morgan Jellet, a descendant of an officer in Cromwell's Army, who later received a land-grant in County Down.

Many of the signatures are very difficult to decipher and in places the writing is in faded ink. The Holywood people whom the Society chooses to record are - William Adair, Charles Hall, John Wright, Thomas Reid, Thomas Baillie, Alexander Waddell, John McCormick, John Waugh, John Scott, John McBride, James Fairlie, Thomas Russell, John Pentland, Alexander Gillespie, John Martin, James Webster and John McClelland.

A census of the fifteen Holywood townlands in 1659 indicates that there were forty-four Irish families and one hundred and three families of Scottish and English settlers in Holywood. However, by 1659 peace had been restored. An Irish rebellion and the signing of the Covenant were events in the past history of a rapidly developing society.

In 1641 the native Irish had revolted and a Scots army was brought over to quell the rebellion. We shall look more closely at the Holywood Massacre when we come to the Colmcille story. Rev Thomas Peebles, Presbyterian chaplain to the Earl of Eglinton's Regiment, was inducted into the charge of Holywood in 1645.

When the monarchy was restored in 1660 conformity to the Protestant Established Church of Ireland again became an issue. Bishop Jeremy Taylor, (1661-1667) declared vacant all cures where Presbyterian clergy were in charge. A Conformist, Rev George Wallace, was inducted into the Holywood Parish on 12th December 1661. The Presbyterians were evicted to sing their melancholy metric psalms on the sea meadows at the foot of Shore Street, an area long ago eroded by marine intrusion.

During the next one hundred and eighty years the Established Church worshipped in the Old Priory. The building was little altered until 1800 when the bell tower was erected over the west door.

The third report of the Ecclesiastical Commissioners, 1836, paints an interesting picture of the congregation before its removal to the beautiful Lanyon building on Church Road in 1844. By 1836 the Vicar no longer lived in the Parish House at Priory Park. In 1812, shortly after the induction of Rev William Anthony Holmes (1810 - 1825) a fine new Vicarage was built on the seventeen-acre glebe land situated on Church Road. Some six hundred people claimed membership of the Church of Ireland, although the old building could accommodate only two hundred worshippers. The churches at Craigavad and Ballymaghan had been picturesque ruins for many years. To accommodate the crowds, a gallery was added to the Priory. It has a very narrow entrance, which can still be seen high up on the inside west gable.

Morning and evening prayers were said every Sunday. Holy communion was celebrated bi-monthly and at Christmas and Easter. Tithes belonged to Viscount Dungannon who had bought the title to be our Landlord in 1765. His Lordship graciously returned thirty-six pounds per annum to church funds, which were augmented by various ecclesiastical allowances and rents.

The Select Vestry performed many of the duties for which the North Down Borough Council is responsible today. Twenty members supervised good behaviour in Holywood's many public houses. The Parish owned a hearse; hire of which cost one shilling. To take the hearse out of the Parish cost four shillings! It seems the hearse trade was brisk, for in 1837 the graveyard had to be enlarged. The congregation was extremely generous in its care of the poor and orphans. It was the duty of the Churchwardens to allocate seating and family pews. However, the Bishop of Down claimed for his personal use the *'chair nearest the stove'*, which heated the old building. The Vicar sat beside the holy table. Every few years, the building was whitewashed inside and out. With white tower and graveyard walls glistening in the noonday sun, background of sea and blue hills, our Priory must indeed have been a pretty sight in 1844.

That year the congregation followed the Vicar to the beautiful new church built on glebe land of Church Road. The Priory remained in the possession of the Church of Ireland and provided an exclusive place in which to inter the town's important citizens. In the year 1871 it came under the care of Holywood Town Council. By 1899 the Holywood Urban District Council had assumed responsibility for the old building. Since 1973 it has been in the care of North Down Borough Council.

In the next essay we shall follow the fortunes of the Dissenters in Holywood.

Holywood's Saints

Laiseran, Colmcille, Philip, James
Are very honourable names
To Holywood to do us good
They came, and teach us how we should
Respect each other; live in peace
And pray that others' troubles cease
No child born here has heart of hate
No parent opens up that gate.
Well done, you saints with worthy names,
Laiseran, Colmcille, Philip, James.

C A

THE COLMCILLE STORY

Colum Cille was born in Gartan, Co Donegal about the year 521. While lecturing on Iona, Monsignor James O'Laverty decided to dedicate the church he intended to build in Holywood to this Irish missionary saint. The foundation stone, specially brought from the ruined church at Gartan to our town, was laid on July 28th, 1872.

Columcille, who founded monasteries at Derry, Iona and Durrow, was born into the northern Ui Neill family. In 563 he crossed the North Channel to found Iona, his monastery in the Kingdom of Dal Riada.

Iona remained the centre of the Columban family of Churches until the ninth century, and played an important part in bringing the Pictish kingdom into the Christian Church. After the Synod of Whitby [664], Iona continued to look towards Ireland for inspiration in manuscript art work, stone sculpture and metalwork. In 697 Adomnán, the ninth Abbot of Iona, wrote the life story of his kinsman - Columcille. His book initiated the abundant collection of literature which portrays the illustrious saint.
It seems before he left Derry the saint wrote the hymn '*Altus Prosator*', a copy of which is preserved in Trinity College, Dublin. The words of the hymn were inscribed on the walls of the Holywood church, which was dedicated to Colmcille's memory.

As we have seen, records of the early Christian connections with continental Europe are vague. Nendrum, some ten miles over the Holywood hills, has an early sixth century radiocarbon date. Bangor, the best-documented Christian settlement in Ulster - was founded in 558. Holywood was a daughter-house of Bangor - first recorded in 642. Our other near neighbour, Movilla at Newtownards, is a sixth-century foundation.

Interior of St. Colmcille's Old Church, 1874.

The early communities suffered from the Great Plague of 549, a desolation the Annals of Ulster call *"The Great Mortality"*. The severity of this annihilation may explain the poverty of information available on the infant Celtic Church in the first decades of its missionary growth. No doubt, Holywood suffered severely in the bitterly cold winters of 684 and 695 when the North Channel is reputed to have been frozen.

Another devastating plague which engulfed us, shortly after the Anglo-Norman invasion, was the Black Death (1347 - 1350). In turn, it may explain why England lost command of Irish affairs. Nevertheless, by 1542 Henry VIII was able to dissolve the Irish monasteries, including Holywood, Bangor and Newtownards and by the early years of the following century, James I could establish a viable colony in North Down. The settlement of returning Scots led to the Holywood massacre in 1642.

In the early years of the seventeenth century the Native Irish increasingly were enraged by the daily sight of Scottish settlers occupying the acres of good North Down land they had owned. The feeling spread that they were being made into second-class citizens and forced to accept a series of curtailments to their religious freedom.

Insurrection broke out in 1641; in North Down it resulted in spasmodic attacks on the settlers. The Holywood Massacre took place on January 26th, 1642 at the Island Field, Ballydavey. The village was due south of Carnage or Carney Hill, Craigavad. As happens today, the Government held an official enquiry into all security incidents. We discover the story of the Holywood Massacre from the dispositions of Katharine, Daniell and Owen O'Gilmore on April 28th and May 4th, 1653 – eleven years after the event.

The Government Examiner was Ambrose Bedell. The manuscripts of the Dispositions are preserved in the Library of Trinity College, Dublin. About a dozen families of O'Gilmores lived in Ballydavey village – the headman was Brian Boy O'Gilmore and all were tenants of Lord Clandeboye.

It seems that on October 25th, 1641 Daniell with Brian O'Boy and six or eight other O'Gilmores had been in a skirmish with the *"Scottes"* settlers at Dundonald. About twelve weeks later, Daniell asked a neighbour called James Johnston to accompany him to the mill to get four stacks of corn ground into flour. At the mill some dispute arose over the ownership of the corn and the men did not come home together. Johnston returned with John Crawford of Crawfordsburn, William Damor, Sandy Dobbin, John Watt and four others. Later that evening Johnston's father and Andrew Hamilton of the Fort warned the O'Gilmores that Lord Montgomery's horsemen intended to plunder Ballydavey village. Katharine attested that about two hundred horsemen and settlers attacked the O'Gilmores on that tragic night.

Katharine said James Johnston, Senior, killed her brother Henry and wounded Edmund Neeson. At this point Andrew Hamilton spirited Katharine out of the cottage; she hid herself in the ditch near the front door. From her hiding-place, she saw Abraham Adam kill her husband, James, also Daniell Crone and Thurlagh O'Gilmore. She said Adam took her sister Owna's arm off at the elbow with his broadsword. In all, seventy-three men, women and children were murdered on that wild wet winter night in January 1642. Sandy Wilson helped to get Daniell MacThomas and his father through a hole which he had broken in the cottage wall. Daniell then hid himself at the lower end of the cottage garden, hearing but unable to prevent the slaughter of his family. After half an hour, he fled to the front of James Johnston's house where he managed to parry a pike attack from an un-named fourteen-year-old boy.

Daniell appealed to James Johnston, Junior, to save his life. The Johnstons hid Daniell for three days, then accompanied him to the scene of the massacre where they buried seventeen bodies. Andrew McVolbem and another Scotsman helped Daniell, his mother and brother escape to the Ards Peninsula, and then to Ballynahinch.

Daniell's father was not so fortunate! After his escape through the hole in the cottage wall, he managed to hide in the hills behind Holywood for three days. Then he was taken prisoner by Robert Jackson, the Holywood Constable, who brought him before Captain Alexander Hamilton. The Captain ordered Constable Jackson to lock up the prisoner in Bangor Gaol. However, Jackson killed Daniell on the way home over the Dundonald moorlands.

Owen O'Gilmore avoided death on the fatal night by concealing himself in the lime kiln on top of Ballydavey hill; later he escaped to Glenarm. Owen told the Inquiry that on the night in question their Scottish neighbours were all friendship and very merry till midnight when *"They fell upon ye Irish and strupt them"*. Presumably it was at midnight that Lord Montgomery's horse soldiers attacked the village.

It seems that Katharine O'Gilmore suffered no ill effects from her night in the wet ditch – she escaped to Ballynahinch where the family name continues to this day. At the beginning of the twenty-first century the Island Field is part of Ritchie's farm. The river which ran along the north-east side of the field is culverted, presumably the village well is still there. A local tradition persists that the massacred bodies were buried in the limekiln.

Between 1696 and 1733 various Penal laws were passed by the English Parliament in London and by the Protestant (Anglican) Irish Parliament in Dublin. These were detested by Presbyterian Dissenter and Roman Catholic alike; all deeply resented paying tithes to support the Established Protestant Church in Ireland.

In North Down, the Scottish settlers assured a high Presbyterian majority population – even though many of their wealthy landowners had turned to the State Church for social advance. Parliaments in far away Dublin found it easier to pass Penal Laws than to enforce them in areas where a huge Dissenter majority existed. However, the North Down Roman Catholic population was small and poor. Only one priest was allowed to officiate in the large Holywood parish. He was forbidden to teach the local children and they were forbidden to go abroad to be educated. Roman Catholics could not vote, sit on juries, join the army or practice law. They could not own a horse worth more than five pounds, purchase land, hold a mortgage or rent land on a long lease.

In the later eighteenth century, a more liberal regime ensued. By 1778 laws forbidding land inheritance and long lease holding were repealed and by 1780 the Test Act was abolished.

In 1823 Daniel O'Connell founded the Catholic Association to promote complete emancipation. Two years later, laws were enacted to suppress both the Catholic Association and the Orange Order! In April 1829 the Catholic Emancipation Act was passed by the House of Lords.

The Northern Whig of Thursday, March 19th 1829 records

> *"On Tuesday (Patrick's Day) the foundation stone of a new Roman Catholic Chapel was laid in Holywood by The Rt Rev Dr Colly, R.C Bishop of Down and Connor. A large assembly of persons was present, of different religious denominations, and a feeling of liberality, kindness and cordiality was manifested on this occasion, which is highly creditable to both Protestants and Catholics. It is due to Mr Patton, a Presbyterian, and the person from whom the ground was obtained.*

By 1831 the congregation numbered some 81 souls. In 1744 it seems the only Roman Catholic in the Parish was the coachman of the Isaacs family, who lived in Holywood House. The returns for 1764 record Dissenters - 1750; Established Church - 14; Papists - 7. Before St Patrick's Church was built on Church View, the "Chapel of Holywood" was Mrs Connor's Coach House situated on Mill Street (Church Road) near the corner of Millbrook Street. About 1860 the Coach-house and a row of eighteen cottages were demolished to extend the gardens of Riverston House. Holywood Nursery School occupies the site today. During the summer months, congregations were enlarged by visitors from Belfast. Two other houses where mass was celebrated were Jeremiah Lockhart's cottage at the top of Ballymenoch Hill and Dennis McDonnell's house in the High Street, at the top of today's Sullivan Place. Jeremiah and Dennis were the gardeners at Ballymenoch House and Holywood House.

In 1811 Father Patrick Curran was appointed Parish Priest of Holywood and Newtownards; Father McGlew ministered from 1822 to 1828 when the Bishop himself - The Most Rev Dr Crolly - took charge of the little parish, and organised the building of the new Church. The congregation was attended by the Parish Priest of Ballymacarrett until 1866, when Holywood became a separate Parish under the ministry of Father James O'Laverty, formerly Dean of St Malachy's College, Belfast.

A denominational increase in the 1871 Census indicated the need for a larger church. Mr Robert Read, proprietor of the Belfast Morning News - now the Irish News - offered a site for the new church in High Street, where the *"Lesley Mews Building"* was erected in 2000. The Read family came to live in "Mill Moat" on Victoria Road in 1862; for forty years they were a generous and highly respected Holywood family.

Instead of the High Street site, Father James O'Laverty preferred the green hill at the western approach to the town. He obtained this prime site from Captain Harrison of Holywood House in 1871. The foundation stone of the new church was laid on 25th July 1872. The beautiful building was constructed of white Scrabo and red Dumfries stone. The corbels represented the principal saints connected with the diocese. The nave was decorated in Ancient Celtic ornamentation lovingly painted by Mrs Dillon of Holywood Post Office, whose father, Mr Neeson, crafted the church furnishings.

St Colmcille's was refurbished in 1969. Two decades later came a major Holywood tragedy. The News-Letter for Friday, 25th August 1989 carried the headline - *"Town unites in sympathy as blaze destroys religious landmark".* Thankfully, the headline *"Church rises out of ashes"* followed in Sunday Life of March 21st, 1993

The resultant phoenix is Holywood's most prestigious modern building. It illustrates how the reforms of the Second Vatican Council open vast creative possibilities for ecclesiastical architects and artists.

The re-built St Colmcille's Church gives new meaning to age-old truths in simple ways which call for the response of the whole person in the unity of worship. As The Very Rev

Interior of Parish Church before extension, 1844.

John Stewart, who was inducted as Parish Priest in 1985 records

> *"Quality and appropriateness are present in every part of the new Church".*

The building is circular in shape, enabling the congregation to gather around the central altar. The altar is composed of hand-carved Portuguese limestone, as are the ambo and the baptismal font. The Blessed Sacrament chapel secures the Tabernacle and is illuminated by the magnificent peacock and butterfly window, depicting reconciliation and resurrection. Seven complementary sacramental windows light the ambulatory.

Around the ambulatory twenty-four pillars support the coned cedar ceiling, which rises to a central lantern. The Stations of the Cross, worked in enamel on copper, are approached by the ambulatory. The fourteenth conveys the butterfly symbol, which is continued in the Pascal candlestick and the reredos panel. The modern sympathetic and simple symbolism in the new building recall the High Celtic ornamentation of the 1872 Church.

Fortunately the conflagration of August 1989 did not destroy the tower, which was carefully restored as a campanile. The tower and spire, which rises to 120 feet, were completed in 1891 by a generous bequest from the Read family. Originally glass prisms scintillated in the sun's rays on each of the pinnacles.
Our town is fortunate that it is guarded at each end by ecclesiastical towers and spires.

Outstanding among Holywood's parish priests in Rt Rev Mgr James O'Laverty - (1828 - 1906). Father O'Laverty was made Monsignor in 1904.
Previously he had been elected to membership of the Royal Irish Academy. In 1857 he was appointed Dean of St Malachy's College, Belfast and in October 1866 he was made priest of the newly established Parish of Holywood. Father O'Laverty's major literary work is the "Historical Account of the Diocese of Down and Connor". The scholarship and industry entailed in the preparation were prodigious, especially at a time when there were few sources to consult.

Under the auspices of St Colmcille's, the Church of Christ the King was consecrated on June 29th, 1947 at the corner of Holywood Road and Station Road, Sydenham. Tragically, it was destroyed by terrorist action in September 1973. The congregation bravely continued until 1991. The holy water font and sacarium originally came from St John's Church, Islandmagee, later used in St Patrick's Church, Holywood and then given to the new Church at Sydenham. The cross and a corbel depicting the dove of peace were salvaged from the ruins of the Church of Christ the King. When St Colmcille's was rebuilt in 1995 these were placed in the porch of the new building.

Many members of the congregations of St Colmcille's and Christ the King have greatly enhanced the artistic, scholastic, sporting and social development of the area. Today, Holywood is very proud of the impressive modern church at the head of the High Street which catches the eye of visitors, including those from overseas, as they enter our town. I hope their Holywood visits and holidays will show them that the building symbolises over thirteen hundred years of Christian witness in Ard Mac Nasca on the shore of Lough Laoigh - the town of a thousand welcomes.

DEVELOPMENT AND DISESTABLISHMENT - THE TALE OF ST PHILIP AND ST JAMES

In a previous essay we left the story of the Established Church when the congregation removed to Church Road in 1844. The new church was built on an acre of the glebe land about a quarter-mile nearer the town than the vicarage, which had moved from Priory Park to Church Road in 1813.

The new building was designed by the famous architect Charles Lanyon, who generously gave his expertise voluntarily. It was consecrated by Bishop Mant on 30th April 1844. The Bishop was living in the Palace, which had been built on Belfast Road in 1827, so he took a keen interest in his local congregation. He was an Englishman and called himself *"a perfect stranger"* to the area. He considered that County Down *"resembled many parts of England".* His tendentious High Church opinions did not appeal to the Ulster laity, among whom a growing evangelical tendency was beginning to develop in the middle of the nineteenth century. Nor did he try to endear himself to the two large Presbyterian congregations in Holywood with whom the Anglicans had a very good understanding. Apparently there was mutual accommodation in times of Sunday services, announcements of lectures and so forth. Bishop Mant determined to terminate such fraternisation!

His successor, Bishop Knox, was consecrated in 1849. He was the second son of the Archdeacon of Armagh and knew Ireland and its people all too well! During the thirty-seven years Bishop Knox lived in the Palace the family was involved in every aspect of Holywood town life. He became Lord Primate of All Ireland in 1886, townsfolk of every persuasion rejoiced in his success and grieved when the Knox family departed from the town to the Palace at Armagh. The Bishop's funeral to the Old Priory some seven years later was the largest procession Holywood had ever seen. People of every denomination and none lined the High Street, paying honour to one of our most loved adopted sons.

Here we should go back to 1844 and the story of the new parish church. The clock, some important windows and memorial tables were removed from the Priory to the new building. Later the roof of the Priory was adapted for the new Parochial School, which was opened on the other side of Church Road in 1845. The roof still shelters the Scouts from the elements.

The bell tower and elegant spire of the new building brought dignity to the town, its bells singing *"sweetly to the sea on Sabbath mornings".* Formerly the six bells had vied with Richard Brinsley Sheridan to entertain audiences in Dublin's Crowe Street Theatre. Sold in 1820, they became the playthings of a wealthy Dublin architect. In 1845 they were acquired for the new Church in Holywood. Surgeon Kelly, writing some six years after Lanyon's Church was consecrated says

> *"The new Parish Church is an edifice of striking architectural completeness in the Elizabethan style. It is situated on a most picturesque spot, a few perches east of the village. It is eminently chaste and neat, befitting the sacred purpose for which it is designed."*

In 1852 Telford's of Dublin, organ builders to Queen Victoria, were commissioned to place an organ in the west end of the Church. In 1869 it was re-built but proved unsatisfactory for the larger building. The instrument was sold to Willowfield Parish Church in 1872.
Within a single decade the new building was considered too small to accommodate the growing congregation. Our modern seaside and residential town, served by a railway line in 1846, was rapidly emerging as the capital of the North Down "Gold Coast".

The welcome problem of an over-crowded church was somewhat lessened by the creation of a daughter Parish at Glencraig in 1858. Five years later a second daughter was born at Strandtown where a church was built on Belmont Road. The Belfast Directory of 1863, called it *"Dundela Established Church"* – however St Mark's, Dundela on Bunker Hill was not built until 1878.

Even so, by 1866 the Holywood congregation required a larger building. The firm of Lanyon, Lynn, Lanyon was asked to produce a plan, which would sympathetically extend the 1844 building. Work commenced in 1868. Sunday services continued as usual until the large new nave, chancel and north aisle were completed. Then the old church was opened into the new building. The original chancel became the organ chamber and the old entrance door was removed to the west side of the tower. The Church was consecrated by Bishop Knox on Wednesday, May 19th, 1868. It was dedicated to St Philip and St James, bas-reliefs of whom are carved on either side of the tympanum above the main entrance.

Ten weeks after the consecration service the Irish Church Act became law and Disestablishment was a fact. An Irish Republican Insurrection in 1867 forced the Liberal Prime Minister, William Ewart Gladstone (1868-1874) to consider the Land, Church and Education Reforms, which eventually convinced him that the answer to *"that Irish problem"* was Home Rule. His Land Acts (1870 and 1881) ended the land wars. His Irish Church Act (1869) disestablished the State Church; however his Home Rule Bills of 1886 and 1893 were unsuccessful.

In 1869 membership of the State Church made up a mere eighth of the Irish people. Despite considerable opposition by Queen Victoria, the Conservative Party and many Irish people including the General Assembly of the Presbyterian Church, Parliament passed the Act on 26 July 1869. From 1st January 1871 the State Church of Ireland became a voluntary body governed by the General Synod, with its property and financial affairs vested in the Representative Church Body. It retained the church buildings and school houses. Financial provision was made for clergy in office at the time. The Representative Church Body received some ten million pounds.

The Act meant that Presbyterian clergy would lose the *Regium Donum*, the King's Gift, which enhanced their stipends. To compensate for the diminished salaries, the Presbyterian Central Ministry Fund was established, with a grant of over half a million pounds. The Divinity School of Dublin University and the Presbyterian College, Belfast received about forty-thousand pounds each; St Patrick's College, Maynooth was given over a third of a million pounds. The Non-Subscribing Presbyterian Church received fifty-four thousand pounds. As a result of the Disestablishment of the State Church of Ireland, the Government Commissioners had well over eleven million pounds to dispense – a vast sum of money in those days. Quite rightly, the new representative church body of the Church of Ireland received the lion's share of the fortune.

Over the years parishioners of St Philip and St James have beautified the church interior with memorial windows and other gifts. Such chaste memorials record the considerable number of well-known Ulster business and professional families who have found their spiritual home within the Holywood Church.

In 1872 an enlarged organ was installed by Foster and Andrews of Hull; the same year the vicarage was refurbished. In 1876 John Lanyon designed a pulpit of Caen stone with columns and panels of Connemara, Devon and Cornwall marble. Perhaps this little gem is the finest example of High Victoriana remaining in Holywood – once Ulster's Victorian seaside capital!

That year – 1876 – the Hill Street Mission was opened and the following year the new purpose-built Model School. In 1878 a Church of Ireland mission was opened in the old Presbyterian Church in the Strand.

By 1880 John Baptist Crozier was Vicar of Holywood. He encouraged the Church Choir to attain the superlative musical reputation which it has maintained into the twenty-first century.

In 1883 gas lighting was introduced, on ornate brass standards positioned in the pews. A peal of eight bells was commissioned from Taylors of Loughborough in 1891 – only five of the original peal could be found to send over to England for re-casting. One had been given to St John's, Ballyclare; another to St Saviour's Cathedral in Connor. Some rash commentators think the eighth may have tolled out the passing hours for the Bishop in his Palace on the Belfast Road. That grand house was demolished in 1890 to provide a site for the British Army's Palace Barracks. The Bishops removed their residence to "Ardtullagh" and then in 1899 to "Culloden", gifted to the Church of Ireland by the Robinson family. Culloden, with its proprietary chapel and fine stained-glass windows, continued to be the Bishop's residence until 1920, when "Conway" at Dunmurry became the See House.

In 1894 the walls of the south aisle (the old church) were lined with red brick to resemble the rest of the interior. The year 1912 saw the central aisle pavement laid in richly decorated encaustic tiles. The vicarage was removed from the gracious old house on Church Road to Belfast Road in 1950. The School-House became the Parochial Hall in 1954 with voluntary labour to help equip it for its new function.

In 1965 the organ was re-built by J W Walker of London in the west end above the Baptistry. The former organ chamber became the Choir Vestry.

The bells required a complete overhaul in 1963. They had been singing over Holywood for almost three-quarters of a century. Paul Taylor of the original Loughborough firm personally supervised the project and the peal was dedicated in 1964. The Society of Change-ringers is one of the oldest organizations in Holywood. The change ringers reached their zenith achievement on Saturday, 30 January 1954 when the 5058 changes of "Holywood Delight Bob Major" pealed out over the town for three hours and five minutes.

During the last decade of the twentieth century the church building and parochial hall underwent a complete overhaul and refurbishment. The Grade A listed properties are in exemplary condition and a credit to the congregation, clergy and our town.
The Parish Centre has become the prestigious locale for important local events. Holywood folk of all creeds will long remember with pleasure the great junket provided by the centre which concluded our pilgrimage around the churches to bring in the New Millennium.

HOLY TRINITY CHURCH, GLENCRAIG

"This Church was built in the year 1857 in the reign of Queen Victoria by William Nimick, Builder, Holywood, Mr Farrell, Architect. Mr Samuel J Carson erected this pulpit. Signed by Mr A Boyd, James Rainey, William Spence X - his mark. Dated this 20th day of November, 1857."

This legend was penned in 1857 on an off cut from a plank which had been used in the building of the new Church at Craigavad.

From the days of the closure of the old Cragger Church which was situated beside the present-day twelfth fairway of the Royal Belfast Golf Club, the parishioners had to travel to Holywood or Bangor to attend Sunday services. Miss May Anne Symes of Glencraig House determined that the growing number of families residing at Craigavad, their dependants and retainers, should have a church in the immediate area. The good lady was well known for generosity in subscribing large donations to the people of Holywood in times of illness and difficulty.

Miss Symes came to live in Glencraig House in 1833 – a great Tudor revival mansion all pinnacles, gables and crenellations; she enjoyed her grand house and demesne until her death in 1863. The picturesque little gate lodge was added in 1840, soon to be complemented by the new Parish Church. Beside the entrance gates to Glencraig House on 10th October 1856 Miss Symes -

"granted for ever, free of all rent, the site for the new building to be called Glencraig Church in which the Litany and Rites of the United Church of England and Ireland shall be used and observed."

Miss Symes obtained the necessary deposit into Government funds, the interest on which would provide stipend; she also headed the list of thirty-three subscribers to the building fund which raised £1,164. The original building cost £1,168.

The Church was consecrated by Rt Rev Robert Knox, D D, on Ascension Day 1858. The Newsletter reported -

"The Church has an octagonal tower seventy feet high, springing from a square base and having a bell-cast top. The Church is fifty-four feet long, exclusive of the chancel and twenty-four feet wide and is intended to accommodate 200 people. It has two handsome double-moulded Gothic entrance doors on the south and west sides and is covered with a framed and slop-chamfered roof, stained and varnished in imitation oak, the principals being supported by carved heads. The seats are open and have carved elbows. The chancel is laid with mosaic pavement and the furniture is at once elegant and suitable. The building is heated by a handsome descending stove."

In 1868 the Glebe House was erected, again the builder was William Nimick; it served the parish for almost a century until it was replaced by an elegant Georgian style bungalow in 1961.

Within twenty-six years of the building of Holy Trinity, the growing congregation required an enlarged Church. William Nimick returned to lengthen the nave and place choir stalls in the present chancel.

In 1921 the chancel was extended to provide a sanctuary and an organ chamber was built into the north wall. This area became the Watson Chapel which was consecrated on 2nd July 1972, the organ having been removed to the west end of the Church in 1967. The congregation's centenary had been celebrated by the refurbishment of the Baptistry.

In 1976 the building received a third extension; a fine main entrance porch was erected below the west window.

Sixty-seven parishioners served in the First World War, fifteen gave their lives in action. Two decades later another seven paid the Supreme Sacrifice. Their names are recorded on the Parish War Memorial. In 1994 two members of the congregation lost their lives in the tragic helicopter crash on the Mull of Kintyre.

In 1966 Northern Ireland Railways opened Seahill railway halt, symbolic of the increased population at Martello Park and Seahill. The North Down Area Plan included Seahill in the village settlement hierarchy with an estimated population of 1,100 persons by 1981. Additional houses brought many more children into the area and a larger school became necessary – a new building was erected in the Rockport walled garden in 1965. The old schoolhouse, which had doubled as day school and church hall, now became the Parochial Hall in its own right. The residence became the Sexton's house.

The "village" development at Seahill required re-alignment of Rockport Road frontages of both church and vicarage. The property walls were re-built and title to the car park secured. By the 1980's a purpose-built Parochial Hall was required. It was dedicated on 30th May 1987, at which time the old schoolhouse was sold into the private sector.

It is interesting to note that in the early 1970's Roads Service indicated that the existing dual carriageway from Bangor to Ballyrobert was to be extended to Craigavad Post Office. Glencraig School was to be demolished as it was in the middle of the proposed laneways!

The plan was to link up with the existing dual carriageway from Marino to Belfast – a mere golden mile up the road towards the city! However, in the North Down Plan, the Roads Authority replaced the proposed Bangor dual carriageway with Motorway 3 (the M3) from the Dargan Bridge along Sydenham By-pass through Redburn Country Park and over the crest of the Holywood Hills to meet the Dual carriageway at Ballyrobert.

Holy Trinity Church, Glencraig has always catered for the interests of the young people of the area, especially the Scout Group and the community of Rockport School. In the early 1920's the Craigavad Football and Recreation Club was founded. The field where Glencraig Park is today was rented, a pavilion erected and a pitch levelled. The Club folded in 1954 – the pavilion continued its useful life in the Dee Street adventure playground in Belfast.

The church building is beautifully furnished with memorial windows. Some twenty-four Biblical subjects are depicted in stained glass by various artists. The windows witness to the loyalty and dedication which many members of the congregation have given to their Church.

At first, Helen's Bay Parish was an integral part of Glencraig. The first service in Helen's Bay took place on Whit Sunday 3rd June 1906 - the foundation stone for St John's was laid on 31st October 1909. Helen's Bay became a separate parish in 1962.

In the appendices of William Mercer's excellent book *"Still other seed"* we are allowed a brief look into the personal diaries of Canon Luke, written during the last decades of the nineteenth century. The journals paint a fascinating picture of the Craigavad lifestyle at that time. As the good Canon never imagined himself a biographer, we are given a completely honest view of vicarage affairs. Those who are interested in the Holywood story should read Mr Mercer's little book.

I wonder was C S Lewis thinking of Holywood when he said *"Heaven is Oxford, lifted and placed in County Down."* During the 1950's he spent the first week of his summer holidays in Crawfordsburn. On Sundays he came to Church at Helen's Bay or Glencraig. Lewis must have found Holy Trinity quite in keeping with his idea of Heaven!

METHODIST MEMOIRS

Now our story turns to the Methodist Church in Holywood

'The people called Methodists' already existed in Dublin when John Wesley came to Ireland in August 1747, followed by Charles Wesley two weeks later. By 1752 itinerant preachers had established the first Society in Ulster. Somewhere between 1753 and 1818 Methodism started in Holywood, mostly by those who adhered to the Primitive form, the discipline established by John Wesley himself. In 1838 the Society was meeting in a little chapel situated fifteen feet back from the High Street between the Habinteg Housing Association's Sullivan Close development and Innis Court. It seated about one hundred

Site of the Holywood Massacre, 1642.

worshippers and measured twenty-seven by thirty-three feet. By 1857 the Primitive adherents had sold the chapel to the majority Wesleyan Society.

By 1830 the Wesleyans had organised a community in Holywood and by 1841 they were meeting in *"Miss Rowley's large room"*. Murphy Solicitors' building in the High Street marks the site of Miss Rowley's property. A few years later, the Methodists were holding their services in the Imperial Hotel, where the Lynch Building is today. Sometimes they met in the private houses of the members, and later in the Belfast Hotel, which is now called the Priory Inn. The Belfast Hotel meeting room was twenty-four by twelve feet and straddled the Ballykeel River. It was called *"the room above the bar"* – its High Street door bore the proud signboard "Wesleyan Chapel". Later it became the Holywood Ballroom and in the early years of last century the Holywood Guide Hall.

In 1849 the sign came down and Primitives allowed Wesleyans to worship in their little High Street chapel. However, this arrangement does not seem to have been completely successful. In 1853 we find the Wesleyans were renting the spacious Assembly Rooms on the Marine Parade. Here the Society prospered and in 1858 they bought the Primitive Methodist Chapel with a land lease for 15 years – although the building still remained at the disposal of the Primitives.

In 1868 the Society rented "Church Hill" off Church View as a manse and in 1886 they purchased the house.

In June 1871 a new church was erected on a greenfield site at the Church Road corner of Church View. Within thirteen years the interior was re-modelled to overcome

"its barn-like walls, violent draughts and speaking echo!"

By 1897 a Methodist Mission was meeting in the Bridge Cottages at Craigavad serving a forty strong congregation.

The following year Holywood may have scored an Ulster "first". The world's first cinematograph screening was in Paris on 22nd March 1895, and "movies" soon arrived in Dublin. The Rev Randall C Phillips, who followed the ministry of Rev James Harpur, was taking part in a cinematographic exhibition in the circus at Knocknagoney in 1898, certainly among the first "film shows" in our area.

The Watchnight Service of 1899 saw the opening of an organ commissioned from Gray and Davis of London. In 1922 the Society purchased the field beside the Church and obtained the site of the Holywood Fountain from the Urban Council.

In 1936 the buildings were refurbished and a fine Evans and Barr organ installed. In the year 1952 the manse on My Lady's Mile was purchased. Between 1952 and 1967 mission services were conducted in the Community Centre at Loughview/Redburn.

On 3rd May 1966 a disastrous fire was confined to the Sexton's house. The Centenary Hall enhanced the site in 1971. The congregation undertook a visitation and questionnaire of the Loughview Estate in 1993, the result of which paints a unique picture of that area. The estate was built on the former grounds of Holywood House after the Second World War. By 1983 most of the houses were occupied by the 30-60 age group; there were few families with young children - the majority of young people were in their teens. Half of the families who were visited attended church regularly; other families claimed church connections. Most of the young people were not involved in church life. Although there were few unemployed people on the estate, in general unemployment was considered to be *"a problem"*. Other family pressures were money problems, children's difficulties, communication break-down and loneliness. When problems arose, the minister, relatives or friends were consulted for advice.

In the early 1990's, the congregation completely refurbished the church buildings.

As with all Holywood congregations, the members offered active sympathy to St Colmcille's Church after the tragic fire which destroyed that beautiful building in 1990.

The published annals of the congregation - *"Holywood and the Society of the People called Methodists"* and *"The Continuing Record"* which were set down year by year show why these meticulous people are called Methodists. Today, the Society enjoys a respected place of Christian witness and community service in our town. As they say, *"The best is yet to be"*.

THE SALVATION ARMY IN HOLYWOOD

The doctrines of Methodism inspired the foundation of the best-known worldwide evangelical Christian movement of the nineteenth century.

In 1865 a crowd of inebriated London East-Enders were ridiculing a young Methodist revivalist. It was William Booth. He knelt on the wet pavement and prayed for his persecutors. Such were the humble beginnings of the organization which in 1877 took the name Salvation Army.

J P Birch of Holywood records

> *"On 12th July 1891 the first contingents of the Salvation Army came to Ireland and camped on the mound of the Holywood Rifle Range on the Kinnegar. They had large attendances at their meetings General Booth was present. This was his first visit to Ireland."*

Soon the Holywood Salvationists built a hall in a pretty garden at the top of Hibernia Street.

Here the war cry continued for several years. However, today the special work of the Salvation Army in Holywood is best known through the Sir Samuel Kelly Memorial Eventide Home at Ballymenoch Park.

Ballymenoch House is one of the oldest mansion sites in our town. C J McKissack and J W Kernohan, previous local antiquarians, believe the original house was the proposed building referred to in 1611 by the Plantation Commissioners *"Sir James Hamilton is preparing to build a house at Hollywood and two hundred thousand brickes with other materialles (are) ready at the place where there are some 20 houses inhabited with English and Scottes."* Certainly, a branch of the Hamilton family was living there about 1783, in a residence built or refurbished in the eighteenth century.

The Hamilton family grave was within the old Priory graveyard. However, the memorial stone was removed to the proprietary chapel at Clandeboye House in the nineteenth century.

The mansion was acquired by the Holmes family, who were related to Robert Holmes, the famous Irish barrister. By 1802 it was the residence of Cunningham Greg, Robert Sullivan's sponsor, and in 1863 the it was sold to Sir Daniel Dixon, Belfast's first Lord Mayor.

The year 1913 saw the fine old house destroyed by fire. Sir Samuel Kelly, the famous Ulster shipping magnate and coal importer (1880 - 1937) built the present house on a slightly different site. In 1947 Lady Kelly donated the parklands to the people of Holywood, and the mansion house to the Salvation Army as a Christian residential home for those who no longer wish or are able to live in their own homes.

The house has been carefully maintained and refurbished. In 1997 the new Sir Samuel Kelly home was opened. It provides accommodation for forty people living in five separate family groups, each of which has its own dining and sitting rooms. There are communal lounges, craft and recreation rooms. Magnificent gardens surround the complex. At the Sir Samuel Kelly Memorial, quality care is provided in a homely Christian environment with full consideration for individual needs throughout the community.

PLYMOUTH BRETHREN

Plymouth Brethren in Ireland had its origins in Dublin about 1820 among well-educated religious enthusiasts from Trinity College. They were impatient of rigid denominationalism and intrigued by the study of Biblical prophecy.

The tenets of Unity in Christ and the absence of any form of Ordination attracted a social elite of Anglo-Irish landowners, lawyers and academics as well as more humble folk. Soon the movement spread to the *"black North"*.

The Downshire Road Hall Assembly originated in the building at the corner of Morrow's Lane and Church View. About the year 1858 Morrow's Lane was extended into a long straight track running up the hill to Demesne Road; by 1866 it was called Downshire Road.

The little building had been the offices of Holywood Loan Fund Bank, of which Surgeon Kelly wrote in 1850 *"It has been established for many years to foster habits of industry and frugality*".

By 1855 the Hall became the meeting-house for the embryo Second Presbyterian congregation, which moved into its church on High Street in February 1858. At this time, the building was called *"Mr Johnston's house"* and continued to be used for church meetings until the High Street congregation built its church halls in 1867. Shortly afterwards, it became the home of the Downshire Road Hall Assembly.

A name frequently occurring in the early records is R M Henry, a member of the Belfast Apsley Street meeting and a well-known scholar of the eighteen seventies. His sons were Professor Henry of Queen's University and Paul Henry, the famous Ulster artist. Mr R E Sparks, solicitor to the Ulster Bank, encouraged the young Assembly in its considerable generosity to overseas missions.

After a century of static accommodation, in May 1960 the Assembly removed diagonally to the present purpose-built Hall on the opposite corner of Downshire Road. The old building became the premises of The Golden Age Club which provided social and welfare work among our senior citizens until 1998. At present, it is the business headquarters for a firm of consultant engineers.

The members of the Assembly believe in the Diety of Christ, His perfect Life, Atoning Death, Resurrection, Ascension and Literal Return; the Necessity for Conversion and Belief in Biblical Inspiration and Authority. The Assembly practices the Baptism of Believers by immersion, the weekly celebration of the Lord's Supper and the Priesthood of all Believers.

The purpose of the Assembly is to propagate the Gospel, to practice the principles of the New Testament Church fellowship and to adorn the Doctrine of God. The Assembly relies solely on the promises of God and makes no claim to perfection or monopoly of Divine Truth.

For neigh on a century and a half, the members of the Downshire Road Hall Assembly have contributed generously and positively to the Holywood community, especially in education and youth work.

THE BAPTIST CHURCH IN HOLYWOOD

Before the Baptist congregation came to worship in the red-brick building at the Crescent corner on High Street, it had been used for many years as an Assembly Hall for members of the Plymouth Brethren.

In the 1960's it became The Fisherman – a Youth for Christ mission organised by a group of dedicated young people who sought to help their peers and introduce them into a Christian society. Many years later, in the year 1982, "The Hob", also situated in the High Street, served the same ideal until the end of the century.

Although the Baptists were established in Ireland by the middle of the seventeenth century and greatly strengthened by the religious revival of 1854, a Holywood meeting did not emerge until September 1958, under the auspices of the Mountpottinger Tabernacle.

The twenty-first century finds the Baptist Church one of the largest evangelical and biblical communions in the world, mainly situated in the United States of America. They are distinguished by the belief that Christian baptism should be administered only to believers, and that it should be administered by immersion. Originally they were known as Ana Baptists – *"those who baptize over again"*. that is on the ground that infant baptism is ineffectual.

The original Holywood group met in the Redburn Community Centre, which the Housing Trust built for the residents of the new Loughview and Redburn estates in 1958.

In September, four years later, the members decided to establish the Holywood Meeting as a Baptist Church in its own right. The inaugural meeting assembled in the large hall of the Community Centre on 17th November 1964.

In August 1971 the Fisherman Youth for Christ Hall, at the corner of The Crescent and High Street was given to the congregation *"for the propagation of the Gospel in Holywood"*. Four years later, in June 1976, Rev W Entwistle was called as the first Pastor of the Holywood Baptist Church.

The congregation flourished. Several organisations added to the spiritual life of the membership which increased rapidly in the little hall beside the Johnny the Jig playground. Soon the building was inadequate for the work of the expanding Church.

A prestige property was acquired at Strathearn on the Belfast Road, a short distance from the place where the congregation originally came into being.

A fine new Church was opened on the twenty-fifth anniversary of the foundation of the congregation - 18th November 1989. In 1995 a minor hall was added to the refurbished building.

The happy growth of the congregation over those years speaks volumes for the work and witness of the pastor and officers in the Holywood area. After two decades, the first pastor moved forward into a wider ministry and the Rev Robert Caldwell became minister to the congregation.

The Baptists contribute greatly to the inbringing of God's Kingdom to Holywood; they have gained an honoured place among the Churches of Holywood.

THE CHRISTIAN COMMUNITY

The Christian Community was established in Stewart's Place in 1993. The tall town-house was built in the early years of Queen Victoria's reign and replaced the less opulent properties of John Rowley. The lovely old round-cornered drawing room has been refurbished as a sanctuary chapel.

In Germany the Christian Community dates back to 1922 when students of Rudolf Steiner developed a new practice of pastoral care and understanding of the Gospel. Work commenced in Ireland in 1975. Today, there are communities all over the world. In Holywood another congregation meets at Glencraig, where services are offered in the German language as well as in English.

The life of the Community is centred in the services of the seven Sacraments, by the observance of the Christian Year and in the Gospel and its Creed.

Preparation for men and women who are called to ordination is carried out in the movement's international seminary in Germany.

Rites used by a contemporary community for a modern people are new in character and liturgy. The aim of the Christian Community is to renew religious life through an increased awareness of our need for a spiritual world view as a basis for religious activity.

THE CHRISTIAN FELLOWSHIP

The high houses on Holywood High Street, where once Cowan's garage served the motoring public, had an ecclesiastical connection long before the Christian Fellowship arrived in 1988.

Rev John Poole came to Holywood about 1850, when he retired from Lismore Church and the moderatorship of the former Presbytery of Cork. The Banner of Ulster for 18th September 1855 recorded Rev John Poole *"collected together the scattered members of eighteen different congregations, to form the basis of a new congregation in Holywood".*

The new clerical arrival in Holywood acquired parcels of land between the Shepherd's Path (My Lady's Mile) and Trevor Street; he may have owned the Holywood brick-fields. When Rev John Poole built the houses in High Street, he saw to it that they were the tallest in the town.

Mr Poole was the grandfather of John Poole Birch, and the founder of the famous Holywood Birch family. J P Birch first brought honour to the town when he scored the hit which won the Senior Cricket Cup for Holywood in 1898. He was still batting at Rockport School sixty years later using Ulster's oldest cricket bat - which he had been given in 1892, after a match between "Inst" and Cliftonville.

The title of Paul Reid's interesting little book, from which I glean information on the Christian Fellowship, advances one reason for the origin of the Church. It is called "A New Easter Rising - the Revival of an Individual, a Church and a Nation". In the early 1990's Easter nationwide conferences decided the answer to the Irish troubles was a movement towards *"non-sectarian Christianity through new churches springing up through the length and breadth of Ireland, with a message of peace and love."*

Earlier the Down Christian Trust had formed in Holywood, as an off-shoot of the Bangor Christian Trust. In the mid-1980's the Down Christian Trust became the Christian Fellowship. Headquarters were established in the attractive modern church on the corner of Holywood Road and Belmont Road at Strandtown (Gelston's Corner). By the year 1988 the Holywood congregation was the first to become autonomous.

The statement of the Christian Fellowship proclaims the fundamental beliefs of the Christian Faith, expressed in the evangelical and charismatic character of the members. Although the church seeks the unity of all Irish Christians for peace, it is non-oecumenical. This is why they believe that the planting of new churches is vital in a changing Ireland. It is only through a community, rightly related to Christ and to each other, that society can be influenced by God's love. The Christian Fellowship believes this is needed in every townland, every village, every town, every city, every county and province in Ireland, resulting in thousands of such new communities.

CHURCHES IN THE OLD PARISH BOUNDS

Before we leave ecclesiastical Holywood let us take a passing glance at the congregations which have grown up in the old extended Parish of Holywood or on the borders of the present-day electoral area, to some of which I have referred previously.

The Presbyterian congregation in Dundonald was established in 1644, in connection with the Holywood Church, with which it shared a common ministry for many years.

Ballygilbert congregation was established in 1841, shortly after the formation of the Presbyterian General Assembly.

Belmont Presbyterian Church was dedicated in 1864, happily in time for J H Connop to include its elegant outline on his pictorial map, "View of Sydenham, Belmont and Glenmachan". It served the growing professional population which came to reside in the nineteenth century mansions in the hills beyond Strandtown.

Twelve years later St Mark's, Dundela was built on the eminence of Bunker Hill. Its grand tower remains an outstanding landmark.

Sydenham Methodist Church was founded in 1884 on Palmerston Road, optimistically reserving a large site on Station Road for building expansion. A fine new church was erected in 1958, although the old Victorian Hall continued to serve the congregation at a youth centre until 1997.
Helen's Bay Presbyterian congregation was established in 1897 to serve the Dufferin Estate's development of the seaside village that takes its name from Lady Helen, granddaughter of Richard Brinsley Sheridan.

A decade later Holy Trinity Church, Glencraig, sponsored evening services at the Helen's Bay Hotel and in 1909 St John's Church was built on Fort Road. In 1923 the building was enlarged, and in 1962 the new Parish of St John Baptist was constituted. The Church lies in the townland of Ballygrot, which formerly was part of Bangor Parish. In the 1830's Lieutenant Henry Tucker's Ordnance Survey describes Ballygrot as seven acres of uncultivated land and patches of rock! He makes no mention of the ancient Church recorded on the 1895 (revised 1938) published 1947 O S map beside "Carrig Gorm" on Bridge Road. Today nothing remains of this ecclesiastical site; it may have been a Chapel of Ease in connection with the Great Abbey of Bangor, which was founded in 558.

The Ordnance Survey map records another ancient church on the Whinney Hill Road, about 600 metres from Craigantlet Crossroads; possibly similar to the Ballygrot antiquity. From the early years of the nineteenth century the Holywood Presbyterian Church organised services in its Creighton's Green schoolhouse. After the First World War, Craigantlet Mission Hall and the Boyd Memorial Hall were established; they continue to flourish at the present day.

Towards the end of the Second World War the congregation of the Church of God met in Devon Parade, Connsbrook Avenue and in 1962 it removed to Gelston's Corner at Strandtown. Here they remained for twenty-three years and in 1983 took up residence in the magnificent mansion - Glenmachan Tower on Glenmachan Road. This had been designed in 1863 by architect Thomas Jackson for Sir Thomas McClure, the nineteenth century developer of that area, and was later occupied by the Shillington family. In 1962 the building at Gelston's Corner was acquired by the Christian Fellowship Church.

When the Church of God Strandtown acquired the fine property in the historic Ballymaghan townland, it included the Glenmachan Tower Hotel. In 1959 the Hotel was refurbished, in 1992 it became a private nursing home.

From the early days of the nineteenth century the Holywood Presbyterian Church organised services in its schoolhouse at Knocknagoney. Post-war development demanded a separate Presbyterian parish and in 1950 a Church was established in the stables of Garnerville House. The growing congregation removed to a temporary building at the Holywood Road corner of Circular Road in 1952 and thirteen years later to its spacious building at Glenmachan.

The Church of Jesus Christ of Latter Day Saints opened its building at the corner of Circular Road in 1964.

The Church of the Annunciation at Knocknagoney also owes its origin to the population expansion from Belfast City into North Down. In 1960 parishioners from Dundela and Holywood met in a temporary hall erected in the fields at the back of Knocknagoney House. After four years the flourishing congregation moved into the fine modern Church, designed by Holywood architect - Denis O'D Hanna, at the corner of the Old Holywood Road.

Nearby and also in 1964 the people of the Christian Brethren Gospel Hall converted a farm-house into a place of worship. In 1967 they removed into the present purpose-built hall.

If you require additional information, most of the Churches have their own published histories and many are connected with internet and provide sites on the world wide web.

There has been a Christian presence in our town for over thirteen hundred years. As the twenty-first Christian century commences, there are eleven established congregations in Holywood and several meetings for fellowship in private homes and halls.

Holywood is an ecclesiastical kaleidoscope - a target view of beautiful forms - from the sixth-century Celtic Church of Saint Laiseran to the modern continental church of the twelfth century; onward to days of Reformation in the sixteenth century, the advent of Dissenters and Protestants and now the present day of new Christian philosophies.

Down the centuries, the clergy have brought leadership, education and culture to the town; the churches have given considerable employment through staff and major building projects; the congregations have provided peaceful friendship for members and denominations. In all, they have set a standard of peace, morality and grace which makes our neighbourhood a very pleasant place in which to live.

OLD HOLYWOOD TOWN

A County Down lyric, Holywood town
Comes back to me though old I've grown
My memory glides down the years;
And once again – eyes without tears.
Heart without stain, all innocence,
I feel once more the influence
Of hill and shore.
I'm four again and all is plain
Come down the hill and cross the lane
And there again the Kissing Bridge stands
Let's all clap our hands!
This is the town, quiet and brown
Old and sedate, well out of date
The maypole still neat,
Where the streets meet.

Herbert Moore Pim from "Songs from an Ulster Valley - 1920"

Previous narrative parted from the Presbyterians when the congregation was ejected from the Priory Church for non-conformity and found a new home on the watery wastes of the sea meadows. Dissenters benefited in 1672 when Charles II, (1660 – 1685) ordered an annual payment in lieu of the tithes and glebe lands of which their clergy were bereft. The royal gift created an odd situation – one church was established by law, the other endowed by public funds! The Regium Donum continued until Disestablishment of the Church of Ireland in 1869. A Declaration of Indulgence, 1687, in the reign of James II (1685 – 1689) came too late for the Holywood Dissenters. By it, Penal laws were suspended and several of the boarded-up meeting houses were re-opened for worship. By then, the Presbyterians had the meeting house beyond the foot of Shore Road.

The saga of 1690 is easily followed in the records of that period. For the Holywood connection, suffice is to say that in August 1689 Frederick Herman, Duke of Schomberg, a seventy-five year old exile from the French Army, landed at Groomsport with ten thousand Williamite troops. They took a route over the Holywood Hills, still known as "King William's Road", crossed the Belfast Long Bridge and marched to Carrickfergus Castle. The weight of General Schomberg's artillery collapsed seven arches of the bridge. For several years Holywood people had to go upstream to Shaw's Bridge to get across

Old Priory Church, original foundations 1190, refurbished in 1490, 1615 and 1800.

the Lagan with dry feet! Several commentators record the tradition that *"certain of Schomberg's troops were encamped during the following winter on the Standard Hill above Holywood."*

S Reid, Church historian, describes County Down in 1689 –

> *"plundered houses; horses, cattle and stock carried away; labourers interrupted resulting in scanty harvests".*

The surrounding farming community was hardest hit when an army chose to winter in the area. Such was the case for the farmers trying to make a living in the Holywood Hills in 1689. That inclement winter Williamite and Jacobite armies alike, along with the Irish peasantry, were laid waste by plague, starvation and horrific mortality. In Belfast Hospital 3,762 deaths were recorded between November and May of that *Annus Horribilis*. Two-thirds of the 10,000 soldiers who left Chester for Ireland on 12th August 1689 perished before May 1690 – hundreds of the survivors were disabled. It was reported that several military ships at anchor off Holywood were filled with corpses. Local tradition related

> *"a whole shipload of plague victims, and some of Schomberg's winter soldiers were buried in a field at Knocknagoney, about a mile from the village of Holywood."*

The burial field may have been in the vicinity of the north west corner of Holywood golf course at the former gates to Ardtullagh and adjacent to Redburn Cemetery. A town project should be the erection of a memorial to those unfortunate victims of 1690.

In 1725 the Presbyterian congregation of the sea meadows divided into those who supported and those who did not subscribe to the Westminster Confession of Faith. The Non-Subscribers retained the meeting-house; the Subscribers removed to the Strand, which soon became known as *"Gospel Lane".*

The Society of United Irishmen had many active supporters in Holywood; perhaps Henry Joy McCracken's family had spent many happy seaside holidays in the town. They had local business connections and boated at Cultra. Thomas Russell, a friend of the McCracken family, was *"on his keeping in Holywood"* after Emmet's Dublin Rising in 1803. Russell was given assistance by local families and helped to a futile escape from Craigavad, before incarceration in Downpatrick Gaol, as *"the man from God knows where".*

On Pike Sunday, 10th June 1798, Rev Joseph Harrison, an ardent royalist, was preaching to the winds in Gospel Lane, when an emissary of the 'Croppies' appeared at the meeting-house door. On a given signal, the United Irishmen in the congregation rose in a body, acquired their hidden pikes and marched to take part in the disastrous Battle of Ballynahinch. During the following week, with their Bangor and Dundonald friends, they returned home - dirty, defeated and dejected. How many Holywood men were killed, captured or wounded by Government forces in unknown. Of the local clergy, the minister of Newtownards - James Simpson, lay hidden at Ballymaghan for many weeks before escape to America; Rev James Porter of Greyabbey was executed and Dr Steele Dickson of Portaferry imprisoned.

One of the Holywood divines, Rev Arthur McMahon, was a member of the Ulster Executive of the United Irishmen and possibly Commander of the movement in County Down. Appraised of imminent arrest, he escaped to France and joined the exiles under Wolfe Tone.

Perhaps the most pathetic of the clergy executions came many months after the Rebellion. Rev Archibald Warwick, the twenty-five year old minister of Kircubbin Presbyterian Church, was betrayed to the authorities and hanged at the door of his meeting house. We know that three Holywood men, after trial at Downpatrick, received sentence of transportation to New South Wales or America. They were James Wallace, John Gribbon and William Patton.

After the rebellion Rev Joseph Harrison was glad to see his loyalist principles vindicated. As a member of the Bangor Presbytery he supported the refusal to recognise the Ordination of Licentiates who, having sympathised with the Rebellion, had escaped to America. Joseph Harrison also supported the General Synod's *"Affirmation of Loyalty to King George",* and the Synod's enhancement with a contribution of five hundred pounds to the Irish Treasury, to show the colour of their turned coats. Those now kept silent who remembered the hue of the coat lining in 1782 when the liberal Synodical Resolution of Emancipation and Reform was enacted. Of course, by 1799 the Fathers and Brethren

Original interior of First Presbyterian Church on Bangor Road.

realised that the Regium Donum, which supplemented Presbyterian stipends, could be manipulated in favour of the State!

In 1842 Rev William Blackwood took his congregation from Gospel Lane to the new church on Bangor Road, of which he was the architect. Blackwood mirrored the Priory in the building plans for his church, which overlooks the first home of the Dissenters - the old Priory. The cruciform edifice with Gothic style tower rising some seventy feet, was one of the first new buildings to be opened in connection with the General Assembly of the Presbyterian Church in Ireland. Kelly comments favourably on the singing gallery and the novel use of the chancel

> *"an evident simplicity prevails in every part, yet the general effect is exceeding pleasing".*

The congregation continues to worship in this fine old building to the present day.

Several interesting Holywood people have been connected with this congregation. A daughter of the first Holywood manse married Rev William Tennat who founded "the Log College" in the United States of America. The College was the original school of Princeton University in New Jersey. The Holywood minister was Rev Gilbert Kennedy (1670-1678).

Rev Henry Henderson, 1844-1879, became known as "Ulster-Scot". His nephew was James Alexander Henderson, who owned the "Belfast News-Letter" and "Belfast Weekly

News". One of the paper's features was a weekly article written by Henry Henderson under the well-known Scottish pseudonym. Some of his early pieces were personal essays, without any news content, perhaps forerunners of modern columnists. After 1879 the articles were continued by Henry's son – Rev Alexander Henderson. Another scholarly cleric was Dr Woodburn, 1916 – 1921, who borrowed from his predecessor the title for his famous book, "The Ulster-Scot".

A quiet, unassuming, world-famous scientist came late to First Holywood Church, though he spent many happy Holywood holidays, he retired to our town and was interred in the New Cemetery. This was Sir Joseph Larmor, (1857– 1942) a Fellow of St John's College, Cambridge; Lucasian Professor of Mathematics – a position held by Sir Isaac Newton; Fellow of the Royal Society and Unionist MP for Cambridge. Larmor's work prepared the way for the great advances in Relativity and Quantum Mechanics. His book, "Aether and Matter" was revolutionary, although he is best remembered for his work on Electrodynamics. The Larmor Precession, which orbiting charges undergo when subjected to a magnetic field, paved the way for Bloch's and Purcell's work on Magnetic Resonance, which is used today in Medical Imagery.

Before we consider the story of the Holywood Presbyterians who did not subscribe to the Westminster Confession of Faith, we should look at the domestic affairs of the Subscribers.

Their fourth minister, Rev Thomas Peebles, was appointed Clerk of Ireland's first Presbytery; it convened in Carrickfergus on Friday, 10th June 1642. He had been Chaplain to the Earl of Eglinton's Regiment and was inducted into the United Parishes of Holywood and Dundonald in 1645, a few months after the Solemn League and Covenant had been subscribed by his congregation in Holywood. Sixteen years later he witnessed the Covenant Script being publicly burnt in Holywood by order of the Irish Parliament. Peebles was liacised for non-conformity and escaped to Scotland. Fortunately his Army Commander and friend, the Earl of Eglinton, interceded for him with the Bishop of Down and he was reinstated in Holywood. Thomas Peebles was *"a learned and faithful man, eminent in Languages and History"*. His knowledge may have pleased the Holywood sermon tasters; his *"tossings and distemper"* aroused the ire of the Carrickfergus Presbytery when his hot temper occasioned the loss of their records.

Rev Thomas Cobham was installed in 1678. We read that *"He closed the work"* of the Sacrament at Carnmoney on 26 June, 1698 when a vast crowd of six hundred came to receive Communion. During the troubled year of 1688 Cobham seems to have fled to Scotland, although it is almost certain he was in Londonderry during the 105-day Siege of the City. During his ministry in 1725 the congregation divided. Those who sided with the Synod of Ulster found a new meeting-house in the Strand, which they enlarged in 1745 during the ministry of Rev William Smith.

William Smith was ordained into the Subscribing congregation on 4th November 1729. He died in 1741, the famine year when the farmlands in the Holywood Hills were *"black and barren"*. Lengthy and intense frosts in the early months of 1740 had destroyed the potato stocks. The prices of food soared; famine and disease reigned, in Ireland some 400,000 people perished. Twelve thousand Presbyterians annually shipped from Belfast and Derry for America. They were the proclaimers of liberty, equality and fraternity in their New World; the first to call for independence from Britain, and the kernel of the Pioneers who conquered the continent which lay open to the West.

Rev John King was inducted in the Strand meeting house in Gospel Lane in 1754. Although a pamphleteer and published author, he was noted for his soporific sermons. A local rhyme of the day ran

"I will not go to Holywood today
To hear John King so dull
His meeting-house may be for me
As empty as his skull."

During his ministry tent preaching meetings were in fashion, on the green beside the church. John King asked other clergy to preach the missionary sermons on these occasions. It seems he was very conscious of his own limitations.

As we have seen, Rev Joseph Harrison, who was ordained in Gospel Lane on 4th March, 1788 was a staunch Royalist and supporter of the Irish Parliament. His politics did not endear him to many of his congregation who were members of the Society of United Irishmen. His son William was ordained as successor on March 19th, 1816. He was drowned on September 18th, 1824 while swimming at Cooper's Bay, within sight of his meeting-house windows.

Rev Henry Wallace was ordained on December 5th, 1826. The same year a Sunday School opened in the Strand with over a hundred scholars and sixteen teachers. During his ministry the Church gallery was extended to accommodate worshippers from Dundonald who disapproved of the unorthodox views of their minister. The Sabbath pilgrimage to Holywood ceased when Rev William Graham was ordained in Dundonald in 1834. In 1867 Rev Henry Wallace became Professor of Christian Ethics in the Assembly's College, Belfast.

After Rev Henry Henderson was ordained in Holywood on September 25th, 1844, he took a lively interest in local education and encouraged his parish schools at Knocknagoney (1811), Creighton's Green (1847) and Ballymiscaw (1855). He won the admiration of his people when a mid-century cholera epidemic struck the town. In 1869 the traceried south windows and the vestry and school rooms were demolished to facilitate the erection of a large lecture hall.

In 1878, Glenside, the first house built in High Holywood, was acquired by the Kirk Session. After renovation, it became the manse for Rev Henry Halliday who was appointed Assistant and Successor on January 8th, 1878.

With the opening of the Palace Barracks in 1898 the Church and congregation were favoured with the bands and soldiers of the Scottish regiments, Henry Halliday being the officiating Chaplain to Her Majesty's Forces. He died in the Post Office on Church Road on April 6th, 1907. The obelisk on the green in front of the Church was erected to his memory.

The congregation intended to celebrate their Tercentenary in 1915 by refurbishment of the Church buildings; the work did not commence until the end of the Great War. While waiting for steel beams *"the roof lay open to the sky for most of a year – grass growing among the pews"*. The Church was re-opened in October 1921, two months before Rev John Kyle was installed as minister. In 1937 a Hammond electric organ was installed which was replaced by a fine Davies of Northampton instrument in 1958. In 1965 the new Halls complex was built and named after the popular minister of that time – Rev Robert Houston (1939-1972). During 1975 the Church interior was completely refurbished. The old high back pews with their individual doors and umbrella stands were removed and given to the Ulster American Folk Park at Omagh. In 1991 the Manse was replaced by a house built in the grounds, nearer to the Victoria Road. A further three ministries brings us to the present day.

TO SUBSCRIBE OR NOT SUBSCRIBE - THAT WAS THE QUESTION!

The original Presbytery of the Church in Ireland assembled at Carrickfergus on June 11th, 1642 and received application for membership from the several congregations already established in Ulster. Of course, Holywood was among the leaders. At that time the Irish church accepted the Scots Confession of 1560.

On July 1st, 1643 an Assembly of Divines met at Westminster, London. Except for two French Reformed clergy, all were members of the Anglican Church. In August the Scottish Assembly sent Commissioners to the Assembly. They could deliberate but were without voting rights. The Assembly produced a Confession and other Directories. These were adopted by Acts of the General Assembly of the Church of Scotland and became the practice of the Presbyterian Church in Ireland.

Ministers and Elders elect in Ireland were not required to sign the Confession of Faith until 1698. In 1705 the 'Belfast Society' was formed by clergy who opposed subscription to 'man-made' confessions or *"Tests of Orthodoxy"*. Synod met in June 1721 and resolved by a large majority *"that all members should sign the Confession of Faith"*. The twelve clergy and four elders who refused to sign were separated from the General Synod without any feelings of animosity. In 1726 they were placed within the Presbytery of Antrim. Rev Michael Bruce of Holywood was one of those so placed. As a result, the Holywood congregation divided, after a century of united work, worship and witness.
The Non-Subscribers or "New Light" sympathizers retained ownership of the meeting-house situated out on the sea meadows, beyond the end of Shore Street. About the same time as the "Old Light" adherents were building their church in Gospel Lane (1740), their co-religionists moved from the wet and windy foreshore to a more agreeable site at the corner of Shore Street and the Marine Parade. At that time Rev John Beatty was minister, (1737 – 1799).

In 1790 a new meeting-house with school-room was erected on the same foundations at the corner of Shore Street. It is interesting to note that in 1852 the Holywood Baths Company took over this prime location when the Assembly Rooms were built. The building became the Maypole Cinema from 1917 to 1940, when it was destroyed by fire. The site was acquired for commerce – at the beginning of the twenty-first century it awaits development.

The Non-Subscribing congregation's present Church on the High Street was dedicated on Sunday, 23rd September 1849. The architect was Charles Lanyon, who also designed the Courthouse on Crumlin Road (1850). The facades of both buildings are very similar. The Church is built in the Classical style with Corinthian pillars and massive parapet. It is one of Holywood's finest listed buildings; architecturally, its interior and exterior are of considerable merit. The property is in its original pristine state and it is beautifully maintained. The congregation joined the Remonstrant Synod in 1830 and in 1910 it was incorporated into the Non-Subscribing Presbyterian Church.

The most colourful of its clergy was Rev Arthur McMahon, 1794-1798; the most scholarly Rev C J McAlester, 1834-1891.

Arthur McMahon, a friend of Henry Joy McCracken and Thomas Russell, was one of the seven colonels of County Down's United Irishmen. A contemporary description paints the picture of a determined revolutionary, courageous, daring and pugnacious, impatient of defiance or opposition. His Reverence possessed very red hair and was a very fine-featured man.

McMahon was a leading member of the Ulster Committee of the United Irishmen. His activities frequently took him away from pastoral duties in Holywood. To cover necessary absences on active service, he claimed persecution by the Londonderry family of Mountstewart, which eventually forced him to flee to Scotland from Bangor Harbour, and then to France in 1798. Colonel McMahon advocated immediate insurrection in 1797, without waiting for the French Army to join the Irish Freedom Fighters. After his escape to the continent, he became an officer in the Irish Legion of the French Service. He did not return to his Holywood Parish.

Rev C J McAlester ministered to the Non-Subscribing congregation from 1834 to 1891. No other resident has given a greater life of service to the town. He was born in 1810, became a student and then a master of the Belfast Academical Institution.

Rev C J McAlester was inducted into his Holywood pastorate in August 1834 when the congregation was meeting in the old Shore Road Church. There he founded a school to continue his pedagogical prowess. When he led the congregation to the beautiful new church in the High Street in 1849 two spacious classrooms were built to accommodate his select preparatory school for girls and boys. No doubt he sought the good advice of his friend, Dr Robert Sullivan, on the organisation of the new school. Locally it became known as the "*Underground Academy*" because it was under the level of the High Street.

Among the distinguished students were Robert Lloyd Praeger and his sister Rosamund, Lord Craigavon and Sir Dawson Bates.

Rev C J McAlester's long ministry brought him membership of every social committee in Holywood. In 1835 he became a member of the Parish Vestry– the local Council of those days – and remained a member till the Act of Disestablishment (1869) which precluded non-Anglicans from membership.

He was editor of "The Bible Christian" and Clerk of the Northern Presbytery until his death in 1891. The obelisk in the Church forecourt was erected in his memory.

The congregation's best-known members are the Holywood Praeger family. William Emil Praeger of The Hague, Holland married Maria, a daughter of the celebrated Patterson family of Holywood. The Praegers moved to Woodburn House on the Croft Road after a short stay in The Crescent. Their son, Robert Lloyd Praeger, studied at Sullivan Upper School, the Royal Academical Institution and Queen's University. A graduate in Arts and Engineering, his upbringing by his grandfather Robert Patterson, FRS, made him choose a career in Natural Science. Robert became Chief Librarian of the National Library and President of the Royal Irish Academy. Queen's, Dublin and the National Universities honoured him with Doctorates. However, no honour gave him more satisfaction that election as the first President of the National Trust for Ireland. Among his many publications *"The Way that I Went"* earned him the title *"Ireland's best loved naturalist"*.

Robert's famous sister Sophia Rosamund was born on 15th September 1867. She studied at Sullivan Upper School, the Slade School and in Paris, winning prestigious awards and scholarships during her apprenticeship. We shall follow Rosamund's career with other Holywood artists in the essay on that subject. Rosamund spent her life with the good of children in mind. She bequeathed the Hibernia Street studio *"to benefit the children of Holywood"*. Praeger's field at Seapark was given as a children's playground. Johnny the Jig, her favourite work, invites children into the High Street playground.

The beautiful Lanyon Church building received a complete refurbishment at the end of the twentieth century, after the sale of the Manse property on Croft Road. As the congregation approaches four hundred years of Christian witness, it maintains the liberal approach to theology which its clergy and people have always proclaimed in the town.

HIGH STREET PRESBYTERIAN CHURCH

Rev Henry Henderson was ordained in First Holywood Church in 1844. He was an avid educationalist, a strong conservative and a gifted journalist in the Belfast News-Letter, which the Henderson family owned.

Unwittingly his exuberance seems to have been the cause of some discord within his large congregation. In August 1855 fifty-two heads of households memorialized the Belfast Presbytery to establish a new congregation in Holywood. The "Banner of Ulster" for 18th September 1855 claims these were the *"scattered members of eighteen different congregations"*. A Commission of Presbytery examined the circumstances, made exhaustive enquiries and eventually recommended that *"the prayer of the Memorial be granted and the Memorialists organised into a congregation"*. Thus was born the third Presbyterian Church in our town. In 1856 the new congregation met for worship in the Loan Fund Office at the corner of Morrow's Lane and Church View – the first minister was Rev James S Denham.

Minutes of the September 1857 meeting of the Methodist congregation, then on the look-out for a meeting-place, record –

> *"A large commodious place in a central part of Holywood, recently erected and now occupied by Rev Mr Denham for preaching, being likely to be soon vacant in consequence of the present congregation removing to its new house, it is believed the owner would sell his interest on moderate terms."*

Alas the asking price was too high. Eventually the Plymouth Brethren meeting took over the little hall. Later it became the premises of the Golden Age Club.

Building work started on the new Presbyterian Church in May 1857, after a row of little cottages in the High Street had been demolished. The attractive stone building was in the Early English style with bell cote and cupola. The architect was Robert Young, formerly a Lanyon apprentice, later the founder of the firm Young & Mackenzie. It was built by Samuel Moore of Morrow's Lane, the fine plasterwork was executed by William Hayes of Marino, the stuccoer who undertook most of the ceiling ornamentation for which Victorian Holywood was famous.

The Church was consecrated by the Presbytery of Belfast on 28th February 1858. Rev J S Denham ministered to the new congregation until his death at the age of 29, as a result of typhoid fever. Rev Henry Osborne was installed in August 1858. During his ministry the Church was enlarged and a lecture hall erected. In July 1873 Glenavon, a residence on the banks of the Ballykeel River was acquired as the Manse.

In 1903 the Kirk Session commissioned the installation of an organ. The High Street Church was among the earliest in North Down to introduce instrumental music into the worship service. The introduction of *"a kist of whistles"* by the Enniskillen congregation in 1868 initiated a fierce debate in the General Assembly. The fathers and brethren divided into "Liberty" and "Purity" parties. The proposed introduction of a hymnbook to complement *"the Psalms of David sung to the Tunes of David"* similarly aroused the ire of the "Purists". Holywood was ever a leader in liberty.

Rev Dr David Maconaghie served the congregation and the Holywood community for many years.

During the long and popular ministry of Rev J Ross Gamble (1937 - 1976) the sanctuary was scrupulously renovated. In recent years the Halls have been refurbished to provide an efficient suite of ancillary buildings.

Very Rev Dr John Ross (1976 - 2000) became Moderator of the General Assembly in 1995.

High Street Church is enhanced by many memorials to former members of the congregation, tastefully designed in stained glass.

Before we leave the story of the Presbyterian Dissenters, we should look at their interest in the Irish language. The Holywood Bryson family provide a good example of the discipline.

It seems the Bryson family first settled in Donegal, where John was born in 1685. His association with the ministry of the local Presbyterian congregation assured practice and fluency of the Irish language. He died in Holywood on 23rd November 1788 - at the great age of 103 years.

His son Rev James Bryson was born in Holywood in 1730. He was ordained in First Lisburn Church on 6th June 1764 and later ministered to Second Belfast (Rosemary Street) and Fourth Belfast (Donegall Street) congregations. It seems James continued the family tradition of using the native tongue when required.

Rev Andrew Bryson was the second son of James. He was licensed by the Presbytery of Bangor on 6th September 1785 and ordained in Dundalk on 15th August 1786. He was *'versed in the language and antiquities of the Nation'*. Andrew's younger brother, Samuel, was born in Holywood on 9th March 1776, the twenty-first son of James Bryson! He became a Licentiate of the Royal College of Surgeons and practiced from 50 High Street, Belfast. He was Collector and Transcriber of Irish Manuscripts and a major authority on Irish place names. He died on 28th February 1853 and was interred in the family grave in Holywood.

Samuel Bryson M D (1810 - 1858) succeeded his father in the family medical practice, his son Samuel (1847 - 1906) was interred in the Priory cemetery. The sons of the family attended the Academical Institution in Belfast, where the Irish language was on the curriculum. In later years the Bryson family lived in Woodbank, Croft Road. Today, Woodbank Lane runs over the site of the old house and gardens.

Correspondence in the Belfast Newsletter of 25th November 1872 recorded the inscription on the Bryson memorial stone -

John Bryson died 23 November 1788 aged 103
Ann Bryson died 1704 (recte 1804) aged 106
Alicia Bryson died April 17th, 1840 aged 73
Samuel Bryson died February 28th, 1830 (recte 1853) age 77

Non-Subscribing Presbyterian Church from Killops' Court on the High Street, 1849.

The old stone appeared to have been replaced by a new Bryson memorial erected on plot 20 in the Priory graveyard.

Another fluent Irish speaker with Holywood connections was Thomas Wilson Dougan (1852 - 1907). His father was Rev John Dougan, ordained in Lough Mourne, Co Monaghan in 1847. Professor Thomas Dougan, School of Classics at Queen's College, Belfast, came to live in Salernum, Croft Road.

Like the Brysons and Dougans, many other Holywood families have shown considerable interest in the study of the Irish language. In his excellent essay on the Rev Henry McManus (1817 -1864), Dr Roger Blaney of Holywood illustrates the Dissenters' support for such ecclesiastical interlocution.

In 1830 the Presbyterian Synod resolved that all its Divinity students should learn the Irish language. At that time the Dissenters were prepared for Ordination at the Belfast Academical Institution, where a Professor of Classics, Hebrew and Irish was in residence.

Dr Blaney points out that sixteenth century written Irish and Scottish Gaelic are essentially the same language, and that the first book printed in Irish was Presbyterian John Carswell's translation of the John Knox Book of Common Order. General Synod of 1710 recorded the availability of Irish translations of the Bible and the Presbyterian Confession of Faith. Then in 1716 General Synod commissioned Patrick Simpson of Dublin to print a Catechism in Irish with a short appendix relating to the rules of Irish grammar. Each Member of Synod was obliged to buy thirty copies of the little book. Two years later, Synod noted that the Catechism had been published and reprinted; it was to be distributed among the Presbyteries. I wonder did Rev Michael Bruce of Holywood pay for his thirty copies and what use was made of them in our town.

In 1836 the Psalms of David were published in Irish. The title page dedicates the book to King William IV and records *"the Psalms of David in the Irish language now for the first time rendered into metre, for the use of the Native Irish by Norman McLeod, D D, Minister of St Columba's Parish, Glasgow."*

By the year 1841, the General Assembly was able to give patronage to the publication of *"An introduction to the Irish Language compiled at the request of the Irish teachers and dedicated as a tribute to those who have preserved and extended the knowledge of our beloved mother tongue."*

The year 1893 saw the establishment of the Gaelic League to establish Irish as a spoken and literary language. In 1915 the League passed a Resolution supporting the desire for independence from the United Kingdom. This breach of the former non-political Constitution led to a certain cooling of the Presbyterian ardour for the Irish language.

Here we depart from the story of the Dissenters. Now, let us take a look at the Garrison town...

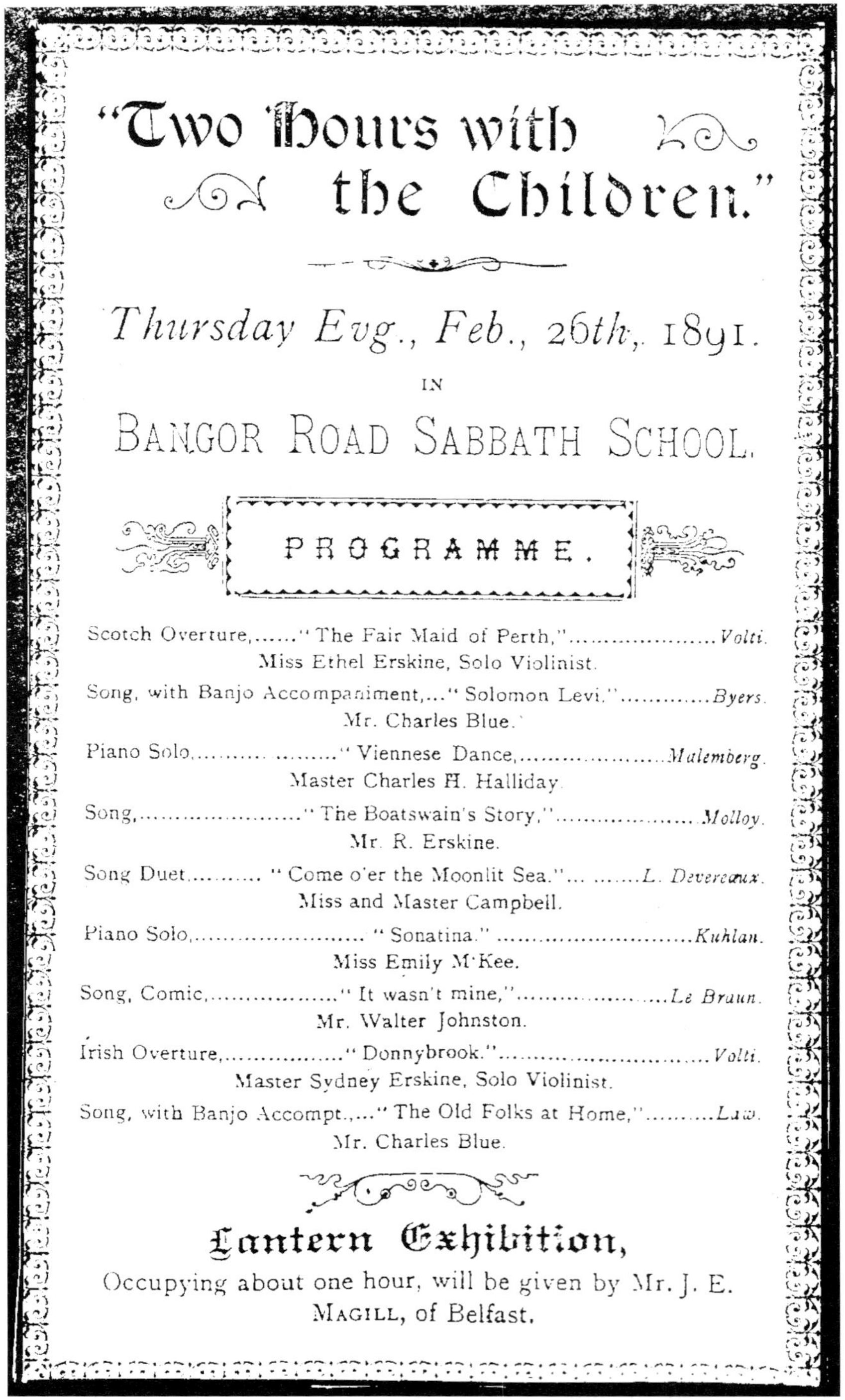

"Two Hours with the Children."

Thursday Evg., Feb., 26th, 1891.

IN

BANGOR ROAD SABBATH SCHOOL.

PROGRAMME.

Scotch Overture,......" The Fair Maid of Perth,"...................*Volti.*
Miss Ethel Erskine, Solo Violinist.

Song, with Banjo Accompaniment,..." Solomon Levi."...........*Byers.*
Mr. Charles Blue.

Piano Solo...................." Viennese Dance,..................*Malemberg.*
Master Charles H. Halliday.

Song,......................" The Boatswain's Story,"...................*Molloy.*
Mr. R. Erskine.

Song Duet.......... " Come o'er the Moonlit Sea."... ....*L. Devereaux.*
Miss and Master Campbell.

Piano Solo,........................ " Sonatina." ....*Kuhlau.*
Miss Emily M'Kee.

Song, Comic,................." It wasn't mine,"......................*Le Braun.*
Mr. Walter Johnston.

Irish Overture,................" Donnybrook."............................*Volti.*
Master Sydney Erskine, Solo Violinist.

Song, with Banjo Accompt.,..." The Old Folks at Home,"..........*Law.*
Mr. Charles Blue.

Lantern Exhibition,

Occupying about one hour, will be given by Mr. J. E. MAGILL, of Belfast.

ESSAY XVII - HOLYWOOD - A GARRISON TOWN

ULSTER MEMORIES

Hills of Antrim, misty green or gleaming,
Granite Mourne where sea and mountain meet
Lovely loughs by Enniskillen dreaming
Lovely Sperrin and the heathery peat.

Rugged coast road on the cliff side perching
Drenched in winter with the driven spray
Fairy glens where nature goes a-searching
Lovelier blooms to crown each coming May.

Sombre sentinel on Scrabo keeping
Guard oe'r Strangford's studded bays;
Keep of Carrick, in whose walls lie sleeping
Pomp and pageantry of Norman days.

Causeway laid by legendary giant
Caverns where Atlantic rollers beat,
Orange days and drums that shout defiant
Bands and banners; tramp of marching feet.

Glimpses golden of a finished duty,
Memories mellow of a sojourn past
Unforgettable in all their beauty -
These are Ulster, these are dreams that last.

A soldier's Ulster memories written by Major M C Cooper, later Regional Director – Post Office, Northern Ireland. He left Holywood for appointment as Regional Engineer, Bristol. Major Cooper was awarded the Military Cross in the First World War and took part in the evacuation of Dunkirk in 1940.

My first visit to the Palace Barracks was at the tender age of three years. I had fallen off the chesterfield in the Clanbrassil sitting room where my grandmother was instructing me in the gentle art of reading. I yelled my head off claiming that my wrist was broken. Dr Gaussen was called, and within minutes I was under X-ray cameras in the Palace Barracks hospital. That memory comes to mind from over sixty years - even then the Army was providing an emergency service for Holywood civilians, which the Health Service is unable to emulate today!

As there has been an Army presence in Holywood during at least six of our thirteen centuries of recorded history, the garrison town essay requires a rapid resume of the salient military episodes in our story, some of which we have explored in other essays.

The Norman Knight, John de Courcy, conquered Ulster in 1177, apparently without Royal Licence. The one hundred miles march from Dublin, over treacherous countryside, was accomplished in a mere four days. The last King of Ulster, Ruaidri Mac Donlevy, submitted as Vassal to the Norman Conqueror.

> *"The horses, the steel armour and the cloth-yard arrows of the Norman bowmen were more than a match against the odds of the half-naked Irish kernes."*

Soon de Courcy had overcome both Down and Antrim, protecting his newly acquired possessions with a chain of castles, mottes and baileys. His best memorial in Holywood is the Priory Church, which he commissioned his agent Thomas Whyte to build in 1190 for the Order of Hermits of Saint Augustine.

De Courcy fell from royal favour in 1204. His replacement, Hugh de Lacy governed the area for King John. Like de Courcy, de Lacy's unbridled ambition led to his downfall. He was chased out of Ireland to Scotland in 1210. The King's determined intention to pursue a personal reconnaissance occasioned a spectacular military occasion for our Garrison Town. The event was recorded in State records for the year 1210 kept in the Tower of London -

> *"Thursday, 29th July at Holywood to Geoffrey Luterell to make a present to mariners of a ship from Bayonne – sixty shillings. Same day to the same to make a present to mariners and galley-men seventeen pounds."*

King John crossed the Belfast Lough from Carrickfergus Castle to Holywood on that memorable summer day. It must have been the most important royal military occasion Holywood has ever witnessed. His army was stationed on Ardshane, John's Hill, later called Windmill Hill. Generations of Holywood children remember being taken to see the oak tree in Tudor Park "to which John tied his horse". To this day, King John's Road winds its way over the hills to Dundonald, to which motte the army marched after the Holywood encampment. Part of it, known as King John's Walk, is a public right of way [Access to the Countryside (N I) Order 1983], joining Princess Gardens with Creighton's Green Road via "the Hooks."

Tradition tells us King John was accommodated in the bailey on the motte beside the Ballykeel River. However, the little wooden castle may not have been erected until King Henry III [1216 – 1272] confirmed *"John de Saukvill in the lands de Sancto Bosco in 1217."* The de Saukvill family seems to have garrisoned Holywood for the next century. During these years the town suffered under the Scottish Bruce Invasion of 1315 to 1318. In 1333 our forbears saw the murder of William de Burg, Ulster representative of King Edward III (1327 – 1377) at the Belfast ford over the Lagan. De Burg was passing through the area to join the King, who was campaigning in Scotland.

In the 1340's the Black Death spread from Asia to Europe; Holywood did not avoid the epidemic. The Archbishop of Armagh, Richard Fitzralp [1346 – 1360] preaching before the Pope in August 1349 claimed that the plague had decimated two-thirds of the English population, but had not affected Ireland or Scotland to the same extent. Modern estimates suggest between a third and a half of the local population was exterminated. The English garrisons which had protected the lands held by Anglo-Irish colonists abandoned their posts as army numbers dwindled. Their Irish manors, villages and rural boroughs were almost deserted. A viable economy disappeared with the population; the result was massive social disorder in Ireland.

A petition to King Edward in 1360 suggests the native Irish country-dwellers were less affected than their town dwelling Anglo-Irish neighbours. Whether this was true or not, what was left of the Irish *"came back into their own"!* The O'Neill's of Tyrone expanded their control into the Kingdom of Dalriada, assuming the title "Kings of Ulster". One branch of the family established itself in Clandeboye. First mentioned in the annals in 1319, they settled on the northern shores of Lough Neagh. By 1420 they had expanded into the vacant lands of South Antrim, to which territories they had added North Down by 1460. The O'Gilmores became the Overseers of Holywood.

For two centuries the authority of the English Crown counted for little in Ireland. Visits by King Richard II, in 1394 and 1399 were completely ineffectual. From 1399 to 1534 a succession of magnates dominated the land, nominally representing the English Crown, actually they were independent princes solely concerned with their own interests.

When the crumbling house of Plantagenet gave way to the modern Tudors, Henry VII (1485 - 1509) saw an Irish threat to his absolute monarchy and took measures to re-establish the Crown's authority. Henry VIII (1509 - 1547) continued his father's Hibernian aspirations. For personal reasons he wished to control the Church and saw the financial capital required for his several projects accruing from the dissolution of the wealthy monasteries. The State Church of Ireland came into being in 1537; the Kingdom of Ireland in 1541. Canny Conn O'Neill (1484 - 1559) acknowledged the Crown and accepted the title "Earl of Tyrone" in 1541. His yellow-haired cousin of Clandeboye nodded, and then continued to maintain an independent chieftainship in South Antrim and North Down.

In 1567 Sir Brian Phelim Bacagh O'Neill finally accepted an English knighthood, only to be killed in opposing English settlements on the Ards Peninsula and the Glens of Antrim. By that time the Virgin Queen was on the throne. It was an Age of Aquarius - adventure and exploration were in vogue and the proper garrisoning of Ireland became a challenge.

Queen Elizabeth had been playing a double game with Sir Brian O'Neill of Clandeboye. While accepting his allegiance as a true subject, the perfidious woman was sending English adventurers to settle in his estates. The same year in which Sir Brian accepted the Queen's accolade, she was considering Sir Thomas Gerrard's proposal to capture Clandeboye with a force of five hundred soldiers. Fortunately the project was too expensive for the penny-wise Elizabeth! Three years later the Queen's secretary recorded the adventures of the bold Captain Barrow and his merry men in Clandeboye. It seems

Palace Barracks guardhouse c. 1922, showing cannon and resident regiment's emblem.

Lieutenant Goodrich was guarding Castlereagh, the O'Neill mansion, with a garrison of fourteen men who sallied forth every day to fetch water, despite some five hundred Irish, incapable of retaliation! This dubious story may have encouraged the Royal secretary to think "easy pickings" were available in North Down.

Sir Thomas Smith sought the Queen's permission for a crusade on Clandeboye. Permission was granted as the project's expenses were not to be levied on the State coffers! Sir Thomas Smith got as far as making copious martial plans. A campaign map drawn in 1572 shows the areas on either side of the Holywood Hills and depicts three elaborate encientеd fortresses to guard the Newtownards end of the Ards Peninsula. These seem to be established on the old Anglo-Norman mottes: Ballyrichard - a couple of miles from Comber, Dundonald and Ballymaghan, a mere two miles from Holywood, which is carefully marked on the map.

Young Thomas Smith, the secretary's son, landed at Strangford on 10th August 1572 with his army. He marched the old road from Downpatrick to take possession of Clandeboye. In October Sir Brian O'Neill, devastated by the treachery of the English queen, torched the old monasteries of Newtownards, Bangor, Movilla and Holywood, in case Smith would use the buildings as barracks for his army. A year later, in early October 1573, Thomas Smith was shot at Comber, apparently by another member of the English Army.

Walter, first Earl of Essex, [1541-1576] who was Resident Commander in Carrickfergus in 1573, wrote

> *"20th October 1573 - At my coming I received letters from Mr Moore, the pensioner, and from a brother of Mr Secretary's, that his son, Thomas Smith, had been slain in the Ardes that afternoon with a shot, and was stricken in the head. His men, finding his house scant guardable, have sent unto me for a band of horsemen to convey them to Mr Moore's at Holywood, which this day I have sent to them."*

Possibly the young English soldier, son of the Secretary to Queen Elizabeth, was laid to rest in an unmarked grave in the Priory cemetery. By 1573 Holywood had regained its reputation as a garrison town, Lieutenant Moore being in command of the local gendarmerie, appointed by Walter, Earl of Essex. Perhaps Essex had an envious eye on a North Down land grant from the Queen; perhaps another Smith stuck his thumb in the opulent pie - none of the adventurers succeeded.

The Queen, who never suffered fools gladly, now reversed her tack and returned her favour to the O'Neill's. In 1586 Sir Con O'Neill was granted a royal patent for Castlereagh - that portion of North Down stretching from Belfast to within a few miles of Portaferry. In 1589 he was succeeded by his cousin, Con McBrian Fertagh O'Neill and Holywood was garrisoned by the Irish O'Neill's until 1606. By then a new king was on the throne. The Stuarts had replaced the Tudors, and James expected much of the new century.

In the first decade of the seventeenth century Sir James Hamilton established a Scots Militia recruited from his tenants and re-established law and order in Holywood. In 1641 the Town Constable was Robert Jackson, the military forces in the area were under the jurisdiction of Captain Alexander Hamilton and under the command of Lord Montgomery. Fear of an Irish Rebellion made Sir James Hamilton, now Lord Clandeboye and an octogenarian, obtain government permission to raise a North Down regiment of foot- soldiers and a troop of horse soldiers. The main recruiting centres were Newtownards, Bangor, Dundonald and Holywood. Soon it was evident that their lordships' militarism was unable to control the Irish Risings, so the Government *"brought over forces from the mainland to control the situation"*.

In the wet winter month of February 1642 the native Irish marched up the Ards Peninsula from Portaferry to attack and defeat Montgomery's fencibles at Mountstewart and went on to sack Newtownards town. Their compatriots moved up the other side of Strangford Lough from Killinchy, but were routed near Comber, in a field now called Battletown. Thus they were prevented from joining their victorious friends at Newtownards. Two months later, April 1642, a detachment of 2,500 Scottish soldiers landed at Carrickfergus under the command of General Robert Munro, to quell the rebellion.

On 22nd August 1642, the Civil War began in England. At first Charles I attempted to secure aid from Ireland. After the King was executed in 1649, all the Irish political parties united (a very rare event) to recognise his son as King. Consequently, in August 1649 Oliver Cromwell came over to subdue Ireland - a project he executed with savage efficiency. Cromwell took the title "Protector" as Head of the Commonwealth of Ireland, Scotland and England during the years 1653 to 1659 He considered the Roundhead Army was a divine instrument to crush those responsible for the 1641 attack on Protestants and those who had allied themselves to King Charles I. The crimes of canting Cromwell computed the loathing which English Essex had contrived. Frustrated mothers still use Cromwell as the bogeyman to threaten errant children!

One incident of the Commonwealth period portrays an interesting local connection. Some months after "the Protector" had started his reign of terror, Lord Clandeboye's son, James was leading the local tenantry in a battle with the Roundheads near Lisburn. The North Down men were beaten into the ground; rumour has it that young Squire James *"sunk in a bog - being corpulent"* Whatever the cause of his obesity, he lived to make peace for another day. James surrendered to Cromwell and paid a fine of £9,000 to keep the Clandeboye estates. It says much for North Down that it could provide such a huge figure in sterling to maintain the *status quo ante bellum*. A more intriguing question is what retribution would Cromwell's army have extracted from North Down and particularly Holywood, if the estate had been unable to pay the fine? Nine thousand pounds was a king's ransom in 1650. The loss of such a sum from the Clandeboye coffers may well explain the future financial difficulties of the Hamilton family.

Restoration of the monarchy came in 1660 and in 1685 James II succeeded Charles II. In the early autumn of 1689 Schomberg's army marched King William's Road to the south of Holywood. During the winter, part of the army bivouacked on Standard Hill overlooking the town. There they ravished the local farms for sustenance. A local reminder of those days is a field in the old Holywood Demesne to the southeast of the Palace Barracks. Here were interred the bodies of plague victims - soldiers of the Williamite army and sailors from the military ships anchored in the lough off the Holywood Bank.

Another interesting repository for the bones of Williamite soldiers lies further along the Old Holywood Road at the Belmont road junction. When a mansion house was built on the adjoining site, it was given the name Schomberg, to commemorate the great General himself.

As we have seen, the 1798 Rising of United Irishmen received considerable support from Holywood Presbyterians. A squad of local volunteers fought in the Battle of Ballynahinch on 12th June 1798. They were thoroughly defeated by the troops of General Nugent. More that one refugee was protected in the area. At that time the town was garrisoned by the Earl of Westmeath's Yeomanry. Their defended barrack buildings were situated at the corner of Downshire Road and High Street, the site presently occupied by Claire House.

Over a century ago the British Army established a permanent presence in Holywood. From the mid 1880's the Army had been using the area as a training ground for regiments stationed in Belfast. The Kinnegar camp could accommodate more than 400 personnel under canvas. Over the years, the regiments which bivouacked on the sand hills were the Gordon Highlanders, the Highland Light Infantry and the Queen's Own Regiment. The Royal Irish Rifles enjoyed the salubrious seaside situation in the early summer of 1885. Their return visit in 1897 was a complete contrast – a virtual Kinnegar washout!

The Belfast News-Letter for 17th June 1897 describes life at the Kinnegar camp during that extremely inclement Irish summer :

> *"Reveille – 5.30 a.m to dress for one hour of Regimental Parade; additional parades at 10.15 a m and 2.0 p m. Each day two companies are struck off for instruction in Musketry. On Tuesdays and Thursdays the Brigades are drilled en masse. On Saturdays between 300 and 400 men are allowed out of camp on pass till Monday morning, but they must be back in camp by 10.30 p m. The remainder of the men attend Divine Service in the town churches.*
>
> *On Tuesday, 15th June 1897 the men of the 3rd and 4th Battalions had a very rough experience when a regular hurricane prevailed and the large marquees were blown down. The orderly room marquee was completely wrecked and regimental documents blown all over the camp. The sergeants' mess marquee, which was fitted up at great expense, was destroyed; all the delph and the mess utensils were smashed. The men were on alert from 2.30 a m in order to prevent their tents being swamped. Indeed, had it not been for the energetic efforts of Colour Sergeant Hull, the whole encampment would have been swamped. This officer, who had been a sub-marine miner, made a large drain through the centre of the camp to enable the escape of excess storm water."*

When the War Office acquired the land in 1887 the Royal Belfast Golf Club, founded in 1881, was charged an annual rent of sixty pounds by the Government. This was rather surprising as the Army officers and their ladies were keen golfers. The War Office did not take into consideration that formerly Squire Harrison provided the golf course to the members free from rent!

On 1st March 1887 the Bishop's Palace and the surrounding 67 acres of parkland were sold by public auction at the salerooms of Messrs H A C Clarke & Son, Rosemary Street, Belfast. By happy coincidence formerly the land has belonged to the family of Thomas Jonathan Jackson (1824 – 1863) U S Confederacy General, nicknamed "Stonewall" for his expertise in the American Civil War.

The Government acquired the Palace for the erection of a permanent military barracks. It complemented the camp on the Kinnegar, which the new building site overlooked. Some years later, Westbrook – former residence of the Sovereign of Belfast - was added

The Barrack Square c. 1922. Clock tower marks site of the Bishop's Palace.

to the Palace Barracks campus. The grounds of Westbrook bordered the west side of Jackson's Road; eventually its grand entrance was replaced by the Linley gates. Both mansions were demolished to make way for the most advanced military establishment of its day.

Oakley House and grounds were requisitioned by the Government on 6th May 1940 to support the war effort. Situated on the east side of Jackson's Road, the house became an officers' mess. Part of the grounds were used to build officers' quarters, the remainder was meticulously maintained as gardens by German prisoners from the neighbouring prisoner of war camp. A wooden annex was added in 1974 to accommodate the increased officer strength occasioned by the 1969 emergency.

Oakley House was built around 1860 in the High Victorian Classical style. Its fine cornices and ceiling roses were typical of Holywood mansions. The central hall, staircase balustrade, cupola and marble fireplace surrounds were exceptionally good. Mess membership included officers of the Ordnance Depot; Royal Electrical and Mechanical Engineers; Territorial Units and R A F Sydenham.

Squadron Leader Paddy Hughes recorded a sighting of the Oakley ghost.

> *"One evening I was sitting alone in the mess, wide awake and stone cold sober. A young lady wearing a long Victorian dress silently came into view, passed through a solid stone wall and disappeared from sight."*

The Ministry of Defence ordered the demolition of Oakley in September 1978. The grounds, the Palace, Westbrook and Oakley make up the campus of the modern Palace Barracks. The mansions were three of the finest nineteenth century houses in the Holywood area.

In 1897 the first permanent unit to occupy the new barracks was the King's Liverpool Regiment. As the initial occupants, the officers thought it necessary to entertain on a lavish scale. Holywood families were only too happy to participate in the fun. The equestrian Dunvilles of Redburn looked favourably on their new neighbours across the Old Holywood Road. Some of them seemed as Irish as the Irish as far as horses were concerned.

On one occasion Captain Sheppard, who kept several hunters and a pack of beagles at the Palace Barracks for his personal use, was hunting in the Holywood Hills. The dogs got into the town reservoir, which had been constructed some sixteen years previously. The following day the Captain called at the Town Hall to apologise for the canine intrusion. The Town Clerk objected verbosely on behalf of the ratepayers; his tirade was cut short then Captain Sheppard told him to send him the bill for a new reservoir!

The Belfast News Letter for Thursday, 17th June 1897 reported

> *"The men of the 3rd, 4th and 5th Battalions of the Royal Irish Rifles stationed at the Kinnegar Camp and the Palace Camp, Holywood, have behaved in the most exemplary manner since their arrival and no disturbance of any kind has taken place."*

Some time before the local press had commented on some of the young soldiers from the Kinnegar Camp who had been celebrating their Holywood postings too enthusiastically!

The problem raised its head at various times over the years : in 1900 Holywood's Town Clerk complained to the War Office concerning *"the heavy drinking habits of the Royal Reserve Regiment who were in residence at the Palace Barracks"*. The War Office replied that the Urban District Council should lay a restriction on the number of liquor licences it issued for public houses in the town. A century later, on 11th June 1989 the Newsletter reported :

> *"Army clamp-down on troops leaving Barracks. Hundreds of on-lookers watched in amazement as carousing soldiers of the 3rd Battalion of the Parachute Regiment fought out a drunken brawl in High Street, Holywood. One soldier had to be hospitalized after a punch-up with 'squaddy' colleagues. The manager of the Seahorse Inn said the soldiers were in high spirits but caused no trouble!"*

The town always overlooked the peccadilloes of the visiting regiments. Holywood was not the only town in the United Kingdom which understood the exuberance of young soldiers far from home. About the year 1870 Elsie Sandes, CBE, brought her idea of Sandes Soldiers' Homes into fruition. A lass from County Kerry, educated at the French School in Bray, she was Superintendent of Soldiers' Homes in England, Ireland and India for sixty-six years. Sandes Soldiers' Homes were intended to supply more salubrious surroundings than local public houses and places of ill repute, in which soldiers could pursue recreational activities. The Holywood Sandes Home was built in 1903 on the hilltop a few hundred metres from the Palace Barrack gates on the way into the town. For many years it provided hospitality for resident regiments. The fine Arts and Crafts building was destroyed by fire in the recent troubles.

A Newsletter cutting for June 1897 reads :

> *"With reference to the Jubilee celebrations in London, six men from each of the 3rd, 4th and 5th Battalions of the Royal Irish Rifles will proceed today from Holywood en route for London to make arrangements, under the command of Major Montgomery of the 4th Battalion, for the encamping at Battersea Park of the detachment which will represent the Regiment on the 22nd inst."*

In 1897 Queen Victoria had reigned longer than any other British sovereign; every part of the Empire was represented by statesmen and soldiers for review by the Queen. It is interesting to note that over twenty men from Holywood were present on that famous occasion.

The Royal Scots Regiment replaced the Royal Irish Rifles in 1899. Quarrels between Dutch and British settlers in South Africa led to the Boer War (1899 - 1902). The Boers were successful until Lord Roberts and Sir Robert Baden-Powell turned the scales in favour of the United Kingdom. The Royal Scots Regiment trained in the Palace Barracks immediately before the voyage to fight in the second Boer War. Later both leaders visited Holywood; Lord Roberts to attend the inauguration of the maypole which Henry Henderson presented to the town in 1902 and Colonel Baden-Powell to inspect the First Holywood Scout Troop (Sir Robert Kennedy's Own) when their new headquarters was opened in 1915.

From the outset, the Palace Barracks gave a considerable fillip to the Holywood Cricket and Lawn Tennis Club. Three officers played a significant role in the Club's first victory – winning the senior Challenge Cup in 1899. The beagling Captain T W Sheppard scored 40; Lieutenant Charlie Harrington opened the first innings with 46 runs and Lieutenant Harry Potter scored 38, the three officers claimed 124 of the first innings total of 189 runs! Charlie became General Sir G H Harrington, Governor of Gibraltar, and Harry became Colonel H C Potter, Commander of H M Forces in Northern Ireland. The Cricket Club's centenary book records *"These three were among the trail-blazers in a bond between the Club and members of the Forces stationed at Palace Barracks."*

The centenary book of the Royal Belfast Golf Club expresses a similar sentiment :

> *"By 1886 some forty officers from the regiments stationed in Belfast began to use the course at Holywood, Kinnegar, and co-operated with the members in improving it. Colonel Lyon-Campbell, in particular, played an outstanding part in laying down new putting greens and teeing grounds. So began the happy and friendly relationship between the military and the Club members which exists to this day."*

In the early days, padres and medical physicians to the resident regiments were the local clergy and doctors; the schoolhouse on the campus was taught by local teachers. There were frequent leisurely liaisons between soldiers and the town's young ladies which often resulted in marriage.

The campus school which the children of the early regiments attended had closed by the 1930's, then the children were conveyed by Army trucks to the Sullivan National School on Holywood's High Street. After the Second World War the Colonel's lady decided that "bussing" children into Holywood was both dangerous and undesirable. In the 1950's a primary school was opened in an Army hut within the precincts of the Barracks and under the authority of the Down County Education Committee.

At first it was operated by a Principal and a dedicated teacher from the Sullivan School; later the numbers required a second assistant teacher. Although equipment and furnishings were spartan, official inspections considered the teaching standards in the school were superlative. However, one inspector thought the young lady teacher should conduct the physical education classes on the Barracks drill square - an invitation which she declined considering the entertainment it would have provided for the surrounding army personnel!

In the 1960's, house building programmes on the parklands of Redburn and Holywood House necessitated the erection of a new purpose-built public school on a greenfield site. Since the opening of Redburn Primary School, the children of families from Palace Barracks have joined with local boys and girls at Redburn. This has proved to be a very satisfactory arrangement for everyone - children, school staff and parents.

Over the century the number of buildings on campus has grown into a small town in its own right. The General's house formerly stood in splendid isolation on the western perimeter, bounded by private gardens and driveways. Now it is surrounded by specialist accommodation for military personnel. The number of buildings around the original barrack square has increased although the campanile still marks the former site of the Bishop's Palace. This clock tower is a fine example of the Arts and Crafts Movement, of which there were so many examples in the Holywood area.

The original guardhouse, now heavily disguised, still presents the Barracks' face to members of the public passing on the dual carriageway, although the main entrance to the complex now opens from the Old Holywood Road. In former days the rather elegant guardhouse had a glass-covered veranda, along which the guard marched with immense precision. A huge First World War cannon dominated the lawns to the west of the guardhouse. On the gently sloping bank which rose from the road to this piece of antique artillery, each resident regiment created its badge and emblem in flowers. Holywood was very proud of this floral tribute at the entrance to our town.

Like the two smaller cannon which guarded the War Memorial in Redburn Square, the huge Palace Barracks cannon commemorated the victories of regiments which had been stationed in Holywood.
One of the campaigns which the cannon commemorated was the Battle at Mons, an event which is still recalled annually in the town. Early in 1914 the Norfolk Regiment was in residence at the Palace Barracks. At 11 p m on Tuesday, 4th August 1914 Britain entered the War against Germany in order to defend Belgium. The Expedition Force of 70,000 men included the Norfolk Regiment which arrived in France directly from Holywood. The regiment was involved immediately in the great retreat at Mons on Sunday, 23rd August. The German First Army, with twice the number of combatants was completely out-manouvred. With few machine-guns, but with excellent rifle fire, the British regiments inflicted so great damage that the German Army was deceived as to the actual strength of their opponents.

In 1940, the three Holywood cannon disappeared with all the town's iron railings and gates for the Second World War effort.

Apart from the garrison hospital, the building Holywood people knew best was the Garrison Church. It was built in the early years of the last century, a small and simple edifice surrounded by shrubbery and flowerbeds. Childhood memories recall flowers blooming in every season at the Palace Barracks - no doubt there was an everlasting supply of enthusiastic gardeners to keep the campus evergreen! The gracious little church was elegantly furnished with carpeted aisle and individual chairs for the members of the congregation. The rather austere pulpit bore a plaque proclaiming -

> *"Presented by Mrs John Dunville to the Glory of God and in memory of John Spencer Dunville, V.C, 2nd Lieutenant Royal Dragoons, who died of wounds - June 19th, 1917, aged 21 years."*

The simple wooden communion table always displayed a floral tribute - even in the darkest winter days. For many years the organist of the Garrison Church was Miss Ena Cunningham. Her father, a lay preacher, had been a member of the Army Military School. Appropriately, the organ was the gift of the Somerset Light Infantry in 1921. I say appropriately, because many of that regiment had married Holywood girls in the little church. That very popular regiment was stationed at Palace Barracks in the early years of the First World War. After demobilisation, many of the men came back to Holywood, married and made their homes in the town. At one time, the local regimental association had more than fifty members.

In the 1960's the Army decided to replace the little chapel with a modern structure – St George's Garrison Church. Buildings of similar design were erected at Lisburn, Omagh, and Ballykinler. The unusual structure, reminiscent of airport architecture, has a hyperbolic timber roof supported by concrete and brick walls. Its construction posed a number of design problems for the Engineering Department of Lyttle and Pollock of Duncrue Street, who won the building contract against stiff cross-channel competition. The interior of the building is lit by deflected natural light, individual chairs are provided for the congregation and the communion table occupies a central position.

The most harrowing event in the town's association with the military families living at the Palace Barracks, occurred on Saturday evening, 22nd April 1933. That tragic night, five children between the ages of two and nine years died in their beds in flat 13. They were the entire family of Lance-Corporal Harry Poole of the Border Regiment, and his wife Mary. The regiment had returned from service in India the previous year. On the fateful Saturday evening, Harry and Mary Poole had gone out for an evening's entertainment, leaving the children to look after themselves. They returned home before midnight, checked to see all was well in the children's room and opened the window a little bit further as there was a slight smell of gas. The five children died of asphyxiation following gas poisoning about three hours later. Three years before the event the flats in Block B had been converted from gas to electric lighting. At that time, the old gas pipes were reported to have been sealed and disconnected from the gas mains. At the inquest it transpired that seven or eight pipes were without plugs. On Friday, 21st April a new gas cooker had been installed in one of the other flats in the block. The gas fitter had turned on the mains when the job was completed without checking the outlet pipes.

The funeral of the five Poole children took place on Wednesday, 26th April 1933. More than ten thousand mourners lined the road from the gates of the Palace Barracks to the New Cemetery beside the Old Priory Church. Whatever little road traffic there was on the Belfast to Bangor Road in 1933 was held back as far as Strandtown and Clandeboye.

After a memorial service in the Garrison Church, the poignant funeral procession assembled in the grounds of the Palace Barracks. The military band of the Border Regiment led the way with long spaced beats on the black-draped drums captured from the French in the Peninsular War at the Arroyos Dos Molinos. The band preceded the three black-plumed horse drawn hearses in which the five little white and silver coffins made their final journey. General Girdwood, GOC (N I) led the procession with the general staff, and the officers and men of the Border Regiment. The wives of the soldiers who lived in the married quarters walked in the procession to support Mrs Mary Poole. Fifty N C O's, each carrying a suitable floral tribute, made up the wreath party. In the centre of Holywood the Union flag, which had been flying at half-mast since the tragedy occurred, was lowered on to each of the stationary hearses at the maypole. The gates of the cemetery had to be closed because of the huge crowds of weeping mourners moving towards the open grave.

All the clergy of the town and representatives of every organisation in the town assembled in the cemetery. The five little coffins were buried in a single grave after a simple service conducted by the Garrison Chaplain. In order to place the two little girls into their separate caskets it had been necessary for Major Gillespie, Royal Army Medical Corps, to break apart their firmly linked hands. In the horrors of asphyxia, Jean and Margaret, who slept together, before death had clenched each other's little hand.

The memorial stone is inscribed :

> *"Sacred to the memory of the children of Harry and Mary Poole*
> *Joseph 9, David 8, Harry 6, Margaret 4, Jean 2.*
> *All called home together on 23rd April, 1933.*
> *Our loss is Heaven's gain."*

If you walk by the grave now, almost seventy years after the tragedy, you will find flowers laid in memory of the five little children from over the water who were left behind in Holywood when the Border Regiment returned to the mainland.

The story of the Garrison Town and the Palace Barracks must include a short reference to the sad times of the Irish Troubles during the second part of the twentieth century, when the Army was called upon to defend the town from terrorist activity.

For the first time in a hundred years security precautions prevented traditional Holywood hospitality. As late as Christmas 1973 soldiers of the 1st Battalion, Middlesex Regiment were the welcome guests to many Holywood Christmas Day family dinner parties. The Belfast Telegraph reported :

> *"Assistant Adjutant Captain C H Gladden says an Army camp at Christmas can be a pretty dismal place for single soldiers. All the camp parties and concerts do not compensate for a Christmas away from home and invitations help the unit to make friends in Northern Ireland."*

However, as terrorist activity increased in the Province, Holywood people had to understand the necessary separation between civilian and military lifestyles for security reasons.

Belfast Telegraph reported on 2nd September 1971 –

> *"A 15 lb bomb was discovered in the toilets of the NAAFI - a shopping facility filled with women and children at lunchtime. One possibility is that the gelignite was smuggled into the Palace Barracks in small quantities, and the bomb assembled by a civilian worker on site."*

We read on 27th January 1972 –

> *"At 11 pm a 15 lb bomb exploded in the transport park, destroying three Parachute Regiment vehicles. A second bomb was defused beside the Officers' Mess."*

Then on all Fools' Day 1977, during the 1st Battalion Gordon Highlanders' third term of duty in modern times, a civilian driver attempted to bring a proxy bomb onto the Palace Barracks campus. The diligent sentry on guard duty refused entry and the car exploded a few minutes later on the Holywood dual carriageway. Records of prisoners' escapes from top security detention, civilian workers receiving death threats and accusations of brutality were the coinage of the camp in those days of terrorist outrage. The Palace Barracks has taken triumphs and tragedies in its stride, served with exemplary consideration and, now, a large village itself, it had benefited and protected Holywood for over a century.

As our town is proud of its garrison status, equally we respect the men and women of Holywood who paid the Supreme Sacrifice in the Wars and whose names are recorded on the Holywood and District War Memorial.

Saturday, 28th January 1922 was a very special day in the town. At three o'clock on that cold winter afternoon, a huge crowd packed Redburn Square for the unveiling of the War Memorial. A large party of ex-Service men was on parade, attended by a full contingent of Boy Scouts.

The Commandant of the British Legion, Sgt Major Webster read the roll call, the names of the dead each followed by a beat on a muffled drum. Buglers of 1st Battalion Somerset Light Infantry sounded "The Last Post". The three buglers sounded "Reveille" after Mrs Elliott of Sullivan Street had placed the public wreath at the base of the new memorial. Mrs Elliott had lost three sons in the War.

The unveiling ceremony was performed by Mrs Dunlop of St Helen's, widow of the town's popular medical practitioner; their eldest son had been the first flower of Holywood's youth to be cut down in the Great War. That afternoon a great garden of private wreaths was planted around the Holywood soldier on his Portland stone plinth.

Many voluntary subscriptions had commissioned sculptor L S Merrifield to design the bronze statue of the soldier "in full kit" in "on guard" position.

A bronze plaque proclaims *"In grateful memory of the men of Holywood and district who gave their lives in the Great War 1914 - 1918". "Their name liveth for evermore."*

Soon the names of Holywood combatants killed in the 1939 - 1945 War were added to the Roll of Honour.

In 1972 the traditional parade ground in front of the War Memorial was sacrificed to road development, when the Holywood throughpass ate its voracious way through the town. In recent years, the Borough Council has created a pleasant garden of remembrance in Redburn Square and replaced the ornamental lamp posts around the War Memorial. Our Holywood soldier continues to defend this Garrison Town from nautical attack!

Sandes Soldiers'Home (1903). It became the Loughview Hotel and later the Strathearn Hotel.

The next generation is well represented in the Garrison Town by the Army Cadet Force, the Air Training Corps and the Sea Cadet Unit.

The **CADET MOVEMENT** is the oldest uniformed youth organisation in the United Kingdom. Although it was formed one hundred and forty years ago, it did not extend into Northern Ireland until 1943. Of course, our town was one of the first in the Province to form an **A C F** platoon. It was inaugurated under command of Lieutenant J Riley and affiliated to the Royal Ulster Rifles in 1943. For many years the platoon met in accommodation on My Lady's Mile. The A C F hut was situated to the east of the tennis courts, on the path which is now called Norwood Lane. In the early 1960's a welcome removal was made to the new Territorial Army Centre at Kinnegar. In 1957 a second unit was formed in Holywood. It is the Sullivan Upper Detachment, affiliated to The Royal Signals. This large and successful unit is restricted to school students and is commanded by Lieutenant Karen Loughrey.

The **AIR TRAINING CORPS** was formed in 1941, at the very height of the Second World War. A massive expansion took place during the war years to provide the large number of potential recruits necessary for maintenance of the Royal Air force. Today there are 940 squadrons throughout the United Kingdom with about 37,000 cadets. The Corps recruits from ages thirteen to eighteen. Cadets may stay on until they are nineteen, or twenty-two for Cadet Warrant Officers.

Proximity to local aerospace manufacturers and the City Airport has always engendered interest in aeronautics by teenagers from Holywood.

Over the years regiments at Palace Barracks have been good neighbours to the Royal Air Force and up until 31st March 1978 Officers of R A F Sydenham were welcome members of Oakley House Officers' Mess. Belfast R A F Careers Office is situated within the Palace Barracks.

2178 Holywood A T C Squadron was formed as a detached flight in 1943. This was at the instigation of Lord Londonderry whose family still lives over the Holywood Hills at Mountstewart. At first, the DF (Direct Flight) met in the Sullivan School building, which in 1954 became Holywood Technical College.

In 1946 the DF was awarded Squadron status. About 1960, 2178 (Holywood) Squadron removed to the A T C Hall on Sullivan Place. The hall was situated between the N I Fire Authority building and the Queen's Hall complex. In the 1960's squadron membership stood at over fifty cadets. It became the royal guard of honour for Northern Ireland, equipped with 36 drill purpose Lee-Enfield .303 rifles. The squadron provided the guard of honour for Royal visits and Lords Lieutenant functions around the Province.

After five years residence in the Sullivan Place hall, the Squadron removed to purpose-built premises adjacent to the Territorial Army Centre at Kinnegar. This was a wooden hut, standardized throught the U K, and was a complete disappointment after the Cadets' palatial location on Sullivan Place.

On 26th August 2000, 2178 (Holywood) Squadron Air Training Corps removed once again - fifty-seven years after inception as a DF. On this occasion the move was a mere five metres - into the Kinnegar Territorial Army Centre. The Centre had been vacated by the Royal Military Police Company (T A) as part of the draw down of U K Reserve Forces. Again the Squadron has spacious accommodation for expansion and looks forward to equaling its 1960's strength in numbers of Cadets. It is vigorous and successful, currently it includes among its members the Lord Lieutenant's Cadet for County Down and the winner of the Best Cadet Award for Scotland and Northern Ireland.

The **SEA CADET MOVEMENT** dates back to the days of the Crimean War when home-coming sailors organised Naval Lads' Brigades for orphans of fallen comrades. Two World Wars developed the movement into a vibrant network of 400 units throughout the U K, sponsored by the Royal Navy. The movement seeks to prepare young people to meet the challenges of the future. Training is based on boatwork; seagoing experience under sail and power; team competitions and individual skills achievement - more worthwhile than trivial leisure pursuits and computer games!

Each unit is organised within the finest traditions of the Senior Service, adding value to proactive community involvement by relating directly to the local social conditions. The **Holywood Sea Cadet Unit** was formed in 1999. As we see the traditional, yet trendy, uniform around the town we are reminded of Holywood's long maritime connections.

Indeed, we are proud of our long history as a garrison town and welcome the local programme of service provided for Holywood's next generation.

HOLYWOOD GYMNASIUM.

GYMNASTIC DISPLAY AND MILITARY TOURNAMENT,

Under the distinguished patronage of COL. JENKINS and OFFICERS 1st BATT. RIFLE BRIGADE,

In TOWN HALL, HOLYWOOD, Saturday, 6th April, 1907,

W. E. WILLIAMES, Esq., J.P., presiding.

PROGRAMME.

1. VAULTING HORSE ... ... BY MEMBERS.
2. INDIAN CLUB EXHIBITION BY COL.-SERGT. SMYTHE (1st Batt. Rifle Brigade).
3. HORIZONTAL BAR ... ... BY MEMBERS.
4. HEAVY-WEIGHT LIFTING ... ... MR. J. TELFORD.
5. COMPETITION, BAYONET v. BAYONET (1st Round), for Gold and Silver Medals, By Men of the 1st Batt. Rifle Brigade.
6. DUMB-BELL DRILL ... ... BY MEMBERS.
7. EXHIBITION OF BOXING By THE BROTHERS PHILLIPS (Aldershot School), Army Midget Champions.
8. COMPETITION, BAYONET v. BAYONET (2nd Round).
9. PARALLEL BARS AND TABLEAU ... ... BY MEMBERS.
10. VIOLIN SOLO ... ... BY MR P. M'DOWELL.
11. COMPETITION, BAYONET v. BAYONET (Final).
12. GYMNASTIC BALL GAME ... ... BY MEMBERS.
13. DISTRIBUTION OF MEDALS.

GOD SAVE THE KING.

LIST OF MEDALS:

GYMNASTIC COMPETITIONS (Junior Grade):

1st—Gold Medal, presented by W. E. Williames, Esq., J.P.; won by TOM GREENFIELD (Score, 77 points).
2nd—Gold Centre Medal, presented by Wm. Black, Esq.; won by VICTOR SLOAN. (Score, 64 points).
3rd—Silver Medal, presented by W. J. Dunwoody, Esq.; won by JOS. HARRISON. (Score, 63 points).

BAYONET v. BAYONET (Confined to Men. of 1st. Batt. Rifle Brigade):

1st—Gold Medal, presented by Major T. V P. M'Cammon, J.P.
2nd—Silver Medal, presented by R. A. Shekelton, Esq., M.D.

BOXING:

Silver Medal, presented by Thos. Barbour, Esq

ESSAY XVIII - HOLYWOOD - A MECCA OF CLUBS AND ORGANISATIONS

HOLYWOOD SCOUTS CAMP FIRE CHORUS

Boil, Oh boil the jolly kettle

Fill, oh fill the billy-can
And to put us into fettle
Eat as much as any man!

Tanned by wind and sun and weather,
For all things we're prepared,
Scout-like, stand or fall together
Every joy or sorrow shared.

When for camping we assemble
See the bread and butter fly
And the cows are all a-tremble
For we drain them nearly dry.

All the hens are busy laying,
Churns are working day and night
Folk from Holywood are saying
"Bless us! What an appetite!"

Robert Patterson of Glenbank,
Scoutmaster of 1st Holywood

FREEMASONRY IN HOLYWOOD

Freemasonry traces its ancient origin from the builders of the Jerusalem Temple in the days of King Solomon, to the fourteenth century guilds of travelling masons and stone-workers who used signs and passwords to greet and gain acceptance from brother craftsmen.

Scotland possesses the earliest record of Masons organised into Lodges, about four hundred years ago. The first Irish Grand Lodge was formed in 1723, its members coming from aristocracy, farmers and tradesmen alike; Catholic, Protestant and Dissenter.

The symbolic degrees, rites and ceremonies date from this time. Emphasis is laid on the member's duty to family, country, fellow members and Deity. The Order of the Eastern Star was founded in 1868; it welcomes women relatives of Masons and Master Masons.

In Holywood, Freemasonry goes back to 3rd June 1813, with the issue of Warrant 254 to the Felicity Lodge. The Lodge ceased to exist on 5th July 1856. Originally the warrant had been issued to a Lodge in Co Waterford in the year 1755 Warrant Number 74 was granted to a Holywood Lodge on 11th November 1844 and suspended on 2nd June 1859.

The oldest existing Lodge in Holywood is Victoria Number 254, the warrant of which was issued on 11th August 1868.

On St John's Day, 1813, three weeks after the inauguration of the Felicity Lodge, thirty-one visiting Lodges came to our town for the annual celebration. The procession assembled in Donegall Place, Belfast and was joined by other Lodges on its progress to Holywood, led by bands and many colourful banners.

The religious service of the day was conducted by Rev Brother Joseph Harrison in the old Presbyterian Church in Strand Street, or Gospel Lane, as the wags of that day called the street!

The draughty old Church with its several galleries was packed to the roof for the occasion. Little did the members of Holywood Lodge think that by the mid-1870's the building would be Holywood Masonic headquarters!

The Holywood celebrations for the year 1818 were recorded meticulously by the teenage Robert Sullivan, destined to become Ireland's famous educationalist. He inscribed his song to Holywood Mason Lodge No 254 to be sung to the tune "Burns' Farewell". I wonder does any other Irish Lodge have its own poem written one hundred and twenty years ago? Did that great reader of newspapers, young Robert Sullivan, see the media account of the celebration before he wrote the song?

A SONG INSCRIBED TO HOLYWOOD MASON LODGE NO. 254

"Upon the twenty-fourth of June
When blooming Nature's face is fair,
To hear the feathered warblers tune
Unto the fields I did repair.
I scarce had been one minute there,
When sounds of joy assailed my ear:
Loud acclamations rent the air –
I straight returned the cause to hear.

When, lo appeared a Mason band,
Harmonious music at their head –
In unity joined hand in hand

They marched along with colours spread.
Their Master's robe was costly red,
Quite splendidly they all were drest:
And care from every heart was fled
And pleasure reigned in every breast.

From Holywood they did proceed
To Bangor town, sublime and fair;
Twelve Lodges, I am told, agreed
To meet and to assemble there.
Rich satin aprons they did wear,
On each was wrought the arch and hall,
The rule, the compass and the square,
Embroidered was upon them all.

Majestically they marched along,
Their drums and fifes did sweetly play -
Amidst the praises of the throng
No Lodge could cope with them that day.
Each member graceful was and gay
Just like our town's brave volunteers
That did their seal and worth display
At the reviews in former years.

Robert Sullivan
30th June 1818

The Newsletter of 30th June 1818 described *"the respectable meeting of Masons held in the town of Bangor on the Anniversary of St John"*, which the Holywood Lodge attended. The religious service was held in the old Bangor Presbyterian Church, beside the harbour at the foot of Ballymagee Street. Rev Hugh Wood, who served from 1808 to 1869, delivered a most acceptable sermon on "Peace to all men".

As well as the removal to the former church building, the Lodge suffered many transfers to new meeting places over the years. For the first two decades it met in public and private rooms around the town. In 1843 the Holywood Hotel became its venue.

On 10 July 1856 the Felicity Lodge came to an end. Because the Lodge had assembled in so many places in the town, it had been necessary to carry a floor cloth to delineate the various stations of the Lodge room on its peripatetic meetings. The beautifully restored floor cloth of the old Felicity Lodge hangs in the anteroom of the Masonic Hall in Sullivan Place. The working jewels of Felicity Lodge, its original banner and cancelled warrant document are well preserved. A refurbished antique chair from the old Lodge adorns the present-day refreshment room.

Holywood Gymnasium (1870) on Shore Street. It became the Innis motor garage and was demolished in 1974.

When Victoria Lodge came into being in 1868, under the new warrant 254, its meeting place was Wellington Terrace on the Kinnegar. Soon it removed to the Assembly Rooms; then to Mrs Anderson's house; on to the old Presbyterian Church, and then in 1880 to 5 Bath Terrace. Five years later the Masons transferred to the old National School building on Church View.

The opening of the refurbished schoolhouse took place on 16th November 1885. and was performed by Rt Hon Lord Arthur Hill, MP for West Down, whose family had bought the manorial rights of Holywood in 1705.

Members of the Lodge and visiting brethren, assembled in the Town Hall, then only ten years old, proceeded in full regalia to Church View for the ceremony, returned to the Town Hall for a sumptuous banquet, which was followed by a grand concert. Lord Arthur himself was prevailed upon to contribute several musical items to this very successful event.

At the turn of the century an expanding membership demanded larger premises. Squire Henry Harrison provided land beside the Town Hall in Sullivan Place. Architect Godfrey W Ferguson designed a building suitable for the prestigious site. It was opened on 12th January 1905 as a memorial to Brother Thomas A McCammon.

The building is fine example of Arts and Crafts design. Interesting features are the large semi-circular stained glass window and the square tower topped by a picturesque copper dome. The interior is comfortably designed with spacious lodge room, banquet hall and other facilities, all of which are beautifully furnished. The property is well maintained and is a credit to the town of Holywood.

Charles Grant recorded the history of several other lodges associated with Holywood. The warrant of the County Masonic Lodge 381 was constituted on 12th January 1905 when the new Hall was opened in Sullivan Place.

The warrant of Sharman Crawford Lodge 403 was issued in 1906. Sharman Crawford was a local politician and landowner. The warrant of John B Crozier Lodge 497 was issued to a new Lodge constituted in Holywood on 12th February 1921. The warrant of T V P McCammon Memorial Lodge 540 was issued in 1922. After the First World War it was suggested that a Lodge should be formed in Holywood to perpetuate the spirit of camaraderie which characterised all ranks in the Forces during the Great War. The title commemorates Lieut Colonel T V P McCammon.

As we enter the twenty-first century, twenty-three Lodges, Chapters, Councils and Templars meet at Holywood. Their unadvertised contribution to our community for almost two centuries is monumental.

THE LOYAL ORANGE INSTITUTION IN HOLYWOOD

Holywood members of the Loyal Orange Institution built their grand mansion house at the corner of Sullivan Place in 1879, although the Order had been active in our town in the earlier years of the nineteenth century.

The Constitution was established after the Battle of the Diamond near Loughgall on 21st September 1795, when the Orange Boys, an offshoot of the Peep O' Day Boys, overcame the Defenders, an adjunct to the United Irishmen.

In those days, the Order attempted to unite the various adherents to the Reformed Faith into a homogenous group, with a view to defend religious freedom for all Irishmen.

The basis of the Institution is to support and defend the honour of King William III; the present Sovereign; the Protestant succession of the House of Windsor; the Reformed Religion and the Law of the land.

The Institution unites to defend its own persons and properties, also to maintain the public peace. It rejects intolerance, persecution, injury and the objurgation of anyone on account of religious preference.

The Orange Order is exclusively an association of Christian people who are attached to the religion of the Reformation. Members are required to attend Church regularly, live morally upright lives and be bonded by tolerance towards each other and to those outside their Brotherhood who adhere to a difference religious persuasion.

Several Lodges meet in Holywood - the District L O L 14 encompasses Ballykeel, Ballyrobert, Dundonald and Castlereagh.
L O L 1687 was first registered in Lisburn during the year 1823 and was meeting in Holywood by 1856, although still within the Belfast District. It was established within the Holywood District in 1884. The Lodge is known as McCammon's True Blues commemorating Lt Col T V P McCammon, son of Col Thomas A McCammon. T V P McCammon was Commanding Officer of the 5th Battalion Royal Irish Rifles, who died in action with the British Expeditionary Force in France on 28th April 1917. He is also commemorated in one of the Holywood Masonic Lodges.

Another famous Holywood personality, who name is held in high esteem in both Orders, is John Baptist Crozier (1853 to 1920). He was Vicar of Holywood from 1880 to 1897. In 1897 he was elevated to the Bishopric of Ossory, Ferns and Leighlin, and a decade later transferred to the Diocese of Down, Connor and Dromore. In 1911 he became the Archbishop of Armagh, Primate of Ireland. Crozier Memorial Temperance L O L 1362 recalls his service to the Holywood community.

The Hall provides accommodation for two Royal Black Preceptories - Holywood R B P 177 and Joshua's Chosen Few R B P 174; also Holywood Women's Lodge Number 4. The famous Colonel Henry Baker, Governor of Londonderry, who died during the siege, is remembered by the Apprentice Boys of Derry Holywood Baker Club.

The old building was completely refurbished in 1964, when the main entrance was opened on to Redburn Square. The Orange Order has granted many Holywood organisations use of the Hall. Formerly the Petty Sessions Court and the local office of the Social Security Agency met there. Holywood people have benefited from the generosity of the Orange charities over many years.

OTHER HOLYWOOD ORGANISATIONS

Whereas it seems simple to discover a letter written fifteen hundred years ago by a Holywood holy man to the Pope in Rome, it is very difficult to unearth the origins of some of our associations founded a mere fifty years ago by the equally holy people of the holy wood. I hope I am able to cover a fair example of our activities in this essay. Every time I thought the list had been completed, Holywood, like the Lernean Hydra, grew another head! I am no Herculean chronicler - if your particular interest has been omitted, I apologise and promise to do better in the future.

Indeed there are many clubs, organisations and associations connected with our ecclesiastical, educational and sporting communities, and there are clubs for specialist pursuits such as fishing and beagling. Others have opened, flourished and failed as current fashion demanded. No doubt the people of the Third Millennium will see many more come and go. Down the years all of them show the vibrancy of our living and caring Holywood community.

THE STORY OF THE BADEN-POWELL SCOUT MOVEMENT IN HOLYWOOD

General Robert Baden-Powell (1857 – 1941) discovered the value of employing soldiers as scouts, during his campaigns in the Boer War (1899 – 1902). He wrote a little book called *"Aids to Scouting"*. It became a textbook for Boys' Brigade leaders who requested the 1908 *"Scouting for Boys"* as a training manual. An experimental camp had been organised the previous year and patrols of Baden-Powell Scouts started to appear in Belfast Boys Brigade companies and Y M C A youth groups from 1907.

Soon the Scouts became an independent movement requiring its members to be loyal to God and King, helpful to everyone and obedient to the Scout Law. The badge was taken from the 'Nort Point' in map reading and the motto – *"Be Prepared"* – came from the South African Constabulary in which Baden-Powell had served. Within two years the movement had spread around the world.

Baden-Powell was no stranger to our area. The Belfast Street Directory for 1896 lists him among the residents of No 2 Eno Villas. This was the officers' mess of the Hussars, who were stationed in Willowbank Barracks before embarkation to South Africa. B-P often spoke of *"beautiful suburban Belfast"* and his enjoyment in *"hiking on the Cave Hill"*.

It was not long before the Scouts came to Holywood; it is thought a troop was founded in 1908 by Rev W J Archer of High Street Presbyterian Church, possibly in connection with the Boys' Brigade Company. The first recorded reference appears to be a members' subscription list for June 1910. The following month the notebook diary of Scoutmaster Martyn Downing gives the format of the local committee. The little notebook is an amusing list of the antics of mischievous boys; the price of food and fares; in fact, the record of an emerging organisation, and an authoritative archive of Holywood youth a century ago.

The first big event for the embryonic troop was a visit to the King's Rally at Windsor Park, London from 30th June to 5th July 1911, camping at Harrow. It was an exciting time for R Beverland, R Curley, H May, J Mawhinney, Donald Fox, Tom McCleave, James Steel and Albert Robinson, under the leadership of Scoutmaster W Martyn Downing. It cost the boys £2 each. Local subscriptions came to £35 – total expenses were £29, leaving a profit of £6. All this is meticulously recorded with a visit to Madame Tussaud's wax exhibition, and a boat trip on the Thames. Sir William Ewart generously treated the boys to a sight seeing tour of the capital, which cost him £7 – that is £350 at today's monetary value. The boys must have remembered Sir William's treat for the rest of their lives!
In the early months the troop was peripatetic, meeting in Rollo House, the Holywood gymnasium, the Town Hall or the Hockey Club. In 1915 the Scouts refurbished the former Masonic Hall, primarily as a drop-in centre for soldiers from the Palace Barracks, for those were the war years. It became a commodious headquarters with a hall and patrol rooms, and received a special visit from B-P himself.

In 1912 Robert Patterson of Glenbank was Holywood Scoutmaster. Glenbank is the redbrick house beside the Croft Burn at the top of Victoria Road. The Pattersons allowed the Scouts to build a camping cabin in the Glenbank orchard, which became the troop's first permanent home. Robert Patterson's first camp was on Mid-Island in Strangford Lough, 12th to 20th July 1912 – the project started his long association with Scouting in Holywood and U K. In 1920, when he was Deputy Provincial Commissioner, B-P invested him with the coveted Silver Wolf. The following year he became an Assistant Camp Chief at Gilwell Park Training Centre on the edge of Epping Forest. Holywood's loss was U K's gain.

Holywood Scouts gained an enviable reputation for their ability to perform at concerts and raise funds for special projects. On 15th March 1913, Viscountess Bangor opened a mammoth Sale of Work in Holywood Town Hall. According to the Northern Whig, Lady Kennedy's stall *'had a splendid collection of unusual items from Russia, the West Indies, Italy and France'*. The Whig continued -
"Doubtless there will be a large attendance of ladies from Belfast anxious to pick up some of the unique articles." The sale raised over £100 – a vast sum of money in March 1913.

Appropriately, the 1st Holywood Troop was known as "Sir Robert Kennedy's Own". Newsletter for 10th May 1913 recorded that Sir Robert had given the troop a hut in the Cultra Manor woodlands. Henry Ballagh (1905 - 1998) remembered it very well – a hut measuring sixteen feet by twelve, where many happy weekends were spent camping. Sir Robert frequently visited the camps - one weekend he brought his friend Sir Robert Baden-Powell with him. To mark the occasion the Chief Scout attached a large brass Scout badge to a tree beside a blazing campfire in front of the hut.

To show his continued interest in his own troop, Sir Robert Kennedy presented colours and a silver dolphin, the Kennedy emblem, as a flagstaff top. The beautiful silver dolphin is used today as a trophy for Ulster Scout aquatic activities.

Sir Robert also encouraged the formation of a flute band and a team of buglers for the Holywood troop.

In June 1913 the troop was given a special reception at Cultra Manor. The First Norfolk Regiment had organised in Belfast the annual province-wide flag signalling championship, competing for the Lady Jaffe Challenge Shield. Holywood Scouts won the day. When H J Dunne and A R Parsons got back home they were chaired through the town, accompanied by the flute and bugle bands – the precious shield held high for everyone to see. The merry procession wended its way to Cultra Manor where the shield was graciously received and given a place of honour in the hall under the portraits of

King Edward and Queen Alexandra. After the customary Manor hospitality, the troop marched back to Holywood behind the flutes and bugles. *"Irish Society"* for 26th July 1913 succinctly captured the event –

> *"Lady Kennedy, who takes a kindly interest in the Boy Scout movement, recently was the recipient of the magnificent challenge shield won by the Holywood troop. Sir Robert Kennedy, who accepted custody in his capacity as President of the troop, said that as all the most valuable things he possessed he placed in the care of his wife, he asked her to take the treasure and guard it jealously. Afterwards the Scouts were entertained by Lady Kennedy, whose health was drunk, together with that of the King and Sir Robert."*

The Belfast Newsletter for 29th April 1913 reported the opening by Lady Kennedy of the new summer camp clubhouse, which Scoutmaster Patterson had erected in his orchard on Victoria Road beside the Croft Burn. The boys did all the work themselves. In her speech, Lady Kennedy referred to the builders as *"young men who would be asked to defend the country against their enemies, if ever the time came"*. The time came fourteen months later, on 4th August 1914 – a war in which every Scout did his duty. The Newsletter for 22nd February 1915 noted that seventeen Holywood Scouts had already enlisted in Lord Kitchener's Army.

Scout troops all over the Province were vitalized by the war effort on the home front. Many projects were undertaken to assist local communities and support the Forces. In 1915 the troop refurbished the former Masonic Hall as a drop-in centre for soldiers from the Palace Barracks. In 1916 the Belfast Telegraph reported the area Scouts' collection of empty bottles and jars which were desperately needed. The project raised £1,233, which was used to build three recreation huts for soldiers on the front line in France and the new Sailors' Club in Belfast.

In Holywood so many boys wanted to join the Scouts that a second troop had to be formed. Rev J T Armstrong became first Scoutmaster of the troop connected with the Church of Ireland in March 1916. Troop headquarters was established in the former Parochial School on Church Road. Although not the oldest group in the district, 2nd Holywood has the longest continuous service record.

One of Holywood's best remembered Scouts is Denis Olver. He was a patrol leader in Kilkenny long before he gave splendid service to the Scout Movement in Holywood.

On 1st June 1918 Denis saved a young boy from drowning in the Lagan Canal. The Earl of Meath congratulated him on the Award of the Gilt Cross.

An eyewitness recorded -

> *"The boy was fishing at the first lock and fell in. His cries brought two bargees, but as they could not swim they merely joined in the chorus and called for help. The boy was on his last gasp when Olver dived in and successfully kept him afloat. Olver's promptitude saved the boy's life as the steepness of the lock made the rescue very difficult."*

The Parochial National School on Church Road (1845). It became the Parish Hall (c. 1878) and the Scout Hall in 1954.

The most exciting post-war event for the Holywood troops was a visit to London Olympia for the 1920 International Jamboree. Nineteen happy Scouts assembled under the canopy of the old Holywood Railway Station for a photo opportunity on 28th July 1920. A special Ulster badge, a red hand on a green shamrock was worn for the first time – the red hand of Ulster spectacular was received enthusiastically by the huge Olympia crowd.

Holywood was represented in the guard of honour which lined the Royal route from the Albert Memorial clock to the Cornmarket when King George and Queen Mary visited Belfast City Hall on 22nd June 1921 to open the Parliament of Northern Ireland.

> *"I speak from a full heart when I pray that my coming to Ireland today may prove to be the first step towards an end of strife amongst the people, whatever their race or creed. In that hope I appeal to all Irishmen to pause, to stretch our the hand of forbearance and conciliation, to forgive and to forget, and to join in making for the land which they love a new era of peace, contentment and goodwill"* -

Such were the words of King George V on that summer day some eighty years ago. In such a spirit of toleration, the Belfast Rotary Club subsidised the delegation to the 1924 Imperial Jamboree held in connection with the British Empire Exhibition at Wembley.

The Holywood troops were well to the fore among the eleven thousand Guides and Scouts who joined in *"the howl of welcome that rose to a terrific crescendo and rolled thunder-like away to the Hills of Antrim."* This was the florid report in the Northern Whig on 10th June 1929, which described the Balmoral welcome given to Lord and Lady Baden-Powell.

Fifty thousand Scouts participated in the Coming of Age World Jamboree at Arrow Park, Birkenhead. It is best remembered as a *"Mudboree"* and for *"woggles"*. The Australian delegation wore scarf fasteners made from native gum nuts to replace the ordinary scarf knot. Woggles were simulated in thin rings of leather and soon became a popular addition to Scout uniform everywhere.

Holywood Scouts were also well represented at the Silver Jubilee celebrations of May 1935. After a great assembly of youth organisations at Balmoral, thirty-six Ulster bonfires joined the seven hundred beacons ignited around the United Kingdom.

The following Royal occasion was the 1937 Coronation visit of King George VI and Queen Elizabeth – for once Balmoral was bathed in magnificent Irish July sunshine.

Then came the year 1939 and another World War. The Chief Commissioner sent a letter to all Scout troops in the Province, seeking support for the Government's request for help in the National emergency. The Scout messenger service was revived, war effort projects were prodigious and a very great number of Scouts joined the security forces.

As before, in war time, interest in Scouting was revived. In 1943 a third Holywood Scout troop came into existence. The first Scoutmaster was Stewart McCadden and the meeting place was the loft of a building behind the old Post Office in High Street. Today, Strand Mews occupies the site. After strenuous fund-raising projects, land at the top of Ean Hill was acquired for a headquarters in 1949, and a temporary hall opened there two years later. The present purpose-built headquarters was built there in 1966, and the Craigantlet Cottage acquired in 1970.

Bob-a-job Weeks were introduced in 1944 – a "bob" was a shilling, or five pence after the decimalisation of our currency. The scheme was revived in 1949 to raise funds for the Scout movement. Holywood householders were well served by the number of boys seeking gardening and garage jobs, many of which were executed with skill and courtesy. *"Would that we had such a reasonable labour force today!"*

Crawfordsburn Camp Site welcomed its first open day visitors in 1949. Holywood is very fortunate to have an international camping and leadership training centre a mere 750 metres beyond our district boundary. The Holywood troops are proud to have the Heasley Memorial Chapel at Crawfordsburn Scout Centre named after a scout who cheerfully contributed much of his life and time to the movement in Holywood and throughout the Province.

When Canon Hill came to Holy Trinity Church, Glencraig in 1948 he found an almost extinct Scout Group in Helen's Bay, which he attempted to revive without success. He started a Wolf Cub Pack at Glencraig which, with the present day troop – 1st Craigavad, continues to flourish. The little book *"Still other Seed"* pictures the good Canon seated on a pile of logs with his young Wolf Cubs. They are gathered around a campfire in the plantation of tall trees where the new Church hall is situated. Eventually land was given for a headquarters – the Churchill Hall, which was erected on a former milk collection centre about 1950. Recently the building has been refurbished with grants from the Parish Church and the Borough Council. The 1st Craigavad Scout Group provides a generous and useful community service by allowing other organisations to use the hall. In 1999 Craigavad Guides came to the fore once again, and now have their meetings in the Churchill Hall.

For a short time, about the year 1950, we had a 4th Holywood Scout Troop which met in a cottage at Knocknagoney, behind Monty's Spout, the sweet spring water supply for the surrounding cottages. In 1931, as a memorial to her son Bobbie, Mrs Violet Dunville of Redburn converted the spout into a drinking fountain, a trough for thirsty horses with a bowl at ground level for tired dogs. Later the troop's meeting place was nearer Holywood at Redburn. It continued for a decade and was re-activated when Jim Mulligan was District Commissioner. It served boys from the Loughview and Redburn areas, but ceased to operate in 2000.

Before the Holywood Urban District Council acquired Redburn House and sixty hectares of woodlands in 1950, one of the many suggestions for its use was a recreation and camping ground for youth groups. Perhaps Crawfordsburn eclipsed this project. However, over the years Holywood Scouts continued to enjoy the use of the house and grounds for summer fetes and camps.

In 1958 Holywood joined in the spirited welcome to the Chief Scout, Lord Rowallane, when he came to visit Crawfordsburn. In 1961 Baden-Powell House, London, was opened by Her Majesty Queen Elizabeth II as a memorial to the founder. Five Queen's Scouts from Northern Ireland were in the guard of honour.

Holywood was represented at many of the world jamborees and summer camps took Holywood boys all over Europe. To celebrate seventy-five years of Scouting in the Province, an international camp was held at Castle Archdale, Co Fermanagh – officially called Lakeland 82. This was the time of the "troubles". Holywood Scouts with their peers showed the world the normality of life in Northern Ireland and the hospitality of our people. Over 30,000 people visited the camp. The Chief Scout, General Michael Walsh, wrote in the camp newsletter "The Lakelander" –

> *"As the only honorary member of the Lakeland Troop, I am delighted to have been able to be with you. Thank you for inviting me to Northern Ireland. I look forward to coming back soon."*

And he did.

Subsequent Chief Scouts have also visited this area. Garth Morrison, who succeeded Michael Walsh, was a sheep-farmer from the Scottish Highlands. On a visit to a Beaver

Scout Rally at Crawfordsburn, he was presented with a blackthorn thumb-stick, made by Jim Shannon from Holywood, which he treasured as a momento of his visit, and which features in many photographs during his term in office. The current Chief Scout, George Purdy, is no stranger to County Down, he hails from Donaghadee.

Scouts and their leaders should be congratulated that within this decade Holywood Scouts will be celebrating their centenary among the townspeople to whose positive lifestyle they have liberally contributed.

14TH DOWN AND CONNOR SCOUT TROOP

The inaugural meeting of 14th Down and Connor Scout Troop took place in May 1972 and the first investiture was held in St Colmcille's Church on Sunday, 2nd June 1972.

The organising committee determined that the troop should have its own "Den" where the Scouts could keep Troop property, camping equipment and records in a place of their own. Accordingly a wooden hut was erected in the old St Patrick's school yard, and here were trained the leaders who have carried the traditions of Scouting to future generations.

The first of many annual summer camps was held at Lough Key, County Roscommon in July 1974. The following year 14th Down and Connor was well represented at Rome during the Holy Year 1975.

Eventually the "Hut" fell down and the Troop transferred to accommodation in St Patrick's Hall on Church View. An exciting ambition is that one day the Troop will be able to re-build its own special "Den".

Twenty-two boys joined the Troop when it came into being in 1974. By the end of the decade girls were welcomed into the Group. Now 14th Down and Connor has over sixty members and a twenty-first century project is to establish a Venture Scout Group for those who wish to continue the Scouting way of life.

THE GIRL GUIDE MOVEMENT IN HOLYWOOD

When Sir Robert Baden-Powell inspired the formation of Boy Scout Troops in 1908 he discovered that thousands of girls wanted to enrol in the movement. They were encouraged by articles for "Girl Scouts" in "Home Notes" – a fashionable ladies' magazine of the day. In 1910 Miss Agnes Baden-Powell was commissioned by her famous brother to set up a parallel organisation to which the title "Girl Guides" was given.

The movement spread through the world; in France it was called *"Les Eclairuses"* and in the U S A after 1915 the girls were known as "Girl Scouts".
The trifoliate badge represents the three-fold promise – duty to God and country; duty to assist others, duty to obey the Guide Law. Audrey Smartt, daughter of a Newry doctor, applied to London for membership; her card signed by Agnes Baden-Powell certifies her as Ireland's first Girl Guide.

The first Ulster Guide Company was formed in St John's Church, Whitehouse; the second was in Richmond Lodge School, Belfast. That grand old firm, Robb's of Castle Junction, a Holywood family, tailored the uniform. It was designed by the girls themselves – navy blue serge and hats piped with red. The girls carried staves and white haversacks.

Guiding rapidly spread through Ireland, after 1916 younger sisters eagerly became Brownies and older guides remained in the movement as Rangers. The Province of Ulster Girl Guides was formed officially in 1920. The first Holywood Company pre-dated this by three years.

During the closing years of the First World War - on 26th September 1917 – Miss M L Davis of Abingdon on Demesne Road registered the 1st Holywood Guide Company. The Brownie Pack followed two years later. Meetings were held in that quaint little building which was part of the Old Priory Inn – *"the room above the bar"*. Having served Holywood as "the Ballroom" and "the Methodist Chapel" it was unnecessarily demolished in 1982.

4th Holywood Guides were attached to St Philip and St James Church. The company was formed in 1936. When disbanded their colours were laid up for safe-keeping in the Church in 1984.

3rd Holywood Guides were formed in 1988 and some nine Brownie and Rainbow units organised between 1934 and 1989.

Soon the Guides removed from "the room above the bar" to a purpose built hall in Park Drive. The girls were very proud of this improvement in status and gave Lady Baden-Powell's name to their new property – Olave Hall. Unfortunately the building was destroyed by fire the night before the 1946 summer camp to Strangford Lough. In 1952 accommodation was found in the former headquarters of the Royal British Legion, an old army hut situated between the Orange Hall and the King Edward VII Memorial Hall in Sullivan Place. After many fund-raising projects, by 1977 the Guides were able to erect the present commodious building on the same prestigious Sullivan Place site.

Holywood Sea Rangers were commissioned on 26th June 1945 and stood down on 25th October 1948. Rene Hawthorne, now Mrs Dawson Moreland, was Skipper. They took the name Sea Ranger Ship "Powerful" and followed with interest the exploits of H M S Powerful, especially during the many hilarious summer camps. S R S Powerful met in Somerset Hall on High Street, a room above the former Savings Bank building, which they shared with the Air Training Corps.

The fascinating logbook of S R S Powerful is carefully preserved in the archives of the Friends of the Holywood Library. It supplements a considerable collection of photographs of Holywood Guides and their many interesting adventures. The Friends of the Library welcome the donation of local records and assures their preservation from loss or destruction, for the use of our Holywood posterity and heritage.

The Holywood Branch of the **Trefoil Guild** was founded in 1965. The group keeps guides and guiders together and provides a rich source of advice and assistance for the Guides of today. In the year 2000, when Holywood Guild hosted the Annual General Meeting for Guilds from all over Ireland in the new Parish Centre, the great hall was filled to capacity. The visitors commented favourably on the convenience and accessibility of our town.

THE PROVINCE OF ULSTER GUIDE ASSOCIATION, LORNE ESTATE, CRAIGAVAD, HOLYWOOD

In the early years most Ulster Guiders went to England for leadership training. In 1944 Knocktarna, near Coleraine became a permanent training camp, then in 1947 the centre removed to Lorne, on Station Road, Craigavad.

The campus of 8.5 hectares provides one of the finest leadership training centres in the United Kingdom. As *"Drusilla"* recorded in the magazine *"Ulster Housewife"* in the September 1948 issue, the Guides were "coming home" when they acquired the Lorne Estate from the Campbell family. Temporary training camps had been held in the grounds of Craigavad House, the home of the Mulholland family, before the estate was sold to the Royal Belfast Golf Club in 1925. In the 1930's training weeks were hosted at the neighbouring Rockport School, during the long vacation.

The inaugural meeting of the Lorne Committee was held at the former Ulster Headquarters on 25th January 1946. After feverish fund-raising efforts and a grant from the Ministry of Finance, the Mansion House, the 21 acres of parkland and the cottages were acquired for £6,000. By coincidence, a similar figure had been paid by the Royal Belfast Golf Club for the neighbouring Craigavad House some two decades earlier!

A further thousand pounds had to be found to furnish Lorne House, before the official opening by the Duchess of Abercorn on 3rd June 1947. The Duchess was able to lighten that extremely inclement summer day with the good news *"that every Brownie, Guide and Ranger had personally raised a minimum of one pound towards the achieved target fund"*. This was a considerable amount of money for a little girl in those days.

Here I should say something of Henry James Campbell (1813 to 1889) and the grand seaside house he built for his retirement in 1873. Campbell removed to Lorne from Belmont House, after an outstandingly successful life spent in the Ulster linen business. Belmont became the site for Campbell College; he called his retirement residence after the valley in Scotland traditionally known as the home of the Clan Campbell. The emblem of the Campbells - a boar's head - is represented in both Campbell College and his Craigavad residence.

The architect of Lorne House is not recorded. However, the mansion bears the characteristics of the firm of Lanyon, Lynn and Lanyon, designers of many of the grand houses in the Holywood area.

Lorne House, with its impressive tower, was built in 1873 in the Scottish Baronial style using fashionable yellow polychrome brickwork, similar to the Sullivan National and Upper Schools (1862 and 1872) and the Holywood Town Hall (1876).

The main stairway and hall windows are features of the house; the spacious rooms are ornamented by the usual spectacular ceiling plasterwork found in Holywood.

The grand solarium, now carefully restored, is one of the few Victorian ironworks remaining in the Province.

In June 1984, a glorious summer day, as Mayor I represented the people of North Down when Princess Margaret visited Lorne. It was delightful to hear our royal visitor, President of the Association, express her sincere admiration for the magnificence and perfection of the mansion house and the camping grounds.

The purchase of the Lorne Estate by the Guide movement was extremely fortunate for the Holywood area. As well as providing one of the finest training centres in the United Kingdom, it preserved a beautiful house and 8.5 hectares of green parkland. Recently, the buildings at Lorne have become the headquarters for the Guide Movement in Ulster.

I shall take an opportunity in this essay to congratulate the several organisations and private owners who have preserved many Holywood mansions as examples of our heritage in *"the days of the merchant princes"*.

If the Guide movement had not acquired Lorne in 1947, the fine house would have been demolished, like so many others, and the 21 acres covered with an expensive suburban housing development.

Similarly, Church authorities maintain Craigdarragh, a Lanyon mansion, and The Firs on Holywood's Belfast Road, a fine example of Arts and Crafts movement architecture. Redclyffe, now the police station, is another example of that style. The Policy Authority also maintains Knocknagoney House - an ostentatious illustration of local High Victoriana. The Salvation Army has preserved Ballymenoch House in its original form; the Folk Museum keeps Cultra Manor in pristine style.

Many of the grand Victorian terraces are conserved by careful owners, as are the huge semi-detached houses, which are peculiar to the Holywood area. Three of our parsonages remain in commendable condition, although long since deserted by their ecclesiastical environmentalists! To be fair, I should say that the congregations have maintained their places of worship assiduously, so that our town is special in its selection of beautiful churches.

High Holywood, lying between the Croft and Ballykeel rivers; Church Road, Shore Road, Demesne Road and My Lady's Mile have retained their peculiar Victorian and Edwardian character, despite the odds, and the worst that modern planning and transport have been able to envisage.

The Guide movement has shown us the way of environmental conservation at Lorne - we thank them for *"coming home"* to Holywood.

We have taken a brief look at several of our sporting activities - the yacht clubs, the cricket, rugby and tennis clubs. Here we shall talk about many of the other associations which make us a very sociable and friendly community. It is well said that in Holywood on every afternoon and evening of any week there is an excellent selection of activities from which to choose!

Over many years the town has benefited greatly from the generosity and perception of the **Business and Professional Women's Association.**

Holywood is fortunate to be one of the two dozen towns in the Province to have a long-established and very successful **Citizens' Advice Bureau.**

When **Holywood Probus** meets in the Yacht Club the upstairs room is filled with virulent members. We have an energetic **Lions Club** in the town and a **Northern Ireland Widows' Association** and an enterprising **Retirement Association**. **Holywood Round Table** continues and the **Road Safety Association** maintains a strong voice for the benefit of our people.

In Holywood we are favoured in hosting three societies which provide for people who no longer wish or are able to live alone, but seek companionship and an independent lifestyle within a secure and happy environment. **Abbeyfield**, which first began in Walmer Terrace, has refurbished the lovely old house on Church Road which was built as a Nurses' Home, in memory of Dr Dunlop. **Habinteg Housing Association (Ulster) Limited** has a purpose-built complex in Sullivan Close, built in Dr Magowan's former garden. **Fold Housing Association** provides two complexes in the town, Spafield Fold (on the site of Spafield Terrace) and Loughview Fold - on the site of Burke's Field. Both Fold and Habinteg have honoured the town by locating their headquarters offices here.

The **Holywood Irish Society** has been meeting in the town for almost a century. It was founded in 1902 by The Rt Rev Monsignor James O'Laverty who became parish priest in November 1866, and through whose efforts the beautiful old church of Colmcille was built. A keen historian and Gaelic scholar, he was elected a member of the Royal Irish Academy in 1869. The Irish Society is a branch of the Gaelic League, the Irish language organisation established in 1893. It sought to revive Irish as a spoken and literary language, and this continues to be the object of the Holywood Society. Classes are organised in the Library for three levels of competence. In its aim to maintain Irish as a spoken language in our town, the Society provides scholarships for members to study at the Irish College in the Donegal Gaeltacht - a collective name for areas where Irish is spoken as the first language.

Withers and Henderson Memorial to members of the Rowing and Swimming Club drowned in 1873.

The Society, into which all sections of our population are welcomed irrespective of creed, class or political preference, organises various social and cultural activities during which the language is practised.

Most national charities have flag days in the town - our citizens are reputed to be among the most generous donors to the call of the rattled collection tin! Three charities have shops in the High Street - **Oxfam**, **Cancer Research Campaign** and **Marie Curie Cancer Care**.

Those whose special interests are music, drama and dance have a wide choice of quality pursuits. We have the annual **Jazz Festival** which is rapidly gaining a place of importance for *"occasions at which to be seen is cool!"* **Ballykeel Flute Band** adds sparkle to the many local events it attends. The **Holywood Music Festival** has a long and interesting history and **Holywood Players** are known throughout the length and breadth of Ireland for their vivacious performances.

Holywood Players are one of the longest running and most celebrated dramatis personae in the town. They have been treading the boards since 1936, giving entertainment and bringing kudos to Holywood with international drama awards. As many of the thespians were off stage serving in the Forces during the War, the Players rested until 1946. Then the Play Reading Society was revived and Norwood Tennis Club became the venue for rehearsals and even the playhouse for ambitious productions. However, gas lighting and the absence of a back stage and proscenium made theatrical life rather difficult for the actors.

Soon, productions were staged in the Non-Subscribing Presbyterian Church Hall - a more salubrious location. The Players removed headquarters to a coach house stable with upstairs loft off High Street; the Tesco supermarket covers the site today. The ancient stone building was painstakingly refurbished with willing hands and much sweat - only to be destroyed by fire a few years later. Shortly afterwards, Stewarts' Cash Stores developed the site. By that time, productions were being staged in the Queen's Hall. A new clubhouse was found on the Kinnegar. Many plays were rehearsed and many triumphs celebrated in the two Kinnegar huts, before they fell to "Holywooditis" - land development for additional housing and apartment buildings.

This time the Players removed to their most imposing rendezvous - the Grainger building in Redburn Square. Shortly after re-organisation of local government had placed Holywood within the Borough of North Down, the Grainger Company headquarters was acquired as a town amenity site. The smart red brick office building got new tenants - Holywood Players. The halcyon days terminated in 1998 when Holywooditis raised its ugly head once again and the Players were evicted, without provision of alternative accommodation! But for the kindness of the Rugby and Cricket Club, the Players would have been peripatetic street artists and buskers - after a half century's service to the town.

Each year the Players rehearse three plays: in winter for the important drama festivals; in autumn for the Christmas season and in spring for the summer theatres.

For many members, the Players have become a way of life; for others a training school for confidence in life itself. They have made the name Holywood synonymous with excellence in drama all over Ireland. Their fully documented archive indicated a wealth of success. Like so many other organisations, the Players require a book to themselves, rather than a mere section in a Holywood essay.

The Players fully deserve the support the town has always given to them. Long may they continue to bring thespian credit to Holywood!

HOLYWOOD MUSIC FESTIVAL

The best way for me to re-capture the early heady days of the Holywood Music Festival is to give you the words of Mrs Nana P Houston (nee Nana Ward) who has contributed so generously to the cultural life of our town :

"TO BEGIN AT THE BEGINNING ....

To begin at the beginning, we need to go back beyond the first festival in 1947, to the dream in the heart of its founder, E Godfrey Brown.

> *"We are the music-makers,*
> *And we are the dreamers of dreams" wrote O'Shaughnessy.*

Godfrey Brown was one of that company. Nor did his thoughts about inaugurating a Music Festival in Holywood remain a dream. He had the vigour and the leadership qualities to start a train of action whereby others were enthused to work with him to bring it to reality, and to continue it, not only in his day, but long after his death.

A meeting of some people thought likely to be interested was called. At a guess, there might have been thirty or forty of us. I can remember Mrs Gaussen with her two little Scotties at her feet, somewhere to the left in front of me, Canon Barber (not Canon at that time, I suppose) in the row behind me, and, of course, Mr Godfrey Brown in the chair. He put the proposition to us, and soon the fact had to be faced that we had lost our fine Town Hall by fire, and were without a major hall suitable for the holding of a Festival such as he envisaged. For this was no mere idea of a few solo classes functioning easily within a church hall. Godfrey Brown, conductor of Belfast Philharmonic Society, loved choral work, and the choral side of this dreamed-of Festival was to loom large. How was the difficulty to be met? He had his answer. "What we need - is something like Grainger's contractor's shed". I can't remember who spoke first.

This shocking suggestion, however, led to the establishment of a fine Festival, the choral section of which was remarkable. That huge galvanized iron structure down by the railway station was emptied, and prepared for use as a concert hall. A platform was set up on a foundation of tar barrels, draped with black-out material (war-time effects were still around) and finished with large potted palms. I am not sure whether it was an upright or a grand piano we brought in that first year. What about heating? There simply was none. That is why the Festival was originally set for May.

Proximity to the railway station led to some unscheduled minor intervals, so to speak. A performer would be on the platform, and a train would herald its arrival with the usual sound effects, whereat the adjudicator would perhaps ring his bell, and indicate that the performance had better be delayed for a few minutes. This was all just part of the pattern, and was accepted with amused good humour.

Day-time sessions, of course, were accommodated in church halls, I suppose that from the beginning the music and speech and drama sections functioned concurrently in different premises, but evenings saw a coming together.

In those early days, we looked forward to the day when we would have a fine new hall in Sullivan Place. And that day came, but there was a uniqueness about those early hopeful days. Sometimes we thrive in adversity."

And thereby hangs a tale, which like other Holywood organisations requires a book to itself.

HOLYWOOD RESIDENTS' ASSOCIATION

The Residents' Association was formed at a public meeting in the Queen's Hall on 22nd January 1970. It aims to provide a forum in which residents may raise matters of local concern, to procure improved amenities for the area and to discuss issues relating to the local environment.

The Association was instrumental in the formation of the **Community Council** and the **Citizens' Advice Bureau.** The annual "Keep Holywood Tidy Campaign" is one of the many projects undertaken by the members which have brought victory to the town in the Best Kept Town Competition.

In 1992 Holywood was Ulster's best kept large town. In 1994 we were the best kept medium town in the Province. In the interval, "medium" had changed its meaning to connote towns with a population between 8,000 and 15,000 inhabitants.

The Association seeks to act in a professional manner in representing the views of the community. Two public meetings are organised annually, to which all residents are invited in the hope that they will raise the important issues which concern them.

Over the years the Association has been a catalyst for the attention of the Borough Council. Perhaps its best contribution has been the provision of a local chamber for the positive debate of Holywood issues, a chamber which we lost when the Urban District Council was assimilated into the Borough Council meeting in Bangor.

The people of Holywood have formed a number of residents' associations for special areas, often at specific times. Helen's Bay, Seahill and Strand Associations look after local problems; Cultra and Kinnegar Associations - perhaps dormant - can awake when called upon.

Belfast Road residents successfully won their battle over the Strathearn Hotel, and are now represented by the **Loughview and Redburn Forum**. The Forum is extremely active; it provides an inter-agency group where specialists from Government bodies, Translink, N I Housing Executive and Police regularly consult with the members.
In Holywood a wide variety of platforms are available for the discussion of residents' problems and successes, irrespective of income level, creed, colour or political preference. They will always be heard with courtesy and consideration.

HOLYWOOD AND DISTRICT COMMUNITY COUNCIL

The Holywood and District Community Council was established in 1973 to preserve the special identity of Holywood after the town's assimilation into the larger Borough of North Down.

Delegates from every organisation in the district are welcome members of the Community Council,. All opinions are encouraged for discussion. All members work together for the benefit of our town.

The major inaugural event was the first Holywood Community Festival - Saturday, 27th April to Wednesday, 1st May 1974. The ambitious programme included a morning fair, a cartoon show, a rugby match, the friendship service, disco, schools concert and a grand festival ball with gourmet supper.

On May Day down the years, traditional dancing has been staged around the maypole in the presence of our Holywood May Queen. The custom had been discontinued during the war years; Belfast Telegraph applauded its return in May 1949.

> *"At sundown, the Band of the Royal Regiment of Wales*
> *celebrated the colourful display "Beating the Retreat". The Regiment's dance band*
> *provided music for the Festival Ball,*
> *which closed the programme of events."*

In 1978 the Community Council organised the extremely ambitious "Then and Now" exhibition. On this occasion the Mayor of North Down, Mrs Mary O'Fee, praised the town.

> ***"You are the pace-setters in fostering civic pride in the***
> ***Holywood community, a quality of citizenship which is sadly***
> ***lacking in many communities in this present day and age.***
> ***Your leadership, example and success I am sure will give encouragement to other***
> ***communities in the North Down***
> ***Borough to follow suit."***

Over succeeding years the Community Council has arranged the famous Annual May Day Fair, a greatly enlarge genus of the original morning fair.

On May Day, a traffic-free Holywood High Street becomes the community fairground, where forty or fifty local organisations set up publicity and sales stalls. Colourful competitions occur and the maypole becomes the cynosure of neighbouring eyes.

The event reminds the reader of the May Day spectacle described by Holywood Surgeon Kelly in 1850, of which I have told you in a previous Holywood essay!

The whole affair is peculiar to our town – long may it continue!

SCOTTISH DANCING

Holywood children have a unique opportunity to develop their talents in Scottish dancing. The class was established by Mrs Jean McCadden (nee McArdle) in 1963 and continues to meet weekly in the Non-Subscribing Church Hall. The boys and girls have been extremely successful in competition work. There is an adult group which meets monthly to practice demonstration and exhibition displays.

Helen's Bay led the way in Scottish dancing in our area – there the group has danced its way to success for over forty years.

ST VINCENT DE PAUL SOCIETY

The **Saint Vincent de Paul Society** was founded in Paris in the year 1833 in response to the mass poverty of that period in France and inspired by the salient example of Vincent de Paul (1580 – 1660). The Society extended to Dublin in 1844 and was established in Holywood in 1896 by Rt Rev Mgr James O'Laverty.

Originally the Society was an exclusively male organisation. However in 1969 the Ladies' Conference St Laiseran of Holywood was founded. The two conferences merged in 1971.

The aim of the Society is to help any one in need with finance, advice and guidance, irrespective of class or creed. Membership is open to all denominations and special training necessary to carry out the voluntary duties is supervised by the North Down Council of the Society.

St Vincent de Paul runs Clare House in Newcastle as a holiday home for senior citizens and organises seaside holidays for younger people who require a break from regular routines. It cares especially for those who fall through the net of State provision or those who prefer the assistance of a voluntary helper.

For over a century in its own quiet and unobtrusive way the Society has brought comfort to many Holywood people.

HOLYWOOD CREDIT UNION

The local headquarters of the **Credit Union** is the gracious old house on Church View which was built in 1895 (for £650!). It was the Reading Room., Parochial Library and Sexton's residence of St Colmcille's Church. *"Many a game of billiards was played within its walls and half-pennies won or lost at the turn of a card!"* Temporarily it was used as the schoolhouse and then as the Parish Youth Centre. In 1990 when the house was adopted by the Credit Union, an old Holywood custom was revived.

In his comments on the economy of the villagers in 1820, Rev William Holmes records *"In Holywood wealth is the only qualification which commands implicit respect; no other merit appears entitled to any."* Thirty years later Surgeon Kelly claimed, *"The Holywood Loan Bank has been established for many years to foster habits of industry and frugality. Its condition speaks highly of the population."* The local Fund Office was in the old National school building in Church View – a few doors down from the Credit Union of today.

The Credit Union movement started in Germany in 1849 to assist people to help themselves recover from debt or poverty. By the beginning of the twentieth century, the movement had expanded to North America and from there it spread to Ireland in 1958. Today, the Council of Credit Unions is an international body serving many million members.

In Ireland Credit Union is recognised as a unique and practical expression of self-help through co-operative endeavour. It is a non-political non-sectarian voluntary movement, which encourages thrift to help its members to use their resources to the very best advantage. It creates a source of credit for the benefit of its members at a fair rate of interest and promotes the welfare of the community.

The Credit Union deals only with its own members; they own it, control it and decide on the distribution of its surpluses. Such distributions often include donations to local charities, educational pursuits and very imaginative archaeological preservation.

HOLYWOOD WOMEN'S INSTITUTE

Holywood Women's Institute is the lineal descendant of the original group of rural women who founded the first institute in Canada in the year 1897. The movement came to North Wales in 1915 and to Garvagh, Co Londonderry in 1932.

During the 1930's Institutes were formed in towns and villages all over the Province; establishment as a Federation in 1942 showed the importance of W I during the war effort.

"The aim of the Federation of Women's Institutes is to unite in promoting any work which makes for the betterment of our homes and the development and improvement of the conditions of rural life by providing a centre for educational activities and social intercourse. The movement is strictly non-political and non-sectarian."

In 1948 a number of families came from England to live in North Down; among those who came to Holywood was a very keen member of the W I in Kent. In 1950 a public meeting was called in the old A T C hall in Sullivan Place and the Holywood W I was organised under the presidency of Mrs Potter of Abingdon.

Soon a drama group was formed; it rehearsed in the beautiful old Riverston House which was demolished in the late 1950's to make way for the Area Telephone Exchange.

The Drama Group's Festival successes encouraged the W I to organise a Choral Group. Later both groups united to produce hospitality night spectaculars - the singing sailors, black and white minstrels, music hall and pantomime. Among the many interests covered in the monthly programmes were floral art, craft work, cuisine, gardening, quiz games, art, embroidery and Scottish dancing. The number of W I voluntary services to our community has increased year by year over the half-century.

Holywood Women's Institute soon removed from the A T C hall and at various times held its meetings in the Orange Hall, the King Edward VII Memorial Hall, Holywood Primary School, Holywood High School and, at present, in the Non-Subscribing Presbyterian Church Hall. Now it is a thriving organisation with about fifty members, all of whose families continue to back the good work and aims of the Federation of Women's Institutes.

CITIZENS' ADVICE BUREAU

The aims of Holywood Citizens' Advice Bureau ensure that individuals do not suffer through lack of knowledge of their rights and responsibilities and available services, or through an inability to express their needs effectively.

The Bureau seeks to exercise a responsible influence on the development of social policies and services locally and nationally.
Headquarters are within the Queen's Hall on Sullivan Place. There are Outreach Centres at the Health and Care Centre on High Street and at the N I Housing Executive office in Abbey Place. A special "Housebound Service" is available for sick, disabled or elderly people.

In Holywood we are fortunate to have a team of specially trained advisers who give their time voluntarily to help people in difficult situations. The Citizens' Advice Bureau provides a completely free, independent, impartial and confidential service of information, guidance and support to the people of Holywood.

HOLYWOOD ROAD SAFETY COMMITTEE

The Road Safety Committee was founded in 1952 as part of a province-wide network charged with the aims of increasing awareness to traffic danger, to methods of abatement and to ways of making our roads safe for use by the public.

Under the aegis of the Holywood Urban District Council, local committee members brought parochial expertise of their own areas. Schools, residents' associations, churches, youth organisations and sports clubs were encouraged to send representatives to the meetings.

The Holywood Committee developed into a vibrant force in our community. After re-organisation of local Government the North Down Borough Council sent two representatives to the Road Safety Committee and the D O E Roads Service provided practical advice. Local Police and Traffic Branch continued to bring specialised knowledge for consideration and action.

Vivid media publicity and "Safe Driver" events alert Holywood drivers and pedestrians to the urgent necessity of individual participation in road safety. Slogan and poster competitions in our schools and youth organisations seek to protect the next generation.

Over the half-century since its inception, the Committee has instigated many road improvements, especially at Marino and during the invasion of the through-pass. Signage melioration has been a special success in our area.

The members meet monthly and always welcome visitors who wish to discuss road safety problems and successes.

PROBUS IN HOLYWOOD

If you take the first three letters of the words Professional and Business, the result is **Probus** - the name adopted some 30 years ago for a continuation for senior members of the better-known Rotary Club.

Individual Probus Clubs are largely autonomous, and most devise programmes involving talks, discussions and visits, with occasional highlights such as "away-days" and a Christmas lunch.

Holywood Probus was founded in 1996; its first president was Mr John Frost, former Headmaster of Sullivan Upper School.

The Club meets in Holywood Yacht Club on the second and fourth Mondays of each month, except for July and August. The Ladies' Branch meets at the Golf Club.

Holywood people are fortunate to have a wide selection of societies for those who have attained the retired lifestyle. Perhaps this is why so many sons and daughters return home for the sundown years!

RETIREMENT ASSOCIATION

A branch of the Northern Ireland Retirement Association was formed in Holywood shortly after 1980. In January 1991 it became an independent group with its own constitution. It is a cross-community organisation unattached to the denominational churches or political parties. Its aim is to further the interests and status of retired people and senior citizens. The group arranges an interesting programme of talks, field trips and debates on relevant subjects.

The Holywood Group hopes to re-vitalise its appeal to senior citizens with an expansion of activity and sedentary pursuits. The members meet every month in the Queen's Hall.

WIDOWS' ASSOCIATION

The Queen's Hall Complex is also the venue for Holywood Widows' Association. It was founded in 1986 to help its members approach the difficulties of bereavement.

HOLYWOOD SPORTS, SOCIAL AND RECREATIONAL CLUB

The Sports, Social and Recreational Club meets in the King Edward VII Memorial Buildings, which were erected by public subscription in 1912.

Holywood is one of the few towns in the United Kingdom which honours the reign of Queen Victoria's successor with a prestigious monument - possibly this resulted from Edward's association with the local yachting and golfing societies. The King and Queen Alexandra were very popular in Holywood. In 1885 the townsfolk *"brilliantly illuminated the hills above the town, from Knocknagoney to Craigavad"* when Edward, then Prince of Wales, visited the Province.

Rosamund Praegar sculpted the plaque above the main entrance doors to the Hall. It represents two working men looking at an open book which records *"Be just, temperate, brave and free"*. The purpose of the memorial buildings was to provide the headquarters for a social and recreational working men's club and a meeting hall for the fashionable "Catch my pal" total abstinence movement.

In Holywood the years before the First World War were noted for exuberance and self-expression by youths and some residents. The Newsletter for 19th December 1903 describes "A Holywood outrage. The Town Hall, the Railway Station, the Sullivan Schools, the Post Office and some private residences were daubed with pitch and pithy slogans. The spiked railings around the Police Barracks (then at the corner of Downshire Road) were decorated with apples and pears stolen from the Marsh family orchards at Glen Lyon. Here the tar-inscribed graffiti read *"Ass leep as usual"*!

The year 1907 saw the downfall of the Ratepayers' Association, because of its failure to tackle the lawlessness situation.

Much of the mischief was attributed to the considerable consumption of alcohol by "the lower classes" in the many Holywood public houses. The 1897 Belfast directory records four flourishing temperance societies in Holywood - Band of Hope, Total Abstinence, Parochial Temperance and the Band of Hope Abstinence.

It was thought that education, activity and religion for working men would solve the problem. The King Edward VII memorial buildings became a purpose-built location for "the redemption of society". In passing, I should add (tongue in cheek) that I can find no contemporary reference to the inabstinent lifestyle of the Holywood "upper classes" during the early years of the twentieth century.

After the War, the hall became famous for its temperance and social facilities for working men. It was used as the local Courthouse, and for many years it was a gymnasium for Sullivan Upper School pupils.

By the middle of the century, class discrimination and social distinctions were rapidly disappearing and a temperance club for the improvement of the working classes was no longer viable.

The Working Men's Club committee purchased the site of the Memorial Hall to enable the premises to be held rent-free for ever. In November 1955, after the deaths of George F Trimble and Miss Rosamund Praeger it was decided to commemorate all the benefactors with a memorial plaque and wall panelling in the Main Hall.

The **Holywood Sports, Social and Recreational Club** was formed to continue and expand the activities. A bar licence was granted, and the memorial buildings were extensively refurbished for modern club use.

HOLYWOOD FOOTBALL CLUB

Over the years various teams of Holywood lads have played football at various locations in the town. A field on the north side of Ardlee Avenue was a favourite pitch before it became building sites for superior houses. Henry Ballagh remembered playing on a field behind Holywood House.
In the early twentieth century the field on the Belfast side of the main driveway leading to Holywood House, now Abbey Ring, was the playing grounds for Holywood Swifts and Holywood Rangers Clubs. As the Holywood boys shared the field with the Lough family's famous tuberculosis tested herd of cows, they often came home smelling rather like vegetables! Play ceased in 1940 when the Army used the area to erect a prisoner-of-war camp.

In 1983 the happy amalgamation of the Loughview Stars, founded in 1961 and Holywood Town, 1972, resulted in the Holywood Football Club. Players will remember that Holywood Town and Holywood Olympic had come together some years before 1983.

The "back field" of Loughview Estate was the Stars' winning venue and the Town team played at Seapark.

The 1983 union enabled Holywood Football Club to field four teams; two in the Amateur League and two in the Down Area League. In 1990 the first team won the I F A Junior Cup and received promotion in the Intermediate League. The Club's other teams have won an impressive collection of divisional leagues and trophies. In 1996 an "under 18" team was founded to play in the North Down Youth League - in its first year it won the Cup and League double!

Nothing succeeds like success, and in 1986 a prestigious Social Club was opened in High Street beside the Library.

In the twenty-first century, the Club looks forward to establishing its own grounds in the Holywood area. At present the four senior teams play home matches on the Borough Recreation Grounds at Seapark, where the traditional Holywood colours of green, red and black continue to bring credit to our town.

GOLF CLUBS

We left the story of **The Royal Belfast Golf Club** when it removed from Kinnegar to Carnalea. Here the members leased 50 acres of the Ker Estate where the nine-hole course in a magnificent seaside setting attracted increased membership. A contemporary member described the Club – *"Life was uneventful and the members did not want it otherwise, we formed one big happy family"*. In 1921 the layout was thoroughly re-constructed into an excellent nine-hole course of some 2,700 yards. (Extended to eighteen in 1927).

Army invasion had forced the club to quit the Holywood Kinnegar; now invasion by holiday-makers and sightseers forced the members to seek a third location. In 1925 the Royal Belfast returned to the Holywood area. Craigavad House with its 140 acre parkland was acquired and a magnificent eighteen-hole course carefully constructed and extended twenty-six years later. In 1958 and again in 1978 the mansion house was refurbished to provide one of the finest clubhouses in Ireland. Six first hard tennis courts and two squash courts complete the excellent sporting amenities.
Helen's Bay Golf Club course is located just beyond the Holywood electorate. In 1896 a meeting of golfing enthusiasts met in the Temperance Café and decided to explore the possibility of renting Dufferin land in the village. The Marquis replied affirmatively from his Paris Embassy on 6th February 1896 and accepted the invitation to become the new club's first patron.

> *"Ideally situated for the holiday golfer, Helen's Bay is a popular summer rendezvous for lovers of the game. Though not the most difficult of courses, it includes holes which can bring our the best in any player and really make the game enjoyable."*

Social activities in Helen's Bay have been unusual. Formerly the members 'migrated' to the Copeland Islands on the Twelfth of July every year, a rare bird on these flights was Lynn Doyle, the famous novelist. Another rare bird featured in the members' "Goose Club" – an annual dinner with an anserinae menu. In the 1920's the versatile members organised the Golf Club Regatta – voted *"one of the most successfully country regattas ever had on the Lough"*.

Over the years, three buildings have served as clubhouses – "The Nest", "Point House" and the present commodious headquarters which have been refurbished on several occasions to make excellent accommodation for members and visitors. We hope this picturesque nine-hole course by the sea will long continue to beautify the North Down coast line.

Holywood Golf Club

The Royal Belfast removed from the Kinnegar in 1892. Twelve years later a group of local businessmen interested in the game decided to form a club in Holywood town. They approached Squire Henry Harrison who leased to Hugh Littlewood Garrett and others 42 acres lying to the south of Demesne Road at £65 per annum for 21 years from 1st May 1904. The Squire inserted a plethora of instructions regarding the club's tenure of the lands.

The original nine-hole course was laid out in the corner of the area nearest to the town, approximately where Demesne Park and Avenue are today. The first of four clubhouses was erected and the course officially opened in September 1904. Harold Reade, top amateur of that time won the first scratch prize, members and visitors enjoyed the Holywood Gala Opening Day. The lands included two quarries, a gravel pit and access on to Church Road to the south of St Valentine's.

The club flourished, and additional land was acquired to the west to provide the players with 90 acres for an excellent eighteen-hole course. A stylish clubhouse was built at the top of the Nun's Walk in good time for the opening by Lord Justice Wilson in September 1922.
The course has an elevated situation overlooking Belfast Lough from the Holywood Hills. It commands a panoramic view from Black Head to Belfast City, and is described as *"fairly difficult with plenty of hazards for the average golfer; very dry and well patronised"*. Water Hagen called it *"a well-groomed course"*.

Soon the committee bought out the original curtilage. Membership was increasing and the hillside course was on top of the world. Then, in October 1945 the fine club-house was completely destroyed by fire. The war had ended on 7th May 1945 and Ardtullagh had been vacated by the Women's Royal Air Force. That grand old mansion, formerly a Harrison residence and even the Bishop's Palace before the Church inherited Culloden, became the new club-house.

Rapidly the big house was converted into an elegant headquarters with every imaginable comfort for the 400 members and their friends.

In 1962 a purpose-built club-house was erected on the old central fire-scarred site. It provided necessary additional social amenities for a growing club membership and required further extension in 1971.

Over the years Holywood Golf Club has a brilliant record in inter-club competitions and exceptional success in coaching potential junior champions.

GAELIC FOOTBALL IN HOLYWOOD

Gaelic football received its first set of authorised rules in 1885, although there are Irish references from the seventeenth century onwards, to *"a form of football where various shaped balls are kicked and carried"*.

Rural de-population in the mid-nineteenth century unpopularised the game; in urban areas rugby and cricket became popular. However, in 1887 the Gaelic Athletic Association revived Gaelic Football with a highly publicised national competition.

By 1915 the team size had been reduced, the ball lightened and hand passing encouraged. Soon the game became the most popular spectator sport in Ireland.

The first club in Holywood was organised in 1927; carrying the proud name of St Colmcille. Like the New Zealanders, the Holywood players were known as the *"all-blacks"*, because the team's strip was black shorts and black shirts with white collars. This early youth club also sponsored a handball team and a drama club.

Although successful in the early days, the club continued for a mere decade. It was revived in 1948 under the title - St Laiseran's - Holywood's patron saint, who had established our Priory in the seventh century. The revived club lasted for another decade but withdrew from the League in 1956.

The highly successful Thomas Russell Gaelic Club was formed in 1962 and soon earned the name *"the Holywood Giant-Killers"* Early success did not continue - the club struggled on until 1976 when it was decided to withdraw from the Antrim League.

The next milestone in the story is the foundation of St Paul's Gaelic Football Club in 1979. St Paul's is an amalgamation of the Holywood, Bangor and Newtownards Clubs. The Bangor Club was founded in 1963, some thirty-three years after Holywood and the same year as the Scrabo Harps was founded in Newtownards. From its inception, St Paul's has been a very successful club, fielding five teams in the Down All County and East Down Leagues and Championships.

Originally the Holywood teams played on a small pitch known as Burke's Field, situated on the town side of Spafield Terrace. Later a move was made to Maguire's Field, which remained the Holywood Gaelic pitch for many years. It was small, only 92 metres by 60 metres, uneven and marshy - virtually unplayable for nine months of the year! The field was below the ancient raised beach of Belfast Lough, between Pebble Lodge (now *"The Parks"* apartment building) and the town dump at Spafield. This was never a salubrious place for an athletic field as broken glass from the dump frequently came to the surface and grazed the knees of the players.

After the horrific storms and tidal flooding of the Kinnegar in 1885, Squire Harrison had given the Holywood Cricket Club the equally swampy lands on the south side of the railway embankment. The Church authorities owned the higher portion of the area adjacent to the Belfast Road. In 1972 Roads Authority decimated the cricket grounds by driving the Holywood through-pass over the pitch. The Gaelic Football Club generously allowed the Cricket Club to use parts of their land to continue the honourable game.

In 1985, when the North Down Borough Council developed the Spafield recreation grounds, outline planning permission was granted for a purpose-built Gaelic pitch between the second rugby pitch and a football ground. This did not materialise, and an all-weather hockey pitch emerged where planning permission had been granted for the Gaelic football grounds.

By this time, St Paul's was well established. The Club realised that the inferior playing facilities of the old Maguire's Field were completely unsatisfactory to meet the growing player participation in Gaelic football. The Foundation of Sport and Arts promised a grant of £50,000 to upgrade the ground. This was dependent on the Club raising from its own membership a minimum of £10,000.

In 1997 work was started on the new grounds. A playing area of 130 metres by 85 metres has been created.

A grant from the Sports Council has provided a state of the art players' pavilion. Spectator accommodation will be provided on the natural banking alongside the Belfast Road.

The magnificent green sward, with its back-cloth of Belfast Lough shimmering in the sunlight below the Antrim Hills is supervised by the fine campanile of St Colmcille's Church. This is indeed an imposing approach to our town, and a worthy tribute to the members and friends of St Paul's Gaelic Football Club, whose goal is to provide facilities to compete with the best.

I am unable to understand why local residents tolerated the offensive and odiferous rubbish dumps which despoiled the entrance to our town in the first half of the twentieth century. The town dump was beside the old Gaelic pitch - now it is covered by Spafield car park. The other disgrace was operated by the Rural District Council beside Kinnegar Halt. Now it is the works operation site of Phoenix Natural Gas Ltd. Formerly, similar refuse disposal areas were to be found on the outskirts of every town. Happily, health and safety regulations have rendered them untenable. Although we are wont to complain about the destruction of our town by alleged progress, we should remember the environmental, vehicular, health-giving and communal projects which have ameliorated our neighbourhood. Most of the improvements arise as a consequence of very hard work undertaken by the clubs and societies we have considered in this essay. All the voluntary officers warrant our gratitude and their organisations deserve our support.

ESSAY XIX - HOLYWOOD IN THE PRAEGER TRADITION

A TOWN OF ARTISTS

"Away down the river
A hundred miles or more
Other little children
Shall bring my boats ashore."

The words are from R Lloyd Praeger –

The river is the Croft Burn at the bottom of Woodburn House gardens.

The boats are the works of Lloyd, Rosamund and all Holywood artists who give pleasure to future generations.

Holywood is a town where artists feel at home and where their work is appreciated; the town basks in the reflected glory.

In this essay we meet many of the artists who have lived in Holywood. Hopefully it portrays a comprehensive account of visual artists, past and present, ranging from amateur to professional. One example which shows their social camaraderie has not been confined to Holywood is the Northern Ireland Group for Art as Therapy which began life in our town under the aegis of the Rosamund Praeger Workshop.

BRIAN BALLARD, R U A, was born in Belfast, and lived in Holywood for many years. He has exhibited in Belfast, Dublin , Cork and London. Ballard enjoys travelling to capture on canvas *"objects in the landscape and the sea in its many moods"*.

BALLARD, ELIZABETH - craft bookbinder, works from her home on Downshire Road. Previously she owned an art gallery on Shore Road, where the work of local artists and craftsmen was displayed.

ELAINE BRADY, who lives in Windsor Avenue, paints in both water colours and acrylics; she enjoys putting figures, especially children, into her landscapes.

SIMON BRIDGE lovingly maintains the historic manse of the First Holywood Presbyterian Church on Victoria Road. Although he is a financial consultant, he has an active interest in architecture and often features buildings in his water-colour landscapes, many of which are local scenes.

Woodburn House on Croft Road where the Praeger family lived. Croft Burn runs through the garden.

MICHAEL CLARKE was born in Bangor and has lived in Church Avenue for many years. He is a natural draughtsman, an architect by profession and sensitive water-colour artist. Much of his work captures the brilliant versatility of the colours of Donegal. Michael Clarke has served the local community on the Borough Council and the Road Safety Committee.

JOHN COCHRANE of My Lady's Mile, is a skilful water colourist, who delights in painting miniature-like pictures of local and provincial buildings, often in a subject series. Recently the Belfast City Council chose Cochrane's multiple image of prominent Belfast buildings for the official Christmas card.

ROBERT T COCHRANE was born in Ballymoney lived on Bangor Road for many years. He studied architecture and became a design draughtsman at Short & Harland's with painting, photography and boat-building as his special hobbies.

DAVID CRONE lived in Holywood's Church Hill Terrace. He made a great impression on the Ulster art scene with dramatic intrusion of colour and the human figure, held in an artificial framework.

LEO DONAGHY is an accomplished water colourist whose paintings have been accepted by the Royal Ulster Academy. He lives on Belfast Road and manages an art gallery in Walmer Terrace.

MARGARET ERSKINE was a member of a well-known Holywood family. She became the leading designer of the Moygashel Linen Company. Her designs for Irish linen tea towels brought world acclaim to the Province. Margaret introduced many Holywood children to a deep appreciation of art in her classes in Sullivan Upper School, where she was a member of staff for many years. She lived in a cottage on the Upper Whinny Hill Road, where she cultivated prize cyclamen plants for the horticultural trade.

ROWEL FRIERS, M B E, R U A, was born in Belfast and lived in Millbank on Victoria Road for many years. His cartoons and illustrations are familiar to everyone in Holywood, where Rowel was held in deep affection by the townsfolk. He exhibited in Belfast, Dublin, London and Limerick. In 1993 he was appointed President of the Royal Ulster Academy. During *"the Troubles"* his political cartoons provided much needed humour to the Ulster public. Rowel Friers worked with the B B C, U T V and the local press. He illustrated more than thirty volumes, including his autobiography "Drawn from life (1994)". His work has appeared in Punch, London Opinion, Dublin Opinion and in many Irish collections.

JOHN FROST, a former headmaster of Sullivan Upper School and one of our talented local musicians, has painted in water colours for many years. His preference is landscapes, which he accomplishes with great freedom and freshness.

MABEL FROST, John's wife, also paints landscapes in water colour with considerable skill

HELEN GALWAY, a sister of John Cochrane, lives at Ballymiscaw, and is a water colourist of considerable ability. Her preference is landscapes, often having considerable scope of view. Here her subtle use of natural colours achieves a restful and accurate depiction. Helen also paints intimate partial views of farmyard corners and cottage interiors with great skill.

COLIN GIBSON attended Holywood Secondary School, now Priory College, where he first showed himself to be a competent artist. He trained as a graphic designer and worked for the Belfast Telegraph before becoming a professional painter. He has exhibited in Belfast, Bristol, Chester, London and Dublin. Gibson's topographical works included town, village and harbour images and recently London street scenes. He now lives in Bangor.

BETTY GREER who lives on Victoria Road uses the watercolour medium to accomplish the true artist's compulsion to paint for pleasure. Betty produces pleasing prospects of everyday items, which immediately claim the viewer's interest.

MORRIS HARDING, O B E, R U A [President], R H A. Before coming to Ireland, Morris Harding was a well-known sculptor and painter, having exhibited at the Royal Academy and the Glasgow Institute. In 1925 he received a commission to work on the nave columns, corbels and west front of St Anne's Cathedral, Belfast. He brought his family to live in Church Hill Terrace. He worked with Rosamund Praeger from her studio in Hibernia Street. Other examples of his work can be seen in St Peter's Church; Telephone House, Belfast; Parliament Buildings, Stormont; Queen's University, Belfast; Government House, Hillsborough; and the Ulster Museum. In 1938 he was responsible for the execution of the frieze (150 feet by 4 feet) in the Ulster Pavilion at the Empire Exhibition.

RANDAL HAYES has lived in Alexandra Park for many years and is a highly respected member of the medical profession. His landscapes in water colour, very often schemes of Donegal, have a simplicity of line and colour which tends to conceal the expertise required to achieve such pleasing results.

OLIVE HENRY, R U A, was Ulster's best known woman stained glass artist. A student at Victoria College and Belfast School of Art, she worked with W F Clokey and Company in her chosen profession. Olive Henry exhibited in Dublin, Belfast, and in England and was a founder member of the Ulster Society of Women Artists. Examples of her work can be seen in the Holywood Presbyterian Churches and Sullivan Upper School. Olive Henry lived in Cultra Avenue until her death in the 1970's.

DEIRDRE HISCOCKS has lived in Torgrange for many years; she is a teacher of art in a Belfast school. Deirdre's water colours of flowers and floral arrangements are painted with great skill and accuracy, and are highly prized. Deirdre is a member of the Ulster Watercolour Society and has exhibited at the Royal Ulster Academy.

W A HUME is an extremely skilled watercolourist with a special affinity for seascapes, with yachts so accurately painted that they appear to move! In past years his paintings of Kelly's coal boats featured on their business calendars. His paintings have been accepted to exhibition by the Royal Ulster Academy and the Ulster bank.

ERSKINE IRVINE, an unusual and highly skilled artist, lives in Invergarry Avenue. His style has a photographic technique without being stiff. He uses water colour, pastels and pencil to achieve extremely individual paintings, often of close-up groups of figures.

HELENA KAUSHAL lives in Pi-Kai on Glen Road. Originally from Finland, she came to the United Kingdom as an art student, where she met her artist husband, Depak Kaushal of the University of Ulster. Now Helena is a revered member of the Holywood community. Her glass installations, examples of which adorn the homes of Hillary Clinton, wife of ex-President Clinton; President Mary Robinson and the American Kennedy family., are highly favoured by discerning collectors.

ALEX KENNING, formerly Principal of Holywood Primary School, is an accomplished water colourist with a preference for painting scenes composed of substantial buildings or seascapes with delicately depicted beached boats.

JOAN KENNING has lived in Holywood for many years and is a former staff member of Sullivan Upper School. She is a fine water colourist, mainly of landscapes incorporating indigenous cottages in the Mournes and Donegal Highlands. Joan is a member of the Ulster Watercolour Society; her work has been selected by the Belfast City Council for the official Christmas card on several occasions.

GAIL KERR has lived in Holywood all her life and is married to Tom Kerr. Gail uses watercolour to paint intimate partial views of farmyards and gardens incorporating animals and birds, with considerable delicacy and naturalness.

TOM KERR was born in Holywood, an architect by profession, he took up painting as a hobby in 1968. He has exhibited at the Royal Ulster Academy. Tom Kerr is a member of the Council of the Ulster Watercolour Society. He has published four collections of his poems illustrated by colour reproductions of his works. They include "*The Melodeon Man*" (1991), "*After a while*" (1992); "*The Quiet Shore*" (1994)" and "*On Painted Strings*" (1997)". He produced a millennium calendar illustrated with his paintings and related poems. A feature of the Holywood art scene is the Kerr Art Group and its well-attended exhibitions in the Sullivan Library. Tom and Gail Kerr live on Demesne Road.

GEORGINA MOUTRAY KYLE was born at Craigavad, studied at the Lolakossi Studio in Paris and travelled widely. She exhibited in Belfast, Paris, Glasgow, Liverpool, Dublin and in the 1924 Wembley Exhibition. Miss Kyle was an Academician of the Ulster Academy of Arts. Examples of her work are on display in the Ulster Museum, Armagh Museum, Queen's University and in the North Down Collection in Bangor Castle.

CAROL McEVOY was born in Canada and now lives on the Holywood Kinnegar. A water colourist of considerable skill and boldness, Carol tackles a great variety of subjects with great freedom.

BEVERLEY McGEOWN was born in the West Indies and has lived in Braemere for many years. She is a talented painter with an individual use of water colour. Beverley enjoys working on a wide variety of subjects from landscapes to floral arrangements.

Johnny the Jig by R. S. Praeger. A memorial to all children killed in road accidents.

SHIRLEY MAGOWAN of Ardmore Road has recently retired from the Faculty of Stranmillis University College. While a fine water colourist for many years, retirement has afforded her the necessary time to develop further her undoubted ability in landscape painting.

FRANK McKELVEY, R H A, R U A, was born in Belfast and worked as a poster designer before entering the Belfast School of Art, where he became Dux. His first important commission was to paint pictures of "Old Belfast" which collection is in the Ulster Museum. Frank McKelvey became a leading portrait painter and was represented in the "Irish Portraits by Ulster Artists" exhibition. Examples of his work are on display in municipal galleries all over Ireland. In 1936 Dutch people living in Ireland presented three McKelvey landscapes to Princess Juliana as a wedding present. In his later years he lived on My Lady's Mile.

GORDON McKNIGHT is a well-known Ulster architect whose work is ecclesiastical and domestic. His office is on Shore Road, and his home for many years has been at

Carney Hill, Craigavad. Gordon McKnight is a first rate water colourist. His works have been accepted by the Ulster Academy over a number of years. On several occasions Belfast City Council commissioned Gordon McKnight to illustrate the official Christmas card.

H ECHLIN NEILL's landscapes of the North Down coast line and his years in Abbeyfield on Church Road provide a Holywood connection with this Ulster landscape painter. He studied in the Belfast School of Art and by profession became a lithographic artist. He was an Honorary Academician of the Royal Ulster Academy and exhibited in Belfast and Dublin. Neill continued his profession to the end of his life. Examples of his work can be seen in the Ulster Museum.

ANDREW NICHOLL, R H A Perhaps it was when he lived or lodged on Demesne Road that his painting of the Holywood windmill from the old mill dam was executed; today the picture may be seen in the Ulster Museum. He exhibited in Dublin, London and Belfast and is represented extensively in British and Irish galleries. Nicholl was one of the artists who illustrated Hall's History of Ireland (1841 - 43). In 1896 he enjoyed a sketching vacation to Sri Lanka (then Ceylon) - some of his Singhalese paintings came home to Holywood. The amount of his extant work is prodigious. While Nicholl lived in Holywood, he appears to have taught landscape drawing in Belfast.

CAROL PANTRIDGE has been a Holywood resident for many years. Her still-life studies and landscapes in water colour display an uncomplicated and natural style to great effect.

GLADYS PETO was born in England and came to live in Holywood during the Second World War. Her work shows delicate line drawing with colour washes added. Before coming to Ireland she had written and illustrated travel books on Malta, Cyprus and Egypt. During her stay in Ireland she may have worked as an illustrator with a local publisher. Examples of her work may be seen in Holywood.

SOPHIA ROSAMUND PRAEGER, O B E, M A has already appeared in our Holywood essays as a very active member of the Non-Subscribing Presbyterian Church and benefactor to the local community. Rosamund Praeger was the daughter of William E Praeger, a linen merchant from Holland who married into the well-known Patterson family of Holywood. At first Maria and William lived in The Crescent, then moved to Woodburn House on Croft Road, where Rosamund was born in 1867. There she played with her brothers in the gardens, which ran down to the Croft Burn. The best known of the boys was Robert Lloyd Praeger. Rosamund was educated at Sullivan Upper School, the Belfast School of Art and the Slade School, London, where she won the silver medal of drawing.

Her professional career began in a studio at 1 Donegall Square West in Belfast. Here she illustrated at least fifteen children's books, many of which were written by herself. One of the best known was a Child's Picture Grammar (1900). Other publications were Nursery Rhymes; Things We Thought of (1902); To School and Back; A Sunshiny Holiday; A Visit to Babyland (1896); The Olde Irishe Rimes of Brian O'Linn (1901); Old fashioned Verses and Sketches; The Red Letter; The Adventures of the Three Bold Babes (1898); The Tale of the Little Twin Dragons (1900); "How They Went to School (1903); How They Came Back from School (1911); How They Went to the Seaside (1909); Me (Baby Writes a Book); Wee Tony –a Day in his Life (1913); The Naughty Ninepins and Wee Tony (1913); Billy's Garden Plot (1918). Further Doings of the Three Bold Babes (1898); The Young Stamp-Collectors; Fearful Land of Forgets (1921). Rosamund had a natural understanding of the way in which a child's mind works - she spent her life drawing and sculpting young people and was always immediately accepted by them. Rosamund's most famous work came in 1920. This was *"The Philosopher"* modelled on a neighbour's child from Croft Road. The original was bought at the Royal Academy, London by an American collector and is in the Colorado Springs Museum. Copies were sold all over the world - the proceeds of which paid for the erection of the St Brigid's Studio in Hibernia Street, Holywood.

Rosamund encouraged Morris Harding to come to Holywood; she allowed him to share her Holywood studio and worked with him on the adornment of St Anne's Cathedral, Belfast. Her best ecclesiastical work is in the Cathedral's Baptistry and the Justice pillar in the nave. Rosamund exhibited in Belfast, Dublin and London. She was an Academician of the Ulster Academy of Arts and served as President. In 1953 Rosamund agreed that her favourite work, Johnny the Jig, be erected in the High Street, the original of which is in the North Down municipal collection in Bangor Castle. A removal from the large house on Croft Road took the family to Derryquin, Old Cultra Avenue, then to Rock Cottage, Craigavad, after the death of her mother, to whose care she had dedicated her life.

Examples of her work may be seen in the Holywood Sullivan Library; Sullivan Upper School, Campbell College; Royal Maternity Hospital; Stormont Presbyterian Church, Giant's Causeway school-house; Ulster Museum; Bangor Castle; The National Gallery; Priory Graveyard; Methodist College, Belfast; Ulster Folk Museum; Ulster Hospital, Dundonald; Belfast Central Library; Non-Subscribing Presbyterian Churches in Comber and Holywood; Riddell Hall; Hillsborough Parish Church; Downey House School; The Memorial Hall, Comber; Holywood Parish Church and in the homes of many of her Holywood friends, to whom she was a gracious, generous and lovely lady.

DAN RAINEY is a particularly talented water colourist whose major interests are shipping and architecture. He spent his life as a working horticulturalist in the Cultra and Craigavad areas and lives in the upper of the unique pair of gate-lodges leading to Ardnalee on Station Road. Dan Rainey's gardening expertise and knowledge of local history are equalled only by his outstanding artistic talent. A considerable quantity of his work remains in the Holywood area.

HELEN ROSS was born in Belfast and studied there and in Norwich. She exhibited in Belfast and Dublin. One of her favourite themes was children at play. Helen Ross lived with her sister in The Crescent, next door to the original home of the Praeger family. Many of her paintings remain in the Holywood area.

BETTY RUSSELL of Braemere Heights is a naturally gifted water colourist who paints relatively small works, featuring groups of people in a free impressionist style, and formal arrangements in a similar personal manner.

ERIC RUSSELL is the other half of this gifted duo. He has an eye for architectural groupings and nautical scenes which he paints in water colour with a freedom of style and colour.

NICOLA RUSSELL opened her gallery on Church Road in December 1998. It is devoted to the exhibition and sale of her portraits and paintings in oils of horses, birds and flowers. Her work "Wild Irish Colt" is part of the Royal Collection. Nicola was a British School at Rome scholar in 1994 and in 2000 has been awarded a Rotary International Scholarship to return to Rome. Her work is found in collections in Belfast, Dublin, Tokyo, Stockholm and San Diego.

MARK SHIELDS was born and educated in the Holywood area and now lives at Craigantlet. He is an accomplished and highly rated painter in oils with a distinctive and subdued Victorian style. Mark Shields has exhibited in Belfast and in London; his paintings have been accepted by the Royal Ulster Academy over many years.

KENNETH DENTON SHOESMITH was a marine artist who painted striking posters and publicity illustrations for the Royal Mail Shipping Company. Some of his best works were the murals on RMS Queen Mary I. The family retired to the Cultra area and donated a large collection of his paintings to the Ulster Museum.

A C STANNUS was living in Tudor Park in 1895. Although born in Belfast, he spent most of his working life in England. He exhibited in London, Belfast, Dublin and Cork. Examples of his work, mostly landscapes, marine and architectural subjects can be seen in the Ulster Museum, the Harbour Office and the Victoria and Albert Museum. When Stannus was living in Holywood he was President of the Belfast Ramblers' Sketching Club, to which all the artistic fraternity belonged - no doubt they met at Tudor House. He was an honorary member of the Belfast Art Society.

SAMUEL C TAYLOR was a talented designer and professional artist. This unassuming Holywood resident worked from his north-lit studio which adjoined Pebble Lodge, recently demolished to erect "The Parks". His daughter Anne was a competent water colourist.

GEORGE THOMPSON was born on the Antrim Coast, to which he returns to find inspiration for fine landscapes in oils. He has lived in the Holywood area for many years and is the creator and first Director of the Ulster Folk Museum at Cultra. In his retirement Dr Thompson has developed his painting skills to a professional standard; he is a highly respected member of the Holywood community.

JOHN TURNER, R U A was born in Belfast and attended Belfast College of Art and the Slade School of Fine Art in London. On returning to Ireland he taught in several Ulster schools. Turner was interested in the revival of old painting techniques, and became one of Ulster's most successful portrait painters. There are many examples of his work in Belfast City Hall, Magee University College, Armagh and Ulster Museums, also in the Arts Council Collection. John Turner lived in Birch Drive and more recently on My Lady's Mile.

JOHN VINYCOMB, R I A, was living in "The Scriptorium", Riverside, Church Road in the early years of the twentieth century. He was a talented artist, designer, illuminator and an international authority on bookplates and heraldry; he published several books on these subjects. Vinycomb was very popular with his colleagues; on learning he was to leave Holywood for England in 1909 they presented a purse containing 100 guineas and for his wife a silver candelabra. Vinycomb was the founder of the Belfast Ramblers' Sketching Club, which developed into the Royal Ulster Academy of Art. The club organised outings to Craigavad in May 1889 and to the Bishop's Palace in July the same year. After the latter, the Vinycombs entertained the members in "The Scriptorium". Quite possibly the Pattersons, the Praegars, John Ward of Marcus Ward and Company, A C Stannus and other local celebrities were present on that important occasion.

MATTIE WAUGH is yet another artist who has lived in Holywood for many years. Although she paints in oils, her main works are perfected in water colour. Her special niche is the arboreal ability to capture on canvas the beauty of trees in every season. Mattie's work is very well known and widely sought after by collectors. She is a member of the Ulster Watercolour Society.

BEA WILLIAMS, born in the Holywood area, is a talented water colourist who uses subtle blends of techniques in a wide range of subjects. She is a member of the Ulster Watercolour Society.

MARTIN WILLIAMS, a Craigavad resident for many years, paints landscapes in watercolour with great gusto, achieving very bold results in a free flowing style.

LOCAL GALLERIES

As well as Nicola Russell's and Leo Donaghy's [Gallery 148], Charles Gilmore's Galleries are situated on Church Road. It specialises in fine Irish paintings. On High Street we have the Elaine Somers Gallery. Jacquart in Hibernia Street specialises in fine art.

Holywood's artistic skills started in the far away days when religious orders inhabited the Priory and introduced the art of textual illumination to our area.

We are fortunate that, down the years, a small County Down seaside town has been "home" to such a great number of artists and that so many of them have been intimately linked with all the intricacies of the local community.

In this essay on our Holywood story we have met with more than forty Ulster artists who enrich our lifestyle by their sojourn in the town. No doubt I have failed to include all our artists and I crave pardon for any omissions.

Of course, Holywood is not only a mecca of painters and sculptors. We have an abundance of musical, literary and theatrical artists. The memorial stones in the Priory graveyard and our other cemeteries read like a library catalogue of captains of industry and administration, educationalists, theologians and social reformers. In the essays I have attempted to include many Holywood celebrities. There are many more. Readers may like to write other important names on the pages designated for personal notes.

In future years there will be many more whose creative skill will continue to make Holywood a unique place in which to live, bring up our families and enjoy our pleasant and peaceful environment to the full. A worthwhile celebration will be a collection of the works of each of our Holywood artists, permanently on display in the Library for future generations to enjoy.

The Old Townhall on Sullivan Place where Holywood societies met after 1876. It was destroyed by fire in 1940.

ESSAY XX

THE JIGGERY BOY OF HOLYWOOD - WHAT IS HIS FUTURE ?

In Holywood town there lives a wee boy
They call him Johnny the Jig
For strangers who pass him by on the road
He doesn't give them a fig.
But brings glee with his melodeon toy
To children of Holywood
With dancing and prancing, music and joy
Laughter and everything good.
He tells of a Boy Scout killed in the street
And of children everywhere
Who live in parents' memories to meet
In a land beyond sore care.
And of a sculptress who loved children well,
Though she had none of her own
But gave love and talent and life to dwell
Within her Holywood home.

C A

JOHNNY THE JIG

The Belfast Newsletter recorded Thursday, November 5th, 1953 as a very important day in the history of Holywood. Morris Harding,
Chairman, assembled his S R Praeger Memorial Committee at the children's playground in the High Street for the unveiling of "Johnny the Jig". Mrs S Duffin performed the ceremony and Major Addy received the bronze figure on behalf of the people of Holywood. Rosamund Praeger was present and she told us Johnny the Jig was the most appropriate "memorial" she could envisage.

The playground was given to the town by the McCormick family of Cultra House in honour of Hugh McNeile McCormick who loved all children. Miss McCormick was one of Rosamund Praeger's many friends. She though it most appropriate that an artistic work which commemorated children who had been tragically killed in road traffic accidents should be erected at the playground's entrance gates.

Rodney Lunn, a Form I scholar of Sullivan Upper School, recited the poem which Elizabeth Shane had specially written *"to Miss S R Praeger by whose sculpture 'Johnny the Jig' the poem was suggested".*

Up where the meadow-land meets with the hill
And the green world changes her gown to brown
There's a magic light where the shadows spill
As the sun does down.

And shrill and sweet on the limpid air
Comes whistle of homing hare or bird
That lifts and falls – then where ? – somewhere
Is a music stirred.

An elfin music that holds the heart
With its plaintive torrent, whose din might spin
A spell like the piper who played his part
In Hamelin.

Where the mountain meets with the meadowland
Sits Johnny the Jig on a stone, his lone
And the concertina twixt hand and hand
Is bone to his bone.

Oh, the young, little shape of him, straight and slim
As he sits with his shock-head bent, intent,
On the world – old mysteries, known to him
And his instrument.

My love on the bird that breaks the day
That carols from branch or bole his troll
My love on the lad that finds a way
For the tunes of his soul.

What wonderment holds his heart in thrall ?
And why is his face a grin from chin
To mischievious brow, yet wise withal
As an ancient djinn ?

And what does he see that no other sees ?
Ah, that .... stay .....surely there go, tiptoe,
Small folk that frolic about his knees
In the sun's last glow.

Elizabeth Shane

S R Praeger's original sculpture from which the Holywood bronze was copied is in the foyer of the Heritage Centre at Bangor Castle. Three plaques are attached to the plinth from which Johnny the Jig laughs at the visitors, still playing his melodeon.

Centre Panel:

Johnny The Jig
by
Miss S. ROSAMUND PRAEGER
(Sculptress of Holywood)
(1867 - 1954)
WHO LOVED CHILDREN
AND DELIGHTED IN THEIR WAYS
PRESENTED DECEMBER 1957

Left side Panel:

LET US LOOK FORWARD TO THE DAY WHEN MEN AT LAST CONVINCED OF THE SANCTITY OF HUMAN LIFE WILL MAKE THE WORLD A SAFER AND HAPPIER PLACE FOR CHILDREN

Right side Panel:

PRESENTED TO BANGOR BY PAUL AND ELIZABETH MORTON IN MEMORY OF THEIR SON FERGUS SHANE PAUL MORTON WHO WAS KILLED ON THE PUBLIC HIGHWAY AT EASTER 1952 WHILST HAPPILY ENGAGED ON BOB-A-JOB TASKS FOR THE BOY SCOUTS AND OF ALL OTHER CHILDREN WHO HAVE LOST THEIR LIVES ON THE ROADS

There is no conclusion to the story of Holywood - only a toast to the next thousand years, and the torch handed on to a new generation.

I have attempted to encapsulate our history in twenty essays, in such a way that each story is able to stand separately as a tale on its own, for correlative integrity I have found it necessary to repeat historic events from differing aspects. It was not difficult to unearth the information, the problem was to check, correlate and sift it down to a manageable size for publication. I could fill another book with Holywood howlers!

The pencil sketches which accompany the text have been drawn over many years. They indicate an amateur hobby and make no pretensions. I have not included pictures of our rapidly disappearing grand houses. Later I hope they will be published with short individual notes.

Future generations must preserve the remaining important buildings in the town - we have lost far too many for the sake of property development. What is left of the green wedge, which still surrounds the town, must not be further encroached by commercial and domestic buildings.

Our coastline, from where it starts at the white shell beach of the West Kinnegar, must be preserved against further land in-filling.

During the First World War my mother, then a student commuting by rail from Cultra, remembered the high sea waves breaking over Sydenham railway station platform. The lough shore came up to the station's level crossing and Mrs Bruce's sweetie shop. Then the white shell beach was held in the corner made by Victoria Park in-fill and the railway line.

When I was travelling to Belfast as a schoolboy land infill had extended down the line to Tillysburn Halt and nature had removed the beautiful little beach of white shells from Sydenham to Tillysburn, over a mile further down the lough shore. Beside the halt ran the Tillysburn Light Railway. This was the pretentious title given to a system of movable narrow-gauge rails upon which the collectors of green seaweeds ran their little wagons. The seaweed was stacked for use as a garden fertiliser.

By the end of the millennium, land reclamation has extended to the Holywood Bank and the natural white shell beach has removed again to the corner of the present-day infill. In two generations over two miles of reclaimed land has been created from compounded rubbish and dredging from the shipping channel. The beautiful white shell beach can still be discovered by what Surgeon Kelly would have described as *"a salubrious perambulation along Park Road listening to the gentle plashing of the waters"*. It is imperative that future generations do not permit waste disposal to intrude further along Holywood's shore line.

We were given a beautiful place in which to live. We must pass it on to that future generation in, at least, as good an environmental state as that in which we received it.

A short bibliography lists the major books from which much of the data was obtained; with the exception of private collections, most books are obtainable from the Holywood Library. An index is included to enable the reader to find rapidly those facts which are forgotten so easily and frequently required to be recalled to memory on a split second.

So many Holywood people have helped to compile the book that it is quite impossible to give credit to all of them individually - suffice to say **THANK YOU** for the corporate knowledge. However, Norma Cooper, stenographer extraordinary deserves special thanks - without her sagacity the book would never have seen the light of day!

Without doubt, there are mistakes and differences of opinion in the text. I trust readers will let me know where corrections and improvements should be made. I hope you have enjoyed reading the story of Holywood as much as I have taken pleasure in writing the text.

I leave the last word to Dr Robert Sullivan, whose verses have introduced many essays

"My friends, these humble lines excuse
That sing your well-deserving praise;
Impute them not to venal views,
I scorn all mercenary lays.
May happiness attend your ways -
May social pleasure round you twine -
And when on earth you end your days,
May you attain your grand design!"

CONNELL AULD FECIT Anno Domini - MMII
Martello Corner,
Holywood

APPENDIX ONE

The five Holywood wards of North Down Borough Council are

1 - PRIORY WARD, which includes part of the town, runs to the Croft Burn in the east, Demesne Ward and Holywood Moss to the west and Ballymiscaw Road to the south. Townland and local area names in the Priory Ward are Ballykeel; High Holywood, Holywood Moss, Woodlands, Ballymiscaw, part of Ballymenagh (Ballymenoch), Ardmore, Glenview, The Crescent, The Strand and Priory Park.

2 DEMENSE WARD takes in the larger part of the town and the Kinnegar. It is bounded by Priory and Loughview Wards and includes Wood End.

3 LOUGHVIEW WARD runs to Belfast City Boundary at Tillysburn and Ballymachan and to Ballymiscaw Road towards the south. Here the townland and local area names are Knocknagoney, Ballymachan (part) ; Redburn, Palace Barracks, Loughview, Strathearn and Cedar Grove.

4 CULTRA WARD lies between Priory and Craigavad Wards. Ballymiscaw Road lies to the south. Townland and local area names include Ballycultra, Ballymenagh (part), Marino, Seapark, Creighton's Green, Braemere and Torgrange.

5 CRAIGAVAD WARD extends from the Glen River and Upper Whinney Hill to Craigantlet Road towards the east. The ward is bounded by Craigdarragh Road, Kathleen Avenue and Sheridan Drive in Helen's Bay. Our largest ward covers an impressive list of townlands and local area names - Craigantlet, Ballymoney, Ballysallagh Major, Ballysallagh Minor, Ballydavey, Ballygrainey, Ballygilbert (part), Ballyrobert, Craigavad (proper), Glencraig, Carney Hill, Larch Hill, Seahill, Martello, Rhanbuoy, Rockport and Clandeboye (part). Wards of the Bangor area lie to the east of Craigavad Ward. There are twenty-four wards in the Local Government Area of North Down Borough Council.

APPENDIX TWO

HOUSE, TERRACE AND FARM NAMES IN THE HOLYWOOD AREA

Here I have attempted to collect the names of the Holywood properties which appeared on old maps, principally those of the late nineteenth and early twentieth centuries, as well as in local memory. In the districts beyond the town itself street numbers were unknown. Families used the well-known names of their homes and townlands as postal addresses.

The 266 street names of Holywood in the twenty-first century are recorded in Appendix Three; some are served from the Bangor Office. However, it is important that the old nomenclature is preserved for future generations, and it is good to see so many families continue to present the name of their houses on the garden gates! Many of the houses have been demolished in order to use the grounds as building site for closely packed residences. Fortunately, in a few cases, the grand old mansions were preserved before the surrounding area was divided into building sites. We should be grateful to those who have been able to maintain the family home and gardens; we hope future planning authorities and rates adjusters will start to appreciate their contribution to the Holywood community. It is impossible to trace all the old house names – some have disappeared altogether, others remain only in the memories of those who lived in the houses. We start in the old parish at Connswater and continue along the Holywood to Belfast Road, Holywood High Street and Bangor Road and on to Helen's Bay.

HOLYWOOD/BELFAST ROAD AREA

Connsbrook, Ballyhackamore, Strandtown House, Seville Lodge, Cranthorpe, Sydenham House, Ravensdale, Aspen Villa, Strandtown Lodge, Creevy, Edgecumbe, Clonaver, Norwood Tower, Alma House, Rockville, Ashfield Farm, Marmount, The Moat, Garnerville, Glendhu, Richmond Lodge, Knocknagoney House, Mertoun Hall, Maryfield, The Bishop's Palace (formerly Ashfield – now Palace Barracks), Westbrook, Oakley, Bellevue Terrace, Pebble Lodge, Barn End, Redburn, Garden Lodge, Ardtullagh, Linwood

DEMESNE ROAD AREA

Willesden, Woodville, Kilmore, Woodside, Loughview House, Cornwall Villas, Moffet's Terrace, Annaville, Fernbank, Thelma, Athelstone, Lindisfarne, Abingdon, Harkaway, Farloe, Lemonfield, Inverstraid, Faunmore, Drumadillar, Winshill, High Fernley, Lynwood, Drumkeen, Oakleigh, Ashleigh, Ardlee Terrace, Duncairn, Craigtara

KINNEGAR AND MARINE PARADE AREA

Eldon House, Golf House (Golf Villas), Anchor Lodge, Villa Nova, Kinnegar Villa, Ivy Place, Prospect Terrace, St Leonard's, Pierview Terrace, Pierview Cottage, Marine Place, Gloucester Terrace, Gray's Buildings, Marine Cottage, Bath Terrace

HIGH STREET/CHURCH ROAD AND TOWN AREAS

The Firs, Begthorpe, Laurel Bank, Ardeen, Spafield, Walmer Terrace, Victoria Terrace, St Helen's, Auburn Place, Redclyffe, Grendor, Poole's Buildings, Jubilee Terrace, Loughview Terrace, Archville, Rollo House, Knockagh House, Alma Terrace, Staunton Place, Alexandra Terrace/Place, Birch Drive, Seaview Terrace, Church Hill, Sunnyside Terrace, Parish Alms Houses, Tyrone Villas, Barronville, Roland Place, Yew Place, Quinnville Terrace, Downshire Cottage, Riverston House, Altona, Riverston Terrace, Church Hill Terrace, Riverside Terrace, Riverside, Woodview Terrace, Innisfallen, Marmion Lodge, Benowen, Rialto, Craigmore, Glenavon, The Glebe House, Stanley House, Plas Merdyn, Cuillaire, Glenview Farm, Holywood Hill House, Highland View

HIGH HOLYWOOD AND CROFT ROAD

Victoria Place, Mill Moat House, Millbank, Martello Terrace, Glenside Place, Glenburn, Hillbrook, Easdale – formerly Donnybrook, Brooklyn House, Riversdale, Glenside Manse, Glenbank, Glenlyon, Ardmore Terrace, Claremont, Carn Wood, Glen Lodge, Crofton, Burnleigh, Bel Air, The Lynn, Braeside, Viewforth, Garrycloyne, The Highlands, Orduna, Woodbank, Brook House, Beechcroft, Croft Manse, Croft House, Salernum, Woodburn House, Delgany, The Croft [or Croft Cottage]

BANGOR ROAD

Cherryville, Tig-na-strue [the house by the stream], Seapark Cottage, Seapark, Seapark Terrace, Benedar, Daisybank, Churchfield, Ballykeel, Martello House, Clifden, Tudor Hall, Priory Park Villa, Ballymenoch House, Leawood, Park House, Knocknatten, Linwood, Sherwood, Kildare, Charleville, Culloden, Woodlands, Thornleigh, The Hill, Glenmakieran, Cultra Manor – now Folk Museum, Kennedy Lodge, Dalchoolin [formerly Wellington – now Transport Museum], The Orchard, Birnam Wood, Coolkelure, Melmore, Loughview, Alma Terrace, Ardkeen, Larch Hill, Fenner, Martello, Enfield

MARINO AND BALLYCULTRA

Lanlowlee, Richdale, Marino Villas (formerly Ward's Cottages), The Priory [formerly The Prairie], Marino House, Ardville, St John's, Farmhill, Tara, Inverlough, West Acre, Grace Lodge [sometimes Greenways], Arendal House, Clanbrassil Terrace, The Haven (now The Field of Doves), Greenacre [formerly Grizetta] now Whispers, White Lodge, Murlough, Heather Lodge, Lisheen, The Grange, Drumlough, Derryhale, Derryquin, The Grey House, Ardmoyle, Cultra Farm, Ardreigh, Cultra House, St Fillans, Lenamore, Windwhistle House, Ingledene, Doon, Coill Mara, Bully Banks, Cultra Cottage, Henley, Clanbrassil (formerly Clanbrassil Villas), Mayfield, Rosavo (formerly Culdaff – now Richmond), Coolbeg, Craig Royston, Cherrydeane, Tempora, Luscar House, Ardvara, Skibbereen, Moyrath, Cultra Lodge, Kilmakee, St Catherine's, Chatelar, Seamount, Killymard, Dunratho, Sorrento, Ardavon, Claybrooke, Iva Craig

CRAIGAVAD

Orlindo, The Grey House, Lorne, Olinda, Oranmore, The Ivies, Mosella, Ailsa Lodge, Dunavon, Bramcote, Rosebank, Arnalee House, Craigavad House (now Royal Belfast Golf Club), Craigowen, Glencraig (now Camphill Community), Bree House, Greenloaning, Rockport House (now Rockport School), Glencraig Rectory, Craigdarragh (now St Columbanus), Ballycrenan, Fairholme, The Chase, Banchory, Dalry, Rathmoyle, Four Winds, Guincho, West Winds, The White House, Gulladuff, Hazelwood, Ballydavey Farm, Drumadarragh House, Beech Hill, Grangefield, Old Grangefield

Here are some of the farmhouses in the southern part of the Holywood area

Loughview, Avoca, Mountpleasant, Holywood Moss Farm, Hillcrest, Millbrook, Creighton's Green, Longlands, Eastview, Ash View, Moorpark House, Rock House, Beechmount, Greenacres, Fort View, Sycamore Farm, Seaview Farm, Copeland View, Hillside Farm, Laurelville, Ferndale, The Sheiling, Clanroy Farm, Eden Farm, Cairnside, Ballysallagh Farm, Millbrook Farm, Hillview Farm, Sallagh Farm, Ballymoney House, Drumavaddy, Simla Cottage, Beech Hill, Glencairn Farm, Fairview, Highlands, Craigreagh, Kilwarlin, Ashfield

I have given the names of 333 properties. The list is incomplete and many have disappeared. The printer has provided a page on which you, the reader, may write the other house names which have your personal interest in the Holywood area.

URBAN DISTRICT OF HOLYWOOD

THE MAYPOLE

ERECTED BY THE

DUNN FAMILY of Tudor Hall,
HOLYWOOD

will be Presented to the Town

AT A

CEREMONY

ON

SATURDAY, 15TH OCTOBER

at 3 p.m.

The Programme includes a display of Dancing round the Maypole by local children from the Leila Corry School of Dancing.

APPENDIX THREE

HOLYWOOD AREA STREET NAMES LISTED ALPHABETICALLY

Abbey Place, Abbey Ring, Abbot's Wood, Acorn Gardens, Ailsa Road, Alanbrooke Gardens, Alexandra Park, Alexandra Place, Ardlee Avenue,, Ardmore Avenue, Ardmore Heights, Ardmore Park, Ardmore Road, Ardmore Terrace, Ardnagreena Gardens, Ash Green.

Ballygrainey Road, Ballymonoch Park, Ballymenoch Road, Ballymiscaw Road, Ballymoney Road, Ballyregan Road, Bangor Road, Beech End, Beechlands Park, Belfast Road, Ben Vista Park, Birch Drive, Brook Street, Brown's Brae, Byron Place Mews, Bennett Wood, Bridge Road

Carlston Avenue, Carn End, Carney Hill, Cedar Grove, Cedar Lane, Church Avenue, Church Green, Church Hill, Church View, Church View Mews, Churchland Close, Circular Road East, Circular Road West, Clanbrassil Road, Clarehill Lane, Clarehill Mews, Clive Road, The Close, The Coaches, Coastguard Avenue, Craigdarragh Park, Craigdarragh Road, Craigowen Road, Creighton's Green Road, The Crescent, Croft Close, Croft Gardens, Croft Manor, Croft Meadows, Croft Park, Croft Road Upper, Crofton Glen, Cultra Avenue, Cultra Park, Cultra Station Road, Coastguard Avenue, Craigdarragh Road

Dalchoolin, Dalwhinney Road, Demesne Avenue, Demesne Close, Demesne Manor, Demesne Park, Demesne Road, Dorset Road, Downshire Place, Downshire Road

Ean Hill, East Link, Edinburgh Avenue, Elizabeth Road, The Esplanade,

Farmhill Lane, Farmhill Road, Ferris Walk, Firmount Crescent, Firmount Court, Fort Road, Frenchwood Park,

Gairloch Park, Glen Brae, Glen Road, Glencraig Park, Glenview Avenue, Glenview Road, The Green, The Grove,

Hammond Drive, Hampton Close, Harwell Road, Henderson Close, Hibernia Street, High Street, Hill Street Mews, Hillview Place, Hinchley Avenue, Hoards Road, Hybank Lane

Innis Court, Inver Park, Invergarry Avenue, Invergourie Road

Jackson's Road

Kinnegar Avenue, Kinnegar Court, Kinnegar Drive, Kinnegar Road, Kintyre Avenue, Kirkmichael Park, Knocknagoney Road, Knocknatten Avenue

Larch Close, Larch Hill, Larch Avenue, Larch Drive, Laurel Lane, Lemonfield Avenue, Linley Close, Linley Drive, Lochinver Avenue, Lorne Lane, Loughview Avenue, Lynwood Park

Maple Close, Mara Gardens, Marine Parade, Marino Park, Marino Station Road, Martello Avenue, Martello Drive, Martello Park, Martello Terrace, Moss Road, My Lady's Mile

North Close, Norwood Lane, Nottingham Road, Nun's Walk

O'Neill's Court, Oakley Avenue, Oakley Drive, Old Cultra Lane, Old Cultra Road, Old Holywood Road, Old Quay Court, Old Quay Road, Old Seahill Road, Old Station Road, The Orchard, Orchard Close, Orchard Way, Otway Court

Palace Grove, Palace Mews, Park Avenue, Park Drive, Parkhouse Manor, Patton's Lane, Pine Crest, Pine Grove, Plas Merdyn, Princess Gardens, Princess Park, Prior's Lea, Priory End, Priory Park, Prospect Terrace

Quinville

Rannoch Road, Rathnmoyle Park, Redburn Square, Rhanbuouy Park East, Rhanbuoy Park, Rhanbuoy Road, Richdale Drive, The Ridings, Riverside, Rockport Road, Rockport Rise

St David's Close, St Helen's Close, Saleen Park, Seafront Road, Seahill Drive, Seahill Road, Seahill Road East, Seapark Avenue, Seapark Court, Seapark Road, Seapark Terrace, Seaview Terrace, Short Road, South Close, Spencer Street, The Spires, Station Road, Stewart's Place, Strand Avenue, Strand Mews, Strathearn Close, Strathleven Park, Sullivan Close, Sullivan Place

Tarawood, Three Acres, Torgrange, Trevor Street, Tudor Oaks, Tudor Park

Victoria Road

Waterside Close, West Green, West Link, Whinney Hill, William Close, Windsor Avenue, Wood End, Woodbank Lane, Woodcroft Park, Woodgrange, Woodlands, Woodlands Avenue.

BIBLIOGRAPHY

For those who wish to read on, I have compiled a list of major sources on which the essays are based. The bibliography is yet another Holywood essay. Local writers and those who have lived in the area are specially marked (*). As well as being a mecca for artists, Holywood is a writers' town. Many of the books are obtainable from Holywood Library. Like the book itself, the list could be twice as long as it is printed here! My private papers go back to the collections of my parents and grandparents. Best of all sources are the rich funds of knowledge of other Holywood people and local oral tradition. These, when checked, are the most interesting part of our living history.

Adamson, I – Bangor, Light of the World   Bangor 1974

Agnew, A - Story of the Non-Subscribing Presbyterian Church   Belfast 1964

Ancient Monuments (N I) in State Care   H M S O 1966 et al

*Author's private collections of various articles on Holywood

* Ballagh, H P – Holywood Memories   Holywood 2000

Barkley, J M - History of the Presbyterian Church   Belfast 1959

Bardon, J – A History of Ulster   Belfast 1992

Bassett, G H - Co Down Guide and Directory   Dublin 1886

* Beatty, A W T – Holywood Yacht Club (1911 – 1990)   Holywood 1997

Beckett, J C The Making of Modern Ireland   London 1966

Belfast Harbour Commissioners Centenary Book   Belfast 1947

Belfast Natural History and Philosophical Society Centenary Volume   Belfast 1924

Belfast Newsletter – Various articles

Belfast Telegraph – Various articles

Belfast and Ulster Directories from 1852

Bell, M - A History of Scouting in N Ireland   Antrim 1985

Benn, G – History of the Town of Belfast   Belfast 1877

Black, A and C – Blacks' Watering Places – "Where shall I go?"   Edinburgh 1871

Black, E – Belfast Harbour Commissioners' Collection of Paintings, Sculptures and Bronzes   Belfast 1983

* Blaney, R – Presbyterians and the Irish Language   Belfast 1996

Brett, C E B – Long shadows cast before   Belfast 1978

Briggs, H – Centenary Diary of N I Electricity   Belfast 1995

* Brown, R – Q U B - Thesis on the Schools of Dr Robert Sullivan   Belfast 1984

Carr, P. – The Most Unpretending of Places   Dundonald 1987

Census Returns – 1841 – 1991 - 1998

* Clarke, R S J and Merrick T – ed. – Belfast Gravestone Inscriptions   Belfast 1984/1986

* Clarke, Janet – Survey of Priory Church Gravestone Inscriptions

Connor, J H – Oil painting of Sydenham, Belmont and Glenmachan 1869 – Belfast Harbour Commissioners

Crosbie, J E M – A Tour of North Down Belfast 1925

Dean, J A K – Gate Houses of Ulster Belfast 1994

Department of the Environment for N Ireland Historic Monuments H M S O 1983

D O E North Down and Ards Area Plan 1984 to 1995 H M S O 1986

Dickson, W Steel – Narrative of Confinement and Exile Belfast c 1800

Encarta – World English Dictionary London 1999

* Friends of the Holywood Library - Archives

* Frost, J – The Continuing Record of Holywood Methodist Church Belfast 1995

Government of N Ireland – North Down Area Plan H M S O 1972

Gibson, W H – Early Irish Golf Oakleaf 1988

Gildea, A L – Guide to North Down Belfast 1979

Gillespie, R – Colonial Ulster : Settlement of East Ulster 1600 – 1641 Cork 1985

Grand Orange Lodge of Ireland: What is the Orange Order ? Belfast 1997

* Graham, D – St Paul's Gaelic Football Club Holywood 1996

* Grant, C W – Holywood Notes Printed privately

Green, E R R – Industrial Archaeology of County Down H M S O 1963

Hamilton, W (ed Lowry T K) The Hamilton Manuscripts Belfast 1867

Hanna, R J – Place Names in the Ards Belfast 1992

Harris, W – Ancient and Present State of County Down Dublin 1744 - reprint 1977

Harrison, J – Ulster Genealogical Review No. 15 Belfast 1999

Hill, G – The Montgomery Manuscripts Belfast 1869

* Holmes, F – The Presbyterian Church in Ireland Dublin 2000

* Holywood Urban District Council – Preliminary Planning Report c. 1965

Irish News – Various articles

Jeffrey, F – Irish Methodism Belfast 1964

Jeffrey, J – Bells and Bellringers of Holywood Parish Belfast 1985

Jope, E M (ed) – Archaeological Survey of County Down H M S O 1966

* Kelly, T T – History of Holywood Belfast 1850

* Keown, M (ed) - Dr Sullivan and Sullivan Upper Holywood 2000

Knox, A – History of County Down Dublin 1875

Lady of the House Magazine for Christmas 1910 London

* Lamont, J A – History of First Holywood Presbyterian Church Bangor 1965

Lewis, A – Topographical Dictionary of Ireland Dublin 1837

* McAlester, C J – Life and Labours of Robert Sullivan
Belfast 1870 – reprint 2000

* McCall, O – Holywood Cricket Club Centenary Book Belfast 1981

* McGurnaghan, J – Parish of St Colmcille Portglenone 1974

* McMeekin, D. - R N I Y C Fairy Class Belfast 1992

Mac Nio Caill, G – Medieval Irish Annals – Dublin 1975

McQuitty, J A – Sketch of Dundonald Presbyterian Congregation
Dundonald 1932

Madsen, L – The Christian Community – Floris Books
Edinburgh 1995

Mason, W S – Parochial Survey of Ireland (including Statistical Account of Holywood Parish by Rev W Holmes) Dublin 1819

* Mercer, W – Still other Seed – Parish History Glencraig 1999

* Merrick, T – Buildings of Holywood Holywood 1986

* Merrick, T – History of the Parish of Holywood (Church magazine) Holywood 1985 - 1988

* Milligan, C F – Bangor and the Belfast Lough Bangor 1976

Murphy, J – The Story of Lorne and the Girl Guides Belfast 1998

Murray's Handbook for Travellers London 1878

Nicholl, J D & Co. (Auctioneers) – Catalogue of Auction of the Furnishings of Redburn Belfast 1940

Northern Whig – Newspaper – various articles

* O'Laverty, J (Monsignor) – Diocese of Down and Connor including special reference to St Patrick's and St Colmcille's, Holywood
Dublin 1880

* Olver, J R D – Holywood and the Society of the People called Methodists Belfast 1971

Ordnance Survey Memoirs of Ireland VII – including G F W Bordes Report on Holywood (1834) with notes by J Scott and M Kertland
Q U B – Belfast 1991

Patterson, E M – Belfast and County Down Railway Belfast 1975

Pike, C E – Life of Robert Cunningham, Minister of Holywood 1615 – 1636 Belfast 1897

Postal Address Book (N I) Portsmouth 1999

* Praeger, R L – Official Guide to Belfast and County Down Railway
Belfast 1898/1901

* Praeger, R L – The Way that I Went Dublin 1937

* Praeger, S R – Illustrated Books for Children Belfast 1896 - 1918

Proctor, E R and Molloy, J – Belfast Scenery (1832)
re-print published Belfast 1982

* Prospecti of the various Schools in the Holywood Area

Proudfoot, L (ed) Down History and Society Belfast 1997

Proudfoot, C V – Rath at Croft Road, Holywood U J A Belfast 1959

Reeves, W – Ecclesiastical Antiquities of Down Dublin 1867

Reid, P – A New Easter Rising Leigh, Lancs 1993

* Robinson, J – Q U B Thesis on Life and Times of Robert Sullivan Holywood 1962

Scott, R – A Breath of Fresh Air – Belfast Parks Belfast 2000

Shane, E – Collected poems Dundalk 1945

Shearman, H – News-Letter 250 Years Book Belfast 1987

* Spectator Newspaper – various articles

* Stewart, J – Parish of St Colmcille, Holywood Belfast 1995

Stevenson, J – Two centuries of Life in County Down Belfast 1920

* Sullivan, R – Juvenile Poems and a Few Songs Belfast 1818

* Tait, D M – The Sanctus Boscus articles on Holywood [in author's private collection]

Townsend, B – Lost distilleries of Ireland Glasgow 1997

Ulster Journal of Archaeology various articles

Walker, B M and Dixon, H – Early Belfast Photographs Belfast 1984

Wallace, H & Co. (solicitors) – Particulars of 1917 Auction of Holywood, Priory Park and Knocknagoney Dublin 1917

*Watson, A – Royal Belfast Golf Club Centenary Book Holywood 1981

* Williams, M – Rockport 1906 – 1986 Holywood 1988

Woburn - House Management Books of the Dunbar Family 1829 – 1840 [author's private collection]

Young, R M – Historical Notices of Old Belfast and Vicinity Belfast 1896

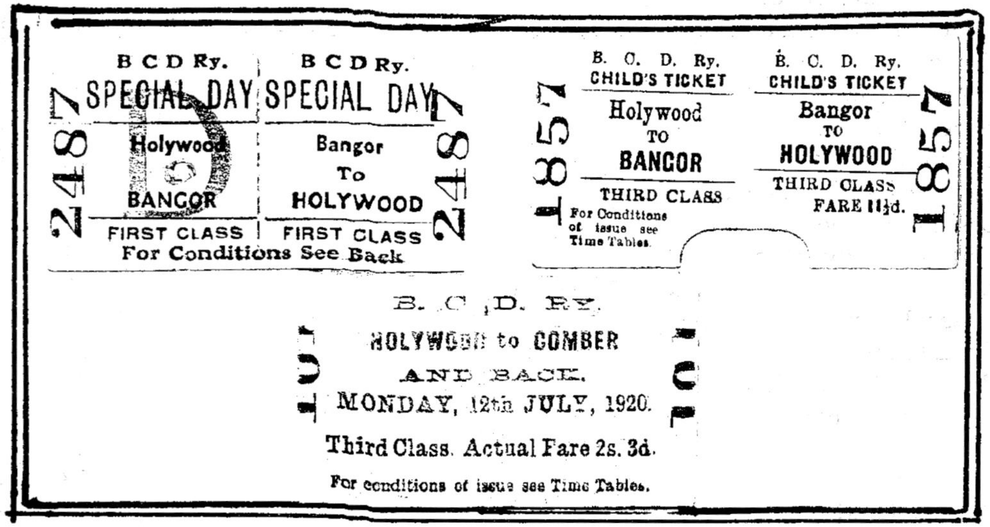

INDEX

NOTES

NOTES